GRAMMAR, VOCABULARY, SPEAKING & LISTENING

Teacher Resources for Blended Learning

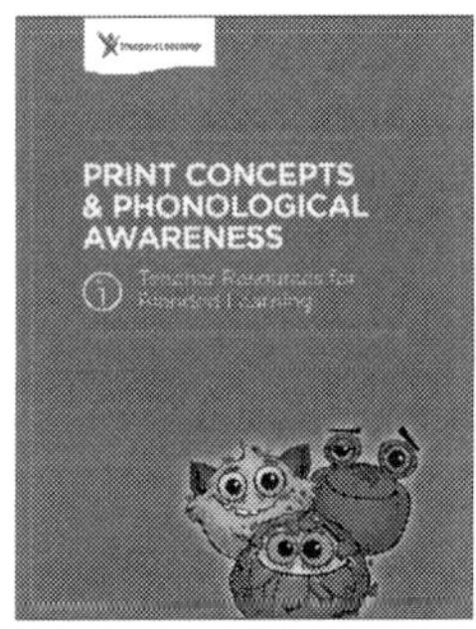

Vol. 1
Print Concepts & Phonological Awareness

Vol. 2
Letter Sounds

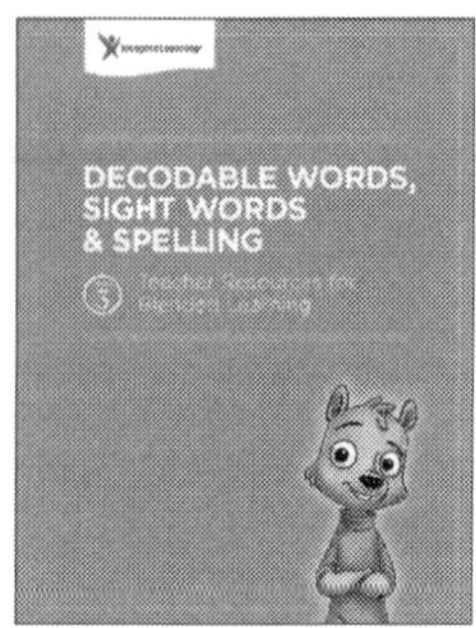

Vol. 3
Decodable Words, Sight Words & Spelling

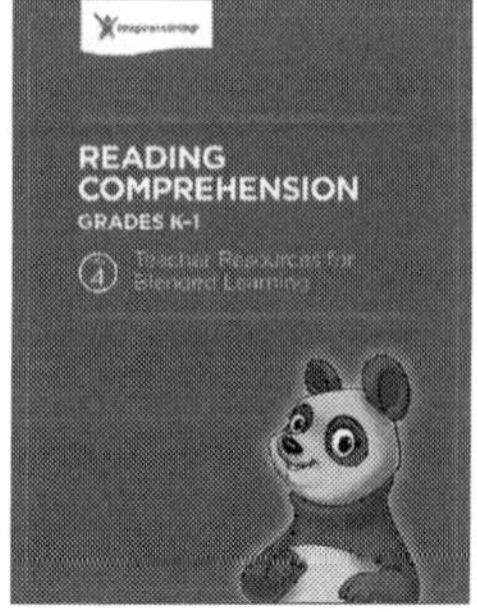

Vol. 4
Reading Comprehension: Grades K-1

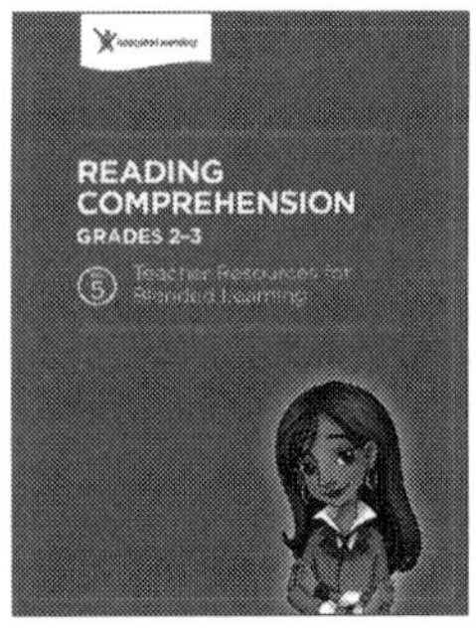

Vol. 5
Reading Comprehension: Grades 2-3

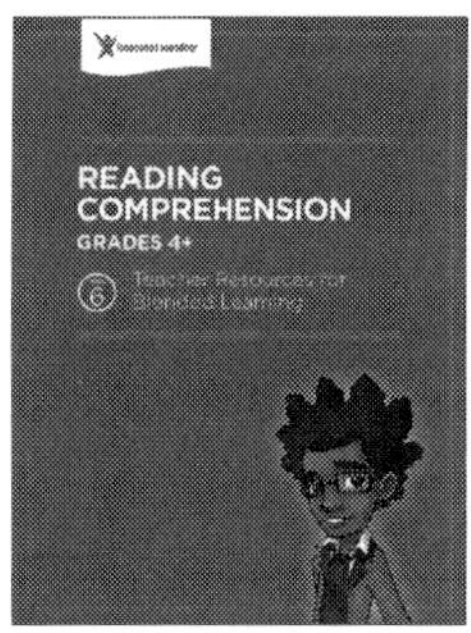

Vol. 6
Reading Comprehension: Grades 4+

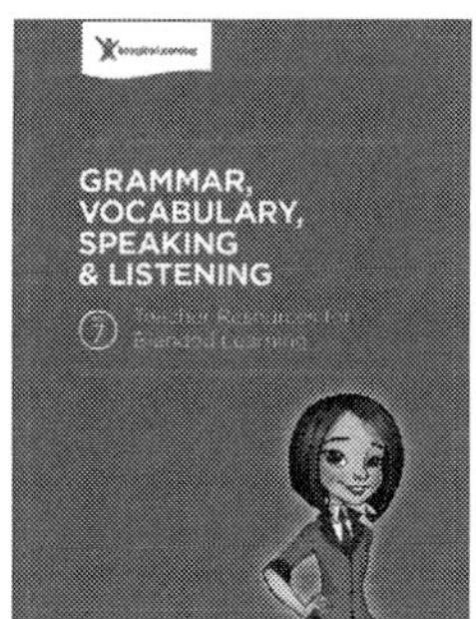

Vol. 7
Grammar, Vocabulary, Speaking & Listening

Available at imaginelearning.com/bookstore

Developed and published by Imagine Learning, Inc.

September 2016 Edition

ISBN 978-1-945460-06-7

CONTENTS

GRAMMAR

This section includes activities, resources, and lessons to help students learn English grammar and use standard language conventions in speaking and writing.

VOCABULARY

This section includes activities, resources, and lessons to help students learn basic beginning vocabulary words, as well as academic vocabulary words that are traditionally used in academic dialogue and text.

SPEAKING & LISTENING

This section includes activities, resources, and lessons to support language production, listening comprehension, and conversation skills and help students learn how to apply them in different conversational situations.

Notes

Using Imagine Learning in the Classroom

Blended Learning with Imagine Learning

Along with the lessons and activities in this volume, Imagine Learning offers a wealth of digital instructional activities. Used together, the offline and online teaching materials provide teachers more flexibility to teach language and literacy within a blended learning environment.

Implementation Options

Offline lessons and online resources can be used for whole group lessons, small group interventions, or individual coaching sessions. Imagine Learning's individualized learning paths also allow students to learn independently at their own individual levels.

TEACHER-LED INSTRUCTION

Because Imagine Learning activities teach key language and literacy skills, teachers can select desired lessons for focused whole-class instruction, practice, and review. Projecting activities or using them with an interactive white board makes it easy for everyone to participate.

ONE-ON-ONE INSTRUCTION

Teachers can use the Action Areas Tool to gain insight on where individual students are struggling and use that information to provide focused instruction. This data is especially helpful as you create an RTI plan and work on skills remediation. Teachers can also extend learning by reviewing student recordings and written responses to offer direct feedback.

SMALL-GROUP INSTRUCTION

The Action Areas Tool pinpoints where groups of students are struggling and immediately creates skill-based intervention groups. The tool also suggests online activities and reteaching lessons that allow for targeted intervention.

COMPUTER BANK OR LAB ROTATION

Imagine Learning provides each student with an individualized learning path by providing systematic, adaptive instruction. This makes it ideal for independent student learning—whether it be at an in-class station or in a computer lab.

Digital Imagine Learning Activities

Teachers can access Imagine Learning's engaging digital activities through the Activity Menu. The Activity Menu is organized by curriculum area. For digital activities that match the skills in this volume, click the corresponding curriculum area. Use the functions below to find the best settings for your class.

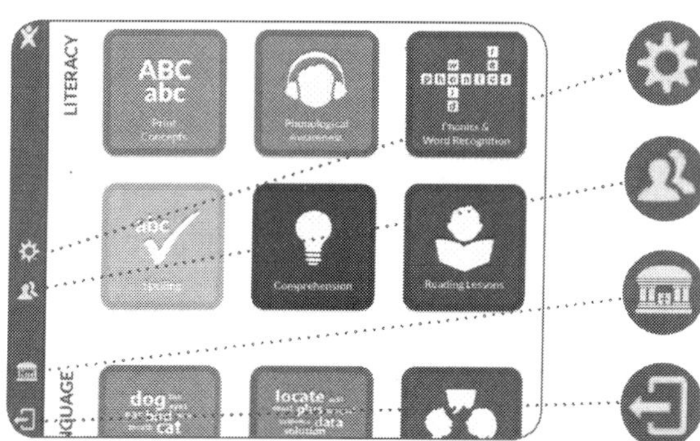

Change **program settings,** including first-language support.

Launch the **Imagine Learning Portal** to find reports, management functions, and additional resources.

Enter the **Imagine Museum** to preview performance-based student engagement features.

Log out of the Activity Menu and return to the **login page.**

Reports and Tools

Tools for setting up the program and monitoring student progress and growth are provided to teachers and administrators. Reviewing data regularly, as well as analyzing student recordings and writings, drives program efficacy and success.

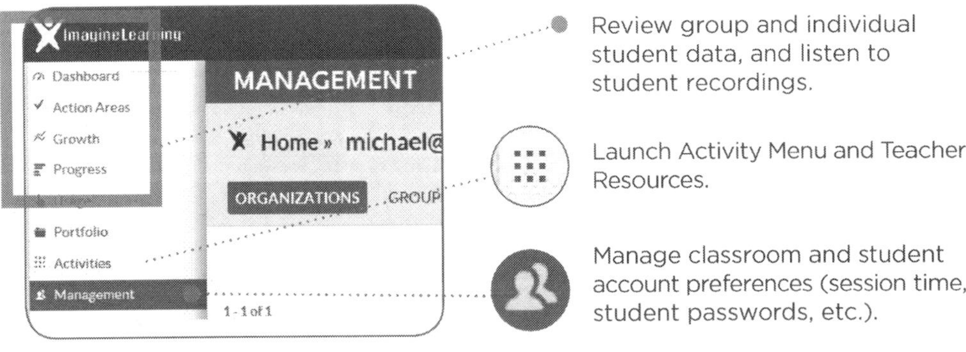

Review group and individual student data, and listen to student recordings.

Launch Activity Menu and Teacher Resources.

Manage classroom and student account preferences (session time, student passwords, etc.).

Action Areas Tool

Use data from the Action Areas Tool to identify individual students or groups of students that struggle with a particular skill. Action Areas will also suggest online activities that can be used to help struggling students.

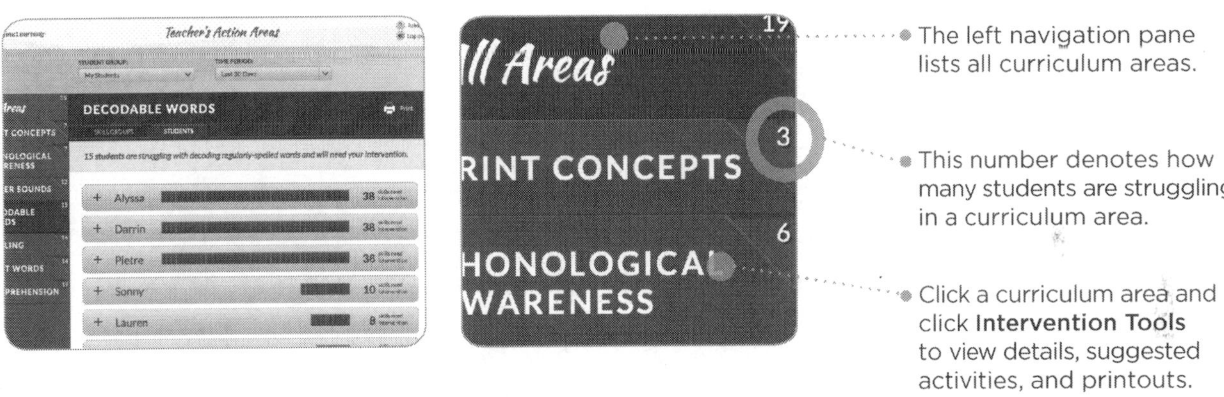

The left navigation pane lists all curriculum areas.

This number denotes how many students are struggling in a curriculum area.

Click a curriculum area and click **Intervention Tools** to view details, suggested activities, and printouts.

Teacher Resources

All Classroom Activities and Reteaching Lessons included in this volume can also be found in the Teacher Resources section online.

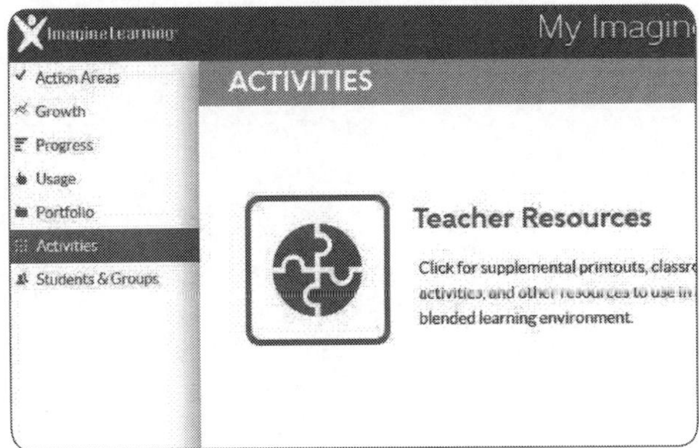

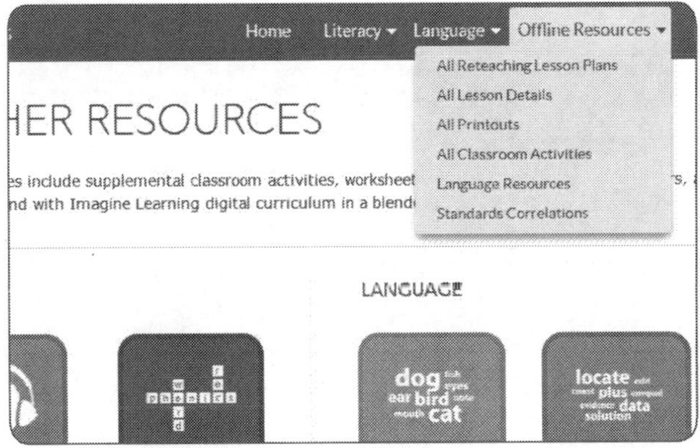

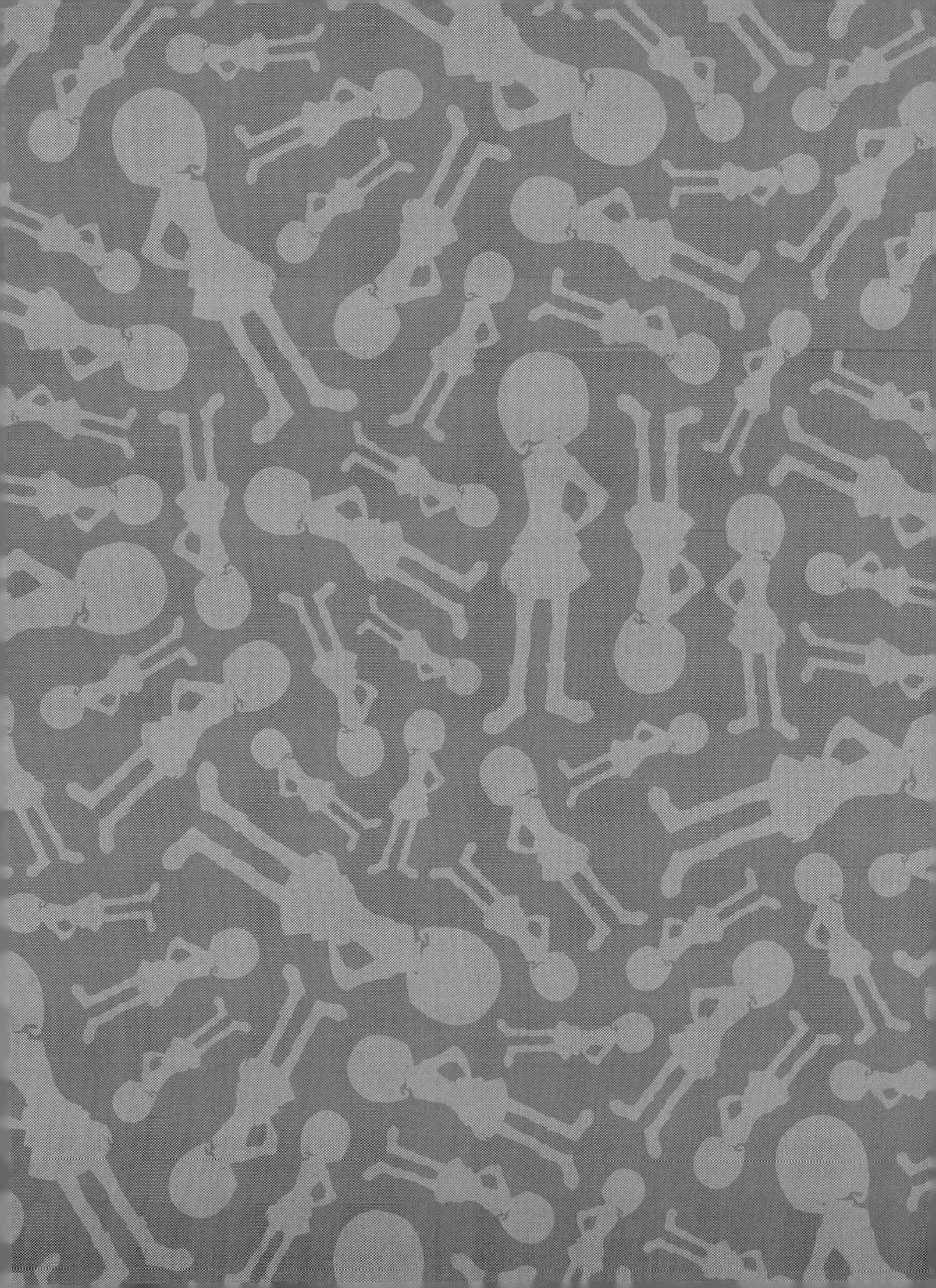

GRAMMAR

RETEACHING LESSONS

Developed with research-based methods, these lessons provide engaging activities and print-ready supporting materials to help students develop basic grammar skills. Each lesson can be used for small group intervention or adapted for whole-class use. Grammar lessons promote oral language production and real-life application of grammar concepts.

Analyze data in the Imagine Learning Action Areas Tool to identify groups of students who struggle with grammar and use the Reteaching Lessons to provide additional support.

- Complete lesson plans with a prior knowledge check, guided and independent practice, and assessment
- Theme-based lessons and art-rich resources and charts that provide reinforcement of grammar concepts
- Standards-based materials that require minimal teacher preparation

Progress Tracking Sheet

Date	Student Name	Lesson/Skill	Intervention Successful (Y/N)	Notes

Progress Tracking Sheet

Date	Student Name	Lesson/Skill	Intervention Successful (Y/N)	Notes

Notes

Reteaching Lessons ✓

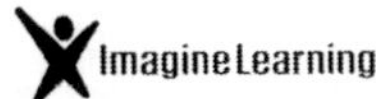

Grammar

Adjectives

Grade 1 | 15 min. | CCSS.L.1.1.f TEKS 110.12.20.A.iii

LEARNING OBJECTIVE: Identify basic adjectives and use them in a sentence.
LANGUAGE OBJECTIVE: Describe fruits and vegetables using adjectives.
PREREQUISITE SKILLS: Know the definition of a noun and be able to identify basic nouns.

Lesson Overview

Teacher reviews rules and examples of adjectives with students. Students describe pictures of fruit to practice using adjectives. Then students play guessing games to practice using adjectives in complete sentences.

Materials	Preparation
• Grammar Chart • Apple Picture Prompt • Fruit Picture Cards • Food Picture Prompt	• Fold the Apple Picture Prompt on the dotted line so that the bottom row covers the middle row and only the top row is visible. • Cut out Fruit Picture Cards. • To print materials in color, visit the online Teacher Resources.

NOTE: Most vocabulary used in this lesson is pre-taught online and a review is included before the independent practice. If students struggle with the words, use the suggestion under differentiation to review and practice.

Reteaching Lessons

Activate Prior Knowledge

Quickly review the prerequisite skill with students and evaluate their proficiency. If students are not proficient with this skill, complete the corresponding Grammar Lesson before continuing.

NOUNS: ***A noun is a word that names a person, place, or thing. Foods are a good example of nouns that are things. If I name something you can eat, that's a noun. I'll say some words. If what I say is a noun, spread your hands toward me like this.*** Extend your arms out in front of you with palms facing up. ***If the word I say is not a noun, fold your arms, like this.*** Fold your arms.

Say each word, pausing for students to react: *open, smash, apple, washed, cake, chop, cooking, soup, squishy, cracker, melon, cheese, yellow.*

Teach and Model

Introduce the grammar principle

Now that you know about nouns, we can learn about adjectives. Adjectives give us more information about nouns.

Work through the Grammar Chart

Use the picture and the caption to present the grammar in context.

Read through the rules.

Explore the examples.

Clarify and correct if needed

When an adjective is right next to a noun, the adjective comes first.

Guided Practice

Say: ***Using adjectives is like painting with words. You can use adjectives to help others see what you are talking about.*** Display the folded picture prompt. Say: ***For example, here is an apple. I can use adjectives to add interesting details about the apple. I can describe how it looks, tastes, or feels, or tell how many there are.***

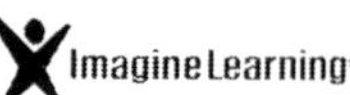

Unfold the picture prompt to display all images. Ask: ***Listen as I use adjectives to talk about an apple. Which picture am I painting with my words?*** Read the following sentences aloud. Pause after each sentence and allow the students to point to the correct picture.

I found a little, wormy apple.

I like shiny, round apples.

We bought many juicy apples.

He has an old, lumpy apple.

Explain: ***If you choose your adjectives carefully, you can describe something that you see and someone else can know what it is—even without seeing it.***

Tell students they will play a guessing game to practice using adjectives. Use the Fruit Picture Cards. Quickly review the names of the fruits on the cards before beginning.

Model the game: Pick a fruit card, but do not show it to the students. Describe the fruit using basic adjectives. Have the students try to guess which fruit you are holding. Repeat with additional fruits. After several rounds have a volunteer pick a card and describe the fruit to the class. This activity will provide sufficient practice after about 8 cards. Select the fruits that your students will be most familiar with.

Bank:

orange: round, bumpy, orange, juicy

grape: small, round, green or purple, sweet, juicy

pear: green or yellow, juicy,

banana: long, curved, yellow, soft, squishy

lemon: hard, bumpy, yellow, sour

cherry: small, red, shiny, delicious,

watermelon: big, heavy, striped, green and red

kiwi: small, brown, fuzzy, round

strawberry: red, squishy, seedy, sticky

blueberry: small, squishy, blue, round

peach: fuzzy, soft, sticky, orange

apple: crunchy, round, red or green,

pineapple: big, long, yellow, pokey, sweet

plum: soft, dark, juicy, smooth

lime: sour, green, lumpy, juicy

coconut: hard, brown and white, crunchy

mango: big, green and orange, sweet, squishy

melon: big, heavy, seedy, round

Alternate Activity

Have students place their heads down on their desks and close their eyes. Tell them to listen carefully to the adjectives and use the thumbs-up signal when they know the fruit being described. After most of the students have raised a thumb, call on a volunteer to guess the fruit.

Independent Practice

Tell the students that they will play a guessing game to practice adjectives. Ask: ***Have you ever been to a store to buy fruit? Imagine a store that sells only one fruit each day and you have to guess what it is.***

The teacher plays the role of the seller and sits or stands behind a desk or a table. The students are the shoppers and will work in groups of two or three. Use the Fruit Picture Cards. Quickly review the names of all the fruits on the cards, and spread them out on the table. Choose a fruit and tell the students when you are ready.

Have two or three students step up to the fruit counter and ask for the Fruit of the Day. Respond: ***If you want to buy fruit, you must guess what it is. You each get to ask one question and each question must use an adjective.*** Answer the students' questions, revealing information that will give them clues but not reveal the answer. For example:

Buyer 1: It is red?

Seller: ***Yes, but it can also be other colors.***

Buyer 2: Is it soft?

Seller: ***No. It is crunchy.***

After the three questions, the students must guess the fruit. They can confer with each other before they make their guess, but they get only one chance. If the buyers guess correctly, they get a point. Repeat the activity with a new fruit and a new group of students.

Differentiation

For more support: Practice adjectives before the game. Say: ***I'll say an adjective, and you say it back with the name of the fruit I hold up: crunchy*** (a crunchy apple); ***juicy*** (a juicy plum); ***squishy*** (a squishy banana); ***sweet*** (a sweet strawberry).

Adjective bank: big, little, soft, smooth, bumpy, red, yellow, orange, purple, green, round, long, sweet, sour, juicy, sticky, fuzzy, crunchy, squishy, light, heavy, delicious

For a challenge: Have the students complete each round of the game by writing an advertising sign for each fruit of the day using a complete sentence and at least two adjectives. For example, a student could write, "The Fruit of the Day is a delicious, red, crunchy apple."

Check Progress

Use the Food Picture Prompt and the following activity to check individual progress made on the target skill.

Say: ***Describe these fruits and vegetables using adjectives.*** Have each student select a fruit or vegetable on the Food Picture Prompt and describe it in a complete sentence that includes at least one adjective. For example, a student could say, "This is a round onion," or "This is a large, purple onion."

If the student can correctly use adjectives to describe two items, consider the intervention successful.

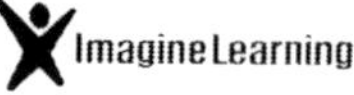

Adjectives

Purple Plums

Flap the rooster
is **big** and **smart**.

He wears **funny** hats
as he works on his art.

He holds **long** brushes
with **fluffy**, **blue** thumbs.

And hums **happy** songs
as he paints **purple** plums.

Reteaching Lessons

Adjectives are describing words; they describe **nouns**.

The big **rooster** paints four, round **plums**.

Adjectives tells us what something is like.

A plum is **sweet** and **smooth**.

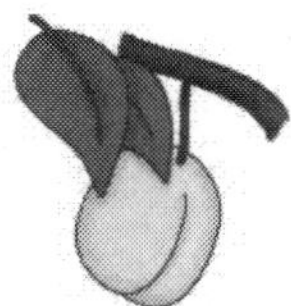

This plum is **small** and **yellow**.

Adjectives tell us "how many" or "how much."

Here are **three** bananas.

I put **all** the bananas in the salad.

apple

Reteaching Lessons

Apple Picture Chart

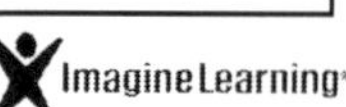

Reteaching Lessons

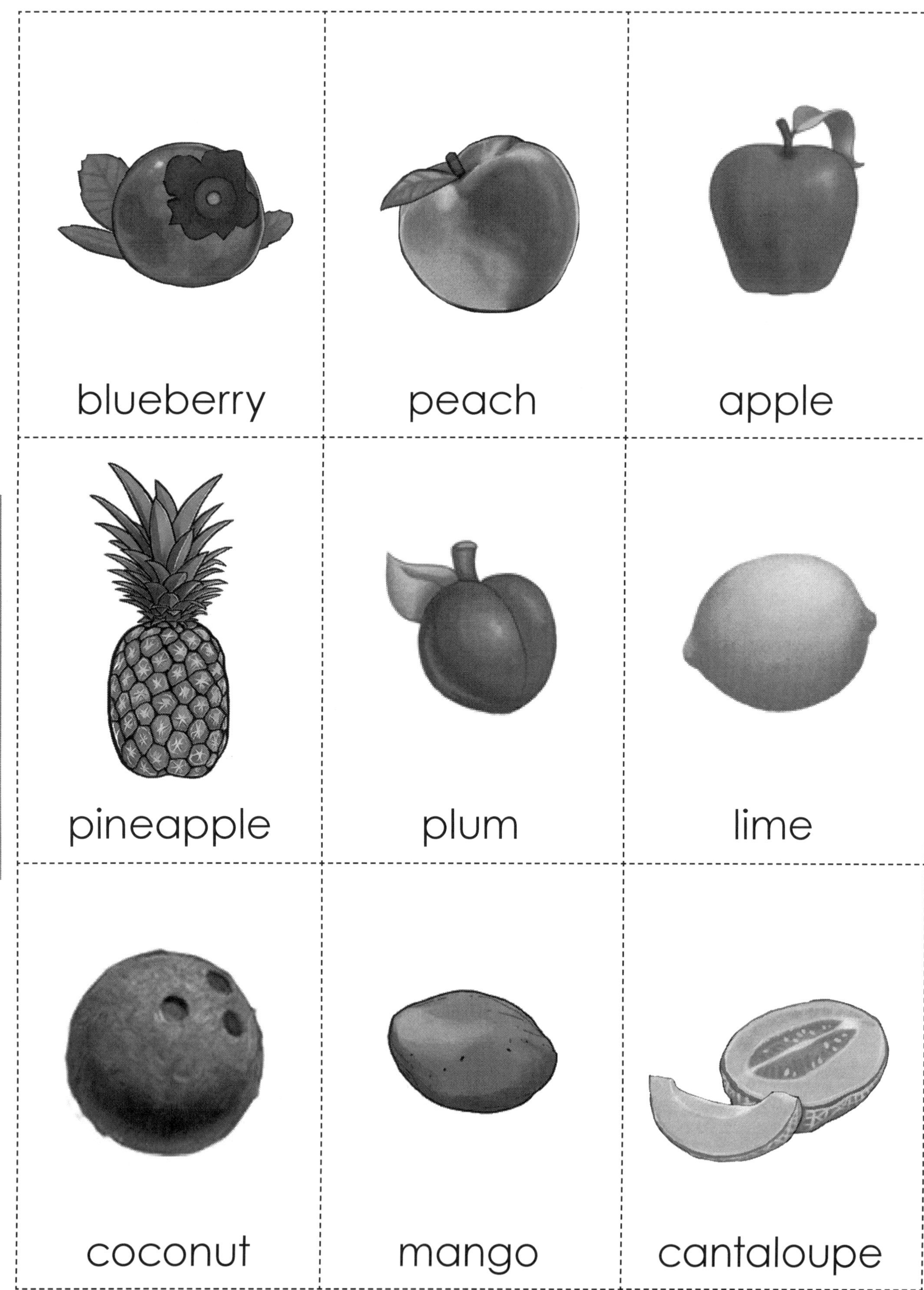

Reteaching Lessons

Fruit Picture Cards

Imagine Learning

Reteaching Lessons

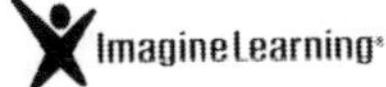

Food Picture Prompt

Grammar

Comparative Adjectives

Grade 3

15 min.

CCSS.L.3.1.G
TEKS 110.15.20.A.iii

LEARNING OBJECTIVE: Identify and use comparative adjectives in complete sentences.
LANGUAGE OBJECTIVE: Compare characteristics of two different animals using adjectives.
PREREQUISITE SKILLS: Know that adjectives describe nouns and be able to identify and give examples of simple adjectives.

Lesson Overview

Teacher reviews rules and examples of comparative adjectives with students. Students use picture prompts and adjectives to compare vegetables. Students then play an animal card game to practice using comparative adjectives in complete sentences.

Materials	Preparation
• Small beanbag • Grammar Chart • Garden Picture Prompt • Farm Animal Cards	• Cut out Farm Animal Cards. (Additional sets of Farm Animal Cards will be needed for the challenge activity.) • To print materials in color, visit the online Teacher Resources.

 NOTE: Adjectives that require the use of *more* ___ *than* rather than the *-er* ending are designated with an asterisk (*).

Activate Prior Knowledge

Quickly review the prerequisite skill with students and evaluate their proficiency. If students are not proficient with this skill, complete the corresponding Grammar Lesson before continuing.

ADJECTIVES: ***An adjective is a word that describes a noun. We can use adjectives to describe what a person, place, or thing is like. For example, this is a pencil. Listen for the words I use to describe this pencil. The pencil is long, skinny, yellow, smooth, pointy, and hard. Those describing words are adjectives.***

Use an object you can toss, such as a small beanbag. Explain: ***I'll name a person, place, or thing. You will all quietly think of adjectives that could describe it. Then I'll toss this to someone who will say the adjective they are thinking of.***

Say a word from the word bank below. Pause to allow students to think. Then toss the beanbag to a student to name an adjective. Have the group repeat the adjective and the noun together. For example, if the teacher says ***flower***, and the student responds *pretty*, the students and teacher repeat: ***a pretty flower***.

Noun bank:

people: a baby, the teacher, your brother, a farmer

places: the school lunchroom (cafeteria), the park, our city, the ocean

things: a chair, a flower, a tree, a spider, a truck, some vegetables

Reteaching Lessons

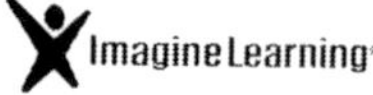

Teach and Model

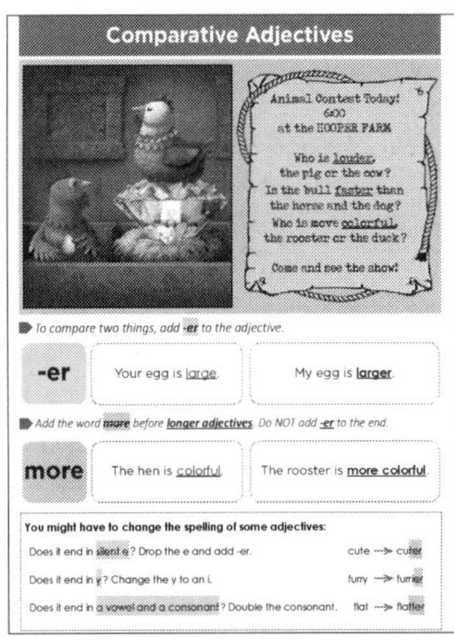

Introduce the grammar principle

Now that you know how to use an adjective to describe a noun, you can learn how to use an adjective to compare two nouns. When you compare, you look at how two things are alike or different. Adjectives can help us do this.

Work through the Grammar Chart

Use the picture and the animal show flyer to present the grammar in context.

Read through the rules.

Explore the examples.

Clarify and correct if needed

- ***The word* than *is usually used with comparative adjectives: The ____ is [bigger] than the ______ .***
- ***Some adjectives have different forms:* good *changes to* better, bad *changes to* worse.**

Guided Practice

Tell the students they will compare two things to practice using adjectives.

Say: ***Everyone at Hooper Farm is busy getting ready for the animal contest. But who is going to take care of the garden? Do you know anything about fruits and vegetables? Can you help me? I'll show you things that grow on a farm, and you can help me to compare them.***

Continue: ***For example, if I say, "Onions are round," you could say, "Peas are rounder than onions." If I say, "Cucumbers are lumpy," you could say, "Potatoes are lumpier than cucumbers."***

Review the fruits and vegetables on the Garden Picture Prompt with the students. Then read the following sentences aloud as you show the picture. Pause and allow the students to use the same adjective to compare the fruit or vegetable you mentioned with another fruit or vegetable pictured. Remind students, as needed, that longer adjectives use the word *more* in front of the adjective instead of adding *-er* to the end.

Sentence bank and possible responses:

Peppers are long. (Carrots are longer than peppers.)

Cherries are small. (Peas are smaller than cherries.)

Corn is sweet. (Cherries are sweeter than corn.)

Tomatoes are juicy. (Watermelon is juicier than tomatoes.)

Potatoes are red. (Strawberries are redder than potatoes.)

Strawberries are soft. (Tomatoes are softer than strawberries.)

Potatoes are hard. (Carrots are harder than potatoes.)

Peas are delicious.* (Strawberries are more delicious than peas.)

Onions are flavorful.* (Peppers are more flavorful than onions.)

Independent Practice

Tell the students they will play a game to practice using adjectives to compare.

Say: ***Imagine we went to the animal contest at Hooper Farm. In each event, two animals will compete for one adjective. You will compare the two animals and decide who wins.***

Review the animals on the Farm Animal Cards with the students. Then shuffle and place the cards facedown in a stack.

Review the adjectives in the bank with the students. Then choose one adjective from the bank and display it for all to see.

Have students draw two animal cards and place them face up on the table.

Reteaching Lessons

Invite a student to form a complete sentence comparing the two animals using the chosen adjective. Based on the comparison, declare one animal the winner. For example, if you choose the adjective *big*, and the student flips over the cow and the hen, the student could say, "The cow is bigger than the hen. The cow wins!"

Keep the same adjective and flip over two new animals, or choose a new adjective from the list.

If students use *-er* when *more than* should be used, help them to self-correct using prompts such as: ***Did you notice the adjective you used was a long word? What do we know about making comparisons with longer adjectives?***

Many of these comparisons will be silly and most of them will be subjective. If necessary, establish the rule that the selected student is the judge and their decision is final (whether others agree or not). This way the focus can be on the correct use of comparative adjectives and the students can have fun and enjoy the silly comparisons.

Adjective bank: strong, long, fast, big, lumpy, brave, soft, cute, clean, loud, nice, messy, smelly, furry, funny, cheerful*, intelligent*, beautiful*, hard-working*, dangerous*, colorful*

Differentiation

For more support: Provide a sentence frame to help the students form a complete sentence:

The ______ is _______ than the _________ .

Practice forming comparative adjectives before the game. Say: ***I'll say an adjective, you add* -er *and say it back. Tall*** (taller), ***small*** (smaller) ***scary*** (scarier), ***cute*** (cuter). Say: ***Now I'll say a long adjective, you add the word* more *and say it back. Amazing**** (more amazing), ***interesting**** (more interesting), ***important**** (more important).

For a challenge: Divide students into pairs and provide each pair with a set of Farm Animal Cards. Have partners alternate making the comparison for each chosen adjective.

Check Progress

Use the questions below and the following activity to check individual progress made on the target skill.

Have each student draw two animal cards to use for the assessment. Explain: ***Imagine that it's time to clean up after the animal show. I'll name a chore that needs to be done. You decide which of your two animals will be able to help with that chore and tell me why, using a comparison.***

For example: ***We need tall animals to take down the decorations. If you have the duck and the horse, you might choose the horse and say, "The horse will do it because the horse is taller than the duck."***

Many of these comparisons will be silly. The purpose is not to make accurate statements about animal traits. If a student can correctly make comparisons using adjectives, consider the activity successful.

Chores: *We need an animal that is ...*

tall to take down the decorations.

short to clean under the tables.

noisy to tell everyone to go home.

confident* to give out the awards.

helpful to pick up trash.

smelly to take out the garbage.

popular* to work at the Lost and Found.

loud to show everyone the exit.

fuzzy to sweep the floor.

smart to count up the tickets.

powerful* to move the benches.

Writing Extension

Shuffle the Farm Animal Cards. Have each student draw two animal cards from the stack.

Explain: ***On your paper write three complete sentences to compare your two animals. Be sure to use an adjective and either add* -er *to the end of the adjective or use the word* more *in front of the adjective to make the comparison. Remember, when you add* -er *to adjectives, sometimes the spelling changes.***

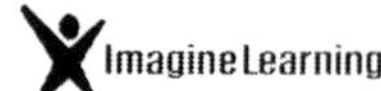

Comparative Adjectives

Animal Contest Today!
6:00
at the HOOPER FARM

Who is <u>louder</u>,
the pig or the cow?
Is the bull <u>faster</u> than
the horse and the dog?
Who is more <u>colorful</u>,
the rooster or the duck?

Come and see the show!

To compare two things, add ***-er*** *to the adjective.*

-er	Your egg is <u>large</u>.	My egg is <u>**larger**</u>.

Add the word ***more*** *before* ***<u>longer adjectives</u>****. Do NOT add* ***<u>-er</u>*** *to the end.*

more	The hen is <u>colorful</u>.	The rooster is <u>**more colorful**</u>.

You might have to change the spelling of some adjectives:

Does it end in silent e? Drop the **e** and add -er.	cute	→	cuter
Does it end in y? Change the *y* to an *i*.	furry	→	furrier
Does it end in a vowel and a consonant? Double the consonant.	flat	→	flatter

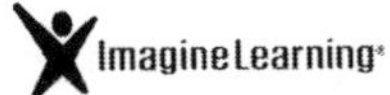

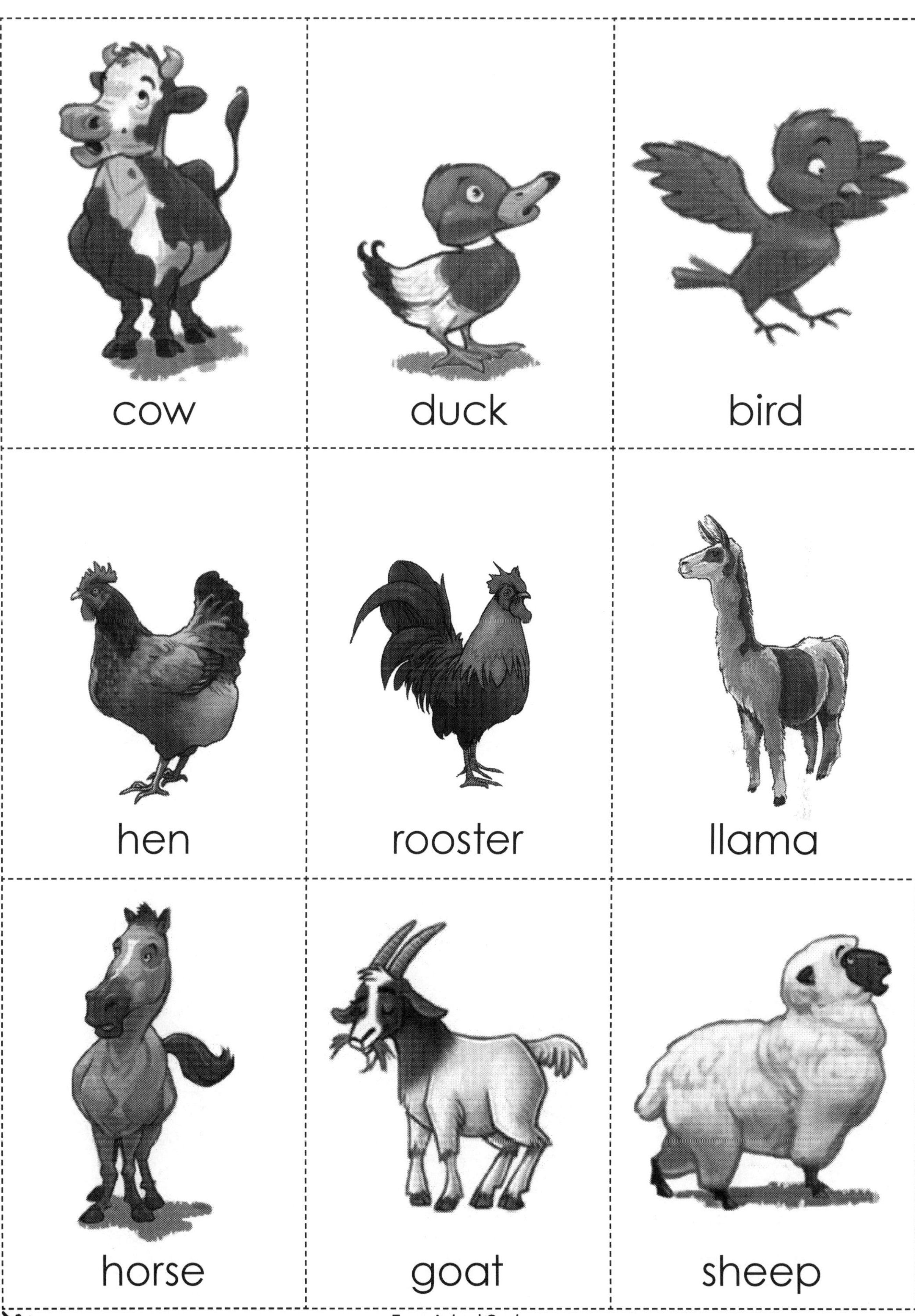
cow
duck
bird
hen
rooster
llama
horse
goat
sheep

Farm Animal Cards

Grammar

Superlative Adjectives

Grade 3

15 min.

CCSS.ELA-Literacy.L.3.1g
TEKS 110.15.20.A.iii

LEARNING OBJECTIVE: Identify and use superlative adjectives to compare more than two things.

LANGUAGE OBJECTIVE: Use superlative adjectives to compare pets.

PREREQUISITE SKILL(S): Know the definition of an adjective and be able to use adjectives to describe and compare nouns.

Lesson Overview

Teacher reviews rules and examples of superlative adjectives with students. Students listen to a story and identify superlative adjectives. They draw pictures and play a game to practice using superlatives to compare various pets.

Materials

- Garden Picture Prompt (from Comparative Adjectives Lesson)
- Grammar Chart
- Blank piece of paper (one per student)
- Beauty Competition Reading Cards (one card per student)
- Superlative Cards (one pair per student)

Preparation

- Cut out the Beauty Competition Reading Cards and Superlative Cards.
- To print materials in color, visit the online Teacher Resources.

NOTE: Many adjectives have spelling changes when used in the superlative form. These spelling changes are not taught in this lesson.

Activate Prior Knowledge

Quickly review the prerequisite skill with students and evaluate their proficiency. If students are not proficient with this skill, complete the corresponding Grammar Lesson before continuing.

COMPARATIVE ADJECTIVES: ***An adjective can describe a noun. Adjectives can also help you compare two nouns. We add -er to most adjectives to show how two things are different or alike. With longer adjectives we often use the word more in front of the adjective instead of adding -er.***

Show students the Comparative Adjective Picture Prompt.

Say: ***Look at these animals. Choose two animals and compare them using an adjective. For example, let's use the mouse and the bear. The mouse is smaller than the bear. Now you try. You will use an adjective to compare two animals.***

Possible adjectives bank: small, big, more colorful, fast, fat, loud, sad, happy, furry

Teach and Model

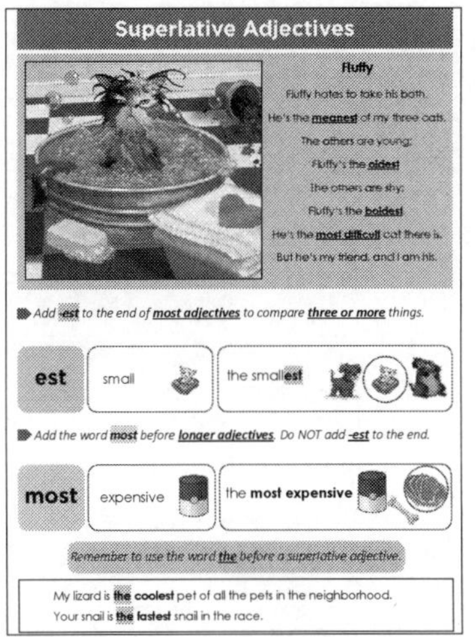

Introduce the grammar principle

Adjectives can help us compare two things. Adjectives can also help us when we compare more than two things.

Work through the Grammar Chart

Use the picture and the poem to present the grammar in context.

Read through the rules.

Explore the examples.

Clarify and correct if needed

- ***Some two-syllable adjectives use the standard** -est **suffix, including adjectives that end in er, le, or ow. For example:*** **narrow / narrowest.**
- ***If a two-syllable adjective ends in y, change the y to i and add -iest. For example:*** **happy / happiest.**

- ***If a two-syllable adjective ends in* e, *add* -st.**
- ***The word the always comes before the adjective.***
- ***Some superlative adjectives are irregular, including:***
  - ***good / best***
  - ***bad / worst***
  - ***old /oldest***
  - ***young / youngest***

Guided Practice

Distribute the Beauty Competition Reading Cards. Tell the students they will read a short story to practice using adjectives to compare three or more things.

Say: ***I will read each sentence. Read along in your head with me. Look at the word in bold. Is it a superlative adjective? Give me a thumbs up if it is and a thumbs down if it is not.***

Stop once or twice during the activity and have students explain their answer, especially if students hesitate or differ on their answers.

A Beauty Competition Just for Pets

1. I entered my pet frog in a **big** contest. (thumbs down)
2. His name is Jumpy and he is very **green**. (thumbs down)
3. Jumpy was the most **adorable frog** there. (thumbs up)
4. He was the **quietest** frog, too. (thumbs up)
5. Jumpy is a **brave** and **gentle** frog. (thumbs down)
6. He is the **most obedient** frog in the world. (thumbs up)
7. He makes me the **proudest** pet owner in the world. (thumbs up)

Independent Practice

Tell the students they will play a game to practice using adjectives to compare pets. Say: ***We are going to use adjectives to describe our pets or our friends' pets. Let's take a minute to brainstorm words we can use to describe pets.*** Write the adjectives on the board. As needed, prompt students to think of adjectives such as these: furry, loving, happy, fat, fast, sleepy, silly, etc.

Pass out a blank piece of paper to each student. Say: ***Now I'm going to give you just one minute to draw a picture of your pet, so work quickly. Try to draw it in a way that shows some of these adjectives. If you don't have a pet, draw a picture of a pet you would want or an imaginary pet.***

Once the students are done with their drawings, arrange them on a table so everyone can see all the pets.

Say: ***Now we are going to compare these pets. Choose three pets to compare. I'll go first.***

Model for the students comparing three pets. For example, to compare a dog, a frog, and a fish, you might say: ***The dog is the fastest.***

Have students take turns choosing three animals and using superlative adjectives to compare the pets.

If students do not use a superlative adjective correctly, use prompts to help them correct it. For example: ***Did you remember to look at how long the word is? What ending do we add if the adjective only has one syllable? What word do we add when the adjective has two or more syllables?***

Differentiation

For more support: If students struggle to come up with an adjective, use this adjective bank to help them:

-est adjectives: large, slow, small, fast, long, short, tall

Most *adjectives:* colorful, boring, beautiful, interesting, expensive, exciting, dangerous

For a challenge: Have students follow the same instructions as above, but after they choose their three animals, ask them to come up with a superlative adjective for each animal instead of just one of the animals. For example, if the animals are dog, frog, and fish, the student could say, "The dog is the fastest. The frog is the roundest. The fish is the smallest."

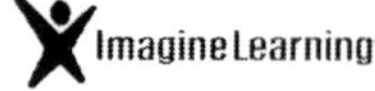

Check Progress

Use the following activity to check individual progress made on the target skill.

Say: ***We are going to change regular adjectives into superlative adjectives.*** Give each student a pair of Superlative Cards (one *most* and one *-est* card). ***I will say a sentence aloud. You choose the card that shows the correct way to change the adjective: add* most *or add* -est. *Keep your card facedown until I count to three. Then we will all hold our cards up at the same time.***

Say a sentence from the word bank. If students need additional support, write the adjective on the board. Have the students hold up their *most* card or their *-est* card depending on what the adjective calls for.

Once everyone has responded, choose one student to repeat the sentence with the superlative adjective and explain why they chose the card they did. Repeat with remaining sentences or until each student has had a chance to respond.

If students can correctly change an adjective to a superlative adjective and explain how and why they did so, consider the intervention successful.

Add *est* to end of adjective	**Add *most* before the adjective**
Your puppy is sweet.	Annie's snake is beautiful.
My owl is smart.	My pet is impossible.
The horse is strong.	The bat is important.
That hamster is round.	Your mouse is adorable.
Tim's parrot is loud.	This cat food is delicious.
This fish is blue.	
Her lizard is bumpy.	
That goat is fat.	

Reteaching Lessons

Superlative Adjectives

Fluffy

Fluffy hates to take his bath.
He's the **meanest** of my three cats.
The others are young;
Fluffy's the **oldest**.
The others are shy;
Fluffy's the **boldest**.
He's the **most difficult** cat there is.
But he's my friend, and I am his.

*Add **-est** to the end of **most adjectives** to compare **three or more** things.*

est	small 	the small**est** 

*Add the word **most** before **longer adjectives**. Do NOT add **-est** to the end.*

most	expensive 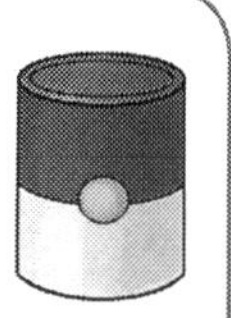	the **most expensive** 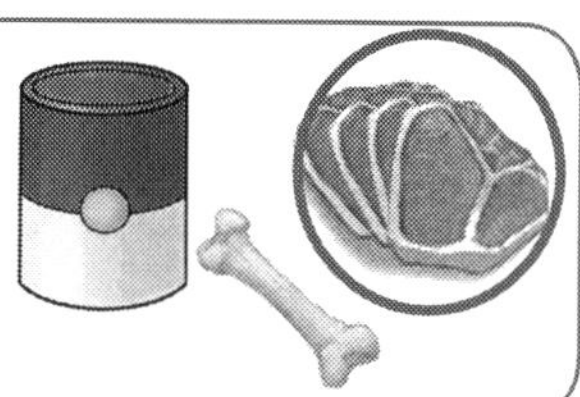

*Remember to use the word **the** before a superlative adjective.*

My lizard is **the coolest** pet of all the pets in the neighborhood.
Your snail is **the fastest** snail in the race.

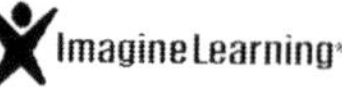

A Beauty Competition Just for Pets

I entered my pet frog in a **big** contest.

His name is Jumpy and he is very **green**.

Jumpy was the **most adorable** frog there.

He was the **quietest** frog, too.

Jumpy is a **brave** and **gentle** frog.

He is the **most obedient** frog in the world.

That makes me the **proudest** pet owner in the world.

A Beauty Competition Just for Pets

I entered my pet frog in a **big** contest.

His name is Jumpy and he is very **green**.

Jumpy was the **most adorable** frog there.

He was the **quietest** frog, too.

Jumpy is a **brave** and **gentle** frog.

He is the **most obedient** frog in the world.

That makes me the **proudest** pet owner in the world.

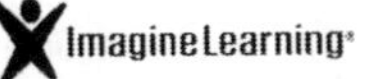

-est	most
-est	most
-est	most
-est	most

✓ Reteaching Lessons

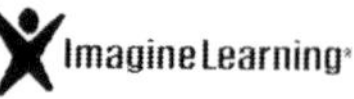

Adverbs

Grade 2

15 min.

CCSS.L.2.1.E
TEKS 110.13.21.A.iii

LEARNING OBJECTIVE: Identify adverbs and use them correctly to modify verbs.
LANGUAGE OBJECTIVE: Describe animal actions using a variety of adverbs.
PREREQUISITE SKILL: Know what a verb is and be able to identify basic verbs.

Lesson Overview

Teacher reviews rules and examples of adverbs with students. Students add adverbs to simple sentences and then play a pantomime game to act out adverbs and use them in complete sentences.

Materials	Preparation
• Grammar Chart • Adverb Picture Prompts • Adverb Cards • Check Progress Sheet	• Cut out Adverb Cards. • To print materials in color, visit the online Teacher Resources.

NOTE: Many words function as different parts of speech, depending on how they are used. Some words are classified as adverbs when used without an object but are classified as prepositions when used with an object. For example, "The bees buzzed outside" (adverb) or "The bees buzzed outside the hive" (preposition). Students at this level do not need to worry about this distinction; accept both adverbs and prepositions

Activate Prior Knowledge

Quickly review the prerequisite skill with students and evaluate their proficiency. If students are not proficient with this skill, complete the corresponding Grammar Lesson before continuing.

VERBS: ***Verbs are action words; they tell what someone or something does. Some actions are hard to see such as think or guess. But many verbs are actions we can do with our bodies. Here are some examples. I'll say a verb, and you show it to me with an action.***

Say each word, pausing for students to react: ***blink, wave, march, eat, dance, jump, wiggle.***

Teach and Model

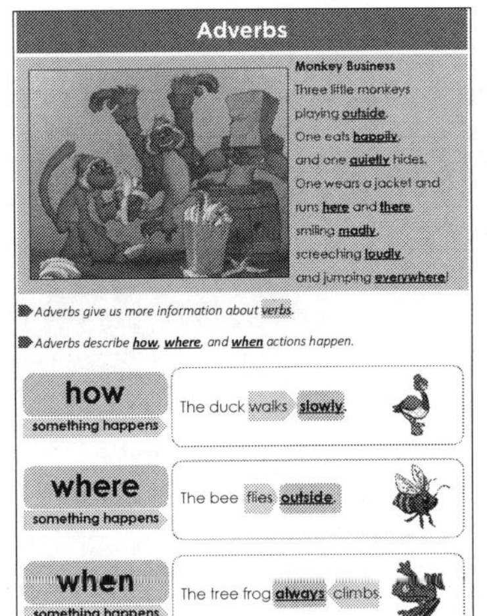

Introduce the grammar principle

Now that you know about verbs, we can learn about adverbs. Adverbs tell us more about a verb.

Work through the Grammar Chart

Use the picture and the poem to present the grammar in context.

Read through the rules.

Explore the examples.

Clarify and correct if needed

- ***Adverbs can come before or after a verb.***
- ***There are different kinds of adverbs:***
  - ***Adverbs of manner: The adverb*** **slowly** ***shows us*** **how** ***the duck walks.***
  - ***Adverbs of place: The adverb*** **everywhere** ***shows us*** **where** ***the bees fly.***
  - ***Adverbs of time: The adverb*** **always** ***shows us*** **when** ***the frog climbs.***

Reteaching Lessons

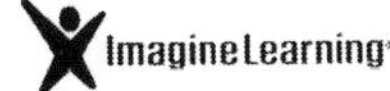

Guided Practice

Tell the students they will add more information to sentences to practice using adverbs.

Say: ***Let's practice giving more information about how, when, and where actions happen. I'll give you a sentence with an action. You tell me an adverb we could add to the sentence that would tell us more about* how, where, *or* when *the action happens.***

Read the sentences from the bank below as you show the corresponding picture prompts. Allow volunteers to suggest adverbs to add to the sentence. After each suggestion, have the group say the sentence with the adverb.

For example: ***The bees buzzed.***

How did they buzz? (loudly) ***Say it with me: The bees buzzed loudly.***

Where did they buzz? (outside) ***The bees buzzed outside.***

When did they buzz? (today) ***The bees buzzed today.***

Guide students as needed to use adverbs correctly. If students struggle to think of adverbs, ask questions to elicit the adverbs from the bank. To help students avoid using prepositional phrases, direct them to use only one-word answers. If a student does use a preposition (by the flowers, in the garden, like a kangaroo) accept it as a correct answer and move on.

Sentence bank:	*Adverb bank:*
The bees buzzed.	noisily, busily, around, everywhere, today, yesterday
The frog is jumping.	quickly, nervously, away, outside
The dog plays.	happily, quietly, excitedly, inside, upstairs, today
Pam's cat purrs.	quietly, calmly, eagerly, always, today

Independent Practice

Note that this activity focuses on the most commonly used adverbs: adverbs of manner.

Tell the students they will play an action game to practice adverbs.

Review the adverbs on the Adverb Cards with the students, and then place the cards in a stack.

Say: ***Imagine we are all monkeys and one person is the monkey trainer. The trainer will tell us an action to do. Before the trainer comes, we will pick an adverb. We will always do what the trainer says, but monkeys like to play around so we will only do it the way the Adverb Card tells us to.***

You might want to establish rules for the monkeys, such as only making very quiet noises or staying in place as they do the actions.

Choose one student to be the trainer. Send the trainer to a different location in the room and have him or her think of actions the monkeys can do. (See action bank for ideas.)

Have a student pick an adverb card from the stack. Read it quietly to the students, but do not let the trainer know the word. Have the trainer return and give the monkeys an action to do. For example: Wave your arms!

Have the monkeys do or pantomime the action in the manner of the adverb. For example, if the adverb chosen was *slowly*, then the monkeys wave their arms slowly.

The trainer then tries to guess the adverb. The guess must be phrased in a complete sentence stating the action and the adverb. For example, "You are waving your arms slowly!"

The trainer can give new commands until he or she can guess the adverb. Repeat the activity with a new student in the role of the trainer.

Action bank: wave your arms, stand, sit, wash your face, eat a banana, climb a tree, bounce a ball, clap, catch a fly, jump, play with a friend, put on clothes, paint a mud picture, shake hands with a neighbor, turn around, make a banana, dance, get a drink from a waterfall, feed the baby, pick up sticks, make a grass pizza, throw a rock, swim in the pond, take a nap, run away from a lion, act like a human

Adverb bank: slowly, lovingly, happily, gracefully, nervously, quickly, angrily, excitedly, sleepily, calmly, silently, sneakily, sadly, powerfully, hungrily, stiffly

Differentiation

For more support: If the trainer struggles to identify the adverb, show three adverb cards as possible choices. Have the trainer choose the correct answer and state it in a complete sentence.

For a challenge: Encourage students to come up with additional adverbs that are not on the cards.

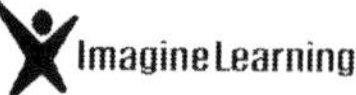

Variation

For more individual participation: Play the game a few times with the whole group. Then divide the students into pairs so there is an assistant trainer and a monkey in each pair. The teacher plays the head trainer. Each assistant trainer thinks of an adverb and whispers it to his or her partner. When the teacher gives the command, the monkeys will do the action. The teacher gets one guess for each pair. The assistant trainer states the correct answer in a complete sentence to indicate whether or not the teacher guessed correctly. For example:

Teacher: ***Sadly?***

Student: Yes, She was eating a banana sadly. Or No, she was eating a banana calmly.

Check Progress

Use the Check Progress Sheet and the following activity to assess individual progress made on the target skill.

Explain: ***The monkeys and their animal friends are busy today. We'll read a sentence together. Then you underline the action the animal is doing and circle the adverb. Then tell me if the adverb describes how, when, or where the monkey does the action.***

Show the student a sentence and read it with them. Have the student identify the action and the adverb. Have them tell you whether the adverb describes how, when or where the animal does the action.

For example: ***The monkey is sleeping quietly.*** The student should underline *sleeping* and circle *quietly*. The student should tell you that quietly describes how the monkey is sleeping.

Say: ***Now I want you to say the sentence again, but this time think of a different adverb you can use.*** The student should repeat the sentence using a new adverb. For example, "The monkey is sleeping today."

Repeat this process with each student, using a new sentence each time.

If the student can correctly identify and use adverbs and say how the adverb modifies the verb, consider the intervention successful.

Adverbs

Monkey Business

Three little monkeys
playing **outside**.
One eats **happily**,
and one **quietly** hides.
One wears a jacket and
runs **here** and **there**,
smiling **madly**,
screeching **loudly**,
and jumping **everywhere**!

Adverbs give us more information about ***verbs.***

Adverbs describe ***how****,* ***where****, and* ***when*** *actions happen.*

how something happens	The duck walks **slowly**. 
where something happens	The bee flies **outside**. 
when something happens	The tree frog **always** climbs. 

Reteaching Lessons ✓

Adverb Picture Prompt

slowly	lovingly
happily	gracefully
nervously	quickly
angrily	excitedly

Reteaching Lessons

Reteaching Lessons

sleepily	calmly
silently	sneakily
sadly	powerfully
hungrily	stiffly

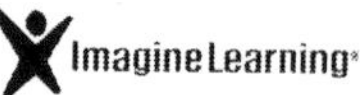

The giraffe eats outside.	
The monkey climbs slowly.	
The frog hangs there.	
The monkey sleeps calmly.	
The gorilla walks around.	
The bird flies high.	
The alligator swims sneakily.	
The monkey jumps excitedly.	
The elephant plays today.	
The monkey sits inside.	

Grammar

Articles A and An

Grade 1

15 min.

CCSS.L.1.1.H
TEKS 110.13.21.A.iii

LEARNING OBJECTIVE: Contrast the indefinite articles *a* and *an* and use them in a sentence.
LANGUAGE OBJECTIVE: Give information about animals using indefinite articles *a* and *an*.
PREREQUISITE SKILLS: Know the definition of a noun and be able to identify basic nouns.

Lesson Overview

Teacher reviews rules and examples of the articles *a* and *an* with students. Students follow picture prompts and choose *a* or *an* to complete a statement. Then students play an animal add-on game to practice using articles in complete sentences.

Materials	Preparation
• Grammar Chart • Parade Picture Prompt • Animal Game Cards • Animal Parts printout	• Cut out Animal Game Cards. • To print materials in color, visit the online Teacher Resources.

NOTE: Most vocabulary used in this lesson is pre-taught online, and a review is included before the independent practice. If students struggle with the animal names, use the differentiation suggestion to review and practice.

Activate Prior Knowledge

Quickly review the prerequisite skill with students and evaluate their proficiency. If students are not proficient with this skill, complete the corresponding Grammar Lesson before continuing.

NOUNS: ***A noun is a word that names a person, place, animal, or thing. All the people, places, and things around you in this room are nouns. I'll say a word. If it is a noun, stand up.***

Say each word, pausing for students to react: *pencil, marching, teacher, happy, sing, school, chair, yellow, ear.*

Say: ***Some nouns begin with consonants, like* b, t, m, s, w, *and others. Some nouns begin with a vowel:* a, e, i, o, *or* u. *I'll say a noun. If it begins with a consonant, circle your fingers in the shape of a* c *for consonant and say "consonant." If it begins with* a, e, i, o, *or* u, *hold your fingers in a* v *shape for vowel and say "vowel."***

Say each word, pausing for students to react: ***b**alloon, **g**ame, **u**mbrella, **p**opcorn, **a**lphabet, **o**tter, **c**at, **a**lligator, **e**gg*

Teach and Model

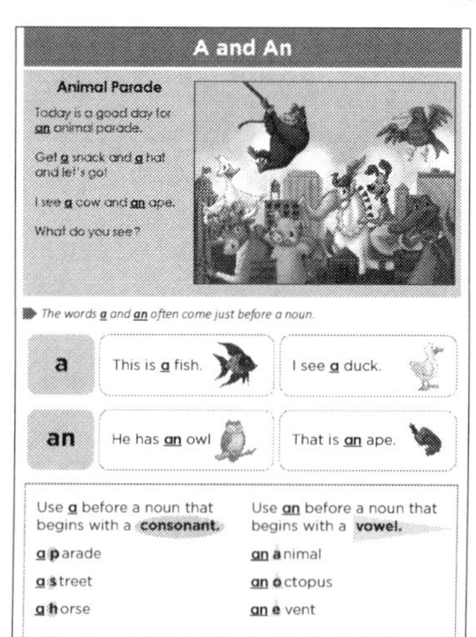

Introduce the grammar principle

Now that we've practiced nouns with consonants and vowels, we can learn about articles. The words* a *and* an *are called articles. They help us identify nouns.

Work through the Grammar Chart

Use the picture and the story to present the grammar in context.

Read through the rules.

Explore the examples.

Clarify and correct if needed

In most cases,* an *is used before words that begin with vowels. Sometimes the pronunciation of the first letter can affect this rule. For example:* u *is sometimes pronounced as* y *(a university),* o *sometimes has a* w *sound (a one), and* h *can be silent (an hour).

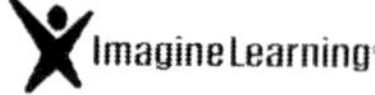

Guided Practice

Tell the students they will complete sentences to practice the articles *a* and *an*.

Say: ***Imagine all the animals had a parade. I'll show some things we could pack to take with us to the parade. You name each one as I pack it. Be sure to use*** **a** ***before a word that begins with a consonant and*** **an** ***before a word that begins with a vowel.***

Show the Parade Picture Prompt. Read the following sentences aloud, pointing to the corresponding image if needed. Pause at each blank and allow the students to use an article and a noun to complete each phrase. Guide students as needed to use the correct articles.

We can sit on ________. (a blanket)

It might rain. I'll take ________. (an umbrella)

We'll need some snacks. Let's take ______ and ________. (a sandwich, an egg)

If it is hot, we will eat ________. (an ice cream cone)

We can take some treats for the animals too. Let's give the horse ________ and the rabbit ______. (an apple, a carrot)

Independent Practice

Tell the students they will play an add-on game to practice the articles *a* and *an*. Say: ***Imagine we went to the animal parade. Let's name the animals we saw.***

Review the animals on the Animal Game Cards. Then place the cards facedown in a stack. Draw a card and place it face up in the middle of the table.

Write the sentence frame on the board and have the students repeat it aloud: ***"I went to the animal parade, and I saw ______________."*** Remind students that when they say an animal name that begins with a vowel, they should use the article *an*. When they say an animal name that begins with a consonant, they should use *a*.

Model the game: Draw a card. Use the sentence frame, filling in the blank with the name of the animal on the card. For example: If you draw the elephant card, say: ***I went to the animal parade, and I saw an elephant.***

Have students take turns drawing cards and adding them, face up to the line of animals on the table. After drawing a card, each student repeats the previous animals and then adds on the new animal pictured on the card. For example: If the next card is a lion, the student says: *I went to the animal parade and I saw* an *elephant and* a *lion.* If the next card is an owl, the student says: *I went to the animal parade and I saw* an *elephant,* a *lion, and* an *owl.*

Differentiation

For more support: Practice articles and animals before the game. Say: ***I'll say an animal, and you say it back with the correct article.***

Say each word, pausing for students to react/respond: ***fox*** (a fox), ***monkey*** (a monkey), ***elephant*** (an elephant), ***iguana***, (an iguana).

For a challenge: Have the students add adjectives to the sentence and make the article agree with the adjective rather than the noun. For example: ***I went to the animal parade and I saw a big elephant and an angry lion.***

Adjective bank: big, tiny, furry, pokey, creepy, colorful, powerful, quick, angry, awesome, enormous, itchy, obedient, orange, unhappy, ugly

Whole-Class Variation

The animal parade can also be used as a whole-class game. Have students place chairs in a large circle. Select one student to be the leader. The leader stands in the middle, and his or her chair is removed, leaving only enough chairs for the students who are sitting. Pass out an Animal Game Card to each seated student.

The leader walks around the inside of the circle and says the sentence frame, filling in the name of an animal. For example, "I went to the animal parade, and I saw ... an elephant." The student with the elephant card stands up says, "I'm an elephant," and follows along behind the leader. The leader continues walking and repeats the sentence with a new animal. For example, "I went to the animal parade and I saw ... a lion." The student with the lion card stands up says "I'm a lion," and follows along behind the leader and the elephant. The game continues with each new animal following along until the leader says, "Rainstorm! The parade is canceled." All students (including the leader) must quickly find a seat and sit down. One student will be left standing. This student becomes the leader.

The students who are seated exchange animal cards and the game starts over.

Reteaching Lessons

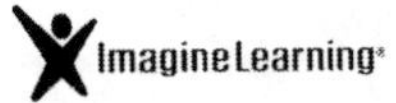

Check Progress

Use the Animal Parts printout and the following activity to check individual progress made on the target skill.

Have the student identify the animal part. Ask: ***What animal part is this?*** (It's an ear.) Have the student explain why he or she chose that article. (Possible response; I used *an* because ear starts with the vowel *e*.)

Then have the student identify the animal. Ask: ***What animal is it?*** (It's a lion) Have the student explain why he or she chose that article. (Possible response; I used *a* because *lion* starts with *l*, which is a consonant.)

If the students can correctly use articles with nouns and explain why they chose the article, consider the intervention successful.

Answer bank: an elbow, a monkey; an ankle, an alligator; a trunk, an elephant; a wing, a bee; a nose, a cow; a tail, a horse; an ear, a lion; an arm, an octopus; an eye, a shark

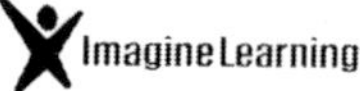

A and An

Animal Parade

Today is **a** good day for **an** animal parade.

Get **a** snack and **a** hat and let's go!

I see **a** cow and **an** ape.

What do you see?

*The words **a** and **an** often come just before a noun.*

a	This is **a** fish. 	I see **a** duck. 
an	He has **an** owl. 	That is **an** ape. 

Use **a** before a noun that begins with a **consonant.**

a **p**arade

a **s**treet

a **h**orse

Use **an** before a noun that begins with a **vowel.**

an **a**nimal

an **o**ctopus

an **e**vent

Reteaching Lessons

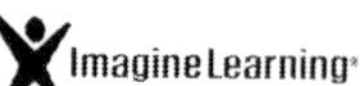
Imagine Learning

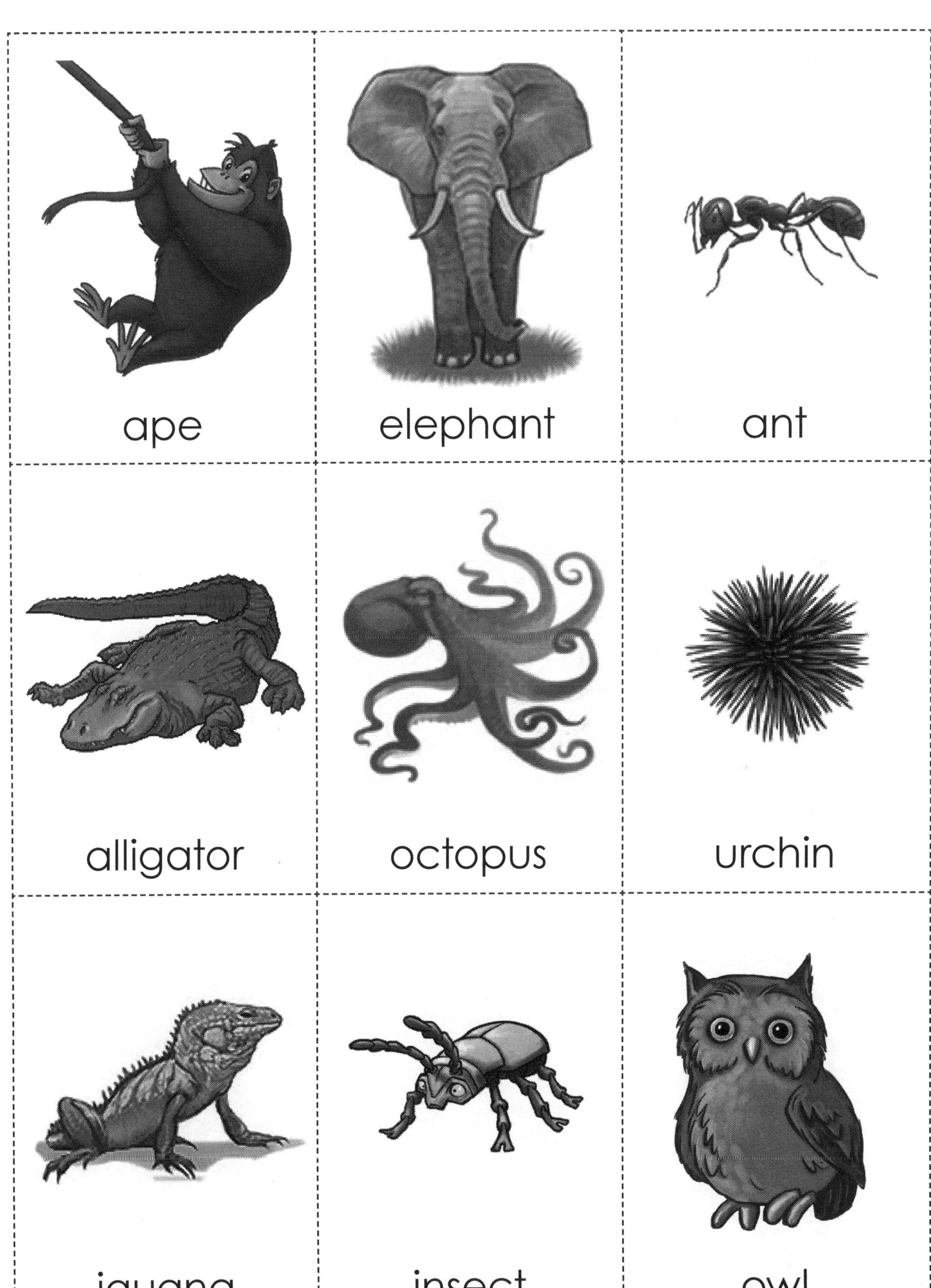
ape
elephant
ant
alligator
octopus
urchin
iguana
insect
owl

Animal Game Cards

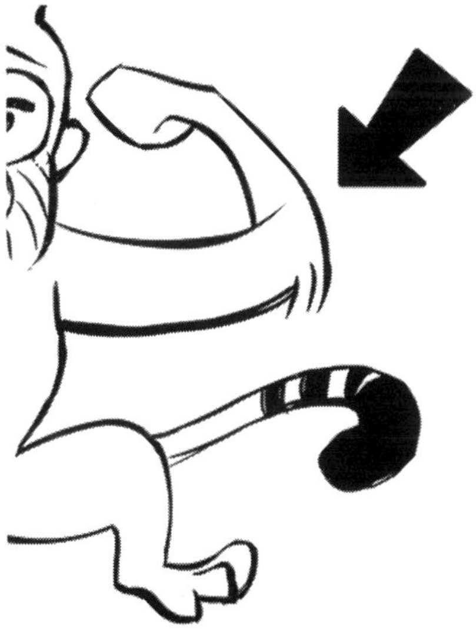

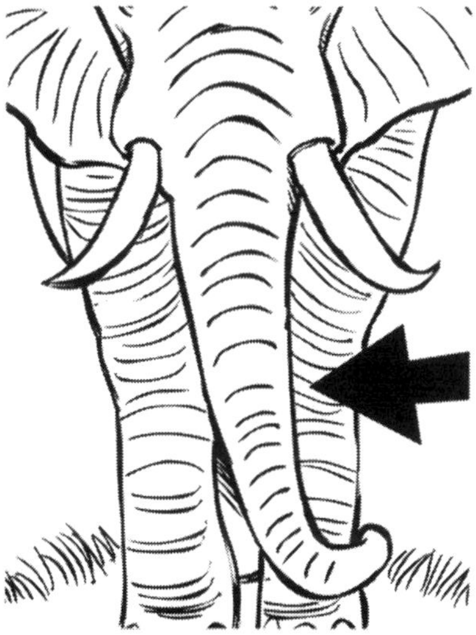

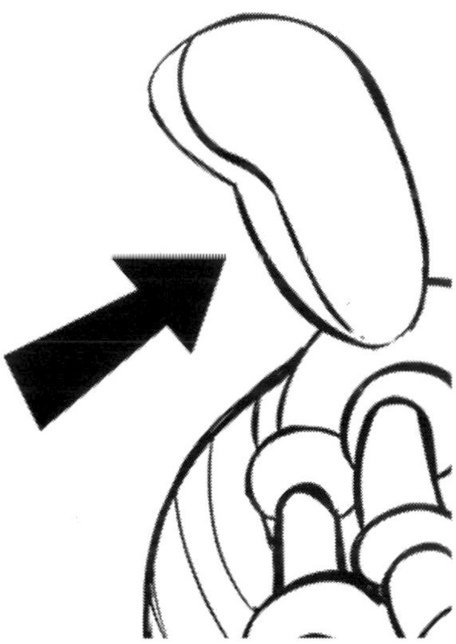

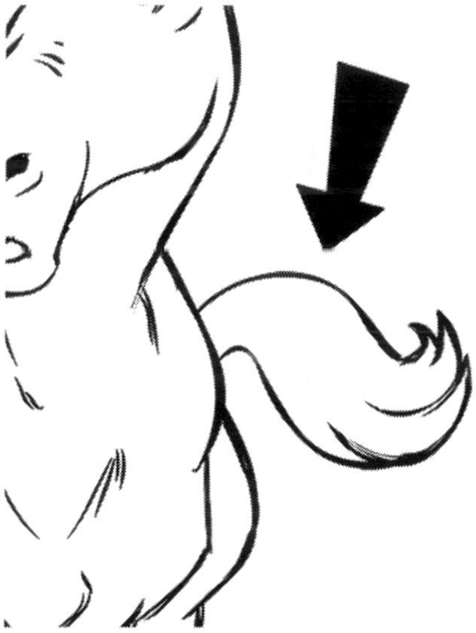

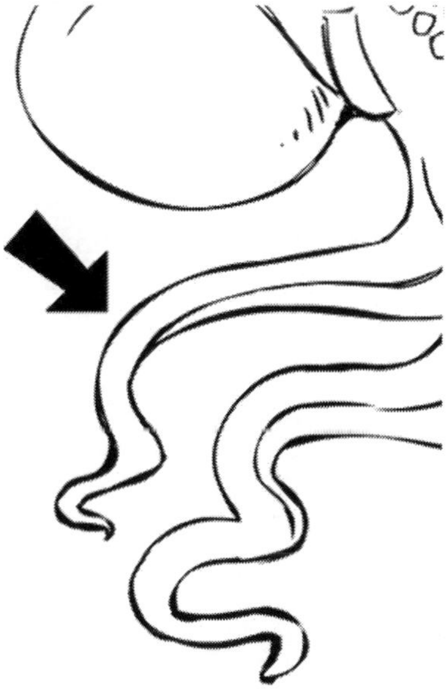

Reteaching Lessons ✓

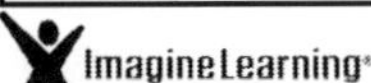

Animal Parts

Contractions

Grade 2

15 min.

CCSS L.2.2.c
TEKS 110.13.2.F

LEARNING OBJECTIVE: Identify and create contractions.

LANGUAGE OBJECTIVE: Combine words to create contractions and use them to talk about a lost pet.

PREREQUISITE SKILLS: Be familiar with personal pronouns. Know what an apostrophe is, and have a sense of formal and informal registers.

Lesson Overview

Teacher reviews rules and examples of contractions with students. Students use a chart to create contractions. Then students play a lost and found game to practice matching contractions to the original forms of the words.

Materials	Preparation
• Grammar Chart • Create a Contraction printout • Contraction Matching Cards • Follow-Up Note (one per student)	• Cut out the Contraction Matching Cards. • To print materials in color, visit the online Teacher Resources.

Activate Prior Knowledge

Quickly review the prerequisite skill with students and evaluate their proficiency. If students are not proficient with this skill, complete the corresponding Reteaching Lesson before continuing.

PRONOUNS: Write the subject pronouns (*I, he, she, it, you, we, they*) on the board. Explain: ***You already know that pronouns can take the place of nouns in a sentence. Let's use a simple sentence to practice using pronouns in place of nouns.***

Write this sentence frame on the board: ____________ like(s) peaches.

Say: ***I'll say the subject of the sentence using nouns, you repeat it with a pronoun in place of the noun.***

My friends like peaches. (They like peaches.)

The new girl likes peaches. (She likes peaches.)

The tall boy likes peaches. (He likes peaches.)

You and I like peaches. (We like peaches.)

Say: ***What pronoun do you use to talk about yourself?*** (I) ***Use I in the sentence.*** (I like peaches.) ***What pronoun do you use to talk directly to someone else?*** (you) ***Use you in the sentence.*** (You like peaches.)

Teach and Model

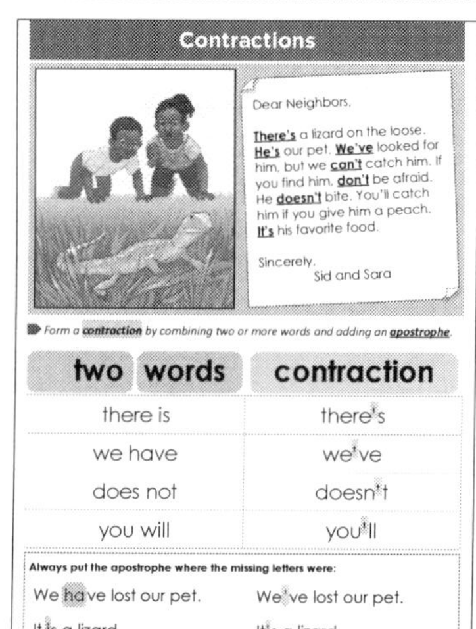
Contractions

Dear Neighbors,

There's a lizard on the loose. He's our pet. We've looked for him, but we can't catch him. If you find him, don't be afraid. He doesn't bite. You'll catch him if you give him a peach. It's his favorite food.

Sincerely,
Sid and Sara

Form a contraction by combining two or more words and adding an apostrophe.

two words	contraction
there is	there's
we have	we've
does not	doesn't
you will	you'll

Always put the apostrophe where the missing letters were:

We have lost our pet.	We've lost our pet.
It is a lizard.	It's a lizard.

Introduce the grammar principle

- ***We use pronouns all the time, especially when we make contractions.***
- ***A contraction is the short version of two words.***
- ***We use contractions when we talk and when we write stories or notes.***

Work through the Grammar Chart

Use the picture and the note to present the grammar in context.

Read through the rules. Explore the examples.

Clarify and correct if needed

- ***We use contractions in informal writing such as a letter to a friend or an email.***
- ***We don't use contractions in formal writing, such as a letter to the principal or a science report***

Guided Practice

Say: ***Now that we know what contractions are and when to use them, let's review how to make contractions.*** Use the Create a Contraction printout and step through the process, asking questions and clarifying any misunderstandings. You might use a sticky note to cover up the answer and reveal it as students move through the steps of forming a contraction.

Ask: ***What happens to the first word when you make a contraction?*** (It stays the same.) ***What happens to the second word?*** (It is shortened.) ***Where do you put the apostrophe?*** (Where we took out the letters.)

Independent Practice

Tell students they will practice contractions in a lost and found game.

Say: ***In this game, we need to help Sid and Sara find all the contractions. Some of you will have a Sid and Sara card with two full words.*** Show the *I am* Contraction Matching Card.

Point to a student and say: ***For example, you may have* I am. *And some of you will have a* lost lizard card *with a contraction.*** Show the *I'm* Contraction Matching Card.

Point to another student and say: ***For example, you may have* I'm. *Those two cards make a match. You will need to look around and talk with other students until you find your match.***

Distribute the Contraction Matching Cards so that half of the students in the group have the lizard cards and the other half have the Sid and Sara cards. Have students find their match and sit or stand next to each other. Once all the matches are made, have each person show his or her card and say what's on the card.

Use new cards, or shuffle and redistribute the same cards, and play a second round.

Differentiation

For more support: Review the contraction matching cards before beginning the game. If you show a card with the full words, have students read them with you and then tell you the contraction. If you show a card with the contraction, have students read it with you and then tell you the full words. Allow students to refer to the Create a Contraction Chart while completing the independent practice.

For a challenge: Once all the matches are made, have each student show his or her card and use the contraction in a sentence.

Check Progress

Use the Follow-Up Note printout and the following activity to check individual progress made on the target skill.

Pass out the Follow-Up Note to each student. Have students read the letter and write the contractions for the words in bold.

Circulate among students to observe each student's ability to form contractions. Ask students to read one of the sentences in which they have created a contraction. Ask them to explain how they made a contraction. If a student does not form a contraction correctly, use prompts to help him or her to correct it.

If students can make four out of six contractions correctly, consider the intervention successful.

Writing Extension

Have students write their own note pretending that they have found the lizard. Challenge them to use three contractions in their note.

Contractions

Dear Neighbors,

There's a lizard on the loose. **He's** our pet. **We've** looked for him, but we **can't** catch him. If you find him, **don't** be afraid. He **doesn't** bite. You'll catch him if you give him a peach. **It's** his favorite food.

Sincerely,
Sid and Sara

Form a ***contraction*** *by combining two or more words and adding an* ***apostrophe****.*

two words	contraction
there is	there's
we have	we've
does not	doesn't
you will	you'll

Always put the apostrophe where the missing letters were:

We have lost our pet.	We've lost our pet.
It is a lizard.	It's a lizard.

Create a Contraction

1. Take two words that you can shorten into one.	**I have**
2. Take out the letters in the second word that you don't need.	**I __ve**
3. Put an apostrophe where the letters used to be.	**I 've**
4. Scoot the letters together, and you've made a contraction.	**I've**

Take out 1 letter	Take out 2 letters	Take out more letters
do + **not** = don't	I + **have** = I've	he + **would** = he'd

Reteaching Lessons

I've found a lizard in my peach tree.

I **don't** know where he lives.

I **can't** take care of him.

He'd love to go home.

✓ Reteaching Lessons

Contraction Matching Cards

 did not	 didn’t
 cannot	 can’t
 I have	 I’ve
 we have	 we’ve
 he is	 he’s

Contraction Matching Cards

have not

haven't

could not

couldn't

she will

she'll

we would

we'd

I would

I'd

Dear Neighbors,

Good news! Our lizard **is not** lost ____________

anymore. **We have** found him. **He is**

____________ ____________

happy to be back home. He had an

adventure, but he **did not** get hurt.

____

We will take care of him so he **does not**

____________ ____________

get lost again.

Sincerely,

Sid and Sara

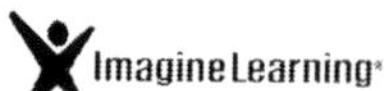

Grammar

Simple Future Tense

Grade 3

15–25 min.

CCSS.ELA-Literacy.L.3.1e
TEKS 110.14.22.A.i

LEARNING OBJECTIVE: Form the simple future tense with the helping verb will and use it correctly in a sentence.

LANGUAGE OBJECTIVE: Talk about activities at a theme park using an action verb and the simple future tense.

PREREQUISITE SKILL: Be able to identify and use basic verbs.

Lesson Overview

Teacher reviews rules and examples of simple future tense with students. Students practice adding *will* to a verb to form the future tense by imagining a field trip. Students play a field trip board game in small groups or pairs to practice the future tense.

Materials	Preparation
• Grammar Chart • Fish World Game Board (1 per group or pair) • Number Cube printout (1 per group or pair) • Field Trip printout	• Cut out, fold, and glue number cubes. • To print materials in color, visit the online Teacher Resources.

NOTE. The independent practice activity is most effective if the number of squares moved per turn is limited to three. The Number Cube printout has only numbers 1–3. To use traditional number cubes, see alternate instructions.

Activate Prior Knowledge

Quickly review the prerequisite skill with students and evaluate their proficiency. If students are not proficient with this skill, complete the corresponding Grammar Lesson before continuing.

VERBS: ***Many verbs are action words; they show what people do. Sentences always have a verb. I'll say a sentence with a verb, and you act it out.***

Say each sentence, pausing for students to act it out:

I wave to my friends. / We eat an ice cream cone. / He climbs the ladder. / They swim in the pool. She sprays water with a hose. / The penguins waddle up the hill.

Teach and Model

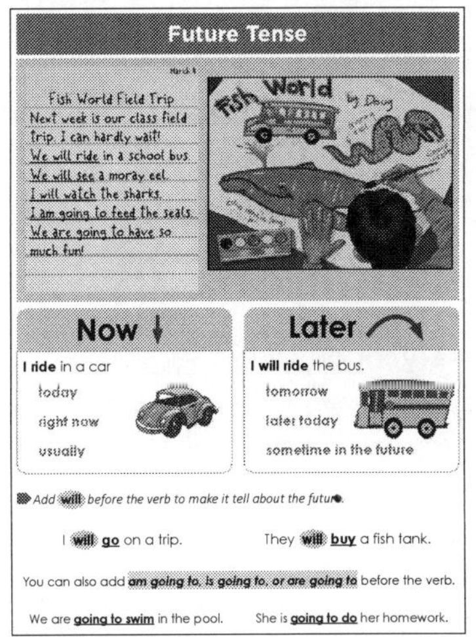

Introduce the grammar principle

Verbs can describe actions that are happening right now, like waving (wave) ***or eating*** (pantomime eating). ***Or they can describe actions will happen later, or in the future.***

Work through the Grammar Chart

Use the picture and the journal entry to present the grammar in context.

Read through the rules.

Explore the examples.

Clarify and correct if needed

An action verb that follows* will *is always used in the base form (not conjugated).

Guided Practice

Tell the students they will do a charades activity to practice the future tense.

Say: ***Imagine we are going on a field trip to an adventure park. What will we do there? I'll act out an activity. You will guess what it is. Then we will use a complete sentence to say that we will do it or are going to do it.***

Act out the phrases from the activity bank for the class to guess. When someone guesses the phrase correctly, guide the group to complete a sentence, using the verb in the future tense. For example, if you act out and the students guess *ride on a bus*, guide the students to form these sentences: We *will* ride on a bus, or We *are going to* ride on a bus.

Activity bank: play baseball, row a boat, climb a ladder, eat a watermelon, fly a kite, play hopscotch, jump on a trampoline, balance on a log/beam, swing on a swing, paint pictures, blow bubbles, drink lots of water

Independent Practice

Tell the students they will play a board game to practice the future tense.

Say: ***Imagine we are going on a field trip to Fish World. There are so many things to see and so many activities to do. Let's play a game to talk about it.***

Pair or group students and distribute the Fish World Game Boards and number cubes. Preview unfamiliar vocabulary from the game board.

Model the game: ***First I will ride the bus to Fish World. I place my marker on the bus by the large arrow. My partner asks me: What will you do next?*** Point out this phrase on the game board and have students repeat it with you.

Explain and demonstrate: ***I roll the number cube and move the number of spaces indicated. Next I use a verb from the middle of the board and the future tense to create a sentence about what I will do next at the theme park. For example, if I land on the shark, I could say, "I will visit the shark tank," or "I am going to learn about the sharks."***

Circulate among students to observe the use of future tense. If students do not use a verb correctly, prompt them to self-correct. For example: ***Did you use the verb will before the main verb?***

ALTERNATE INSTRUCTIONS: If a traditional number cube (numbers 1–6) is used and students finish quickly, have them clear the board and start over. Students could also change partners before starting a new game.

Differentiation

For more support: Review the game board before beginning the game. Have the students choral read the verbs in the dialog box. Point to each square and have the students name each activity. Pair struggling students with a partner that can support them and help them to form complete sentences.

For a challenge: Have students make up two complete sentences on each turn. The first sentence is what they, themselves will do. For the second sentence they must use a new verb and describe what their partner (or another classmate) will do. For example: *I'm going to learn about the dolphins. You are going to swim in the dolphin tank.*

Check Progress

Use the Field Trip printout and the following activity to check individual progress made on the target skill.

Say: ***Let's talk about things we will do when we get back from the field trip to Fish World.***

Have the students repeat the sentence frame: **After the field trip, ________.** Have each student use this frame and ideas from the list (or his or her own ideas) to make complete sentences in the future tense. Give an example: ***After the field trip, we will come back to the school.***

Have students explain how they know the sentence was in the future tense.

If students can correctly use and explain their use of the future tense, consider the intervention successful.

Writing Extension

Explain: ***Plan a trip you'd like to take in the future. It could be an imaginary trip to Fish World, a trip to the store, or even a trip to Mars. Write about at least six things you will do on your trip. When you are finished, read your plan to your partner.***

Future Tense

March 4

Fish World Field Trip

Next week is our class field trip. I can hardly wait! We will ride in a school bus. We will see a moray eel. I will watch the sharks. I am going to feed the seals. We are going to have so much fun!

Now 

I ride in a car

today

right now

usually

Later

I will ride the bus

tomorrow

later today

sometime in the future

*Add **will** before the verb to make it tell about the future.*

I **will** **go** on a trip.

They **will** **buy** a fish tank.

You can also add ***am going to, is going to, or are going to*** before the verb.

We **are going to swim** in the pool.

She **is going to do** her homework.

Fish World

A: What will you do next?

B: I will ____. or I am going to ____.

ride	visit	touch
see	feed	learn
watch	eat	explore
swim	take	play
make	drink	go

kid pool

killer whale

sea urchins

Mr. Fish Movie

crafts

dolphin cove

rare fish

manta rays

cool down

crabs

jellyfish

eel exhibit

water break

whale bay

sea horses

penguin town

rides

snack

tropical fish

shark tank

seals

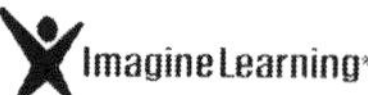

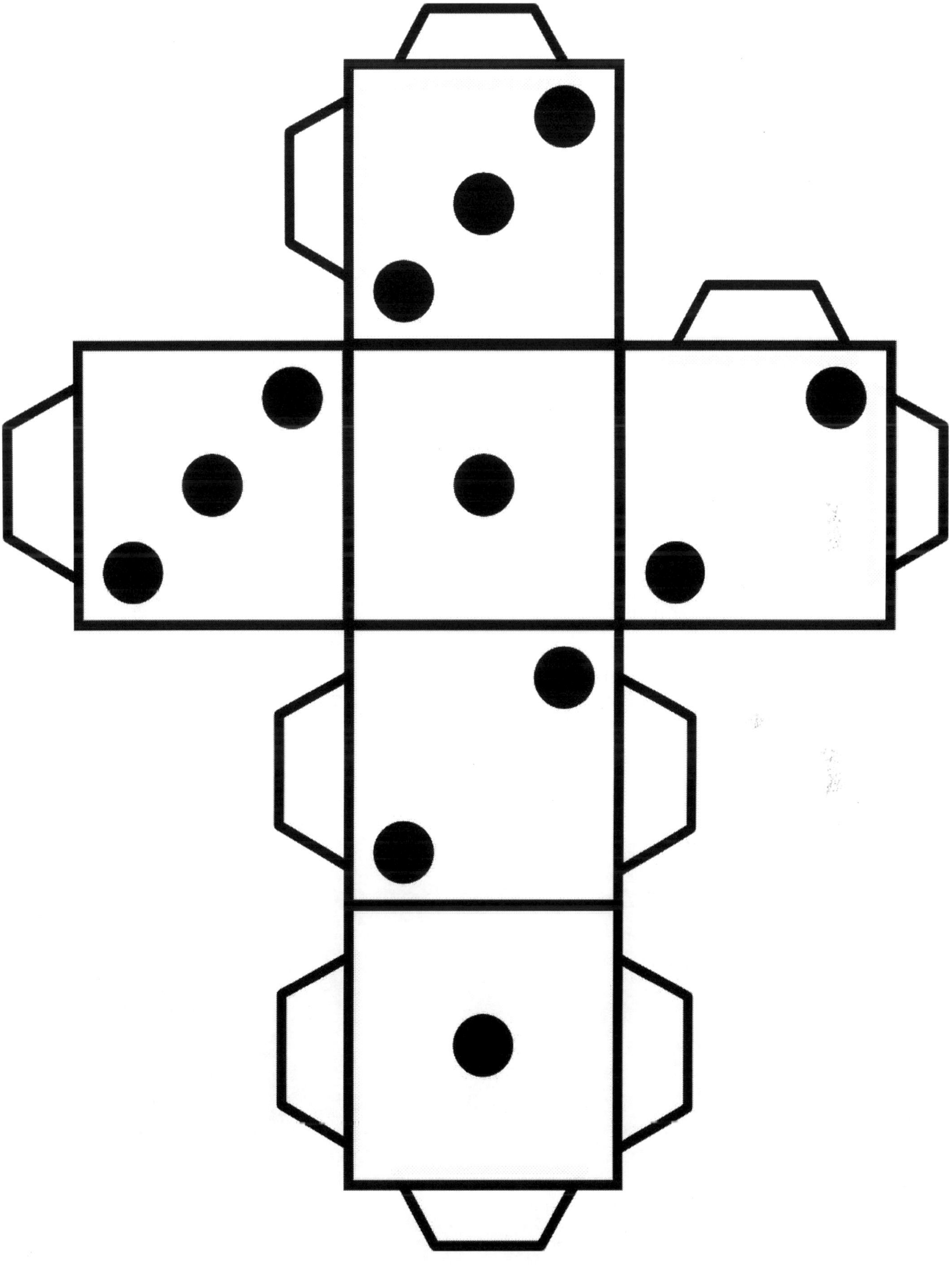

Reteaching Lessons ✓

After the field trip, __________.

clean out the bus

thank our teacher

write a letter to Fish World

talk about our favorite things

read books about fish

do homework

draw a picture

learn more about sharks

write about our trip

tell a friend

take a nap

plan another trip

pack up to get ready to go home

Grammar

Nouns

Grade 1

15 min.

CCSS.ELA-Literacy.L.1.1b
TEKS 110.12.20.A.ii

LEARNING OBJECTIVE: Identify and classify common nouns as person, animal, place, or thing.
LANGUAGE OBJECTIVE: Talk about nouns seen in everyday life on a trip to the beach or park.

Lesson Overview

Teacher reviews rules and examples of nouns with students. Students identify nouns in picture scenes. They play a sorting game and classify noun picture as a person/animal, place or thing.

Materials	Preparation
• Grammar Chart • Picture Prompts 1–3 • Beach Picture Cards • Tape	• Cut out Beach Picture Cards. • To print materials in color, visit the online Teacher Resources.

NOTE: Most vocabulary used in this lesson is pre-taught online.

Activate Prior Knowledge

PLACES: ***Right now we are at school. School is a place. After school we go to other places. Some of you go home. Home is a place. What are some other places you go to after school?*** Allow a few volunteers to name places (child care, homes of other relatives or caretakers, stores, etc.) ***These are all places we go. Say, "places."***

PEOPLE: ***When we are at school or at home, or in other places, we are there with other people. Here at school there are teachers and students, at home you might have a brother or sister. Who are other people that you see each day?*** Allow a few volunteers to name people (mom, dad, relatives, etc.) ***These are all people. Say, "people."***

THINGS: ***Everywhere we go, we see things. I see a book. I see a wall. What do you see?*** Allow a few volunteers to name things in the room. ***These are all things. Say, "things."***

ANIMALS: ***One other thing that we usually don't see at school but that many of us see at home or in other places are animals. I have (I know someone who) has [an animal]. Give me a thumbs up if you have an animal in your home. Give me a thumbs up if you know someone that has animals in their home. Give me a thumbs up if you have been to a place with lots of animals, like a farm or the zoo. Say, "animals."***

Teach and Model

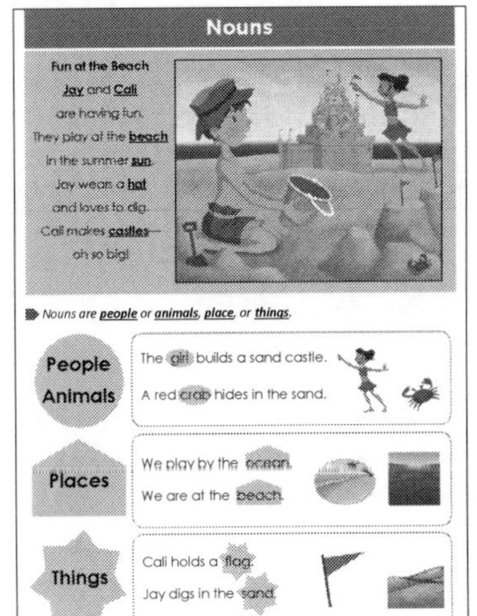

Introduce the grammar principle

A word that names a person, place, animal, or thing is called a noun. Let's learn more about nouns.

Work through the Grammar Chart

Use the picture and the poem to present the grammar in context.

Read through the rules.

Explore the examples.

Clarify and correct if needed

Some nouns can fit into more than one category. For example, some nouns can be both a place and a thing, like a beach. The most important thing is that you know it is a noun.

Reteaching Lessons

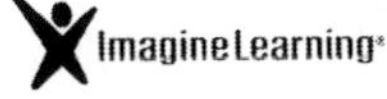

Guided Practice

Tell the students they will look at a picture to practice finding nouns.

Say: ***Cali and Jay are going to the beach. They get in the car with their mom and dad. Cali and Jay look out the window. This is what they see! Look at the picture to find nouns that name people or animals.***

Hold up Picture Prompt 1. Say: ***For example, I see a dog! The word* dog *is a noun because it is an animal. What other nouns do you see in the picture that name people or animals?***

Help students identify as many nouns as possible in the first picture.

Hold up Picture Prompt 2. Say: ***Cali and Jay's car is stopped at a stoplight. This is what they see out the window. Look at the picture to find nouns that name places. For example, I see a store! The word* store *is a noun because it names a place. What other nouns do you see in the picture that name places?***

Identify as many nouns as possible in the second picture.

Hold up Picture Prompt 3. Say: ***Cali and Jay's family made it to the beach! They are in the parking lot. Look at the picture to find nouns that name things. For example, I see a car! The word* car *is a noun because it names a thing. What other nouns do you see in the picture that name things?***

Remember, some places can be things, and some things can be places. For example, *store* could be a place or a thing. Consider either answer correct.

Independent Practice

Tell the students they will play a sorting game to practice telling whether a noun is a person/animal, place, or thing. Put three sticky notes up on different walls of the classroom, each labeled with a different category (person/animal, place, thing). Place the Beach Picture Cards facedown in a stack.

Say: ***Imagine we are at the beach. These are pictures of things you might see there. Tell me where each picture should go. Does it go on the person or animal wall? Does it go on the place wall? Or does it go on the thing wall?***

Write the sentence frame on the board: ***A(n) __________ is a noun because it is a(n) __________.*** Ask students to repeat the frame out loud in unison.

Model the game: Draw a card. Read the sentence frame, filling in the blank with the name of the noun on the card and what makes it a noun. Remind students that a word is a noun if it names a person or animal, a place, or a thing.

Have students take turns drawing cards and using the above sentence frame to determine why the thing is a noun. Have the students walk to the appropriate wall and tape their card to the wall under the category name. For example, if the card is an umbrella, the student says, "An umbrella is a noun because it is a thing." The student then walks to the "thing" wall and tapes the card to the wall.

Person/Animal	Place	Thing
swimmer	store	ball
dog	bathroom	palm tree
fish	lifeguard tower	boat

If students do not identify the noun's category correctly, use prompts to help them correct it. For example: ***Look at the picture again. Think about the three categories. What is this a picture of? Which pile does it belong in?***

Differentiation

For more support: Choose one category to start with (for example, person or animal). Go through the deck of cards and have students identify *only* people and animals. Then move on to the next category (for example, *place*). Go through all the cards again, this time identifying places. Finally, move on to the third category (for example, *thing*) and have students identify only things.

For a challenge: Give each student a turn and time them while they sort the cards on their own. Once they have finished sorting, tell them to think of one additional noun they see in the room (or nouns they can think of around the school) that they could add to each category.

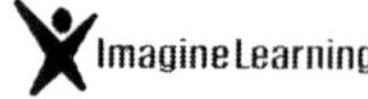

Check Progress

Use the word bank and the following activity to check individual progress made on the target skill.

Say: ***Imagine that we can't go to the beach today because it is too cold outside. Instead, let's take a trip to the park! What people, animals, places, and things would we see along the way? I'll say a word and you tell me if it is a noun.***

Read a word from the word bank. Ask: ***Is this word a noun?*** Have the student give a thumbs up for yes and a thumbs down for no. Then ask the student how they knew if it was a noun or not a noun. For example, a possible response for why *soft* is not a noun is, "*Soft* is not a noun because it is not a person or animal, a place, or a thing." Select additional words and repeat exercise as necessary.

If the student can correctly identify examples and non-examples of nouns and explain why a word is or is not a noun, consider the intervention successful.

Word bank:

Person/Animal	**Place**	**Thing**	**Not a noun**
police officer	bathroom (could also be a thing)	window	hungry
duck	hospital (could also be a thing)	fence	happy
dog	post office (could also be a thing)	table	excited
squirrel	grocery store (could also be a thing)	bench	colorful
baby	gas station (could also be a thing)	flower	quickly

Reteaching Lessons

Nouns

Fun at the Beach

Jay and **Cali**
are having fun.
They play at the **beach**
in the summer **sun**.
Jay wears a **hat**
and loves to dig.
Cali makes **castles**—
oh so big!

Reteaching Lessons

*Nouns are **people** or **animals**, **places**, or **things**.*

People
Animals

The girl builds a sand castle.

A red crab hides in the sand.

Places

We play by the ocean.

We are at the beach.

Things

Cali holds a flag.

Jay digs in the sand.

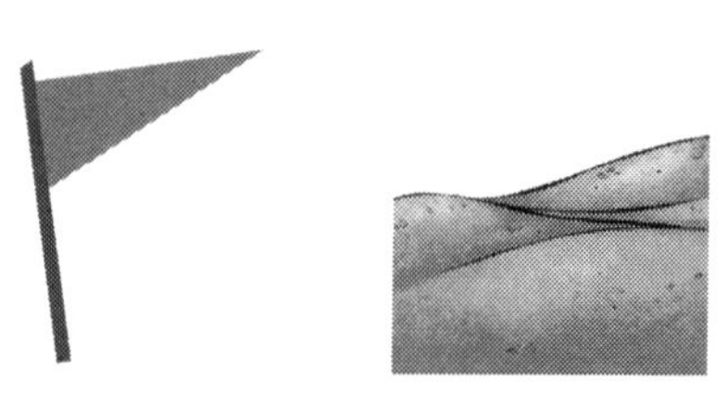

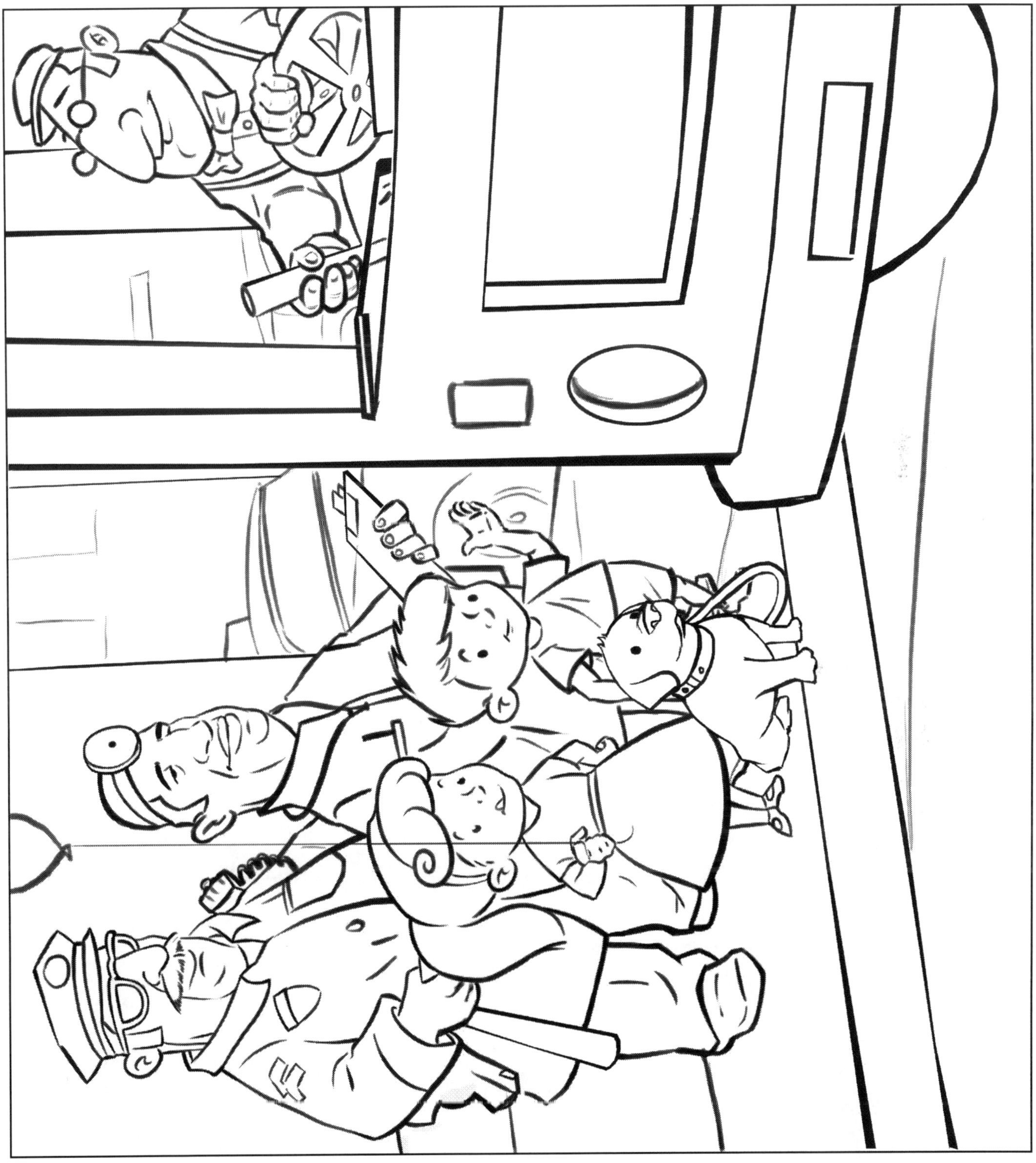

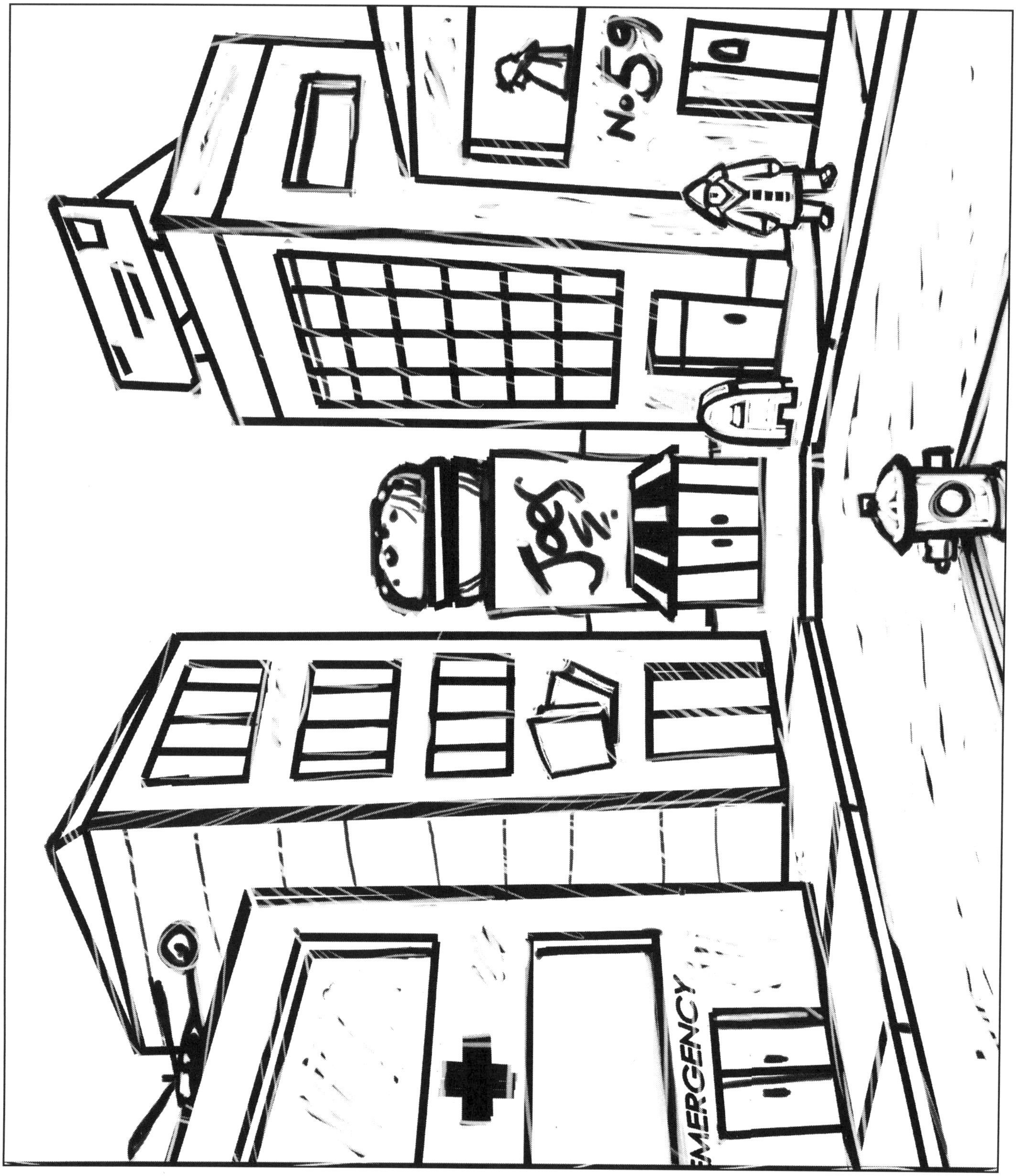

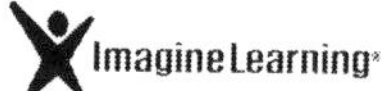
Imagine Learning

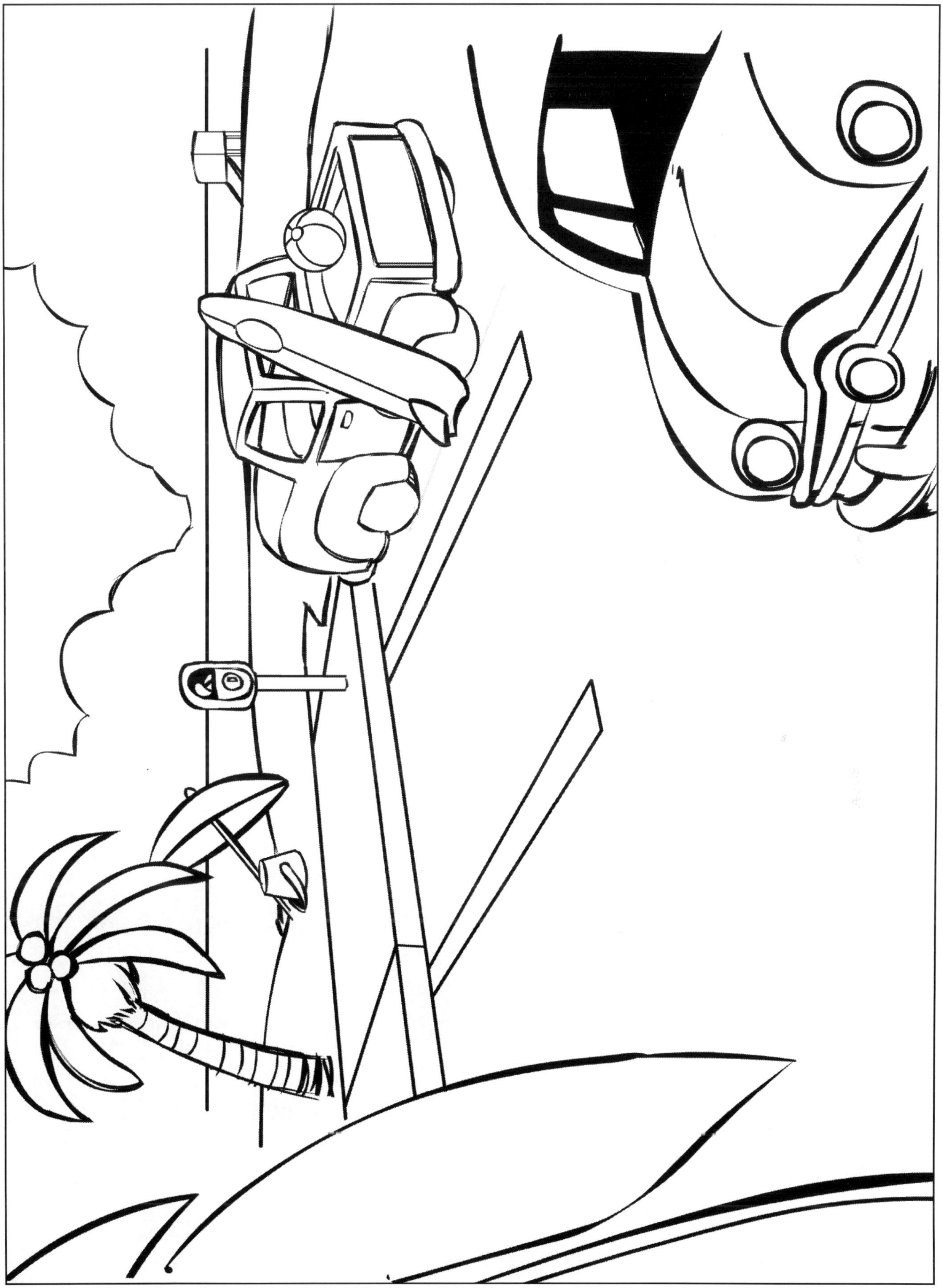

Reteaching Lessons

swimmer	dog	fish
ball	boat	palm tree
 store	bathroom	lifeguard tower

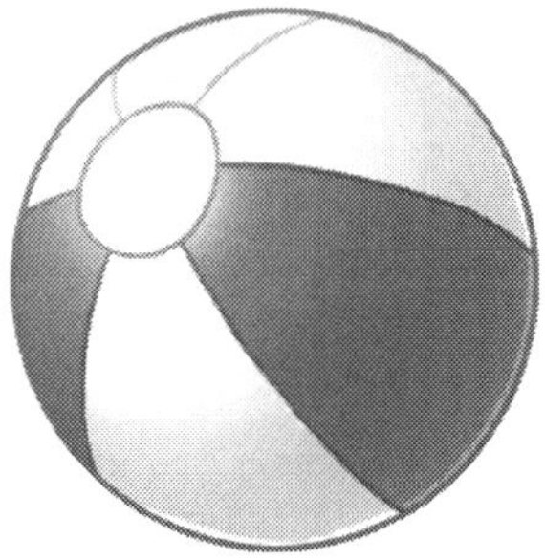

Proper Nouns

Grade 1

15 min.

CCSS.ELA-Literacy.L.1.1b
TEKS 110.12..20.A.ii

LEARNING OBJECTIVE: Correctly identify and use proper nouns.
LANGUAGE OBJECTIVE: Use proper nouns to describe special people, places, and things in the world.
PREREQUISITE SKILL: Know the definition of a noun and identify basic nouns.

Lesson Overview

Teacher reviews rules and examples of proper nouns with students. Students read post cards between two friends to identify proper nouns. Then students play a circle game to practice using proper nouns.

Materials	Preparation
• Grammar Chart • Proper Noun Postcards • Proper Noun Category Strips (optional) • Proper Noun Cards	• Cut out Proper Noun Postcards and fold the picture over to simulate a postcard with the picture on the front and the letter on the back. • Cut out Proper Noun Category Strips or write noun categories on the board (see independent practice activity). • To print materials in color, visit the online Teacher Resources.

Activate Prior Knowledge

Quickly review the prerequisite skill with students and evaluate their proficiency. If students are not proficient with this skill, complete the corresponding Grammar Lesson before continuing.

NOUNS: ***A noun is a word that names a person, place, animal, or thing. All the people, places, and things around you in this room are nouns.***

Write noun classifications on the board: person/animal, place, thing.

Say: **I'm going to point to one of these words: person *or* animal, place, *and* thing. *Think of an example of a noun that belongs in that group. When you have one in your mind, touch your head like this.*** Demonstrate with index finger to the side of head as if pointing out you have an idea in mind.

Alternate pointing between the three categories, calling on a few students each time to name a noun that belongs to that group. If a student incorrectly identifies a noun, ask: ***Think carefully, is [word student said] a person, an animal, a place, or a thing? If it's none of those, what does that mean?*** (It's not a noun if it doesn't belong to one of those categories.)

Note: Some nouns can be a place and a thing. If one is mentioned, allow students to discuss and place it in one category or the other.

Teach and Model

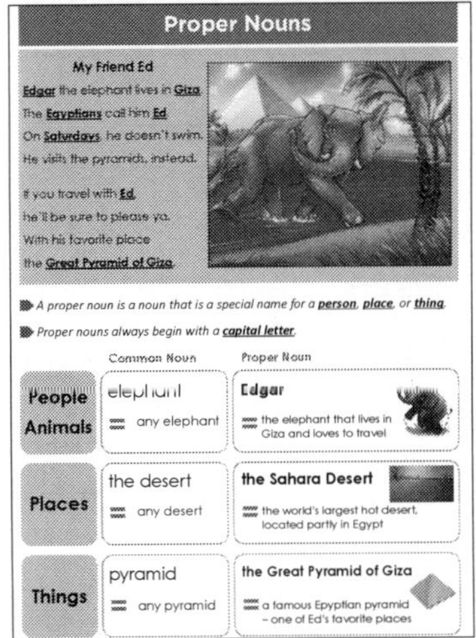
Proper Nouns

My Friend Ed
Edgar the elephant lives in Giza.
The Egyptians call him Ed.
On Saturdays, he doesn't swim.
He visits the pyramids, instead.

If you travel with Ed,
he'll be sure to please ya.
With his favorite place
the Great Pyramid of Giza.

A proper noun is a noun that is a special name for a ***person***, ***place***, *or* ***thing***.
Proper nouns always begin with a ***capital letter***.

	Common Noun	Proper Noun
People Animals	elephant = any elephant	Edgar = the elephant that lives in Giza and loves to travel
Places	the desert = any desert	the Sahara Desert = the world's largest hot desert, located partly in Egypt
Things	pyramid = any pyramid	the Great Pyramid of Giza = a famous Epyptian pyramid – one of Ed's favorite places

Introduce the grammar principle

Now that we have practiced nouns, we can learn about proper nouns.

Work through the Grammar Chart

Use the picture and the poem to present the grammar in context.

Read through the rules.

Explore the examples.

Clarify and correct if needed

- ***People's first and last names are proper nouns.***
- ***Titles of books or movies are proper nouns.***
- ***Days of the week and months of the year are also proper nouns.***

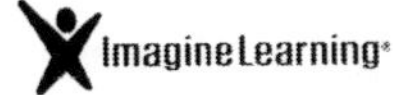

Guided Practice

Tell the students they will practice finding proper nouns: ***I'll say two nouns. One will be a common noun that names a person, place, or thing and the other will be a proper noun that is a special name for a specific person, place, or thing. You tell me which one is the proper noun:*** **city, New York City.**

Point out that *city* is a common noun because it names any place that is a city, but *New York City* is a special name for one specific city.

Repeat with additional examples as needed: *Lake Michigan/lake, boy/Michael, Tuesday/day, park/Central Park.*

Say: ***Remember, proper nouns always start with a capital letter and name a special person, place, or thing.***

Do you like to visit interesting places like Edgar the elephant does? Display the post cards with the image side showing. ***Here are some post cards from people who are traveling. The messages are about special people, places, and things. Let's read one together. I'll read it aloud, and you listen for proper nouns.*** Have the students follow along and signal when they hear a proper noun (give a thumbs up, raise their hand, touch their nose, etc.). Call on a volunteer to identify the proper noun. Have all the students repeat it together.

Students might confuse words at the beginning of a sentence with proper nouns because of capitalization. Help them understand the difference between capitalizing a word because it is at the beginning of a sentence and capitalizing a letter because it is a proper noun.

Say: ***A proper noun is always capitalized. It doesn't matter if it is the first word in a sentence or if it is somewhere else in the sentence. Look at the word at the beginning of the sentence. If you moved this word to somewhere else in the sentence, would it still need to be capitalized? If it would, it is a proper noun. If it wouldn't, it is a common noun.***

Independent Practice

Tell the students they will play a game called Around the World to practice using proper nouns.

Display the Proper Noun Category Strips: months, teachers, street names, cities in our state, superheroes, book titles, students in our class, holidays, and pet names.

Have the class sit in a circle. Pick a student volunteer. Have the volunteer choose a category and tell the class what it is. Have everyone silently think of a proper noun that belongs in that category.

Then have the volunteer student whisper his or her proper noun to you without letting the rest of the class know. Once everyone has thought of their proper noun, the volunteer student stands in the middle of the circle.

The student in the middle goes around the circle and has each student say their proper noun aloud one at a time. The goal is for the student in the middle to get all the way "around the world" without someone saying his or her secret proper noun. If a student in the circle says the same proper noun as the student in the middle of the circle, they trade places. The new student in the middle picks a category and the game starts over. If the volunteer gets all the way around the circle, and no one says the same proper noun, he or she wins and gets to choose a new student to be in the middle.

If a student does not use a proper noun, use prompts to help him or her self-correct. For example: ***Remember to say a word that names a special person, animal, place, or thing.***

Differentiation

For more support: Before beginning the activity, go through each category and ask a volunteer to give an example of a proper noun that would fit in the category. For example, if you point at the *teacher* category, the student would provide the name of a teacher at the school.

Once students have provided an example for each category, move on to the full activity.

For a challenge: Have students come up with additional categories of their own. Then repeat the activity using their categories as prompts for coming up with proper nouns. Examples could be sports teams, days of the week, candy bars, etc.

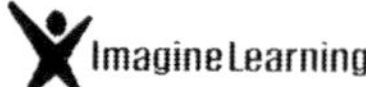

Check Progress

Use the Proper Noun Cards and the following activity to check individual progress.

Give each student a set of noun cards.

Say: ***Imagine we are visiting New York in June. Think of all the fun things we would see! Look at the cards. You will sort them into two piles. One pile is for proper nouns. The other pile is for regular nouns. Put each card on the pile it belongs in.***

When students are done sorting, go over both piles together. Have students explain why the noun is or is not a proper noun.

Answer bank:

Proper noun	**Not proper noun**
Hannah	pizza
Kevin	taxi
Park Avenue	stoplight
The Empire State Building	man
June	woman
Statue of Liberty	building

If the student can correctly identify proper nouns and explain why a noun is proper or not proper, consider the intervention successful.

Reteaching Lessons ✓

Proper Nouns

My Friend Ed

Edgar the elephant lives in **Giza**.
The **Egyptians** call him **Ed**.
On **Saturdays**, he doesn't swim.
He visits the pyramids instead.

If you travel with **Ed**,
he'll be sure to please ya.
With his favorite place
the **Great Pyramid of Giza**.

- *A proper noun is a noun that is a special name for a* ***person****,* ***place****, or* ***thing****.*
- *Proper nouns always begin with a* ***capital letter****.*

	Common Noun	Proper Noun
People Animals	elephant = any elephant	**Edgar** = the elephant that lives in Giza and loves to travel 
Places	the desert = any desert	**the Sahara Desert** 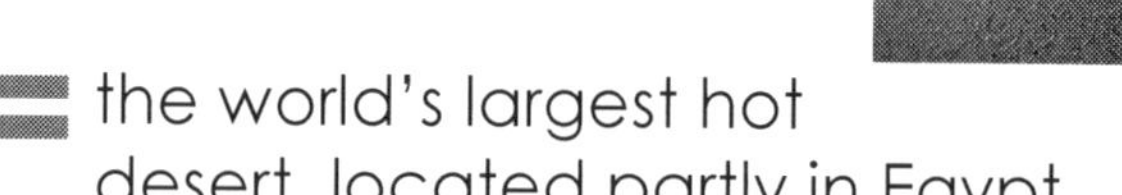 = the world's largest hot desert, located partly in Egypt
Things	pyramid = any pyramid	**the Great Pyramid of Giza** = a famous Egyptian pyramid—one of Ed's favorite places

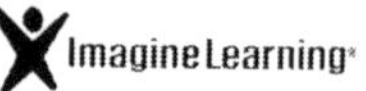

Dear Tisha,

I am so excited for you to come to Italy! Do you still want to take a ride on the Po River? My cousin Marco just got a fishing boat. He named it River Bee.

See you in July!

Kiana

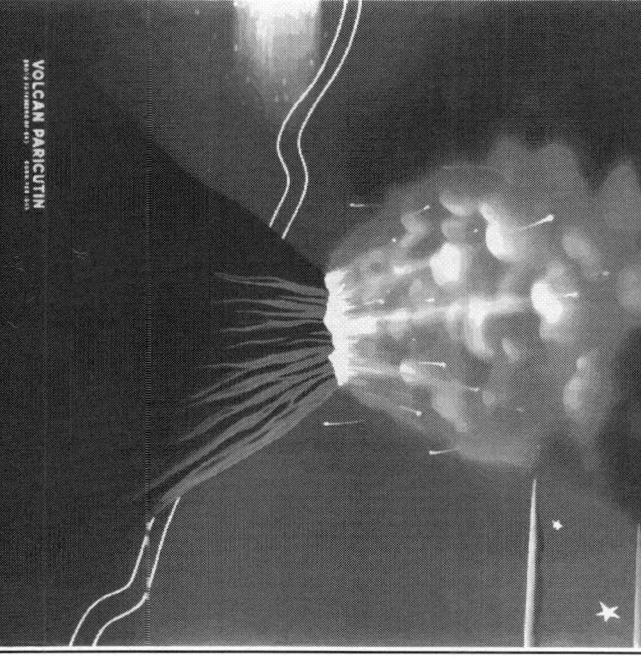

Logan,

You won't believe it! Yesterday I got to hike up the Paricutin Volcano. It was really cool! Tomorrow is November 1st. Mexico has a holiday called Day of the Dead. I'll tell you all about it when I get back.

Love,

Asher

P.S. Jonah says hello!

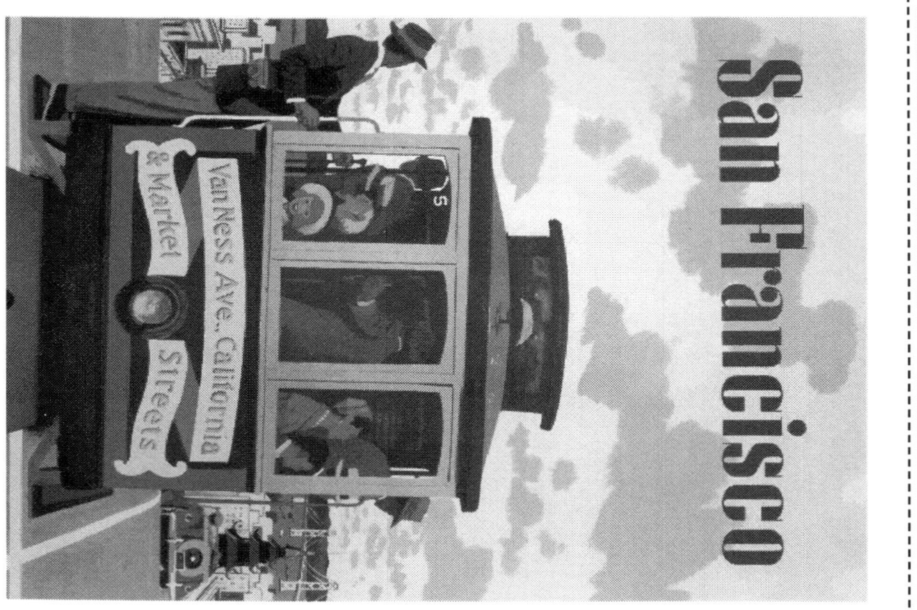

Hi Cam

I can't wait for you to come visit me in San Francisco! The weather is beautiful in May. We can go to Golden Gate Park and play all day. We can also ride to Polk Street and go shopping.

Tell Uncle Quan that we got tickets for him to see the San Francisco Giants baseball game on Saturday.

See you soon!

Kim

PUEBLOS OF THE SOUTHWEST

National Parks & Monuments

Hello Asad!

Here's a post card from our trip to Mesa Verde National Park.

This park was created by President Roosevelt in 1906. We saw wild turkeys, squirrels, and deer. We even saw a Great Horned Owl. We climbed up to houses built into rock cliffs. They were built by the Pueblo Indians more than 700 years ago. I'm sending you a book about it. It's called *The Secrets of Mesa Verde*.

Hope you like it!

Joseph

Months

Teachers

Street Names

Cities in Our State

Superheroes

Book Titles

Students in Our Class

Holidays

Pet Names

Reteaching Lessons

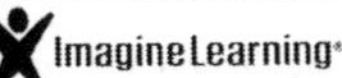

Proper Noun Cards

Grammar

Irregular Past Tense

Grade 2

15 min.

CCSS.L.1.1.H
TEKS 110.13.B.21.A.iii

LEARNING OBJECTIVE: Correctly form and use the past tense of frequently occurring irregular verbs.

LANGUAGE OBJECTIVE: Talk about a trip using irregular past tense verbs.

PREREQUISITE SKILLS: Be able to identify basic verbs. Be able to conjugate verbs in the simple present tense and be able to conjugate regular verbs in the simple past tense.

Lesson Overview

Teacher reviews rules and examples of irregular past tense with students. Students use irregular past tense verbs to discuss a checklist of completed tasks. Then students play an add-on game to practice using common irregular past tense verbs in complete sentences.

Materials	Preparation
• Grammar Chart • Travel Checklist printout • Road Trip Activity Cards • Challenge Cards (optional)	• Cut out Road Trip Activity Cards. • If doing the challenge differentiation activity, cut out the Challenge Cards. • To print materials in color, visit the online Teacher Resources.

NOTE: Because irregular past eanse verbs do not follow a set of rules, mastery comes through repeated exposure and memorization. This lesson includes practice activities for many of the most common irregular past tense verbs. If the Check Progress activity shows that students still struggle with the irregular forms, provide more time and opportunities for students to learn the forms.

Activate Prior Knowledge

Quickly review the prerequisite skill with students and evaluate their proficiency. If students are not proficient with this skill, complete the corresponding Grammar Lesson before continuing.

PRESENT TENSE VERBS: ***Many verbs are action words. For example, walk: I walk down the road.*** Pantomime walking. ***Or wave: We wave goodbye.*** Pantomime waving.

All action verbs show when the action happens. We can use verbs in the present tense to show the action is happening or could happen now or happens often. I'll say an action that we do now or that we do as a routine in school. You repeat the sentence and act out the verb.

Sentence bank:

We read books every day.

We sharpen our pencils when they break.

We eat lunch now.

We work on the computer.

We play at recess.

We always raise our hands.

PAST TENSE VERBS: ***Just as we can use verbs to show an action is happening now or happens often, we can use verbs to show an action happened in the past. The past could mean yesterday, or long ago, or just a few minutes ago. For this practice, let's use yesterday. I'll say a sentence in the present. You add the word yesterday to the beginning and change the verb to the past.***

Sentence bank:

We sharpen our pencils.

We work on the computer.

We play at recess.

We raise our hands.

We look at pictures.

Reteaching Lessons

Teach and Model

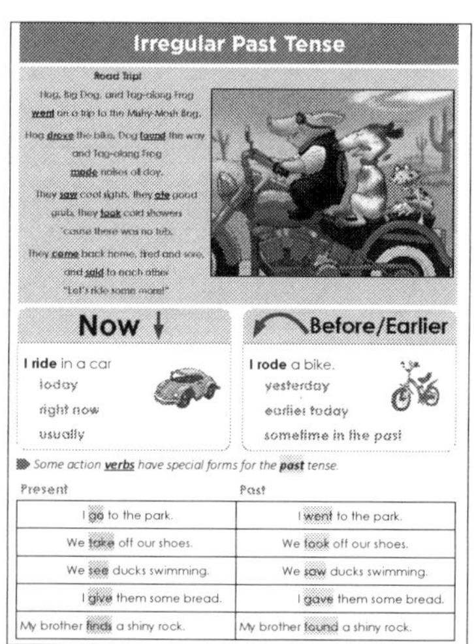

Irregular Past Tense

Road Trip!

Hog, Big Dog, and Tag-along Frog
went on a trip to the [illegible] Bog.
Hog **drove** the bike, Dog **found** the way
and Tag-along Frog
made noises all day.
They **saw** cool sights, they **ate** good
grub, they **took** cold showers
'cause there was no tub.
They **came** back home, tired and sore,
and **said** to each other
"Let's ride some more!"

Now

I ride in a car
today
right now
usually

Before/Earlier

I rode a bike.
yesterday
earlier today
sometime in the past

*Some action **verbs** have special forms for the **past** tense.*

Present	Past
I go to the park.	I went to the park.
We take off our shoes.	We took off our shoes.
We see ducks swimming.	We saw ducks swimming.
I give them some bread.	I gave them some bread.
My brother finds a shiny rock.	My brother found a shiny rock.

Introduce the grammar principle

As you can see from the sentences we just practiced, many past-tense verbs end in -ed: sharpened, worked, played. Some past-tense verbs are irregular. Irregular means that something doesn't follow the normal rule.

Work through the Grammar Chart

Use the picture and the poem to present the grammar in context.

Read through the rules.

Explore the examples.

Clarify and correct if needed

With irregular verbs, you don't add the letters -ed to the end of the verb. You need to change a part of the verb, or sometimes the whole word.

The road trip poem contains the word grub. *Explain to students that it is another word for food.*

Guided Practice

Tell the students they will answer questions to practice using verbs to talk about an action in the past.

Use the Travel Checklist printout. Say: ***Imagine we are going on a trip. Let's go through our checklist to see if we have everything ready. I'll ask you something from the list, and then you can tell me you did it already. Remember to use the special forms for the past tense. If you don't know them, I will help you.***

Read the following sentences aloud as you show the Travel Checklist. Call on individual students to respond. Check off the items as they respond. Guide them as needed to use the past tense in their answers.

Did you ...

... write a list of places to visit? (Yes, I wrote a list.)

... go to the store? (Yes, I went to the store.)

... find the map? (Yes, I found the map.)

... make your bed? (Yes, I made my bed.)

... feed the fish? (Yes, I fed the fish.)

... buy food? (Yes, I bought food.)

... get the suitcases ready? (Yes, I got the suitcase ready.)

... take out the garbage? (Yes, I took out the garbage.)

... tell everyone to get in the car? (Yes, I told everyone to get in the car.)

Independent Practice

Tell the students they will play a game to practice the special forms of the past tense. Say: ***This game is about a road trip. First let's review some fun activities you could do on a trip.***

Review the Road Trip Activity Cards to be certain that students are familiar with the past tense forms of the activity verbs: Remind students that all of the verbs in this game have special forms for the past tense. Tell students you will read the activity card, and you want them to say the activity in past tense, for example: ***Ride a motorcycle.*** (rode a motorcycle) ***Buy a t-shirt.*** (bought a t-shirt) ***Take pictures.*** (took pictures) If students struggle with the irregular past tense forms, use the differentiation suggestions below.

Say: ***Now we are ready to talk about our road trip.***

Write the sentence frame on the board and have the students repeat it aloud.

We went on a road trip, and we _______________.

Model the game: Draw a card and read it aloud. Use the sentence frame, filling in the blank using the activity on the card and the past tense form of the verb. For example, if you draw the *take pictures* card, say: Take pictures; ***We went on a road trip and we took pictures.*** Place your card faceup on the table to begin the sequence of actions.

Have students take turns drawing cards and adding them faceup to the line of activities on the table. After drawing a card, the student repeats the previous actions and then adds the new one listed on his or her card. For example: If the next card is *sing silly songs*, the student says, "We went on a road trip and we took pictures and we sang silly

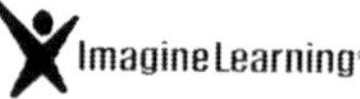

songs." If the next card is buy a t-shirt, the student says, "We went on a road trip and we took pictures, we sang silly songs, and we bought a t-shirt."

When a student draws a *come back home* card, have the student say all the previous actions and add *"then we came back home."* Then clear all cards from the line and start over.

If students use the wrong past tense form, prompt them to correct it. For example: ***Did you use the right form? This verb doesn't end in -ed. Can you think of the special form?***

Road Trip Activity Cards: ride a motorcycle (rode), take pictures (took), drink water (drank), see a famous statue (saw), make lots of stops (made), eat at a restaurant (ate), go to a museum (went), buy a shirt (bought), sing silly songs (sang), find a restroom (found), get snacks (got), get a flat tire (got), ride a bike (rode), take a rest (took), see animals (saw)

Differentiation

For more support: If students struggle with the past tense forms, teach them with the following activity. Divide the group in half. Tell group 1 they will be "present" and group 2 they will be "past."

Say a verb, for example, *ride*. Teach both forms and use them in context, for example: ***In the present, we say* ride. *I ride the bus every day. In the past, we say* rode. *Yesterday I rode a train.***

Point to the students in group 1. Say: ***Present.*** Have group 1 repeat the verb in the present tense. (ride) Point to group 2. Say: ***Past.*** Have group 2 repeat the verb in the past. (rode)

Alternate calling out *present* and *past* and having the groups respond. Do this four to six times. Mix it up by saying *past* twice in a row or saying *present* but looking at group 1. Repeat with additional verbs.

For a challenge: Mix in the challenge cards and play a round with the following new verbs. Have the students create original phrases to go with the verbs.

Challenge cards: bring, break, do, give, keep, run, write, hold, leave

Check Progress

Use the following activity to check individual progress made on the target skill.

Say: ***Think about a trip you have taken. It could be a long road trip or a trip to somewhere nearby, like the park or downtown. I will ask you questions about your trip, and you will answer using complete sentences with verbs in the past.*** Alternate between students, asking questions and requiring them to respond in complete sentences using a past tense verb. For example, if you ask: ***Where did you go?*** The student might respond, "I went to the park." Repeat questions as necessary until all have responded to at least three questions.

Where did you go?

Whom did you go with?

What did you see?

Did you buy anything?

What did you take with you?

Did you make anything on your trip?

Did you ride on a motorcycle?

What did you eat on your trip?

What did you drink?

If students can respond using irregular past tense verbs correctly, consider the intervention successful.

Whole-Class Variation

Have students place chairs in a circle. Select one student to be the leader. The leader stands in the middle and his or her chair is removed, leaving only enough chairs for the students who are sitting. Pass out a Road Trip Activity Card to each seated student. Have students hold their cards facing out so that others in the circle can see it.

The leader walks around the inside of the circle and says the sentence frame, filling in the name of any road trip action. For example, "I went on a road trip and I took pictures." The student with the *take pictures* card stands up, says "I took pictures too," and follows along behind the leader. The leader continues walking and repeats the sentence with a new action. For example, "I went on a road trip and I saw a famous statue." The student with the *see a famous statue* card stands up says "I saw a famous statue too." and follows along behind the leader and the picture taker. The game continues with each new action following along until the leader says, "End of the Road! Everybody go home." All students (including the leader) must quickly find a seat and sit down. One student will be left standing. This student becomes the leader.

The students who are seated exchange cards and the game starts over.

Reteaching Lessons ✓

Irregular Past Tense

Road Trip!

Hog, Big Dog, and Tag-Along Frog
went on a trip to the Mishy-Mosh Bog.
Hog **drove** the bike, Dog **found** the way,
and Tag-Along Frog
made noises all day.
They **saw** cool sights, they **ate** good
grub, they **took** cold showers
'cause there was no tub.
They **came** back home, tired and sore,
and **said** to each other,
"Let's ride some more!"

Now 	Before/Earlier
I ride in a car today right now usually 	**I rode** a bike yesterday earlier today sometime in the past

*Some action **verbs** have special forms for the **past** tense.*

Present	Past
I go to the park.	I went to the park.
We take off our shoes.	We took off our shoes.
We see ducks swimming.	We saw ducks swimming.
I give them some bread.	I gave them some bread.
My brother finds a shiny rock.	My brother found a shiny rock.

Travel Checklist

- ☐ write a list of places to visit
- ☐ go to the store
- ☐ find the map
- ☐ make your bed
- ☐ feed the fish
- ☐ buy food
- ☐ get the suitcases ready
- ☐ take out the garbage
- ☐ tell everyone to get in the car

ride a motorcycle

take pictures

drink water

see a famous statue

make lots of stops

eat at a restaurant

go to a museum

buy a t-shirt

sing silly songs

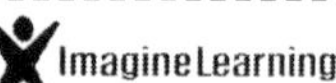

find a restroom

get snacks

come back home

get a flat tire

ride a bike

come back home

take a rest

see animals

come back home

Reteaching Lessons ✓

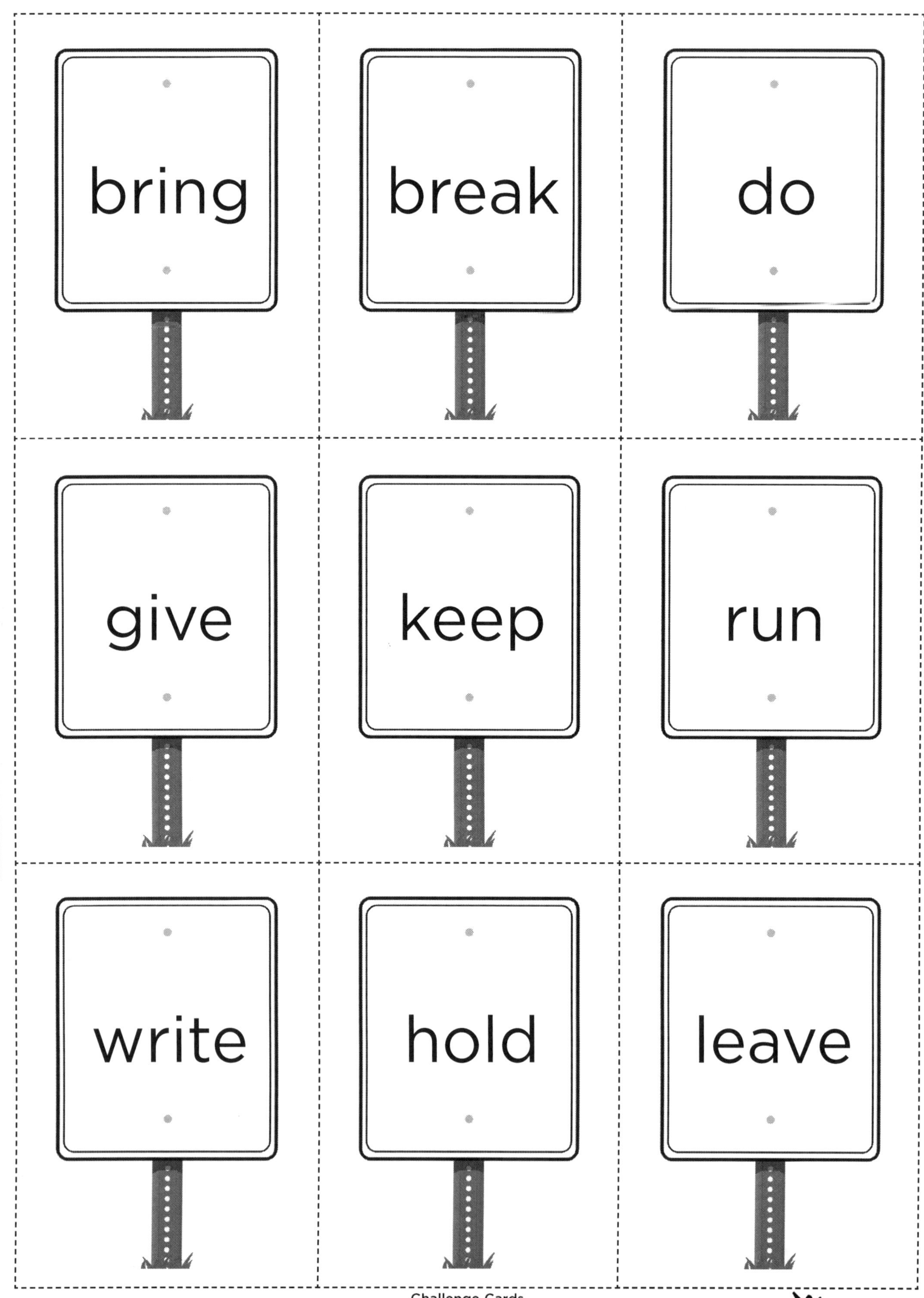

Challenge Cards

Grammar

Regular Past Tense

Grade 2

15 min. 

CCSS.L.1.1.E
TEKS 110.12.3.E

LEARNING OBJECTIVE: Understand and use simple past tense verbs to talk about actions that happened in the past.

LANGUAGE OBJECTIVE: Use simple past tense verbs to talk about celebrations.

PREREQUISITE SKILL: Understand that all sentences have a verb and that the verb shows the action of the sentence.

Lesson Overview

Teacher reviews rules and examples of regular past tense with students. Students talk about celebrations that happened in the past to practice regular past tense verbs. Students play a verb card game and write a past-tense story together.

Materials	Preparation
• Grammar Chart • Party Picture printout • Verb cards • Party Checklists printout	• Cut out Regular Present Tense Verb cards. • To print materials in color, visit the online Teacher Resources.

Activate Prior Knowledge

Quickly review the prerequisite skill with students and evaluate their proficiency. If students are not proficient with this skill, complete the corresponding Grammar Lesson before continuing.

VERBS: ***Verbs are words that tell an action. In the sentence "I smile," the action is* smile. *I'm going to say some sentences, and I want you to act out what I said and say the verb back to me.***

Say a sentence and encourage the students to pantomime the action of the sentence. Then ask students to tell you what the verb is in the sentence.

Sentence bank: I clap my hands. / I dance to the music. / I open a present. / I count three candles. /I look at my watch. / I wave goodbye.

Teach and Model

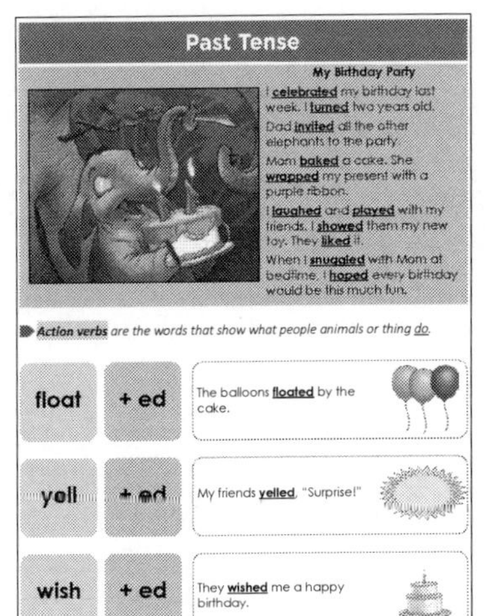

Introduce the grammar principle

Now that you know about verbs, we can learn about verbs in the past tense. Past tense verbs show that an action happened in the past. The past could mean yesterday or long ago or just a few minutes ago. It means the action has already happened.

Work through the Grammar Chart

Use the picture and the story to present the grammar in context.

Read through the rules.

Explore the examples.

Clarify and correct if needed

- ***The pronunciation of words ending in -ed depends on the final consonant sound.***
- ***There are three ways to pronounce -ed: /id/, /d/, and /t/***

Reteaching Lessons

Guided Practice

Tell the students they will talk about something that happened in the past to practice using past tense verbs.

Say: ***Let's talk about a celebration that happened in the past. It could be a birthday or a family party or any kind of celebration.***

Model for students how to talk about a celebration that happened in the past. Say: ***First, I'd like to tell you about [a celebration in the past]***. As you talk, write down the regular past tense verbs you use.

Suggested past tense word bank: danced, played, loved, liked, asked, clapped, looked, needed, started, joked, enjoyed, mixed, piled, hoped, parked, spilled, saved, visited, painted, picked

Direct the students' attention to the list of regular past tense verbs you've written. Ask: ***Who can tell me what all these words have in common?*** (They all end in *-ed*.) Review words with students.

Show students the Party Picture printout. Say: ***Now it's your turn. Here are pictures from a party. Let's imagine that you were at the party, but I wasn't. I want to hear about the party, so I need you to tell me what happened. Use these picture prompts to tell me about the party.*** Give students some time to look at the pictures and think about what to say.

Prompt the students to use the Party Picture page to take turns talking about a celebration that happened in the past. Write down the regular past tense verbs they use. (Only write down regular verbs that end in *-ed*. Irregular verbs will be addressed in another lesson). Continue until all students have had a turn or two.

Say: ***Let's look at the regular past tense verbs you used. What do they have in common?*** (They all end in *-ed*.) Direct students' attention to the list of regular past tense verbs and review some of the words with students.

Party Picture page verbs:

greet (two people greet at the door)

dance (two people dance)

play (one boy plays the guitar)

call (one boy calls the pizza guy on the phone)

watch (three kids watch a video)

pop (one girl pops popcorn)

help (one boy helps clean up)

open (one girl opens a window)

bake (one boy bakes chocolate chip cookies)

pour (one girl pours glasses of juice)

Independent Practice

Introduce the story-writing activity. Say: ***Let's imagine we went to a birthday party together and we want to write a story about it. We'll have to use action words that show it happened in the past.***

Show students the stack of Verb cards and say: ***You'll each get turns to come up with sentences using one of the verbs from this stack. You will take a card from the stack and read the verb. You'll make the verb a past tense verb by adding -ed. Then you'll use that verb to come up with a sentence to add to the story.***

Say: ***I'm going to start the story. I'll write the first line: "Last week we attended a birthday party for our friend." Who can find the word that shows this party happened in the past?*** Have a student underline the word. Talk about how the *-ed* helps you finds the action word that happened in the past.

Say: ***Now you will continue creating sentences for the story using actions from the cards.*** Model the sentence creating by drawing a Verb Card from the stack. Make up the next sentence for the story. Write down the sentence and ask a student to underline the verb.

Have students take turns drawing cards and adding sentences to the story. Let students know it is all right to make up sentences that are a little silly. The focus is on adding *-ed* to the verb, not on whether the story makes sense. Write down each sentence and ask a student to underline the verb. Continue until each student has had a few turns creating sentences.

If a student does not use a past tense verb correctly, use prompts to help him or her to correct it. For example: ***Did you remember to add -ed to the verb?***

Verb Cards: ask, call, look, work, guess, help, love, need, open, use, watch, wish, count, enjoy, fill, peel, save, visit, smile, touch, view, jump, decide, yell, melt, wave, walk

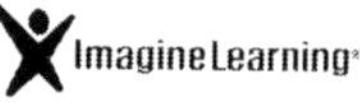

Differentiation

For more support: Have students draw the cards from the stack. Create a sentence for the student using the present tense verb and ask the student to say the past tense version of the verb.

For a challenge: Have students draw two cards from the stack and create a past tense sentence using both verbs.

Check Progress

Use the Party Checklists printout and the following activity to check individual progress made on the target skill. Depending on the number of students, choose one party checklist or use both to allow all students at least two opportunities.

Say: ***Here is a checklist showing all the things you need to do to get ready for a party. Let's imagine that this party already happened and you are telling me about all the things you had to do. I'll read one item from the list and you use it in a sentence to show that it happened in the past.***

Display the Party Checklist(s) so the students can follow along. Read items from the checklist and prompt students to supply the missing verb in a sentence. Ask students to tell you how they know the verb is talking about the past.

If the student can say the past tense verb correctly and explain that adding -ed to regular verbs makes them past tense, consider the intervention successful.

Party Checklist: Birthday Party

- decide who to invite
- plan the games
- shop for food
- color invitations
- mail invitations
- start the party at noon
- play games
- pop balloons
- enjoy cake
- thank my friends for coming to the party

Party Checklist: 4th of July Party

- decide who to invite
- clean up yard, house, or apartment
- invite neighbors over for barbeque
- plan the menu
- shop for food
- shop for decorations
- welcome neighbors to the party
- grill the hamburgers
- serve the food
- watch the fireworks
- thank neighbors for coming to the barbeque

Past Tense

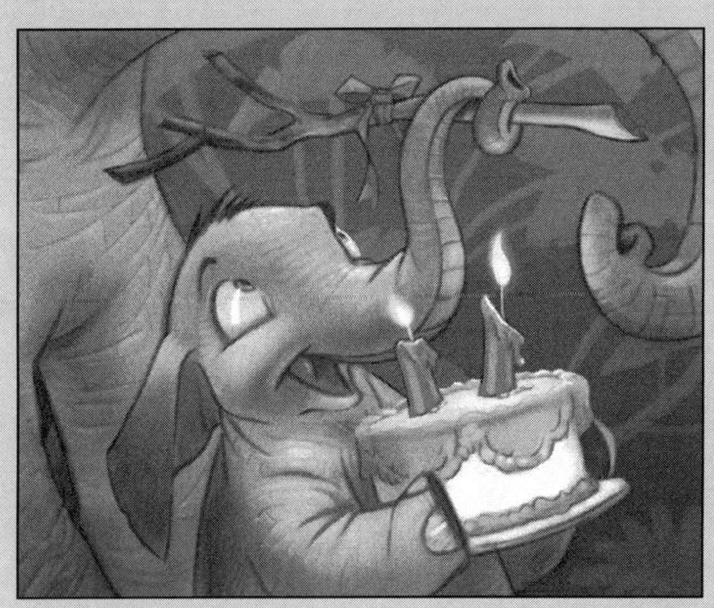

My Birthday Party

I **celebrated** my birthday last week. I **turned** two years old.

Dad **invited** all the other elephants to the party.

Mom **baked** a cake. She **wrapped** my present with a purple ribbon.

I **laughed** and **played** with my friends. I **showed** them my new toy. They **liked** it.

When I **snuggled** with Mom at bedtime, I **hoped** every birthday would be this much fun.

Action verbs *are the words that show what people animals or thing do.*

float	**+ ed**	The balloons **floated** by the cake. 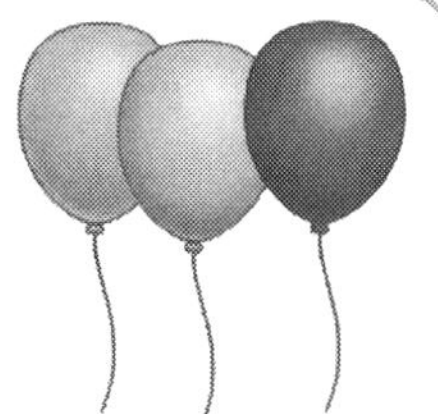
yell	**+ ed**	My friends **yelled**, "Surprise!" 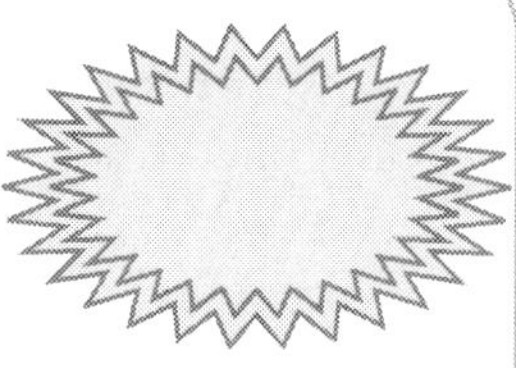
wish	**+ ed**	They **wished** me a happy birthday. 

Party Picture

love	work	ask
need	guess	call
open	help	look

peel	count	use
save	enjoy	watch
visit	fill	wish

smile

jump

melt

touch

decide

wave

view

yell

walk

Party Checklist: 4th of July Party

- [ ] decide who to invite
- [ ] clean up yard, house, or apartment
- [ ] invite neighbors over for barbeque
- [ ] plan the menu
- [ ] shop for food
- [ ] shop for decorations
- [ ] welcome neighbors to the party
- [ ] grill the hamburgers
- [ ] serve the food
- [ ] watch the fireworks
- [ ] thank neighbors for coming to the barbeque

Party Checklist: Birthday Party

- [ ] decide who to invite
- [ ] plan the games
- [ ] shop for food
- [ ] color invitations
- [ ] mail invitations
- [ ] start the party at noon
- [ ] play games
- [ ] pop balloons
- [ ] enjoy cake
- [ ] thank my friends for coming to the party

Grammar

Personal Pronouns

Grade 1

15 min.

CCSS.ELA-Literacy.L.1.1d
TEKS .110.12.20.A.vi

LEARNING OBJECTIVE: Correctly use pronouns in place of nouns.
LANGUAGE OBJECTIVE: Use the correct pronouns to discuss people helping others.
PREREQUISITE SKILL: Know the definition of a noun and be able to identify basic nouns.

Lesson Overview

Teacher reviews rules and examples of personal pronouns with students. Students use picture cards to practice using pronouns to replace nouns. They play a pantomime game to act out scenarios of people doing classroom chores.

Materials	Preparation
• Grammar Chart • Pronoun Picture Cards • Secret Helper Cards • Pronoun Chant • Check Progress printout	• Cut out Pronoun Picture Cards and Secret Helper Cards. • To print materials in color, visit the online Teacher Resources.

Activate Prior Knowledge

Quickly review the prerequisite skill with students and evaluate their proficiency. If students are not proficient with this skill, complete the corresponding Grammar Lesson before continuing.

NOUNS: ***A noun is a word that names a person, place, animal, or thing. All the people, places, and things around you in this room are nouns. I'll say a word. If it is a noun, stand up.***

Write three categories on the board: person/animal, place, and thing.

Say: ***I'm going to point to one of these categories: person or animal, place, and thing. Stand up if you have an example of a noun that belongs in that group.***

Alternate pointing between the three categories, calling on a few students each time to name a noun that belongs in that group. Some nouns can be a place and a thing. If one is mentioned, allow students to discuss and place it in one category or the other.

Teach and Model

Introduce the grammar principle

Now that we have practiced nouns, we can learn about pronouns. Pronouns are important because they can help us not repeat the same nouns over and over.

Work through the Grammar Chart

Use the picture and the story to present the grammar in context.
Read through the rules.
Explore the examples.

Clarify and correct if needed

- ***Use the pronoun that tells the right number of people, places, or things:***
- ***When you talk directly to people:***
  - ***Use you.***
- ***When you talk about people, places, or things:***
  - ***Use I to talk about yourself.***
  - ***Use we to talk about yourself and another person.***
  - ***Use he to talk about one boy/male.***
  - ***Use she to talk about one girl/female.***
  - ***Use they to talk about more than one person, place, or thing.***
  - ***Use it to talk about one place or thing.***

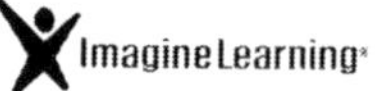

Guided Practice

Display the first Pronoun Picture Card: <u>The boy</u> washes the dog. Say: ***Let's look at some pictures of people and animals that are helping. I'll read a sentence that goes with the picture. You will help me change the underlined noun or nouns to a pronoun.*** Model the correct pronoun for the first card: ***He washes the car.***

Read each accompanying sentence out loud. Have the students replace the underlined noun(s) with the correct pronoun.

If a student does not use pronouns correctly, help them to self-correct using prompts such as: ***What noun are we replacing with a pronoun? Did you notice that there is [only one person, more than one person]? Did you notice that the person is a [man, woman]? What do we know about using pronouns to talk about [only one person, more than one person, a man, a woman]?***

Sentence bank:

<u>The boy</u> washes the dog. (He)

<u>Nate</u> walks the dog. (He)

<u>Pip</u> fixes the fence. (She)

<u>Paul and David</u> sweep the floor. (They)

<u>The girl</u> collects eggs. (She)

<u>Dad</u> carries the baby. (He)

<u>The school bus</u> takes me to school. (It)

<u>The nurses</u> help people who are sick. (They)

<u>The teacher</u> helps me learn math. (He/She)

Independent Practice

Tell the students they will play a game to practice using the pronouns *I*, *you*, *he*, and *she*. Say: ***Imagine our classroom is a mess, and some of you secretly do some jobs to clean up the room. Each of you will get a Secret Job Cards and we'll try to guess who did which job.*** Review the jobs on the Secret Helper Cards with the students.

Display the chant. Say: ***To play this game will need to know a little chant.*** Have the students repeat and practice the chant.

I did?

Yes, you.

No, I didn't.

Then who?

Model how to play the game. First read a job from the bank below, for example: "Clean the floor." Then have all the students ask together: "Who cleaned the floor?" Name a student. Have everyone look at them and say, "You cleaned the floor." Have the student who was named say "I did?" and the group respond "Yes, you." Then the student will say, "No, I didn't," and the group responds, "Then who?" Have the student who was named point to another student and say "He (or she) did." Then the chant starts over:

Group: You cleaned the floor.

Student: I did?

Group: Yes, you.

Student: No, I didn't.

Group: Then who?

Student: He / She did.

Remind the students to point and say *he* or *she*, not names, since they are practicing pronouns.

Explain: ***If you get pointed out and it really is your secret job, you have to say, "You are right! It was me!" But, if I can't guess the right person after three tries, I will ask you to tell me who it is. Then I will pick a new secret job and start again.***

Give each student a Secret Helper Card. Have students look at their card, remember it, and place it face down so that other students can't see it.

Reteaching Lessons ✓

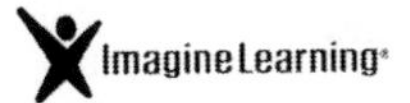

Play the game. If students use a name instead of a pronoun, prompt them to correct it by saying: ***Replace [name] with a pronoun.***

After one round, tell the students you will play again, but this time you will practice the plural pronouns *you*, *we*, and *they*.

Pair each student with a partner. Shuffle the cards and hand out one secret job to each pair. This time as they chant, have student use plural pronouns.

Group: You cleaned the floor.

Students: We did?

Group: Yes, you.

Student: No, we didn't.

Group: Then who?

Student: They did.

Secret job bank: clean the door / put away the globe / wipe the shelves / collect the papers / sharpen the pencils / wash the windows / stack the books / straighten the chairs / erase the chalkboard / clean the computers / water the plant / clean the desks /

Check Progress

Use the Check Progress printout and the following activity to check individual progress made on the target skill

Say: ***I'll show you a sentence and read it aloud. Look at the words in the box. Are they nouns or pronouns? If they are not pronouns, tell me a pronoun you could use to replace the nouns.***

Read each sentence aloud. If the student can identify pronouns and correctly replace nouns with pronouns, consider the intervention successful.

1. The boys clean the room.
2. We rake the leaves.
3. Mom likes to sweep.
4. He wipes the table.
5. Mei helps her friend.
6. The boxes are ready.
7. Mrs. Jones sorts the books.
8. You take the garbage.
9. They feed the cat.
10. Max puts the box away.
11. The teacher cleans his desk.
12. I mop the floor.
13. Ty and Nat pull the rope.
14. My brother and I wash the car.
15. You stack the papers.
16. Dad and I work hard.
17. I water the plants.
18. My friends and I pick up trash.
19. She holds the baby.
20. The dogs get baths today.
21. We are happy to help.
22. All the students wash windows.

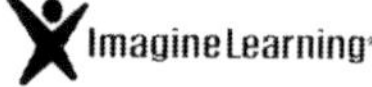

Pronouns

Help!

The bull is mad.

It won't move.

I need help.

My brother and sister will come.

They are strong.

We will work together.

*Pronouns take the place of **nouns** in a sentence.*

One person or thing		More than one person or thing	
I		**we**	
you		**you**	
he 	**she** 	**they**	
it		**they**	

The boy washes the dog.

Nate walks the dog.

Pip fixes the fence.

Paul and David sweep the floor.

The girl collects eggs.

Dad carries the baby.

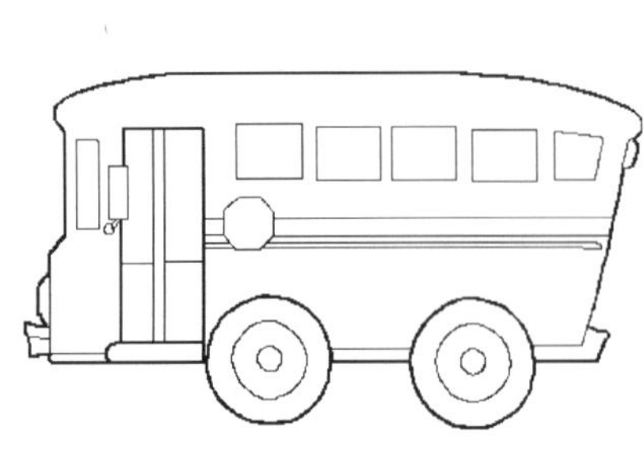

The school bus takes us to school.

The nurses help people who are sick.

The teacher helps me learn math.

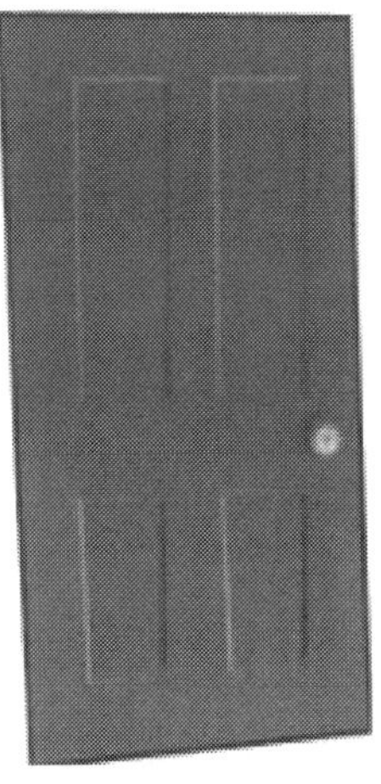

clean the door

put away the globe

wipe the shelves

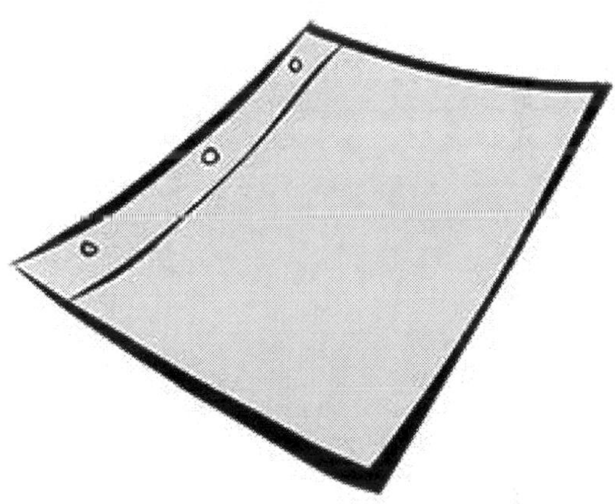

collect the papers

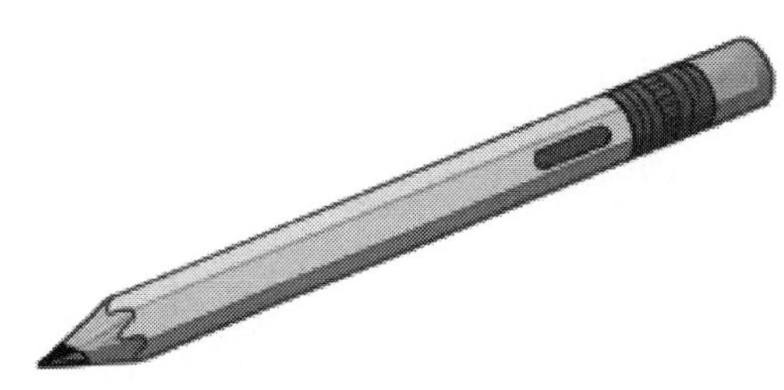

sharpen the pencils

wash the windows

stack the books

straighten the chairs

erase the chalkboard

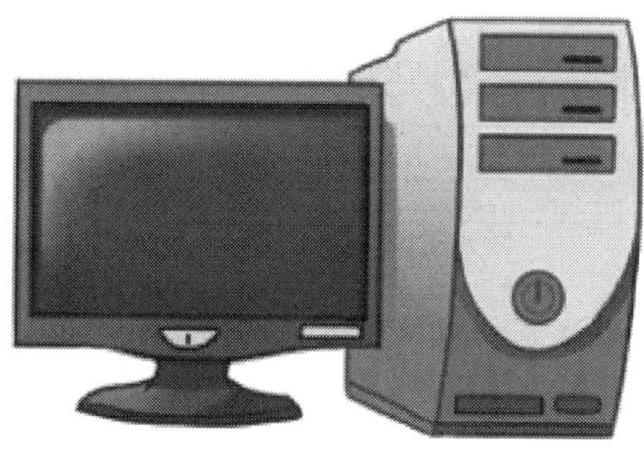

clean the computers

water the plant

clean the desks

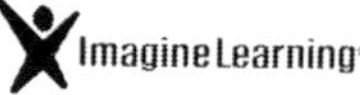

Secret Jobs Singular Pronouns: *I*, *you*, *he*, *she*, and *it*

Who cleaned the floor **?**

You cleaned the floor **.**

I did?

Yes, you.

No, I didn't.

Then who?

He did. / She did.

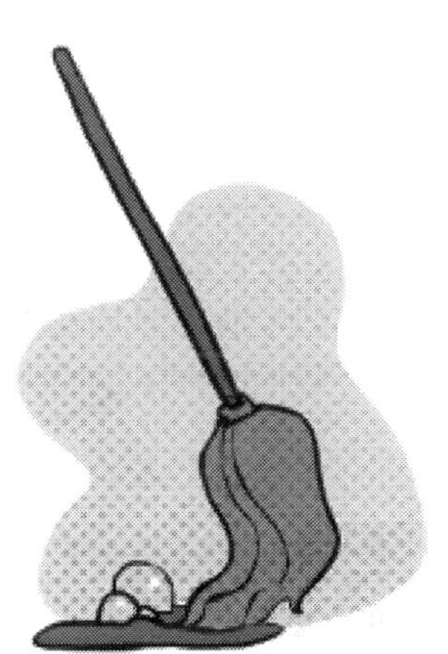

Secret Jobs Singular Pronouns: *we*, *you*, and *they*

Who put away the games **?**

You put away the games **.**

We did?

Yes, you.

No, we didn't.

Then who?

They did.

Reteaching Lessons

Personal Pronouns: Check Progress

1. The boys clean the room.
2. We rake the leaves.
3. Mom likes to sweep.
4. He wipes the table.
5. Mei helps her friend.
6. The boxes are ready.
7. Mrs. Jones sorts the books.
8. You take the garbage.
9. They feed the cat.
10. Max puts the box away.
11. The teacher cleans his desk.
12. I mop the floor.
13. Ty and Nat pull the rope.
14. My brother and I wash the car.
15. You stack the papers.
16. Dad and I work hard.
17. I water the plants.
18. My friends and I pick up trash.
19. She holds the baby.
20. The dogs get baths today.
21. We are happy to help.
22. All the students wash windows.

Plural and Singular

Grade K

15 min.

CCSS.L.K.1.c
TEKS 110.11.16.A.ii

LEARNING OBJECTIVE: Form and use plural nouns by adding -s to regular singular nouns.

LANGUAGE OBJECTIVE: Use singular and plural nouns to talk about classroom and everyday items.

PREREQUISITE: Understand the concepts of one and more than one. It may be helpful if students can read, but reading is not required for the lesson. The emphasis of the lesson is oral language production.

Lesson Overview

Teacher reviews rules and examples of singular and plural with students. Students imagine using magic wands to add *s* to regular nouns to make the noun plural. They practice with classroom items and then play Go Fish with plural and singular picture cards.

Materials	Preparation
• Grammar Chart • Singular and Plural Cards • Singular and Plural Picture Prompt	• Cut out Singular and Plural Cards. • To print materials in color, visit the online Teacher Resources.

Activate Prior Knowledge

Quickly review the prerequisite skill with students and evaluate their proficiency. If students are not proficient with this skill, complete the corresponding Grammar Lesson before continuing.

ONE AND MORE THAN ONE: Show students several pencils. Ask: ***What do I have here?*** (pencils) Pick up one pencil. Ask: ***Now what do I have?*** (a pencil)

Say: ***The word pencils is about all of the pencils, and the word pencil is about one of the pencils. Listen carefully. What sound do you hear at the end of the word pencils?*** (/s/)

Say: ***Now, hold up your hands. I see lots of fingers. Put your hands down. Now, [name a student], show me only one finger. The word fingers is about many fingers, and the word finger is just about one.***

Teach and Model

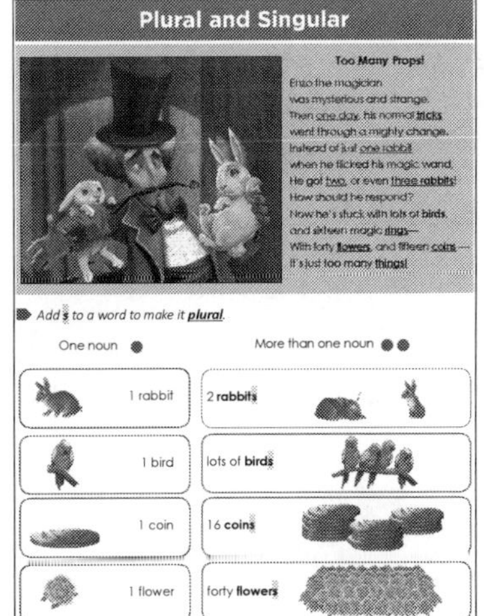

Plural and Singular

Too Many Props!

Enzo the magician
was mysterious and strange.
Then one day, his normal tricks
went through a mighty change.
Instead of just one rabbit
when he flicked his magic wand,
He got two, or even three rabbits!
How should he respond?
Now he's stuck with lots of birds,
and sixteen magic rings—
With forty flowers, and fifteen coins—
It's just too many things!

Add s to a word to make it ***plural***.

One noun	More than one noun
1 rabbit	2 **rabbits**
1 bird	lots of **birds**
1 coin	16 **coins**
1 flower	forty **flowers**

Introduce the grammar principle

Words that are about just one thing are called **singular.** ***Words that are about more than one thing or many things are called*** **plural.** **Singular** ***means one.*** Have students repeat the word *singular*. **Plural** ***means more than one.*** Have the students repeat the word *plural*.

Work through the Grammar Chart

Use the picture and the poem to present the grammar in context.

Read through the rules.

Explore the examples.

Clarify and correct if needed

- ***Most of the time we just add -s to the end of a noun to make it plural.***
- ***Some have special rules for plurals. We will learn those words in a different lesson.***

Guided Practice

Tell the students they will use magic wands to practice making regular nouns plural by adding *-s*.

Say: ***Imagine these pencils are magic wands. Our wands can help us add a magic* -s *to change one thing into more than one thing. Magic* -s *changes the word from* singular *to* plural. Plural *means more than one.***

I'll say a word and you change it into a plural using magic* -s. *For example, I'll say* book. *You repeat* book *and wave your magic wand and say "books." Let's use our magic wands to make a few more words plural.

Continue with more words using the word bank below.

Word bank: desk, door, teacher, crayon, pen, eraser, clock, calendar, ruler, chair, map, notebook, backpack, table

Independent Practice

Show the Singular and Plural Cards. Show a card with a singular image and say: ***The magician has used his magic wand to make things plural.*** Show the corresponding plural card.

Tell the students they will play Go Fish to match singular and plural words. Quickly review the names of all the objects on the cards before beginning the game.

Show the students how to play Go Fish. Explain that to get a match they need to have two cards with the same items in the picture; one card will have just one item and the other card will have two or more. Show them how to look at their cards and find a card they want to match. Practice the question "Do you have ________ ?" and the two possible responses: either "Yes," and hand over the matching card, or "No, go fish!" and the player draws a card from the pile. Use the banana card to model. Clarify that if they have one banana, they will need to ask for the plural: "Do you have bananas?" If they have bananas, they will need to ask for the singular, "Do you have *one* banana?" If they get the singular and the plural cards, either by asking or drawing, they have a match and they place the cards in front of them.

Shuffle the Go Fish cards together and hand out four cards to each student. Put the remaining cards face down on the table. Take the first turn to model the game, then the turn passes to the student on your left.

Remind students to speak clearly and emphasize the /s/ so other students can hear the endings of the words. If a student does not use the plural noun correctly, use prompts to help him or her to correct it. For example: ***Did you remember to add* -s*?***

Differentiation

For more support: Pull six matches from the set of cards, mix them together, and spread them faceup on the table. Have a student find a match, name both cards, and then remove them from the table. Have students take turns until all the card have been cleared. If time allows, repeat with the remaining six matches.

For a challenge: As students play Go Fish, have them make up a sentence for each set of cards they win.

Check Progress

Use the Singular and Plural Picture Prompt and the following activity to check individual progress made on the target skill.

Point to different parts of the picture and ask students to tell you the plural form of the noun.

If the student can correctly say the plural forms of two nouns after looking at a picture, consider the intervention successful.

Word bank: table, candle, card, bag, hat, cube, fan, magic wand, cape, rope, ball, glove, cup, lock

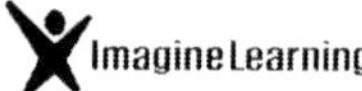

Plural and Singular

Too Many Props!

Enzo the magician
was mysterious and strange.
Then one day, his normal **tricks**
went through a mighty change.
Instead of just one rabbit
when he flicked his magic wand,
he got two, or even three **rabbits**!
How should he respond?
Now he's stuck with lots of **birds**
and sixteen magic **rings**—
With forty **flowers** and fifteen **coins** —
It's just too many **things!**

*Add **s** to a word to make it **plural**.*

One noun 

More than one noun 

One noun	More than one noun
 1 rabbit	2 **rabbits** 
 1 bird	lots of **birds** 
 1 coin	16 **coins** 
 1 flower	forty **flowers** 

Reteaching Lessons

hat

hats

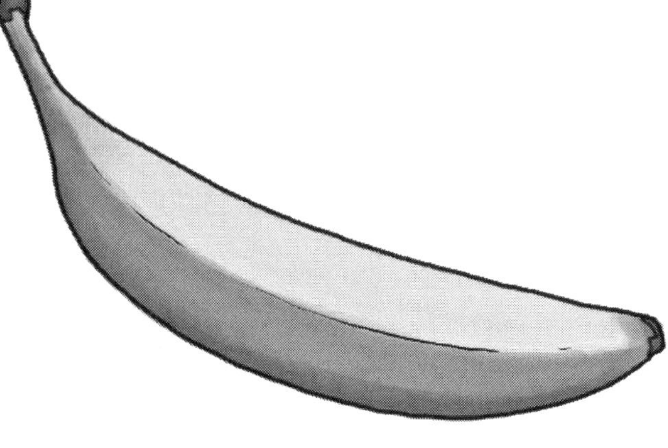

banana

bananas

button

buttons

Reteaching Lessons

Singular and Plural Cards

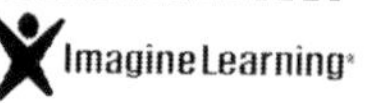

cookie

cookies

dolphin

dolphins

student

students

Reteaching Lessons

boot

boots

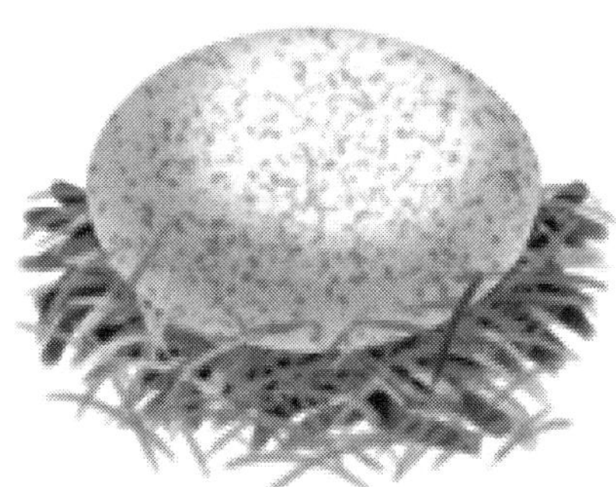

egg

eggs

backpack

backpacks

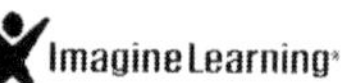

pumpkin

pumpkins

giraffe

giraffes

crayon

crayons

Reteaching Lessons ✓

The Magician's Table

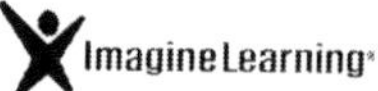

Irregular Plurals

LEARNING OBJECTIVE: Form and use frequently occurring irregular plural nouns.

LANGUAGE OBJECTIVE: Use irregular nouns to talk about people and things you would see in a zoo.

PREREQUISITE SKILL(S): Understand the meaning of singular and plural and know common plural endings *-s*, *-es*, and *-ies*.

Lesson Overview

Teacher reviews rules and examples of irregular plurals (such as *feet, children, teeth, mice, fish*) with students. Students clap to identify plural and singular nouns. Students play a chanting game and substitute irregular plural nouns.

Materials	Preparation
• Grammar Chart • Singular Word Cards • Plural Word Cards • Singular Picture Cards • City Zoo Chant printout	• Cut out word cards and picture cards. • Depending on the age and abilities of your students, you might add hand actions to the City Zoo Chant. You could prepare these ahead of time or have the students help you invent them during the activity. • To print materials in color, visit the online Teacher Resources.

Activate Prior Knowledge

Quickly review the prerequisite skill with students and evaluate their proficiency. If students are not proficient with this skill, complete the corresponding Grammar Lesson before continuing.

REGULAR PLURALS -S -ES AND -IES: ***We know many ways to make nouns plural.***

One hat, two ______. (hats) ***What do we add to make most nouns plural?*** (We add *-s*.) ***I'll say a noun. You add -s to make it plural. Draw an s in the air as you say it. Cloud.*** (clouds) ***Park.*** (parks) ***Boot.*** (boots) ***Flower.*** (flowers)

One dress, two ______.(dresses) ***What do we add to nouns that already have an s sound in the ending, such as nouns that end in /s/, /x/, /ch/, /sh/?*** (We add *-es*.) ***I'll say a noun, you add -es to make it plural. Draw an es in the air as you say it. Glass.*** (glasses) ***Lunch.*** (lunches) ***Brush.*** (brushes) ***Fox.*** (foxes)

One baby, two ______. (babies) ***What do we do with words that end in a consonant plus a y?*** (Change the *y* to *i* and add *-es*.) ***I'll say a noun. You motion with me like this: take off the y*** (make a crisscross motion in the air) ***add an i*** (draw a lowercase *i* in the air)***, then add -es. Ready? Story.*** (stories) ***Sky.*** (skies) ***Puppy.*** (puppies) ***Berry.*** (berries)

Teach and Model

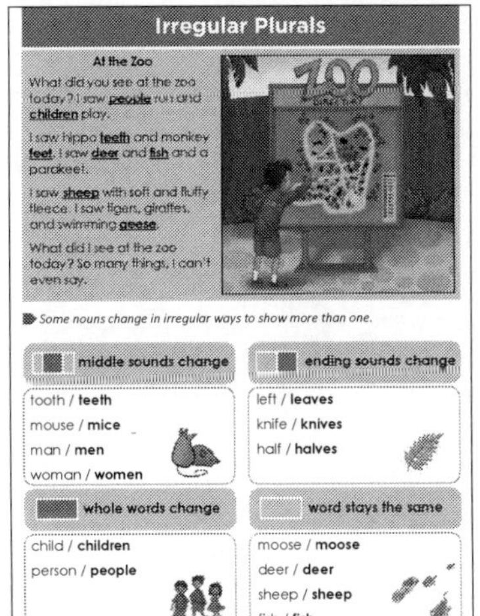

Introduce the grammar principle

- ***A few nouns have irregular plural forms.***
- ***Irregular means it doesn't follow the usual rules.***
- ***This means you will have to memorize how the words change.***

Work through the Grammar Chart

Use the picture and the poem to present the grammar in context.

Read through the rules.

Explore the examples.

Guided Practice

Tell the students they will review and practice the irregular nouns.

Note: If reviewing the Grammar Chart shows that students do not know the irregular forms, use this sorting activity to review. If students are already familiar with the irregular plurals, skip the sorting activity.

Sorting activity: Display Singular Word Cards in a column. Hand out Plural Word Cards to students. Call on students one at a time place each of their plural words next to their matching singular word. Have all students repeat both words as each match is made.

Say: ***Now, imagine we are walking through the zoo. I'll name something I see. You show me by clapping if what I said was singular or plural. If it is singular, clap one time, like this.*** Demonstrate. ***If it is plural, clap many times softly and quickly like this until I signal you to stop.*** Demonstrate, clapping gently.

Say: ***For example, I see mice.*** (students clap multiple times) ***That's right.* Mice *is plural. Now I need a volunteer to change the plural word to a singular.*** (mouse)

Say: ***There is a tall person.*** (students clap once) ***That's right.* Person *is singular. Now I need a volunteer to change the word person to plural.*** (people)

Use words from the bank below in random order. Alternate between singular and plural. Observe student responses, then call on volunteers to change singular words to plural and plural words to singular.

Singular	*Plural*
woman	women
goose	geese
child	children
foot	feet
tooth	teeth
leaf	leaves
man	men
knife	knives
person	people

After students are comfortable with these plurals, say: ***Some words don't change from singular to plural. How will you know if I am talking about one or more than one? Listen to these sentences and see if there is a clue that helps you know.*** Say: ***I see a red fish swimming in the tank. I see many fish swimming in the tank.***

Say the following sentences, the plural directly after the singular. Help students discover that there are usually other words in a sentence that can help you know if something is singular or plural (*a, one, many, all, is, were,* numbers, etc.).

Singular	*Plural*
I saw a tall moose.	The moose were all hiding in the woods
The deer was by the fence.	We saw two deer by the road.
One little sheep is lost.	The sheep stayed together in a flock.

Independent Practice

Tell the students they will learn a chant to help them practice irregular nouns. Set aside the *man* picture card, and place all other Singular Picture Cards facedown in a stack. Display the City Zoo Chant.

One ________________ is walking at the city zoo.

He meets one more, and now there are two.

Two ___________ are walking at the zoo today.

They have lots of fun. Then they both walk away.

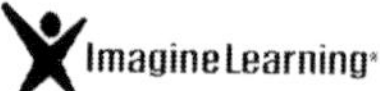

Model the game using the word *man* to fill in the blank: Hold the *man* picture card and read the first verse aloud. ***One man is walking at the city zoo. He meets one more and then there are two.*** Then have students choral chant the first verse with you.

Read the second verse aloud, using *men* to fill in the blank. ***Two men are walking at the zoo today. They have lots of fun. Then they both walk away.*** Have the students choral chant the second verse with you.

Have a student draw a card from the stack and use the singular noun to complete the first verse. The student then points to another student who uses the plural form of the noun to complete the second verse.

After saying the chant, have one student write out the plural form of the noun on the board. If students struggle, have students write the plural form before they chant the verse.

Repeat with new students and new nouns.

Noun cards: deer, fish, moose, person, mouse, child, goose, sheep, woman (in the chant, change *he* to *she*), leaf, foot, tooth (the last three will make fun, silly sentences)

Differentiation

For more support: Use a simplified chant.

One ______ is walking at the city zoo.

Two _____ are walking at the city zoo.

For a challenge: Review additional words not practiced above and add them to the game: elf/elves, wolf/wolves, wife/wives, die/dice, bison/bison

Check Progress

Use the following activity to check individual progress made on the target skill.

Read a sentence and call on a student to change it from singular to plural. Help the students as needed to change *a* to *some* or *many* or to change *one* to a plural number, but require them to change the noun from singular to plural on their own.

Singular	*Plural*
I saw one goose in the pond.	I saw three geese in the pond.
The mouse ran into the hole.	The mice ran into the hole.
The leaf fell from the tree.	The leaves fell from the tree.
The child ran and played.	The children ran and played.
One man cleaned the cages.	Two men cleaned the cages.
I like the hippo with the big tooth.	I like the hippo with the big teeth.
I saw one sheep at the zoo.	I saw four sheep at the zoo.
A woman bought ice cream.	Two women bought ice cream.
I saw a person taking pictures.	I saw many people taking pictures.
A big moose ate the plant.	Three big moose ate the plant.
I saw a deer with white spots.	I saw some deer with white spots.

If the student can correctly change these irregular nouns to the plural form, consider the intervention successful.

Irregular Plurals

At the Zoo

What did you see at the zoo today? I saw **<u>people</u>** run and **<u>children</u>** play.

I saw hippo **<u>teeth</u>** and monkey **<u>feet</u>**. I saw **<u>deer</u>** and **<u>fish</u>** and a parakeet.

I saw **<u>sheep</u>** with soft and fluffy fleece. I saw tigers, giraffes, and swimming **<u>geese</u>**.

What did I see at the zoo today? So many things, I can't even say.

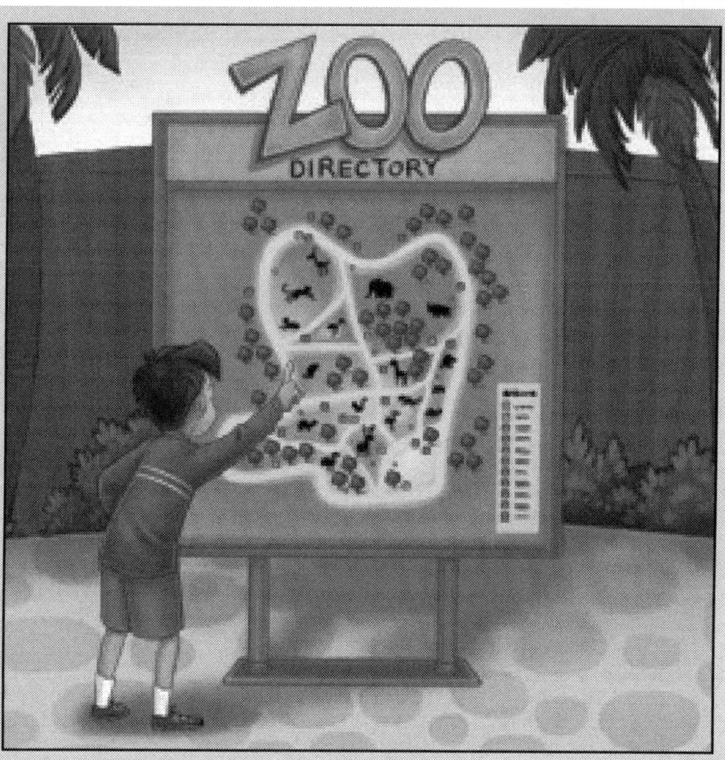

Some nouns change in irregular ways to show more than one.

 **middle sounds change**

tooth / **teeth**
mouse / **mice**
man / **men**
woman / **women**

 **ending sounds change**

leaf / **leaves**
knife / **knives**
half / **halves**

 **whole word changes**

child / **children**
person / **people**

 **word stays the same**

moose / **moose**
deer / **deer**
sheep / **sheep**
fish / **fish**

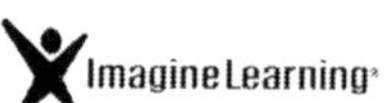

child	goose	woman
leaf	tooth	foot
person	knife	man

children	geese	women
leaves	teeth	feet
people	knives	man

deer

fish

moose

person

mouse

child

Reteaching Lessons ✓

goose

sheep

woman

leaf

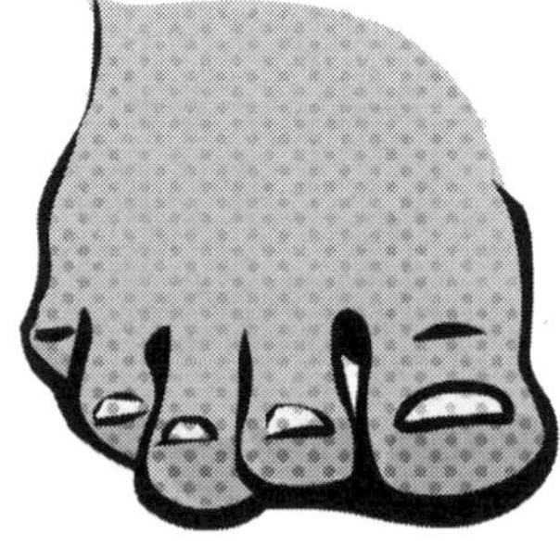

foot

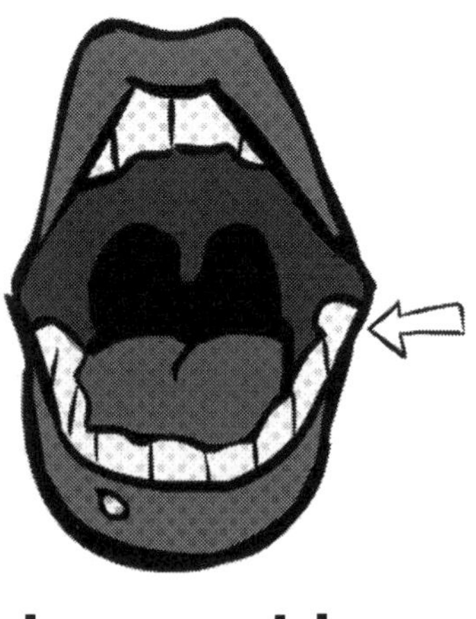

tooth

Singular Picture Cards

One ____________ is walking at the city zoo.
He meets one more, and now there are two.

Two ____________ are walking at the zoo today,
They have lots of fun, then they both walk away.

Grammar

Plural Nouns: -s and -es

Grade K

15 min.

CCSS.L.K.1.C
TEKS 110.13.21.A.ii

LEARNING OBJECTIVE: Form plural nouns by adding -s or -es.

LANGUAGE OBJECTIVE: Use plural nouns that end in -es to talk about packing items into boxes.

PREREQUISITE SKILLS: Know the definition of a noun and be able to identify basic nouns.

Lesson Overview

Teacher reviews rules and examples with students of forming plural nouns using -s and -es (for example: *cat, cats, fox, foxes*). Students use a number spinner to practice plural nouns ending in -s and -es. Students then play a sorting game to practice identifying plural endings and using plural nouns in complete sentences.

Materials	Preparation
• Grammar Chart • Octopus Spinner • -s and -es Boxes printout • -s and -es Picture cards • -s and -es Word Cards	• Cut out picture and word cards. • Cut out the Octopus Spinner. Attach the octopus to the spinner with a brad. • If desired, cut out and attach the -s and -es box printouts to the fronts of two actual boxes. • To print materials in color, visit the online Teacher Resources.

Activate Prior Knowledge

Quickly review the prerequisite skill with students and evaluate their proficiency. If students are not proficient with this skill, complete the corresponding Grammar Lesson before continuing.

SINGULAR AND PLURAL NOUNS: ***A singular noun names one person, animal, place, or thing. For example: finger or book. A plural noun names more than one. For example,* fingers *or* books.**

Say: ***Did you notice that plural words can end in two sounds? A plural noun can have an /s/ sound like in books or a /z/ sound like in fingers. Have students repeat the words and notice the two sounds for plurals.***

Say: ***I'll say a noun, and then I'll signal you like this.*** Gesture or point to group. ***If it is singular clap one time. If it is plural, clap two times.***

Say each word, then gesture to students to clap: ***hats, flower, paper, kittens, schools, banana, pants, students, shirt maps, cookies, dog.***

Teach and Model

Introduce the grammar principle

Now that you know about singular and plural, we can look at two different ways to make nouns plural when we are writing and speaking.

Work through the Grammar Chart

Use the picture and the poem to present the grammar in context.

Read through the rules.

Explore the examples.

Clarify and correct if needed

Words that end in* s, ch, x, *and* sh *already have an* s *sound. If we add* s *to these nouns, we can't hear the plural ending, so we make them plural by adding -es.

Guided Practice

Tell the students they will play some games to practice plurals.

Use the Octopus Spinner. Say: ***Imagine we are helping Ollie Octopus pack his boxes. I'll name a thing, and you will spin Ollie to find out how many we need to pack. Then you will tell us in a complete sentence. For example, the thing we need to pack is*** **chair.** ***How many should we pack? I'll spin the spinner and give the answer in a complete sentence: Ollie says to pack three chairs.***

Word bank: book (books), ball (balls), bus (buses), brush (brushes), hat (hats), floss (flosses), flower (flowers), couch (couches), lemon (lemons), lunch box (lunch boxes), pan (pans), watch (watches)

Independent Practice

Say: ***In this game, you work in a packing factory. Your job is to put items in the right boxes. Here are all the things you will need to pack up. Let's review them.*** Quickly review the items on the -s and -es Picture Cards. If students struggle with the words, use the suggestion under differentiation to review and practice.

Place the *-s* and *-es* printout on the table (or on two boxes). Say: ***Here are two boxes.*** Place the Picture Cards face down in a stack. Say: ***Here are all the items that we need to pack into the boxes. If we need to add*** **-s** ***to the word to make it plural, we'll sort it to this box.*** Point to the *-s* box. ***If we add*** **-es** ***to make the word plural, we'll sort it to this box.*** Point to the *-es* box card.

Continue: ***For this job, I need three workers.*** Have three students stand in a line (student A, student B, and student C). Student A takes a card from the stack and says the item aloud and hands it to student B. Student B says the plural form aloud and hands it to student C. Student C sorts into the correct box: -es or -s.

Tell the students who are not in the assembly line that they are the quality checkers. Have them listen and watch carefully to make sure that the cards are being sorted correctly.

When a student draws an octopus card, he or she calls out, "Break Time!" and the three workers sit down. Have new students rotate into the positions.

When all the cards are sorted, review the words and ask the quality checkers to confirm that they have been sorted into the correct groups.

-es answer bank: sandwiches, benches, bushes, brushes, sixes, crutches, buses, dresses, watches, glasses, matches, radishes, peaches, dishes, foxes

-s answer bank: spots, pencils, socks, apples, rabbits, bugs, brooms, cans, shoes

Differentiation

For more support: Practice plurals before the game. As you review the items on the cards, say: ***I'll say an object, you say it back in the correct plural form.*** **Fox.** (foxes) **Glass.** (glasses) **Game.** (games) **Bench.** (benches)

For a challenge: Have Student A say the word and use the singular word in a complete sentence before passing it to student B. Student B repeats the sentence, making the sentence plural.

Check Progress

Use the -s and -es Word Cards and the following activity to check individual progress made on the target skill.

Have a student draw a card and read the word. Then have the student say whether to add an *-s* or *-es* to the end of the word to make it plural. On at least one word per student, ask the student to explain why he or she chose that plural ending.

If the student can correctly form the plural nouns by adding *-s* or *-es* and explain why, consider the intervention successful.

Answer bank: inches, pens, grasses, taxes, flowers, wishes, kites, boxes, classes, papers, bunches, carts, passes, witches, windows, lashes

Plural: -es

Ollie's Moving Day

It's moving day! I have lots of **boxes**.

I'll pack them up with all my **things**.

Magnets and **matches**, **dishes** and **patches**,

Crayons and **kisses** and octopus **rings**.

Reteaching Lessons

One ●	**More** than one ● ●
 An octopu**s**	 Eight octopus**es**
 One bo**x**	 Lots of box**es**

Add **-s** to most **nouns** to show more than one.

dog **s**

pant **s**

book **s**

eye **s**

Add **-es** to nouns that **end in s**, **ch**, **x**, and **sh**.

dre**s**s **es**

ben**ch** **es**

fo**x** **es**

di**sh** **es**

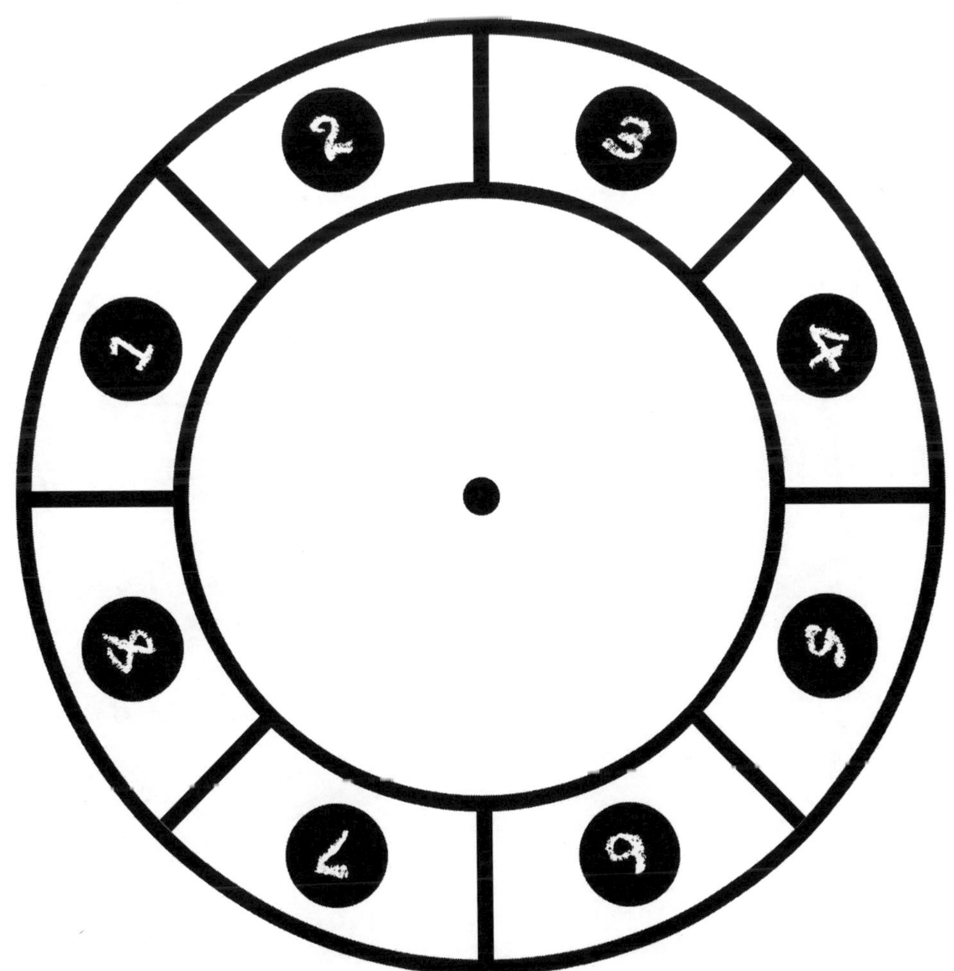

Reteaching Lessons ✓

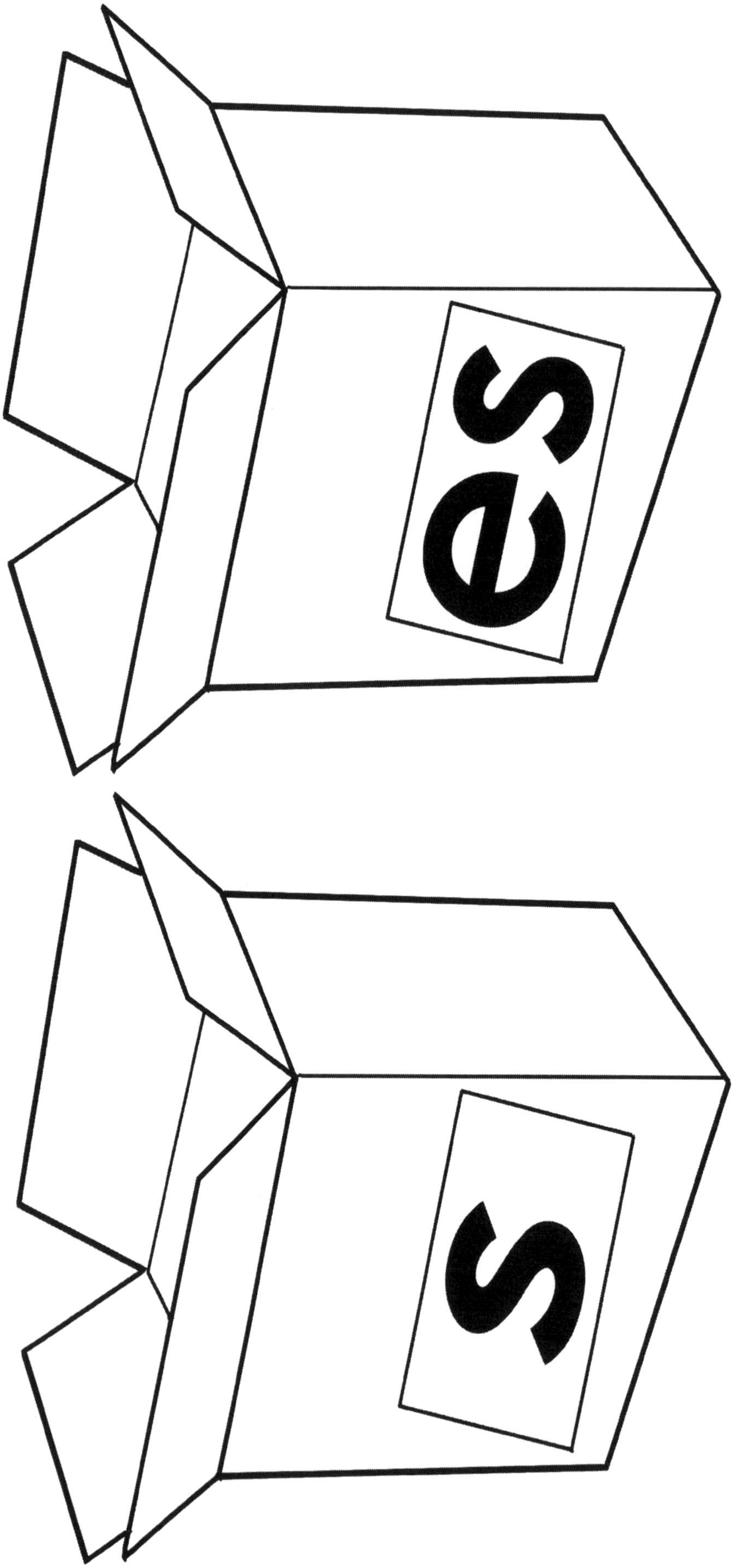

Reteaching Lessons

es

s

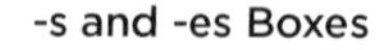

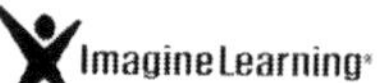

Break time!	Break time!	Break time!
fox	dish	peach
radish	match	glass

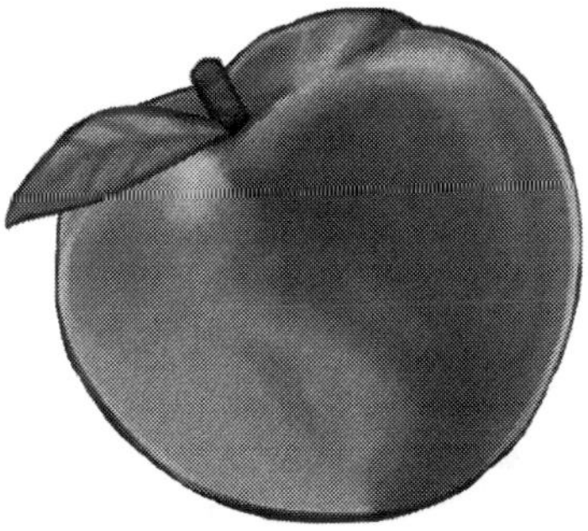

Reteaching Lessons

bus	dress	watch
crutch	six	brush
sandwich	bench	bush

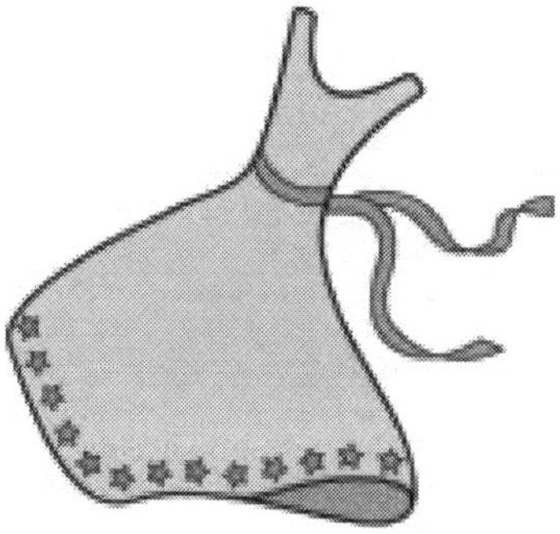

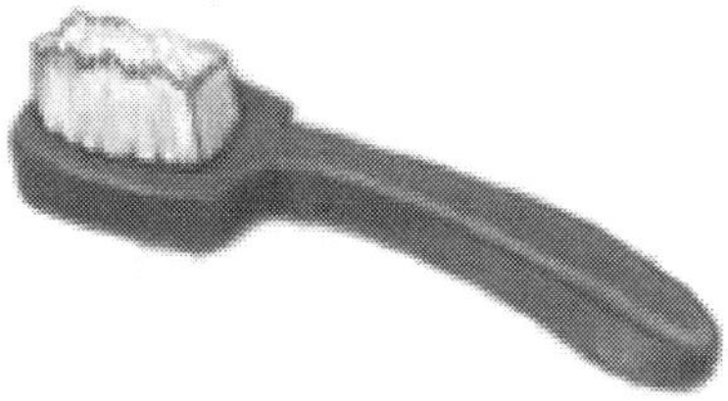

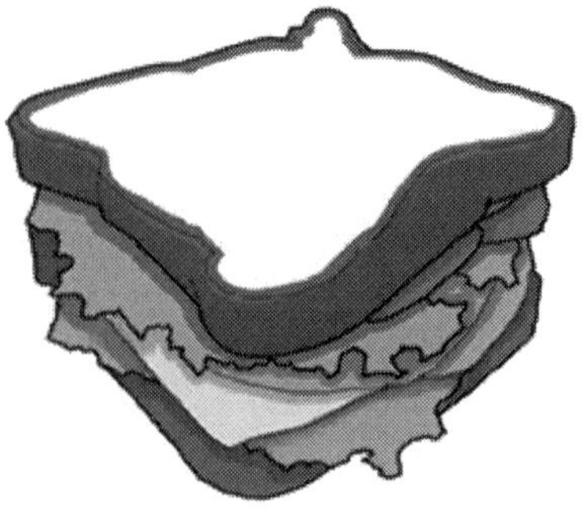

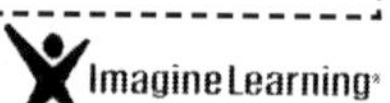

shoe	can	broom
bug	rabbit	apple
spot	pencil	sock

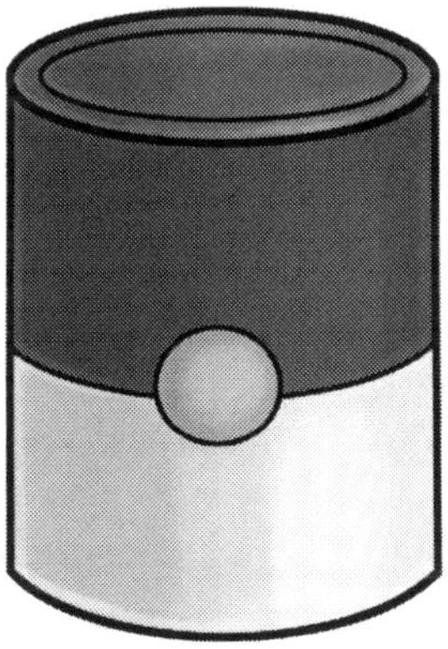

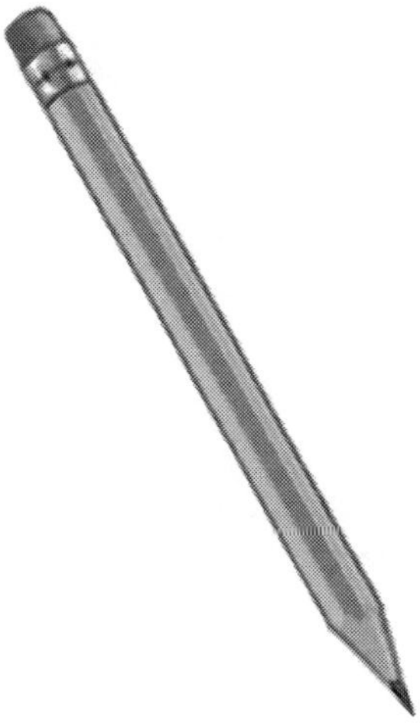

Reteaching Lessons

inch	flower
pen	wish
grass	kite
tax	box

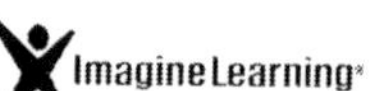

class	pass
paper	witch
bunch	window
cart	lash

Reteaching Lessons ✓

Plural -s and -ies

Grade 2

15 min.

CCSS.ELA.L.2.2.d
TEKS 110.13.21.A.ii

LEARNING OBJECTIVE: Form plural nouns orally and in writing by adding *-s* or *-ies*.

LANGUAGE OBJECTIVE: Use plural nouns that end in *-s* and *-ies* to talk about spies and spy adventures.

PREREQUISITE SKILLS: Be able to identify basic nouns and know the difference between a singular and plural noun.

Lesson Overview

Teacher reviews rules and examples with students of plural nouns with *-s* and *-ies* (for example, *boy, boys, spy, spies*). Students analyze nouns in sentences to determine the correct plural ending. Students then play a quiz-show style game to practice adding *-s* or *-ies* to words ending in *y*.

Materials	Preparation
• Grammar Chart • -s and -ies Game Board • -s and -ies Check Progress printout • White board and marker or paper and pencil (1 per student)	• Cover each square of the -s and -ies Game Board with a sticky note. • To print materials in color, visit the online Teacher Resources.

Reteaching Lessons

Activate Prior Knowledge

Quickly review the prerequisite skill with students and evaluate their proficiency. If students are not proficient with this skill, complete the corresponding Grammar Lesson before continuing.

SINGULAR AND PLURAL NOUNS: *A singular noun names* one *person, animal, place, or thing. A plural noun names* more than one. *Most of the time we make a noun plural by adding s. Sometimes we add* -es.

Write words from the word bank on the board and quickly discuss whether to add *-s* or *-es* to make the word plural.

Word bank: bug (bugs), agent (agents), fox (foxes), stair (stairs), wrench (wrenches), footprint (footprints), address (addresses), glass (glasses)

Teach and Model

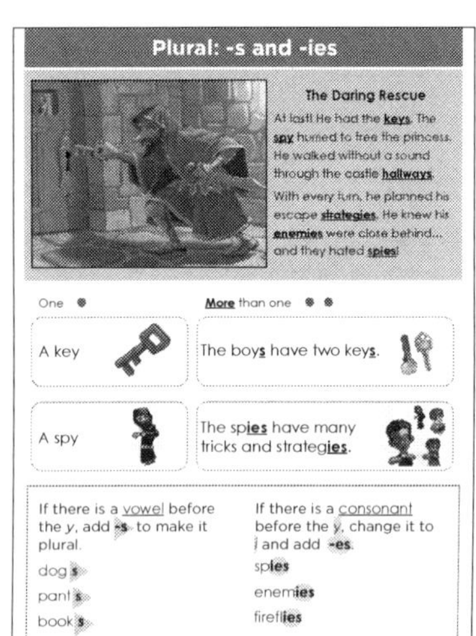

Introduce the grammar principle

There is another group of words that we need to know about when we are making words plural. This group is made up of nouns that end in y. To know how to change these nouns, you look at the letter that comes right before the y.

Work through the Grammar Chart

Use the picture and the story to present the grammar in context.

Read through the rules.

Explore the examples.

Clarify and correct if needed

- ***For words that already end in -ie, just add an -s. For example, movie/movies; cookie/cookies.***

Guided Practice

Say: ***Now it's your turn. I'll write a word on the board and you tell me whether to add -s to make it plural, or change the y to i and add -es.***

Write the first word on the board. Say the plural form of the word in a sentence to help students conceptualize the word as a plural noun, not a verb.

Have a student come up and mark the vowel or consonant right before the *y*. Then have the student write the plural form of the word.

- play: The author wrote three **plays** about a spy.
- fly: The **flies** wouldn't leave the spy alone.
- highway: The police blocked the **highways** while they chased the spy.
- day: How many **days** does a spy work in a month?
- ferry: The police searched the **ferries** looking for the spy.
- way: He knew ten **ways** to disguise himself.
- family: Their **families** didn't know they were spies.
- party: Can spies have **parties** together?

Words ending in -s*:* play, highway, day, way

Words ending in -ies*:* fly, ferry, family, party

Independent Practice

Tell students they will play a game to practice adding *-s* and *-ies* to nouns.

Divide the students into two groups.

Show the -s and -ies Game Board. Say: ***Under these sticky notes are nouns ending in y. Your job, should you choose to accept it, is to tell me if you need to add an -s or change the y to i and add -es to make the noun plural.***

For the first column, you read the word out loud and tell me if the word should end in -s or -ies. For the second column, I'll read a sentence. You read the word under the blank line and tell me whether to add -s or -ies to make it plural. For the last column, I'll say the word in a sentence. You read the word in the box and spell the plural form of the word.

The team with the most spy points will be named super spies.

Instruct students they can choose any square, and that the number of spy points for answering correctly corresponds to the numbers in the left hand column.

Have a student select a sticky note and complete the task written in that square. The turn then goes to the other team. Continue playing until all students have had a turn and all squares have been uncovered. Keep track of points and declare the winners "super spies" at the end.

If a student does not correctly make the noun plural, use prompts to help him or her to correct it. For example: ***Did you remember to look to see if a vowel or a consonant comes just before the y?***

Answer Key:

Spy Points	-s or ies	In a Sentence	Spell it
100	guy (guys)	The spy hid the secret papers under the (trays).	plural of copy (copies)
200	body (bodies)	What (hobbies) do spies enjoy after work?	plural of hallway (hallways)
300	valley (valleys)	The clue was hidden between two (pennies).	plural of city (cities)
400	chimney (chimneys)	Spies like to meet in dark (alleys).	plural of turkey (turkeys)
500	responsibility (responsibilities)	The spy traveled to many different (countries).	plural of trophy (trophies)
600	lady (ladies)	Do spies have to work on (holidays)?	plural of jersey (jerseys)

Reteaching Lessons

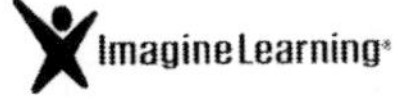

Example sentences for Spell It:

- The spy hid three **copies** of his passport in a safe.
- The spy moved slowly through the laser mazes in the **hallways**.
- The spy had traveled to so many **cities** he couldn't remember where he was.
- She hid in barn with a flock of **turkeys** while her enemies drove away.
- He won three **trophies** at the spy vs. spy field day races.
- The spies wore football **jerseys** as disguises.

Differentiation

For more support: Write the singular form of the noun from the game board on index cards. Have students sort the target word into two categories: words ending in *-s* and words ending in *-ies*. If a student does not correctly make the noun plural, circle the consonant or vowel that comes before the *y*.

Check Progress

Use the -s and -ies Check Progress printout and the following activity to check individual progress made on the target skill.

Give students a white board and marker or piece of paper and pencil. Show the check progress page to the students. Point to the word you want them to spell and instruct them to write the plural form of the noun. Call on a student to explain why the word should end in *-s* or *-ies*. Repeat with each word.

If the student can correctly spell the target words and explain when to add *-s* or *-ies* to words ending in *y*, consider the intervention successful.

Answer bank:

Words ending in -s: toy, cowboy, journey, ray, freeway

Words ending in ies: pony, baby, bunny, cherry

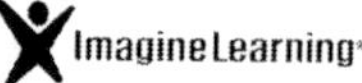

Plural: -s and -ies

The Daring Rescue

At last! He had the **keys**. The **spy** hurried to free the princess. He walked without a sound through the castle **hallways**.

With every turn, he planned his escape **strategies**. He knew his **enemies** were close behind… and they hated **spies**!

Reteaching Lessons ✓

One ●	**More** than one ● ●
A key 	The boy**s** have two key**s**. 
A spy 	The sp**ies** have many tricks and strateg**ies**. 

If there is a vowel before the *y*, add **-s** to make it plural.

dog**s**

pant**s**

book**s**

If there is a consonant before the *y*, change it to *i* and add **-es**.

sp**ies**

enem**ies**

firefl**ies**

Spy Points	-s or -ies	In a Sentence	Spell It
100	guy	The spy hid the secret papers under the ______ (tray).	plural of copy
200	body	What ______ (hobby) do spies enjoy after work?	plural of hallway
300	valley	The clue was hidden in between two ______ (penny).	plural of city
400	lady	Spies like to meet in dark ______ (alley).	plural of turkey
500	chimney	The spy traveled to many different ______ (country).	plural of trophy
600	responsibility	Do spies have to work on ______ (holiday)?	plural of jersey

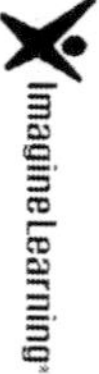

cowboy	freeway	ray
bunny	toy	pony
cherry	journey	baby

Prepositions

Grade K | 15 min. | CCSS.L.1.1.H TEKS 110.13.21.A.iii

LEARNING OBJECTIVE: Identify and use basic prepositions correctly in a sentence.
LANGUAGE OBJECTIVE: Use prepositions to talk about where things and animals are.
PREREQUISITE SKILL: Be able to identify basic nouns.

Lesson Overview

Teacher reviews rules and examples of prepositions with students. Students use the correct preposition to describe the location of a stuffed animal. Students play a matching game and talk about where a mouse is hiding in picture cards.

Materials	Preparation
• Grammar Chart • a small stuffed animal • Preposition Model Cards • Preposition Cards (one card per student) • Preposition Check Progress printout	• Cut out Preposition Model Cards and Preposition Cards. • To print materials in color, visit the online Teacher Resources.

Activate Prior Knowledge

Quickly review the prerequisite skill with students and evaluate their proficiency. If students are not proficient with this skill, complete the corresponding Grammar Lesson before continuing.

NOUNS: ***A noun is a naming word. It can name people, animals, and things. For example,*** **teacher** ***is a noun that names a person.*** Point to yourself. **Cat** ***is a noun that names an animal.*** Put your fingers by your head like animal ears. **Ball** ***is a noun that names a thing.*** Cup your hands together as if you are holding something.

Model the hand actions: ***I'll say a word. If it names a person, point to yourself, because you are a person. If it names an animal, put your fingers up like animal ears. If it names a thing, cup your hands, like this, as if you are holding a thing. If it is not a person, animal, or thing, put your hands in your lap.***

Say each word, pausing for students to react: *teacher*, *cat*, *ball*, hiding, *pencil*, sneaky, *box*, *student*, *mouse*, sing, *peach*, white, *neighbor*.

Teach and Model

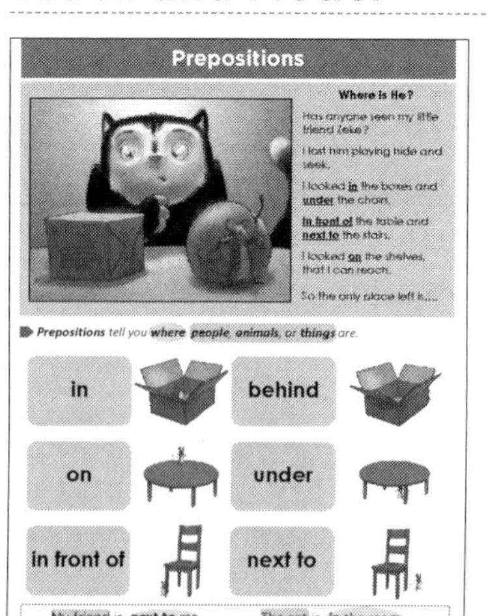

Introduce the grammar principle

Knowing nouns will help us learn about prepositions. A preposition is a word that tells where a noun is.

Work through the Grammar Chart

Use the picture and the poem to present the grammar in context.

To engage the students with the Grammar chart, there is an open ending that the students can fill in. Tell them before you begin that the poem is a like a riddle and they need to pay close attention so that they can finish the last line.

Prompt students to complete the poem with "behind the peach."

Read through the rules. Explore the examples.

Clarify and correct if needed

- ***Prepositions usually come between the noun and its location.***
- ***There are many more prepositions: above, across, against, around, below, beside, between, by, inside, into, off, outside, over***
- ***Many prepositions are single words. Some prepositions are two or more words:*** **on top of, in front of, next to, ahead of, away from, far from, out of**

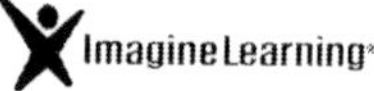

Guided Practice

Tell the students they will listen and respond to practice prepositions.

Show students the small stuffed animal. (In this model lesson, it is a mouse.) Say: ***Let's play hide and seek with this mouse. I'll put the mouse somewhere and then make up a sentence. You show me if what I said is right.***

If I use the correct preposition to say where the mouse is, put your hands up and wiggle them quickly like this. Demonstrate "jazz hands." ***If I use the wrong preposition to say where the mouse is, shake one finger back and forth like this.*** Demonstrate signaling "no" with your index finger.

Put the stuffed mouse under a table and say: ***The mouse is under the table. Is that the right preposition?*** (Students wiggle their hands.) Have students repeat with you: ***The mouse is under the table.***

Put the stuffed animal on your hand. Say: ***The mouse is under my hand. Is that the right preposition?*** (Students shake their finger.) Call on a volunteer to say the correct statement of where the mouse is.

Repeat using ideas from the bank below or creating your own. Alternate between saying the correct position of the stuffed animal and incorrect statements.

Watch the responses and help students self-correct as needed. After you have used each preposition at least once, and you have determined that students understand the meaning of each one, put the mouse in a new location and ask: ***Where is the mouse?*** Have a volunteer create a complete sentence using a preposition.

Idea bank: *on* my head, *in* a book, *in* a box, *next to* a chair, *in* front of [student name], *in front* of the board, *under* the paper, *behind* a book

Independent Practice

Tell the students they will play a matching game to practice prepositions.

Show Preposition Model Card #1. Explain: ***I will give each of you picture that looks like this. It will have a chair, a tree, a rock, and a box.*** Point to each item. ***The picture also has Zeke, the mouse. But Zeke is hiding in a different place in each picture. The game is to use prepositions to find out where Zeke is hiding. Let's practice asking and answering questions with prepositions. I can ask: Is Zeke under the chair? You can answer with a preposition and say yes or no, but do not say where he is.*** (No, he is not under the chair.) ***Is he behind the tree?*** (No, he is not behind the tree.) ***Is he on the rock?*** (No, he is not on the rock.) ***Is he next to the rock?*** (Yes, he is next to the rock.)

Model the game: Hold Preposition Model Card #2, but do not show students. Say: ***I have a new card. You pretend to be my partner and ask me questions using prepositions. See if you can guess where Zeke is hiding. For example, you can ask me: Is Zeke in the box? Is Zeke under the tree?***

Prompt the students as needed to help them ask *yes* and *no* questions with prepositions. Answer in complete sentences using *yes* or *no*. When students guess Zeke's hiding place (behind the chair), show them your card.

Assign students to work with a partner. Explain: ***After I give you the card, do not show it to anyone. That will give away Zeke's hiding spot. You can look at your own card to ask and answer questions, but don't let your partner see it until after he or she guesses the hiding place correctly.*** Give each student a card. Have one partner start first and ask questions with prepositions until he or she guesses the location correctly. Then it will be the other partner's turn. After both partners have guessed correctly, have students rotate to a new partner and begin again.

Differentiation

For more support: Display the Grammar Chart to remind students of the prepositions they can use in their questions. Have one student take a card and stand in front of the group. Have the other students work together to ask questions to find out where Zeke is hiding.

Check Progress

Use the following activity to check individual progress made on the target skill.

Show students the Preposition Check Progress printout. Point out and name the objects in the pictures: box, ball, orange, mouse, pot. Have each student look at an image and use a preposition to create a sentence about the objects in the image. Alternate between images and students until each has at least two opportunities to create a sentence.

If students can use prepositions to describe the locations of the objects in the pictures, consider the intervention successful.

Whole-Class Variation

The preposition card game can be played with a larger group or whole class. Make additional copies of the cards sets so each student will have a card and and that there will be at least two copies of each card. Use the same instructions as above, but let students know that there will be other cards with Zeke hiding in the same spot as on the card as they have. Allow students to move around the room asking questions until they find a student with a matching card. Remind students that they must keep their picture hidden. When two students believe they have found a match, have them come to you, and show you their cards.

If you have extra cards, you can give them to students who find a match early on, so that they can continue playing.

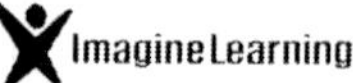

Prepositions

Where Is He?

Has anyone seen my little friend Zeke?

I lost him playing hide and seek.

I looked **in** the boxes and **under** the chairs,

In front of the table and **next to** the stairs.

I looked **on** the shelves, that I can reach.

So the only place left is....

Prepositions *tell you* ***where*** ***people****,* ***animals****, or* ***things*** *are.*

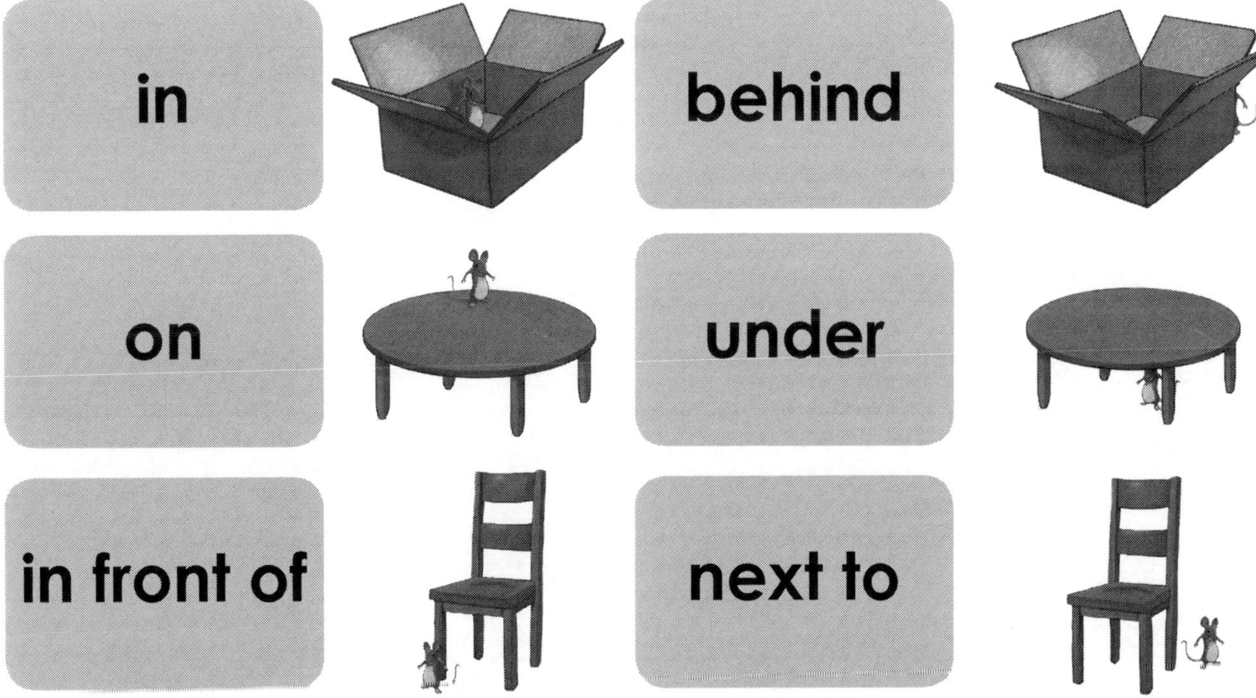

My friend is **next to** me.

The cat is **in** the room.

The teacher is **behind** the desk.

The box is **on** the shelf.

Reteaching Lessons

Preposition Model Card #1

Preposition Model Card #2

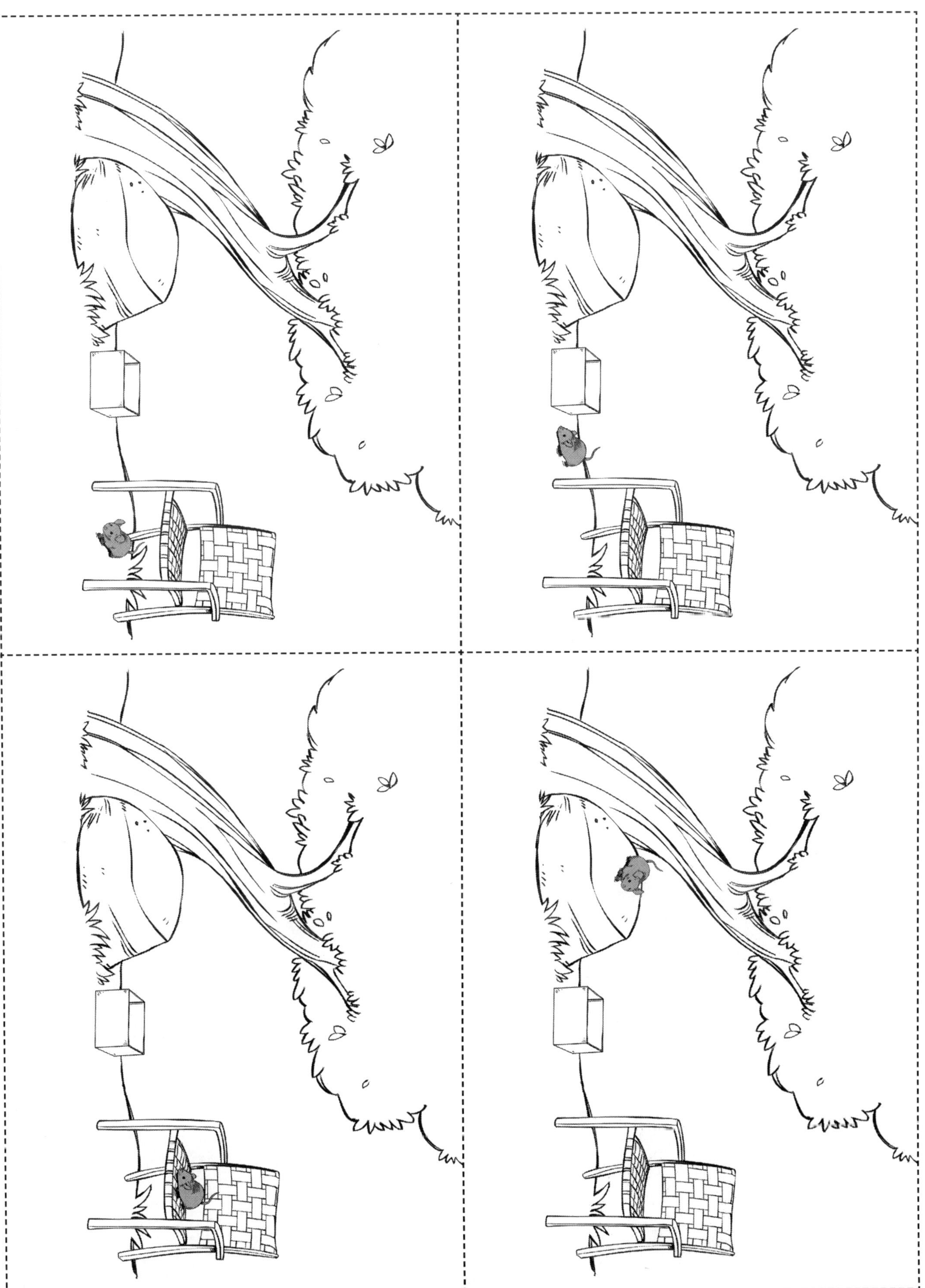

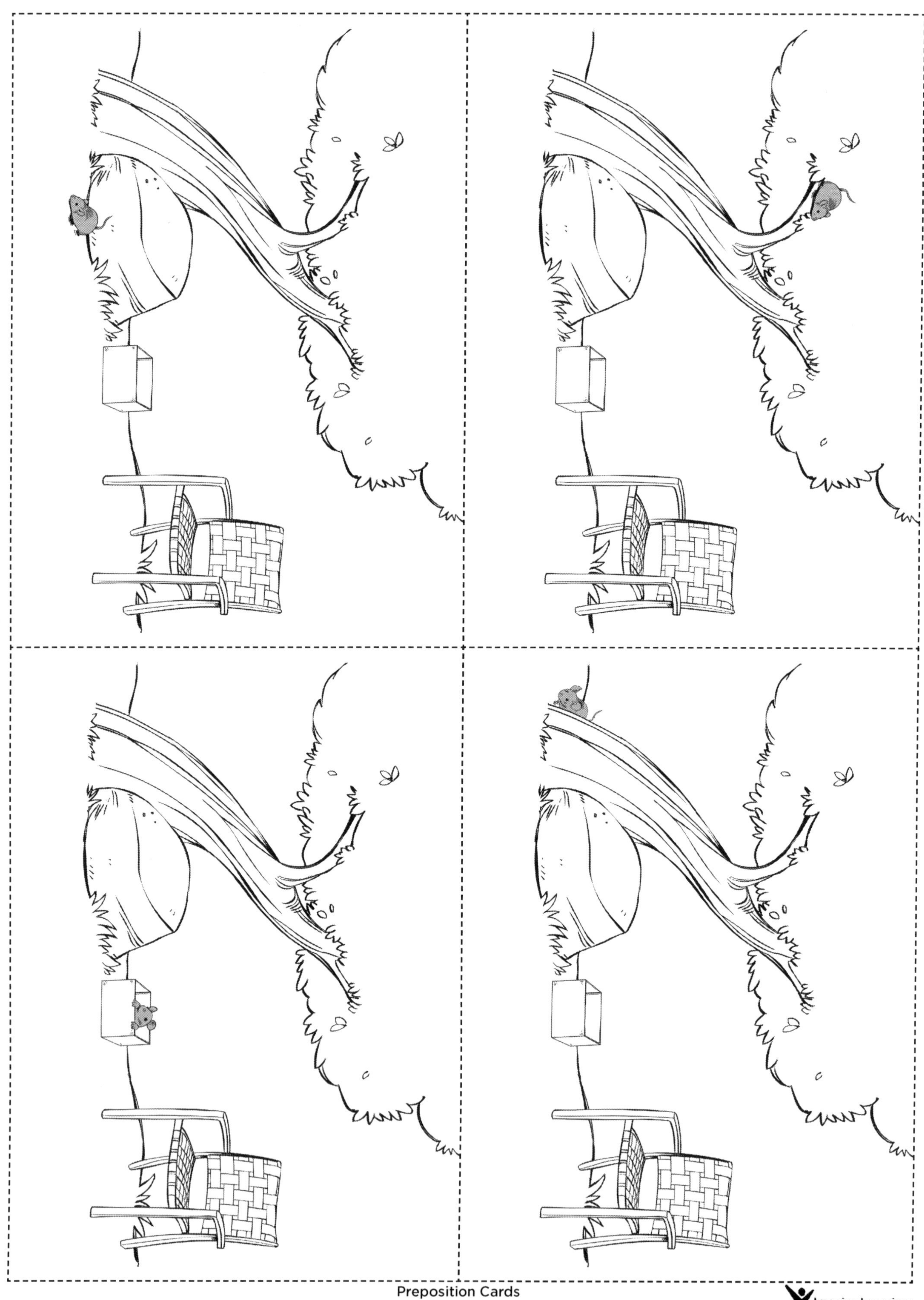

Preposition Cards

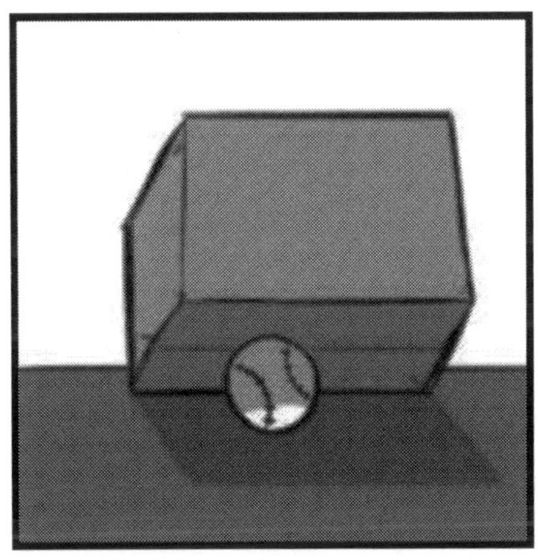

Reteaching Lessons ✓

Present Tense

Grade 1

15 min.

CCSS.ELA-Literacy.L.1.1
TEKS 110.12.20.A.i

LEARNING OBJECTIVE: Use the present tense. Conjugate verbs and ensure subject-verb agreement in a sentence.

LANGUAGE OBJECTIVE: Talk about the different seasons of the year using the correct forms of the present tense.

PREREQUISITE SKILLS: Be able to identify subjects and verbs in a sentence and understand that a subject can be a noun or pronoun.

Lesson Overview

Teacher reviews rules and examples of present tense conjugation with students. Students combine subjects, verbs, and objects from three columns and match the present tense verb to the subject. Students play a spinner game to create present tense sentences.

Materials	Preparation
• Grammar Chart • Sentence Building Chart • Season Spinner Chart • Picture Scenes printout (one per student)	• To print materials in color, visit the online Teacher Resources.

NOTE: This lesson depends on the students' prior knowledge of seasons. If students don't know or struggle with the seasons, briefly review aspects of spring, summer, fall, and winter (weather, seasonal activities, food, clothing, etc.).

Activate Prior Knowledge

Quickly review the prerequisite skill with students and evaluate their proficiency. If students are not proficient with this skill, complete the corresponding Grammar Lesson before continuing.

SUBJECTS AND VERBS: ***To be complete, every sentence needs two things: a subject and a verb. The subject tells whom or what the sentence is about. The verb shows what the people or things in the sentence do.***

Sometimes the subject of a sentence is the name of a person, place, or thing. Sometimes a pronoun replaces the name of the subject.

Read aloud the sentences from the bank below. Ask: ***What's the verb?*** Have students say the verb aloud in unison. Ask: ***What's the subject?*** Have students say the subject aloud in unison. Once the students have correctly identified the subject and verb, ask volunteers to act out the sentence.

Sentence bank:

Pam waves.

She claps.

He snaps.

The dog barks.

We tap.

Ellie and Ethan whisper.

They laugh.

I count.

You hum.

My shoes squeak.

Answer Key:

Verbs: waves, claps, snaps, barks, tap, whisper, laugh, count, hum, squeak
Subjects: Pam, she, he, the dog, we, Ellie and Ethan, they, I, you, my shoes

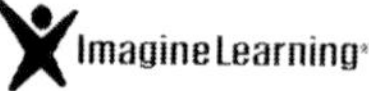

Teach and Model

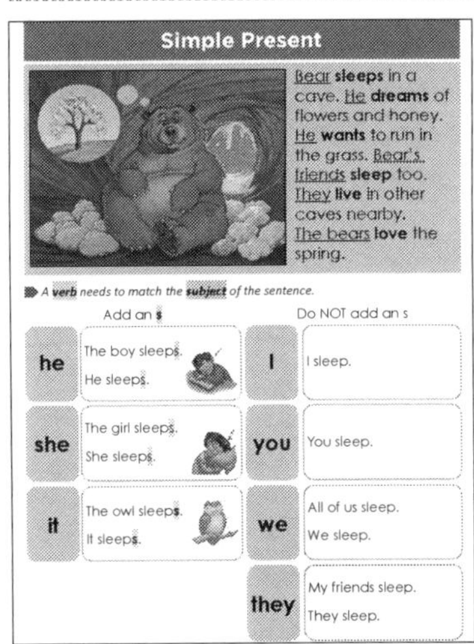

Introduce the grammar principle

- ***When you understand that the subject is what the sentence is about and that the verbs show the action, you're ready to learn about the present tense. Present tense verbs work together with the subject of the sentence.***
- ***They show us that the actions are happening now.***

Work through the Grammar Chart

Use the picture and the story to present the grammar in context.

Read through the rules.

Explore the examples.

Clarify and correct if needed

- ***Whether it is a noun or a pronoun, the subject of a sentence needs to match the present tense verb in the sentence.***
- ***To be sure they match, look at the end of the verb.***
- ***Add an*** s ***to the end of a verb when the subject is*** **he, she,** ***or*** **it.**
- ***Never add the letter*** s ***to the end of a present tense verb when the subject is*** **I, you, we,** ***or*** **they.**

Guided Practice

Tell the students they will practice present tense verbs by talking about what they like to eat during different seasons of the year.

Show the Sentence Building Chart and point to each column as you explain the activity. Say: ***We are going to make sentences out of these word parts. Each sentence needs a subject, a verb that matches the subject, and a food item. I will say a season, and you will make a sentence about what someone eats or drinks during that season.***

Model the activity. For example: ***If I choose they as the subject of my sentence and I want to talk about eating, would I choose the verb*** **eat** ***or*** **eats*****? Let's see:*** **they eats,** ***or*** **they eat*****? Now, what do I want to choose for a food that is eaten in the summer? How about ice cream? So my sentence says, "They eat ice cream."***

Have students take turns making sentences. There are no right or wrong answers with regards to which food goes with each season. For example, students might get silly, saying they eat ice cream in the winter. Allow them to have fun with the game as long as they are conjugating the verbs properly.

Ask students to explain how they made their choice. Use prompts such as: ***Why did you choose the verb that has an s on the end? Why did you choose the verb that doesn't have an s on the end?*** Help them remember the rules they have just learned on the Grammar Chart.

Independent Practice

Tell the students they will practice present tense verbs by talking about what they do during different seasons of the year.

Show students the Season Spinner Chart. Place a paperclip on the dot in the center of the spinner and hold the paperclip in place with the tip of a pencil.

Have a student spin the paperclip to get a subject and a season. Have the student think of something that subject does during the season. Have the student make and say a sentence that combines the subject and what the subject does.

Model: ***For example, if the season is summer and the subject is we, I could say, "We swim in the pool."***

Give each student a few turns making sentences. Make sure students are correctly conjugating their chosen verb to match the subject of their sentence.

If students do not use the present tense correctly, use prompts to help them correct it. For example: ***Did you remember to match your verb to your subject? What do we know about adding an -s when our subject is*** **he?**

Reteaching Lessons

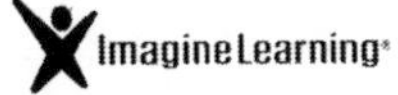

Differentiation

For more support: Before beginning the activity, brainstorm different ideas of what people and things do during each season.

Say: ***Think about the four seasons: summer, fall, winter, and spring. What happens during the different seasons? I will call out a season. You call out things that happen or things that people do in that season.*** (possible responses for winter: people build a snowman, snow falls; for summer: people swim, it gets hot) Review each season.

Check Progress

Use the Picture Scenes printout and the following activity to check individual progress made on the target skill.

Give each student a Picture Scene printout. Say: ***Look at each picture. I will read each sentence out loud. Then you choose the verb that matches the subject.***

Read each sentence and ask students to identify the correct form of the verb. Call on a student to tell you why he or she chose that answer.

If students can correctly choose the correct form of the verb and explain why they chose that verb, consider the intervention successful.

1. The flowers ________ (bloom/blooms).
2. The grass __________ (grow/grows).
3. The sun ________ (shine/shines).
4. The toys ________ (sit/sits) on the sand.
5. He _________ (play/plays).
6. The leaves _________ (fall/falls).
7. They ________ (cover/covers) the ground.
8. The snow ________ (fall/falls).
9. It _________ (look/looks) beautiful.
10. The boy ________ (wear/wears) at hat.

Answer key:

1. bloom
2. grows
3. shines
4. sit
5. plays
6. fall
7. cover
8. falls
9. looks
10. wears

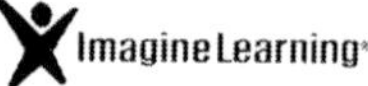

Simple Present

<u>Bear</u> **sleeps** in a cave. <u>He</u> **dreams** of flowers and honey. <u>He</u> **wants** to run in the grass. <u>Bear's friends</u> **sleep** too. <u>They</u> **live** in other caves nearby. <u>The bears</u> **love** the spring.

*A **verb** needs to match the **subject** of the sentence.*

Add an **s**		Do NOT add an s	
he	The boy sleeps. He sleeps. 	**I**	I sleep.
she	The girl sleeps. She sleeps. 	**you**	You sleep.
it	The owl sleep**s**. It sleep**s**. 	**we**	All of us sleep. We sleep.
		they	My friends sleep. They sleep.

Reteaching Lessons

Subject	Verb	Food item
He She It I You We They The boy Sofia Mom The girl	**eat** **drink**	 soup  lemonade  ice cream  apple pie  corn hot chocolate  hamburger 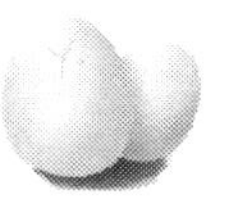 eggs  tomato
	eats **drinks**	

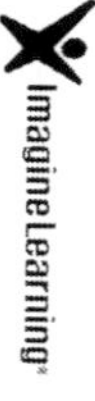

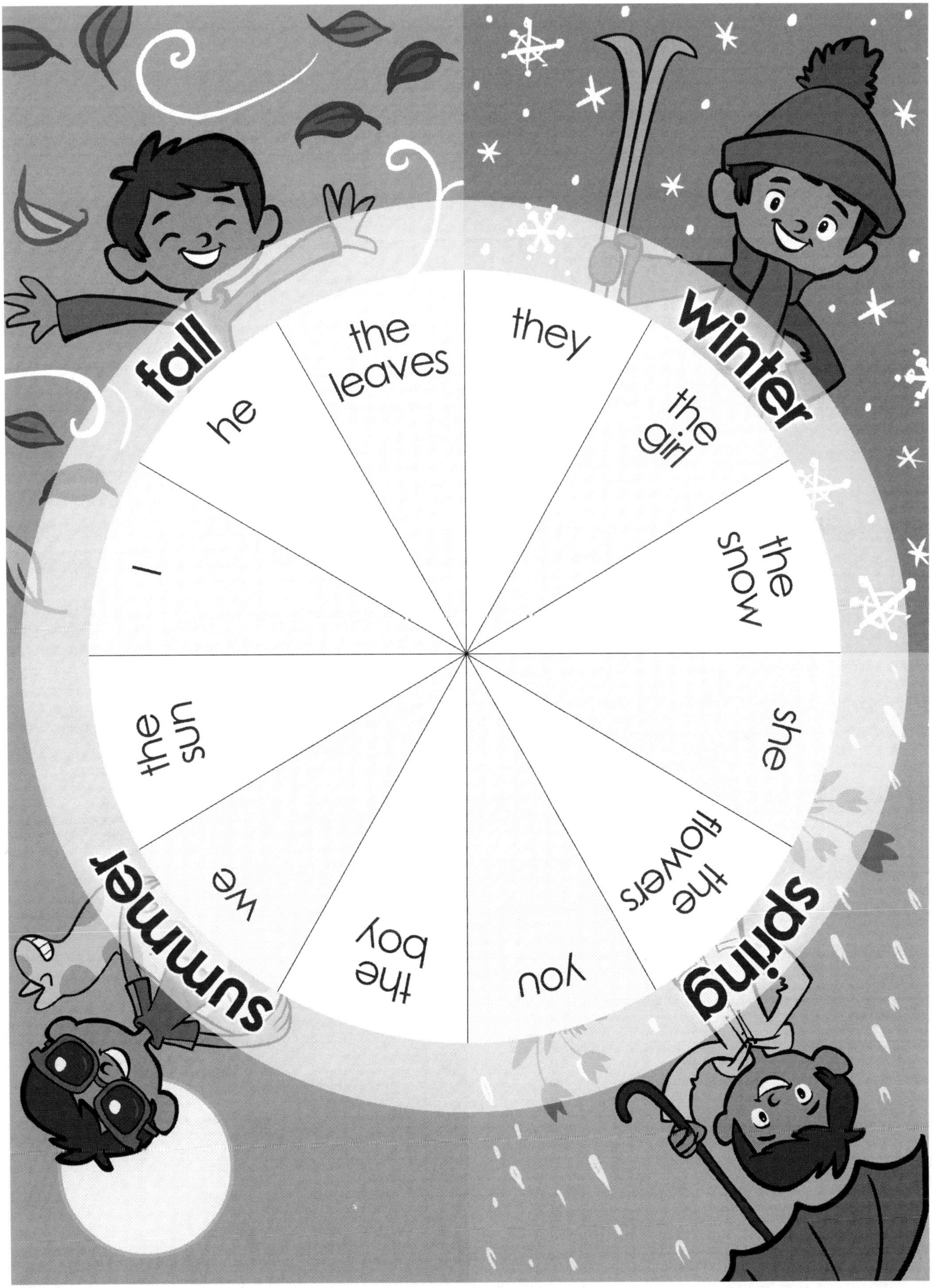

fall
winter
spring
summer

the leaves
they
the girl
the snow
she
the flowers
you
the boy
we
the sun
I
he

Spring

1.The flowers ________________.
(bloom/blooms)

2.The grass ________________.
(grow/grows)

Summer

3.The sun ________________.
(shine/shines)

4.The toys _______ on the sand.
(sit/sits)

Fall

5.He ________________.
(play/plays)

6.The leaves ________________.
(fall/falls)

7.They __________ the ground.
(cover/covers)

Winter

8. The snow ________________.
(fall/falls)

9. It __________ beautiful.
(look/looks)

10. The boy __________ a hat.
(wear/wears)

Grammar

Questions with Auxiliaries

Grade 3

15 min.

CCSS.L.3.1.D
TEKS 110.14.22.A.i

LEARNING OBJECTIVE: Understand and use the auxiliary question words *do* and *does*.

LANGUAGE OBJECTIVE: Ask questions about jobs using helping verbs.

PREREQUISITE SKILL(S): Be able to correctly identify subjects and verbs and understand their functions in a sentence.

Lesson Overview

Teacher reviews rules and examples with students of asking questions with auxiliaries. Students complete questions to review the use of *do* and *does* when asking a question. Students role play job interviews to practice asking and answering questions with auxiliaries.

Materials	Preparation
• Grammar Chart • Do and Does Questions printout • Job Interview Cards • Interview Questions printout • Check Progress printout	• Cut out Job Interview cards. • To print materials in color, visit the online Teacher Resources.

Reteaching Lessons

Activate Prior Knowledge

Quickly review the prerequisite skill with students and evaluate their proficiency. If students are not proficient with this skill, complete the corresponding Grammar Lesson before continuing.

SUBJECT: ***In a sentence, the subject usually comes at the beginning and tells you who or what the sentence is about. The subject can be one word or more than one word. In the sentence, "My brother runs," the subject is my brother.***

VERB: ***The verb is the word that shows the action of the sentence. In the sentence, "My brother runs," the verb is runs.***

Read the sentences from the bank below. Ask a volunteer to identify the verb and subject.

Sentence bank:

She talks to her friend. (subject: she; verb: talks)

They buy new shoes. (subject: they; verb: buy)

I watch the movie. (subject: I; verb: watch)

We share a treat. (subject: we; verb: share)

The office opens at 9 a.m. (subject: the office; verb: opens)

The trucks drive quickly. (subject: the trucks; verb: drive)

Sometimes we use helping verbs with an action verb. Together the helping verb and the "main verb" (the action verb) tell more about the action in the sentence.

Read the sentences from the bank below. Ask a volunteer to identify the main verb and the helping verb.

Sentence bank:

She can talk to her friend. (main verb: talk; helping verb: can)

They should buy new shoes. (main verb: buy; helping verb: should)

I might watch the movie. (main verb: watch; helping verb: might

We could share a treat. (main verb: share; helping verb: could)

The office may open at 9 a.m. (main verb: may; helping verb: open)

The trucks are driving quickly. (main verb: are; helping verb: driving)

Teach and Model

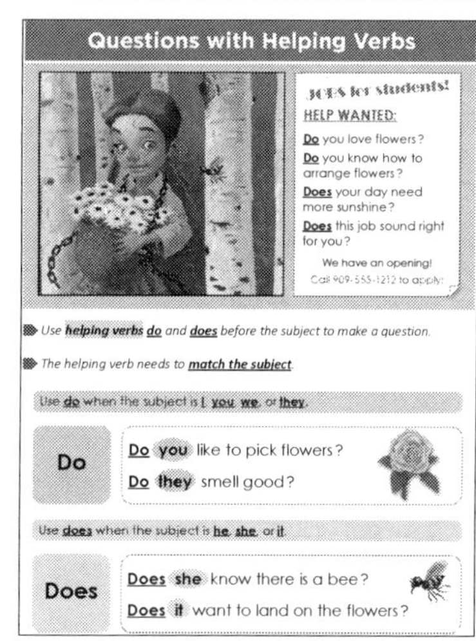

Introduce the grammar principle

Sometimes we use helping verbs to start a question.

Work through the Grammar Chart

Use the picture and the job advertisement to present the grammar in context.

Read through the rules.

Explore the examples.

Clarify and correct if needed

- **Do** ***and*** **does** ***are also used with pronouns that replace subjects.***
- ***The subject comes between the helping verb and the main verb.***
- ***When there is a helping verb, the main verb stays in its base form.***
- ***Base form means the verb is in present tense with nothing added.***

Guided Practice

Tell the students they will practice using *do* and *does* in questions.

Show students the Do and Does Questions printout and say: ***These questions are missing their helping verb. I'll choose a question on the page and read it. Then you tell me the helping verb that should go at the beginning of the question. Remember, the helping verb must match the subject of the sentence. Use*** **do** ***when the subject is*** **I, you, we** ***or*** **they.** ***Use*** **does** ***when the subject is*** **he, she,** ***or*** **it.** ***If the subject is a thing, use*** **do** ***for more than one thing and*** **does** ***for one thing.***

Answer key:

Do you like to work?

Do you have brothers or sisters?

Do they have jobs?

Does a farmer work with animals?

Does the florist shop need a cashier?

Does that computer connect to the printer?

Do the pens go in the supply closet?

Independent Practice

Tell the students they will pretend they are a job interview panel. Students will rotate being on the interview panel or being interviewed.

Introduce the Job Interview Cards. Say: ***We are going to imagine we are in a job interview. These cards have a picture of someone doing a job and a description about the job. You'll use the helping verbs do and does to interview each other for different jobs.***

Your interview questions have to begin with do and does. You'll each take turns asking interview questions and answering the questions.

Introduce the Inverview Questions printout to students.

Sentence frames:

Do you_________?

Do you know how to _______?

Does it sound fun to you to ________?

Do you like _________?

Does he _______?

Does she _______?

Have a student select a job card from the stack and pass it around so everyone can see the picture and read the description. Model how to ask questions using the information on the card and the sentence frames.

Reteaching Lessons

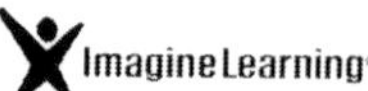

Have students take turns being on the interview panel and asking the interviewee questions using the question words *do* and *does*.

After the panel has interviewed the student, have the panel discuss with each other whether to hire the student for the job. They should use the "Does he/Does she" sentence frames.

If a student does not use auxiliary verbs correctly, use prompts to help him or her to correct it. For example: ***Did you remember to use* [do, does] *at the beginning of the question?***

Differentiation
For more support: Have students practice creating questions using the sentence frames to ask questions about any topic before introducing the Job Interview Cards.
For a challenge: Students make up their own questions about other jobs using do and does.

Check Progress

Use the Check Progress Questions printout and the following activity to check individual progress made on the target skill.

Ask each student to read aloud a job interview question and fill in the blank with *do* or *does*.

If the student can correctly use the target auxiliary verb in the sentence, consider the intervention successful.

Answer Bank:

Do you want this job?

Do you think you will like this job?

Does she take the bus to work?

Does his boss know he is looking for a new job?

Do you speak more than one language?

Does he like to work with other people?

Do you know how to work hard?

Does this job sound interesting to you?

Do you get to work early?

Does she earn more money now?

Do we get a break for lunch?

Do they want to check his work?

Does he bring his dog to work?

Questions with Helping Verbs

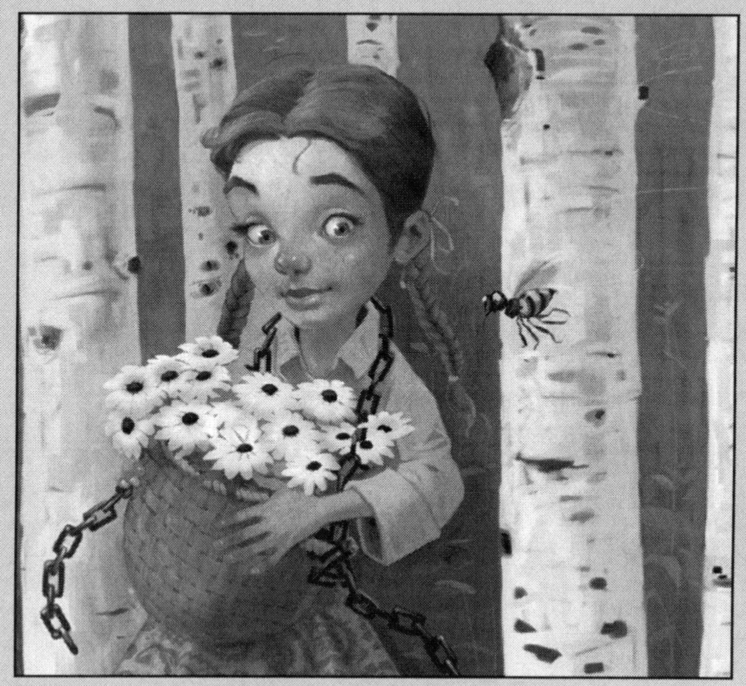

JOBS for students!

HELP WANTED:

Do you love flowers?

Do you know how to arrange flowers?

Does your day need more sunshine?

Does this job sound right for you?

We have an opening!

Call 909-555-1212 to apply!

*Use the **helping verbs do** and **does** before the subject to make a question.*

*The helping verb needs to **match the subject**.*

Use **do** when the subject is **I**, **you**, **we**, or **they**.

Do

Do **you** like to pick flowers?

Do **they** smell good?

Use **does** when the subject is **he**, **she**, or **it**.

Does

Does **she** know there is a bee?

Does **it** want to land on the flowers?

Reteaching Lessons

Do and Does Questions

_____ you like to work?

_____ you have brothers or sisters?

_____ they have jobs?

_____ a farmer work with animals?

_____ the florist shop need a cashier?

_____ that computer connect to the printer?

_____ the pens go in the supply closet?

Reteaching Lessons

Artist: draw, paint, or create art

Chef: make food, work in a restaurant, plan the menu, shop for food

Juggler: entertain people, perform tricks, juggle objects like balls, rings, sticks and clubs

Dancer: perform along with music and other dancers, perform a variety of different styles of dances

Farmer: run a farm, grow food, raise animals, drive a tractor

Astronaut: travel in space, fly a spacecraft, repair the spacecraft, do scientific experiments in space

Dog trainer: teach a dog to do tricks and be obedient, take care of dogs

Auctioneer: run auctions, start a bid, talk fast, get the best price

Miner: dig for ore or metal, work in tunnels and caves, work underground, work in the dark

Clown: make people laugh, make animals out of balloons, do tricks, ride a unicycle

Shoe shiner: clean and polish shoes, remove dirt and grime, use brush and polish to make shoes look clean

Skydiver: jump out of airplanes, help others learn to skydive, do tricks in the air

Interview Questions

Do you _________?

Do you know how to _________?

Does it sound fun to you to _________?

Do you like _________?

Does he _________?

Does she _________?

Reteaching Lessons

Check Progress Printout

_____ you want this job?

_____ you think you will like this job?

_____ she take the bus to work?

_____ his boss know he is looking for a new job?

_____ you speak more than one language?

_____ he like to work with other people?

_____ you know how to work hard?

_____ this job sound interesting to you?

_____ you get to work early?

_____ she earn more money now?

_____ we get a break for lunch?

_____ they want to check his work?

_____ he bring his dog to work?

Grammar

Question Words 1

Grade K

15 min.

CCSS.L.K.1.D
TEKS 110.12.20.C

LEARNING OBJECTIVE: Understand and use question words.

LANGUAGE OBJECTIVE: Get to know other students and the teacher by asking questions using *who, what, where, when, why*, and *how*.

PREREQUISITE: Be able to answer simple yes/no questions.

Lesson Overview

Teacher reviews rules and examples of question words with students. Students do a pair-share activity to practice using question words at the beginning of a question. Students play a ball-toss game and use question words to get to know others in the class.

Materials	Preparation
• Grammar Chart • a small ball or soft toy • Question Words 1 Cards (one set per student pair)	• Cut out Question Word Cards. • To print materials in color, visit the online Teacher Resources.

NOTE: Discuss with students what kinds of questions are appropriate and what questions are inappropriate. Encourage students to respond in complete sentences throughout the lesson.

Reteaching Lessons

Activate Prior Knowledge

Quickly review the prerequisite skill with students and evaluate their proficiency. If students are not proficient with this skill, complete the corresponding Grammar Lesson before continuing.

YES/NO QUESTIONS: ***We ask questions when we want information. Some questions you can answer with either a yes or a no. Let's try it. I'll ask a question. If your answer is yes, do a sign for yes by making your fist look like your head and bob up and down. Demonstrate. If your answer is no, make your fist look like a head shaking back and forth, like this.*** Demonstrate. Ask questions from the bank below and allow all students to respond together by signing their answers.

Question bank: Are you a boy? Are you a girl? Do you have a pet? Do you like bubble gum? Do you like to play in the park? Do you walk to school? Would you like to be one inch tall? Can you touch your nose with your tongue?

Teach and Model

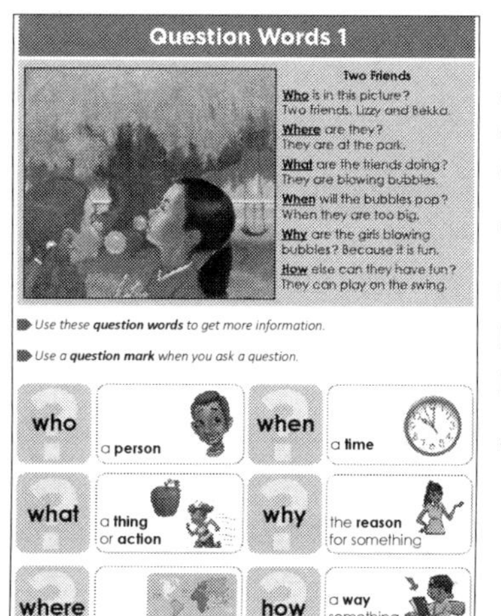

Introduce the grammar principle

Sometimes when you ask a question, you want more than just a yes or no for the answer. We use question words to find out more about the people, places, and things around us.

Work through the Grammar Chart

Use the picture and the questions and answers to present the grammar in context.

Read through the rules.

Explore the examples.

Clarify and correct if needed

- ***Questions end with a question mark.*** Ask students to identify a few question marks on the chart.
- ***We use who to ask questions about a person.***
- ***We use what to ask about a thing or action.***
- ***We use where to ask about a place.***
- ***We use when to ask about time.***
- ***We use why to ask about the reason for something.***
- ***We use how to ask about the way something is done.***

Guided Practice

Tell the students that they will play a game to practice asking questions.

Say: ***Imagine you want to get to know a new friend. You could use question words to ask your friend questions about who they are, what they do, what they like or don't like, and any other questions that would help you get to know them.***

Model the activity. Toss the soft ball to a student and ask the student a question from the question bank below. Have the student say the question word you used and then answer the question. Then have the student toss the ball to another student and ask that student a question.

Question bank:

Who is in your family?

Who is one of your best friends?

What do you like to eat?

What is your favorite color?

What pets do you have?

Where do you go for fun?

Where do you sit to do homework?

When do you play video games?

When do you wash your hands?

Why do you wear shoes?

Why is our school named [school name]?

Why do we follow rules?

How do you get to school?

How old are you?

Independent Practice

Say: ***Imagine you have just met the other students in the classroom. There are so many things to learn about your new friends. Let's use question words to get to know other students.***

Group students into pairs. Give each pair a set of Question Word Cards and have them place it between them with the cards in a stack. Tell students they will have one minute to get to know their partner. Have them take turns drawing cards and using the word on the card to ask their partner a question. Remind students that they need to listen politely to the answer after asking a question.

After 60 seconds, have the students switch partners. If time allows, continue to switch partners every 60 seconds until all students have had a chance to work with every other student.

Circulate among students to observe the use of question words. If a student does not use question words correctly, use prompts to help him or her to self-correct. For example: ***Remember to use the question words at the beginning of a sentence then listen to the answer.***

Differentiation

For more support: If students struggle to come up with questions, have them use the same questions from the ball-toss game.

For a challenge: For each round with a new partner, use a sentence from the bank below or make up a statement and have students ask only questions about the statement.

For example, the statement "I like to play at the park" could prompt the following questions:

Why do you like to play at the park? **Where** is the park? **How** do you get there? **When** do you go to the park? **What** do you like to do? **Who** do you see at the park?

Sentence bank: I eat ice cream. / I go to school. / I read books. / I see an animal.

Reteaching Lessons

Whole-Class Variation

Invite a guest into the classroom (principal, librarian, etc.) and have students use question words to get to know the guest.

Check Progress

Use the Question Words 1 Cards and the following activity to check individual progress made on the target skill.

Say: ***Let's practice the question words with a few more questions. This time you get to ask questions to get to know me!***

Have the students use question words to ask the teacher questions. Remind the students about what is appropriate to ask.

If the student can correctly ask two questions using the question words, consider the intervention successful.

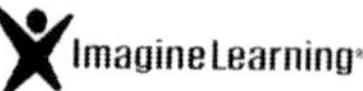

Question Words 1

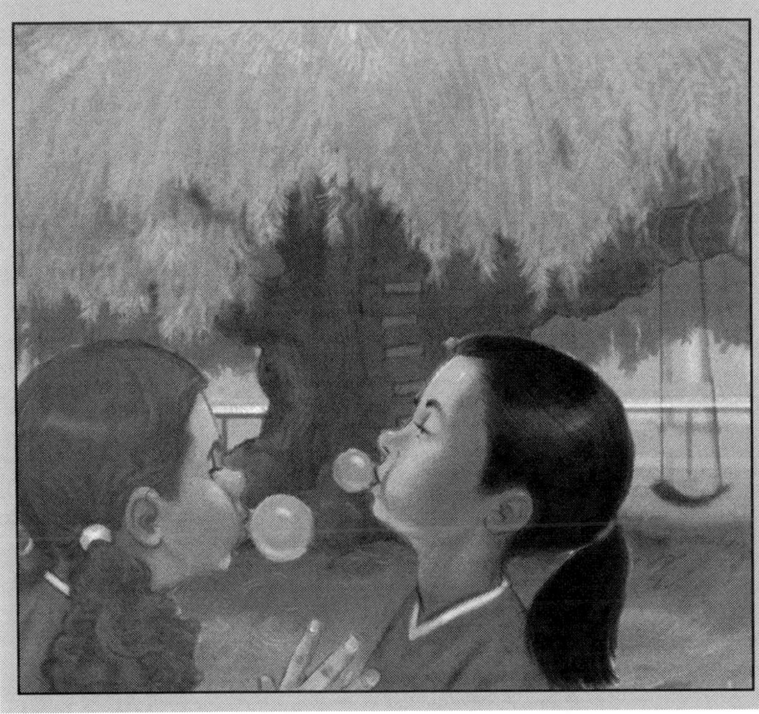

Two Friends

<u>Who</u> is in this picture?
Two friends, Lizzy and Bekka.

<u>Where</u> are they?
They are at the park.

<u>What</u> are the friends doing?
They are blowing bubbles.

<u>When</u> will the bubbles pop?
When they are too big.

<u>Why</u> are the girls blowing bubbles? Because it is fun.

<u>How</u> else can they have fun?
They can play on the swing.

- *Use these **question words** to get more information.*
- *Use a **question mark** when you ask a question.*

a **person**

when

a **time**

a **thing** or **action**

the **reason** for something

a **place**

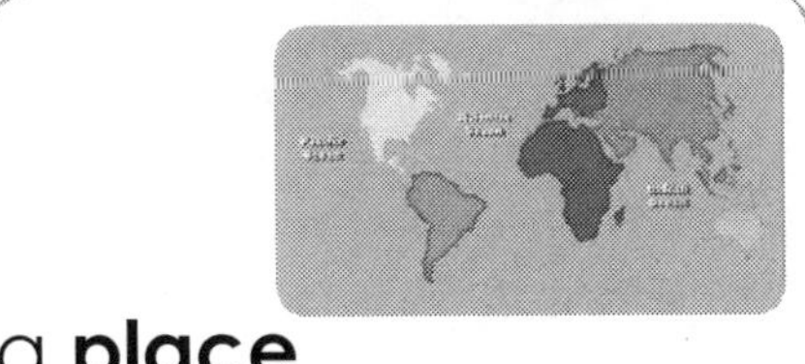

a **way** something is done

Who?

What?

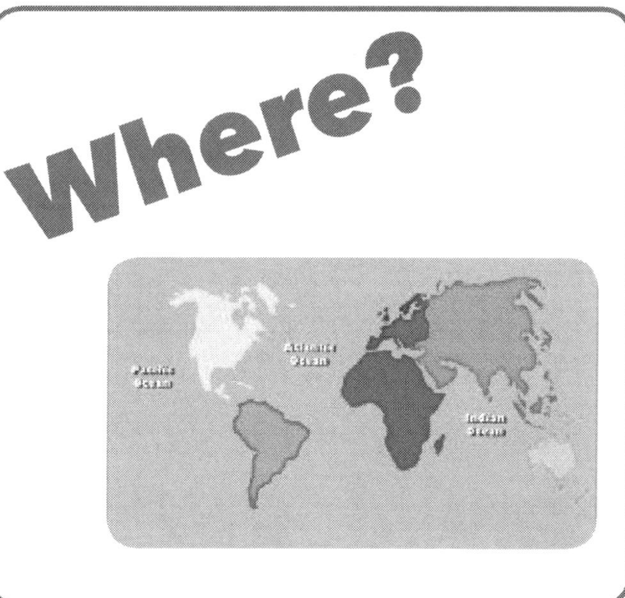
Where?

When?

Why?

How?
3

Grammar

Question Words 2

Grade 3

15 min.

CCSS.L.3.1.I
TEKS 110.14.22.C

LEARNING OBJECTIVE: Understand and use questions words to comprehend text.

LANGUAGE OBJECTIVE: Ask questions about stories using question words.

PREREQUISITE SKILL: Identify question words and answer basic questions that use the question words *who, what, where, when, why,* and *how.*

Lesson Overview

Teacher reviews rules and examples of question words with students. Students use Question Word Cards to find out more information about stories and then play a story cube game to practice asking questions.

Materials	Preparation
• Grammar Chart • Question Words 2 Cards • Story Cube • Story Reference printout • Question Prompt Chart	• Cut out Question Word Cards. • Copy Story Cube page on cardstock, then cut and assemble. • To print materials in color, visit the online Teacher Resources.

Activate Prior Knowledge

Quickly review the prerequisite skill with students and evaluate their proficiency. If students are not proficient with this skill, complete the corresponding Grammar Lesson before continuing.

YES/NO QUESTIONS: ***We ask questions when we want information. Some questions can be answered with "yes" or "no." I'll ask a question. Turn to your partner and quickly answer the question with a yes or a no, then turn back and face me without talking.*** Designate partners. Ask questions from the bank below and allow students to give their response to their partner.

Question bank: Do you have a pet? Can you speak Chinese? Do you like green beans? Is your bedroom painted pink?

Say: ***Sometimes when you ask a question, you want more than just a yes or no for the answer. Question words help us find out more about the people, places, and things around us. I'll ask a question. Turn to your partner and share a short answer, then turn back and face me without talking.*** Ask questions from the bank below and allow students to give their response to their partner.

Question Bank: What is your name? Who is your favorite author? Where do you keep your toothbrush? How did you get to school?

Teach and Model

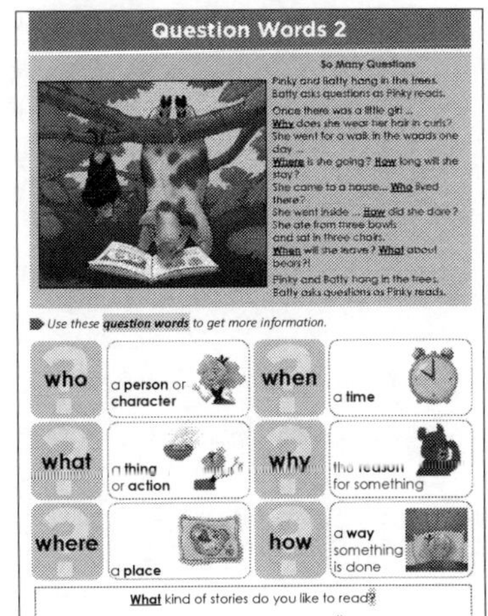

Introduce the grammar principle

Sometimes we want to know more than just yes or no. We can use question words to get more information.

Questions often begin with the words who, what, where, when, why and how.

Work through the Grammar Chart

Use the picture and the poem to present the grammar in context.

Read through the rules.

Explore the examples.

Clarify and correct if needed

- ***We use who to ask questions about a person or character.***
- ***We use what to ask about a thing or action.***
- ***We use where to ask about a place.***
- ***We use when to ask about time.***
- ***We use why to ask about the reason for something.***
- ***We use how to ask about the way something is done.***

Reteaching Lessons

Guided Practice

Show the Question Words 2 Cards and tell the students they will use the Question Word Cards to practice asking questions. Use the Story Reference printout as needed to match story clues to the stories.

Say: ***Books are full of wonderful stories. You may know some of them. I'm going to give you a clue about a story. You will take a Question Word card and use that word to ask me a question. You will ask questions to see if you can figure out what story we are talking about. As I answer the questions, give me a thumbs up when you think you know the story.***

Select a story clue from the bank below. Have a student draw a Question Word Card. Then give the story clue and have the student ask a question using that question word. Guide students as needed to ask questions about the story. Use prompts such as: ***We use who to ask questions about a person. Is there a person in the clue you can learn more about? We use* where *to ask about a place. Did you hear a place in the clue?*** Continue having students draw Question Words Cards until you've given three clues about the story.

Have students put their thumbs up when they think they know the story. After three questions, call on a student to say what the story is. If they don't know the story after three questions, have them use the question word what to ask you to name the story.

As time allows, continue with another story until you have completed three or four.

Story clues bank:

Story 1: A boy climbs a giant vegetable stalk into the sky.

Story 2: A spider saves a pig's life on the farm.

Story 3: A cat comes to play and causes trouble at home.

Story 4: Children use fairy dust and fly to a wonderful place.

Story 5: A little bear has adventures with his friends in the woods.

Story 6: A girl falls down a hole and meets amazing characters.

Substitute stories you have read in class or other stories that are familiar to students as needed.

Independent Practice

Tell the students they will play a Question/Answer game to practice asking questions using question words. Display the story cube.

Say: ***I'm going to use this story cube to tell you the story of the ugly duckling. Pay attention to the story. After we've read it, you'll throw the cube and ask questions using question words.***

The Ugly Duckling

Side 1: Once upon a time there was an ugly duckling. He looked different from his brothers and sisters.

Side 2: They teased him about looking so different. He got tired of them teasing him and decided to run away.

Side 3: He met other animals who also teased him and told him he looked strange.

Side 4: Finally, it was springtime. One day he saw beautiful swans in a pond. He had never seen anything like them. They were so lovely!

Side 5: He knew he was not lovely. He put his head down in shame. He was surprised to see his reflection. He was a beautiful swan!

Side 6: Now he knew why he had looked so different from his brothers and sisters. He had been a swan all along!

Have students roll the dice and use the picture as a prompt for creating a question using a question word. For example, for side 4, they could ask the question, "When did he see the other swans?"

Call on a volunteer from the group to respond. The student who can answer the question gets to roll the dice. Continue as time permits or until each student has had a few turns.

If a student does not use question words correctly, use prompts to help him or her to correct it. For example: ***Remember the question words come at the beginning of the sentence. Think about what you want to know and decide which question word you should use.***

Differentiation

For more support: After going through the story with the story cube once, tell the story again, but stop on each picture. Give the student a question word prompt and have a student ask a question using that question word.

For a challenge: Have students use the story cube to re-tell the story of the Ugly Duckling using only questions.

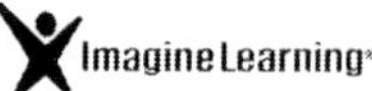

Check Progress

Use the Question Prompt chart and the following activity to check individual progress made on the target skill.

One at a time, have students close their eyes and randomly point to a word or phrase on the Question Prompt. Have students opens their eyes, read the word or phrase in the square, and ask a question using the word from the page and any one of the question words. For example, if a student selects farmer, he or she could ask, "Who takes care of the animals on the farm?"

Have the students explain why they chose the question word they did. (Possible response: I used *who* because I wanted to ask a question about a person.)

If students can correctly use the question words and explain why they chose the question word, consider the intervention successful.

Answer bank: golden goose, morning, long ago, small boy, jungle, bright green, 100, a king, curly, treasure chest, castle, big bear, mountain, run, library book, ride, farmer, yesterday, ocean, talking cow, wide river, summer, midnight, hide, author

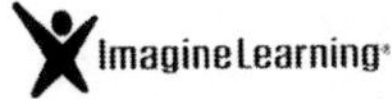

Question Words 2

So Many Questions

Pinky and Batty hang in the trees.
Batty asks questions as Pinky reads.

Once there was a little girl...
Why does she wear her hair in curls?
She went for a walk in the woods one day...
Where is she going? **How** long will she stay?
She came to a house... **Who** lived there?
She went inside... **How** did she dare?
She ate from three bowls
and sat in three chairs...
When will she leave? **What** about bears?

Pinky and Batty hang in the trees.
Batty asks questions as Pinky reads.

Use these ***question words*** *to get more information.*

who	a **person** or **character** 	**when**	a **time** 
what	a **thing** or **action** 	**why**	the **reason** for something 
where	a **place** 	**how**	a **way** something is done 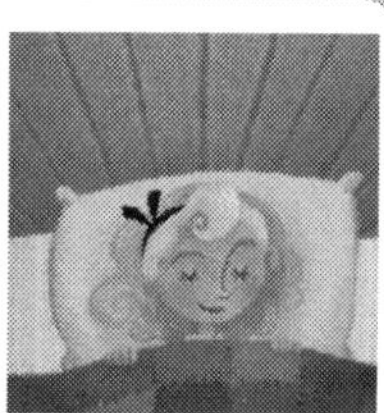

What kind of stories do you like to read?

Who do you read them with?

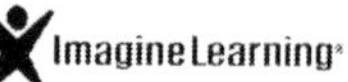

Who?

What?

Where?
N

When?

Why?

How?
3

Story Cube

Story Reference Printout

Story 1: ***Jack and the Beanstalk*, a fairy tale**

Jack and his mother were poor and hungry. Jack's mother tells him to sell his cow to get some food, but he trades the cow for magic beans. Jack's mother is angry and throws the beans out of the window. The next morning there is a giant beanstalk that reaches into the sky. Jack climbs the beanstalk and finds a giant's castle.

Story 2: ***Charlotte's Web* by E.B. White**

Charlotte, a spider, and Wilbur, a pig, become friends when Charlotte writes messages in her webs. These messages convince the farmer to let Wilbur live and not be killed to become food. Wilbur becomes a famous pig and protects the egg sacs that Charlotte has laid.

Story 3: ***The Cat in the Hat* by Dr. Seuss**

A brother and sister who are bored on a rainy day have adventures when the Cat in the Hat comes to their house. They play games, and two creatures called Thing One and Thing Two make messes. The kids try to keep things in order.

Story 4: ***Peter Pan* by J.M. Barrie**

Peter Pan is a boy who never grows up and can fly. Peter brings Wendy and her brothers to Neverland, where they have adventures with mermaids, pirates, and Indians.

Story 5: ***Winnie the Pooh* by A.A. Milne**

A small bear, Winnie the Pooh, lives in the woods where he has adventures with his friends Piglet, Rabbit, Eeyore, Owl, and Christopher Robin.

Story 6: ***Alice in Wonderland* by Lewis Carroll**

Alice follows a white rabbit and takes a magical journey in Wonderland where she meets many interesting creatures like the Cheshire Cat, the Mad Hatter, the March Hare, and the Queen of Hearts.

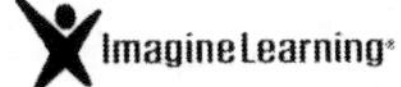

golden goose	morning	long ago	small boy	jungle
bright green	100	a king	curly	treasure chest
castle	big bear	mountain	run	library book
ride	farmer	yesterday	ocean	talking cow
wide river	summer	midnight	hide	author

Sentences

Grade K

15 min.

CCSS.L.K.1.F, 2.A, 2.B
TEKS 110.11.16.C

LEARNING OBJECTIVE: Understand the components of a sentence. Produce and expand complete sentences.

LANGUAGE OBJECTIVE: Build basic sentences to talk about people, animals, places, and things.

PREREQUISITE: Students should have a basic concept of words and that words combine to make sentences. It may be helpful if students can read, but reading is not required.

Lesson Overview

Teacher reviews rules and examples of sentences with students. Students use a picture prompt to complete original sentences. Students play a bean bag toss game to create Silly Sentences.

Materials	Preparation
• Grammar Chart • Silly Sentence Parts • small bean bag • Sentences Picture Prompt	• Cut Silly Sentence Parts apart on dotted lines so that each column is on a single strip of paper. • To print materials in color, visit the online Teacher Resources.

Activate Prior Knowledge

Quickly review with students and evaluate their readiness for this lesson.

Say: ***Sentences are made up of words. Some words tell us who the sentence is about. Some words tell us the action of a sentence. Some words give us other information. We put the words together to make a sentence.***

I'm going to say some words. If you think the words go together to make a sentence, give me a thumbs up. Demonstrate a thumbs up. ***If you think the sentence is missing something, or if it is just words that don't make a complete thought, give me a thumbs down.*** Demonstrate a thumbs down.

Read the complete and incomplete sentences from the bank below and allow students to respond:

Incomplete Sentences	*Complete Sentences*
Dad made	Dad made soup today.
bark, night, the	The dogs bark all night.
in the sky	Birds fly in the sky.
her book after school	Ruby reads her book after school.

Teach and Model

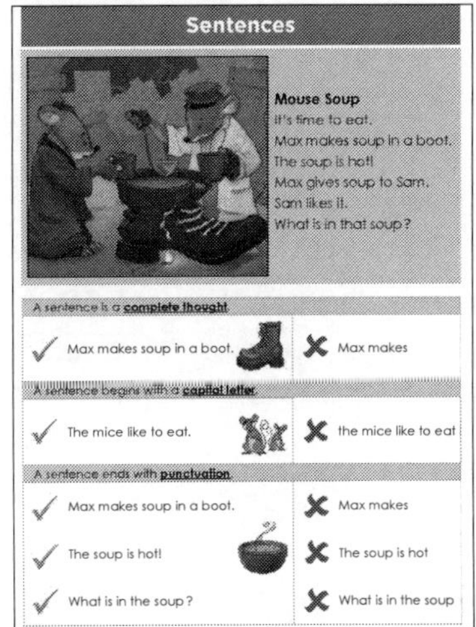

Introduce the grammar principle

- ***Remember, sentences are words put together to mean something.***
- ***Let's learn more about sentences.***

Work through the Grammar Chart

Use the picture and the story to present the grammar in context.

Read through the rules.

Explore the examples.

Clarify and correct if needed

- ***Most of the time we use a period at the end of a sentence.***
- ***We use a question mark when we ask a question.***
- ***We use an exclamation point if we want to show a strong feeling or excitement.***

Guided Practice

Instruct students to use the picture from the Grammar Chart to make new sentences.

Say: ***You've heard a story about Max and Sam and their soup. Let's make up more sentences about the picture. Remember, a sentence is a complete thought.***

Write down student's sentences on chart paper. As you write, prompt students to tell you where the sentence should have a capital letter and which end punctuation to use.

Example sentences:

Sam and Max wear coats.

The match warms up the soup.

The mice have blue mugs.

Max has a flat hat.

The boot is full of soup.

Independent Practice

Tell the students they will play a sentence building game to practice making complete sentences. Place the Silly Sentence Parts in order on a table or floor. Spread them apart to allow room to toss a small bean bag onto the squares.

Say: ***These parts will help us build sentences. We'll toss this bean bag to choose each part of a sentence, and we'll use those parts to make a complete sentence. I'll write down the sentence so we can read it when it is finished. Sometimes we'll make a sentence that is silly.***

Demonstrate sentence building. Working from left to right, toss the bean bag to choose a component from each category until you have created a complete sentence. Say each sentence part aloud and write it on chart paper. When the sentence is complete, read it aloud and have the students repeat it with you

Have each student create a sentence by tossing the bean bag to select sentence components. Write each sentence on chart paper, read it aloud, and have students repeat the complete sentence.

Silly Sentence Parts

Who	Action	Adjectives	What	Where	Punctuation
Rose	flies	a messy	bike	on the school bus	!
Andy	reads	a fast	sandwich	at school	. (period)
Sparky	hops on	a silly	book	in the kitchen	!
The monster	rides	a little	airplane	in the sky	?
Dad	eats	a delicious	skateboard	on the farm	. (period)

Reteaching Lessons

Differentiation

For more support: Use the Silly Sentence pages and work as a group to build one sentence. Have one student choose from the first category, a second student choose from the second category, and so on. Write out the sentence so the students can see it and discuss the sentence annotation (punctuation, capitalization).

Check Progress

Use the Sentences Picture Prompt and the following activity to check individual progress made on the target skill.

Read the sentences to the students. Ask each student to point out punctuation and capital letters from the story.

Have each student make up a new sentence about the picture.

If the student can correctly identify the capital letter and punctuation of one sentence and create a complete sentence, consider the intervention successful.

Writing Extension

Have each student use ideas from the Silly Sentence Parts to write their own sentence on a strip of paper. Have students cut their sentence strip into word cards and mix them up. Then have students trade with another student and put the sentence back together.

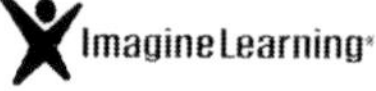

Sentences

Mouse Soup
It's time to eat.
Max makes soup in a boot.
The soup is hot!
Max gives soup to Sam.
Sam likes it.
What is in that soup?

A sentence is a **complete thought**.	
 Max makes soup in a boot. 	 Max makes

A sentence begins with a **capital letter**.	
 The mice like to eat. 	 the mice like to eat

A sentence ends with **punctuation**.	
 Max makes soup in a boot.	 Max makes
 The soup is hot! 	 The soup is hot
 What is in the soup?	 What is in the soup

Who	Action
Rose	flies
Andy	reads
Sparky	hops on
The monster	rides
Dad	eats

Silly Sentence Parts

Adjective	What
 a messy	 bike
 a fast	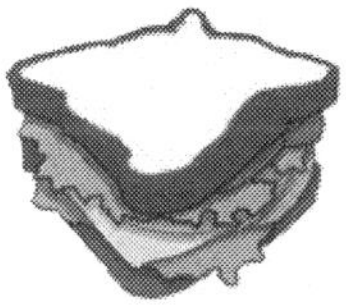 sandwich
 a silly	 book
 a little	 airplane
 a delicious	 skateboard

Reteaching Lessons ✓

Where	Punctuation
on the school bus	!
at school	.
in the kitchen	!
in the sky	?
on the farm	.

Reteaching Lessons

Jonah and Annie sleep by the fire.

The bears sneak in to the camp.

What will the bears find in the cooler?

The baby bear wants cake!

Reteaching Lessons

Grammar

Subject

Grade 1

15 min.

CCSS.ELA-Literacy.L.1.1b
TEKS 110.12.20.A(iii)

LEARNING OBJECTIVE: Identify the subject of a sentence.

LANGUAGE OBJECTIVE: Use complete sentences to talk about people and what they are wearing.

PREREQUISITE SKILLS: Know what a sentence is and understand that it is made up of different parts and words.

Lesson Overview

Teacher reviews rules and examples of subjects with students. Students complete sentences by filling in the subject. Students play a guessing game by describing a subject on a picture card.

Materials	Preparation
• Grammar Chart • Subject Picture Prompts • Subject Cards	• Cut out Subject Cards. • To print materials in color, visit the online Teacher Resources.

Activate Prior Knowledge

Quickly review the prerequisite skill with students and evaluate their proficiency. If students are not proficient with this skill, complete the corresponding Grammar Lesson before continuing.

SENTENCES: ***Sentences are made up of words. We put words together to make a complete thought.***

I'm going to say some words. If you think the words go together to make a complete thought, give me a thumbs up. Demonstrate a thumbs up. ***If you think the sentence is missing something, or if it is just words that don't make a complete thought, give me a thumbs down.*** Demonstrate a thumbs down.

Read the complete and incomplete sentences from the bank and allow students to respond together, showing their answers.

Incomplete Sentences	*Complete Sentences*
girl wears	The girl wears a hat.
hat yellow	The hat is yellow.
the dog	The dog eats the shoe.
buy red	We buy red shoes.

Teach and Model

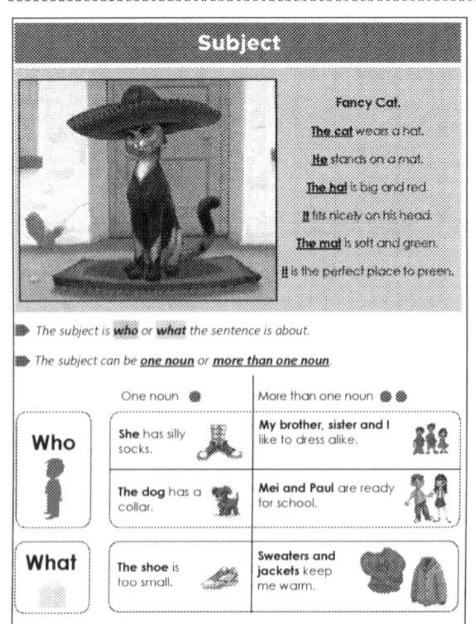

Introduce the grammar principle

Now that you know that words go together to make sentences, you can learn about the parts of a sentence. One important part is the subject. Every sentence has a subject.

Work through the Grammar Chart

Use the picture and the poem to present the grammar in context.

Read through the rules.

Explore the examples.

Clarify and correct if needed

- ***The subject is always a noun. It can be a person, place, animal, or thing.***
- ***Words in sentences follow an order.***
- ***The subject usually comes at the beginning of the sentence.***

The Grammar Chart includes the word *preen*, which is likely to be unfamiliar to the students. Explain that preening is what a cat does to make itself look good and clean.

Reteaching Lessons

Guided Practice

Tell students they will complete sentences to practice subjects. Show the Subject Picture Prompts. Subject Picture Prompts feature characters from Imagine Learning Beginning Books.

Say: ***I'm going to say a sentence without a subject. You will use these picture cards to help you find the subject and complete the sentence.***

Let's look at all the things in these pictures that could be subjects. Remember, the subject is whom or what the sentence is about. In this first picture the sentence could be about the girl. We could also use her name, Pam. Or we could even use she for the subject of our sentence. The sentence could be about her hat or the flower on her hat. Review other items in the picture prompt as needed.

Read the following incomplete sentences aloud as you show the picture prompt. Pause after each and have the students to complete it with a subject.

______ puts on her new hat. (Pam, The girl, She)

______ wears glasses. (He, The teacher)

______ chews the shoe. (The dog, Bob)

______ has a big flower. (The hat)

______ like(s) to skate. (The boy and his dad, Sam and his dad, Sam, Dad)

______ keep(s) Sam safe when he skates. (The helmet, The knee pads)

______ is wearing a little bow tie. (He, The teacher)

______ wear(s) short pants. (Sam, Sam's Dad, The boy)

______ is getting wet and slimy. (The shoe)

Independent Practice

Tell the students they will play a game to practice finding the subject of a sentence.

Lay out all the Subject Cards on the table. Review the people on the cards.

Say: ***I will secretly choose a card in my head and think of a sentence to describe what the person is wearing. But I won't say who or what the subject is, instead, I will say, "This subject..." You will look at the cards and try to guess which person I chose.***

Model the game: ***Ready? This subject is wearing a tall, white hat. Call on a volunteer.*** (Possible response: Is it the baker?)

When a student guesses the correct card, have the class repeat the complete sentence together aloud. (The baker wears a tall, white hat.)

Pick one student to go first. Have the student think of a card but not tell anyone which card it is. The student then says a sentence that describes what the person from the card is wearing, but replaces the person with "this subject." The other students guess who it is and then say the sentence together out loud.

Subject Cards: fireman, swimmer, boy, magician, ballerina, skier, teacher, biker, clown, doctor, builder, runner, baker, skater, baby, scarecrow, duck, cat

Differentiation

For more support: Write these sentence frames on the board for students who struggle: This subject is wearing __________. This subject has __________.

For a challenge: After the students have correctly guessed a card, have a volunteer choose a different object from the same picture. Then have the student describe the object, making it the subject this time, rather than a person. For example, *This subject is floppy and round.* Have the other students guess the subject of the sentence. (Is it pizza dough?)

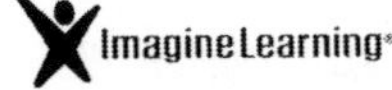

Check Progress

Use the following activity to check individual progress made on the target skill.

Say: ***Listen to these sentences. What is the subject? Think of the answer, and then I will call on someone for an answer.*** Read the assessment sentences. The subjects are underlined in the sentences below.

Lucy puts on her gloves.

The cat is wearing a new collar.

I wear my favorite shoes.

The pants are long.

We love to wear t-shirts.

Her dress is blue and white.

My mom and dad wear glasses.

The boy's shirt is old.

My socks are fuzzy.

She buys a summer swim suit.

The coat keeps me warm.

The baby holds her blanket.

The shoes squeak when he walks.

The teacher is wearing a new hat.

If the students can correctly identify the subjects the sentences, consider the intervention successful.

Reteaching Lessons

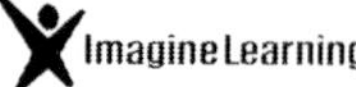

Subject

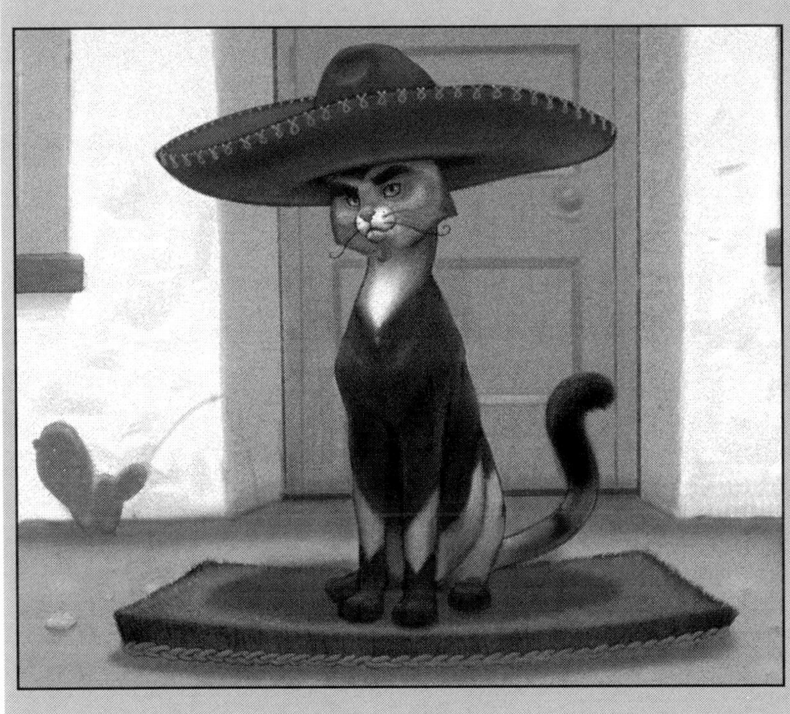

Fancy Cat.

The cat wears a hat.

He stands on a mat.

The hat is big and red.

It fits nicely on his head.

The mat is soft and green.

It is the perfect place to preen.

Reteaching Lessons ✓

*The subject is **who** or **what** the sentence is about.*

*The subject can be **one noun** or **more than one noun**.*

	One noun 	More than one noun 
Who 	**She** has silly socks. 	**My brother, sister, and I** like to dress alike. 
	The dog has a collar. 	**Mei and Paul** are ready for school. 
What 	**The shoe** is too small.   	**Sweaters and jackets** keep me warm.  

Pam

Sam and Dad

Bob

The teacher

fireman

swimmer

boy

magician

ballerina

skier

Reteaching Lessons ✓

teacher

biker

clown

Subject Cards

Subject-Verb Order

LEARNING OBJECTIVE: Use correct subject-verb order when creating sentences.

LANGUAGE OBJECTIVE: Describe things that need to be fixed and the people that fix them using correct subject-verb order.

PREREQUISITE: Be able to identify subjects and verbs in a sentence and understand their functions.

Lesson Overview

Teacher reviews rules and examples of subject-verb order with students. Students put sentence strips in order to create sentences about fixing a table. Students then play a collaborative game to create sentences to describe people that fix things.

Materials	Preparation
• Grammar Chart • Ball • Picture Cards • Sentence Strips • Check Progress printout (one per student)	• Cut out Picture Cards. • Cut out Sentence Strips except for the example sentence strip. • To print materials in color, visit the online Teacher Resources.

Activate Prior Knowledge

Quickly review the prerequisite skill with students and evaluate their proficiency. If students are not proficient with this skill, complete the corresponding Grammar Lesson before continuing.

SUBJECTS AND VERBS: ***Every sentence needs a subject and a verb. What is a subject?*** (Possible response: A subject is who or what the sentence is about.) ***What is a verb?*** (Possible response: Verbs are action words; they show what people and things do.)

Say a sentence from the bank below aloud. Ask a volunteer to identify the subject and the verb.

Sentence bank: She sews. / We sweep. / They work quietly / The door creaks. / I wash the dishes. / He paints houses.

Teach and Model

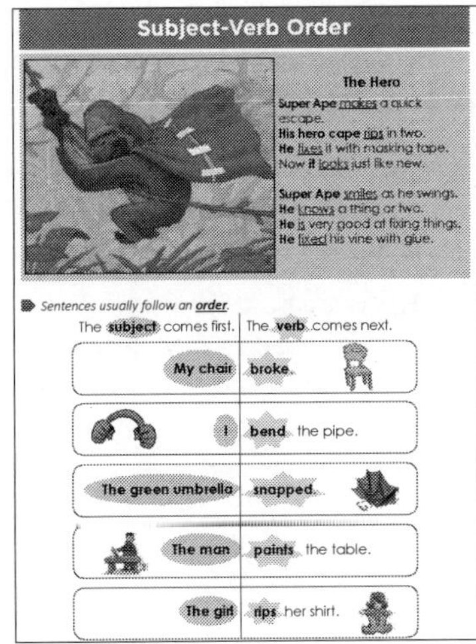

Introduce the grammar principle

Now that you know about subjects and verbs, we can practice putting them in the right order in a sentence.

Work through the Grammar Chart

Use the picture and the poem to present the grammar in context.

Read through the rules.

Explore the examples.

Clarify and correct if needed

- ***The subject is the person, place, or thing the sentence is about.***
- ***The verb shows what the subject does.***

Guided Practice

Tell the students they will make sentences by putting parts together in the right order.

Display the example sentence strip. Point out each part: ***The subject comes before the verb. What is the subject?*** (Pip and Rim) ***The verb goes next. What is the verb?*** (play) ***The rest of the words come after the verb to complete the sentence. How does this sentence end?*** (together)

Say: ***Now you try the next sentence. There are four pieces: a subject, a verb, a sentence ending, and a picture to finish it.*** Lay out the four pieces for the next sentence in mixed up order. Ask for a volunteer to put the pieces in the correct order to form a sentence. Continue one sentence at a time until all sentences have been put in order.

Sentence #	Subject	Verb	Ending
Example	Pip and Rim	play	together.
1	Rim	digs	a big hole.
2	The fence	breaks	in pieces.
3	Pip	sees	the broken fences.
4	She	fixes	it.
5	Pip and Rim	are	happy now.

Independent Practice

Tell the students they will play a word game to practice making sentences with the subject and the verb in their correct places. Use the Picture Cards and ball for this activity. Have the students begin by standing or sitting in a circle.

Say: ***I will show you a picture card of someone who helps fix or build things. We are going to create sentences about the picture cards, one part at a time. The sentence can be about what the person is doing, what the person is wearing, or anything else you notice about the picture.***

Model the activity together with these instructions the first time you play:

Show the picture of the mechanic. Give the ball to a student. Say to that student: ***You will say the subject. For example, "The mechanic" or "She." Or you can even give the subject a name, like "Jane." Then you will throw the ball to another student.*** Have the student say a subject and throw the ball.

Tell the next student: ***You will say the verb. For example, "fixes" or "works."*** After that student says a verb, instruct them to throw the ball to a third student.

Tell the third student: ***You will finish the sentence any way you want as long as it makes sense with the subject and the verb.*** Give the third student an example that works, such as "broken cars," "in the auto shop," etc.

Choose a student to start a new sentence. Continue the game. Have students come up with two or three sentences for each picture card before showing them a new card.

Differentiation

For more support: Give each student a few picture cards. Go around the circle and ask the students to say a sentence about one of their word cards. For example, for mechanic, a student could say, "The mechanic fixes broken cars." Keep going around the circle until all the picture cards have been described. Then play the activity above as described.

For a challenge: Give each student a picture card. Tell students not to show anyone what their card is. Ask the students, one at a time, to say a sentence about their word card without the exact subject. Say a model sentence for the students. For example, if you had the mechanic card, you might say: ***This person is fixing the engine of a car.*** Then have the other students guess who is on the picture card. Continue until each student in the circle has had a turn or until all picture cards have been used.

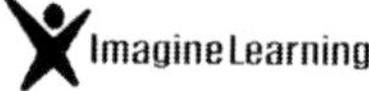

Check Progress

Use the following activity to check individual progress made on the target skill.

Give each student a Check Progress printout. Say: ***Read each pair of sentences. One of the sentences is correct because the subject and verb are in the correct order. Circle the correct sentence.***

Ask for a volunteer to explain why the sentence he or she chose is correct.

If the student can identify sentences that use subject-verb order correctly and explain why the sentence is correct, consider the intervention successful.

*Check Progress**

	Answer A	Answer B
1	**My tooth hurts a lot.**	Hurts my tooth a lot.
2	Go I to the dentist.	**I go to the dentist.**
3	Looks the dentist at it.	**The dentist looks at it.**
4	**He says it has a cavity.**	Says he it has a cavity.
5	Needs he to fix it.	**He needs to fix it.**
6	Fixes the dentist my tooth.	**The dentist fixes my tooth.**
7	**He tells me to always brush my teeth.**	Tells he me to always brush my teeth.

* Correct answers are in bold

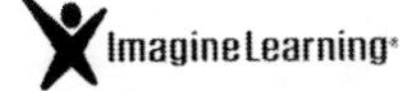

Subject-Verb Order

The Hero

Super Ape <u>makes</u> a quick escape.
His hero cape <u>rips</u> in two.
He <u>fixes</u> it with masking tape.
Now **it** <u>looks</u> just like new.

Super Ape <u>smiles</u> as he swings.
He <u>knows</u> a thing or two.
He <u>is</u> very good at fixing things.
He <u>fixed</u> his vine with glue.

*Sentences usually follow an **<u>order</u>**.*

The **subject** comes first.	The **verb** comes next.
My chair	**broke.**
I	**bend** the pipe.
The green umbrella	**snapped.**
The man	**paints** the table.
The girl	**rips** her shirt.

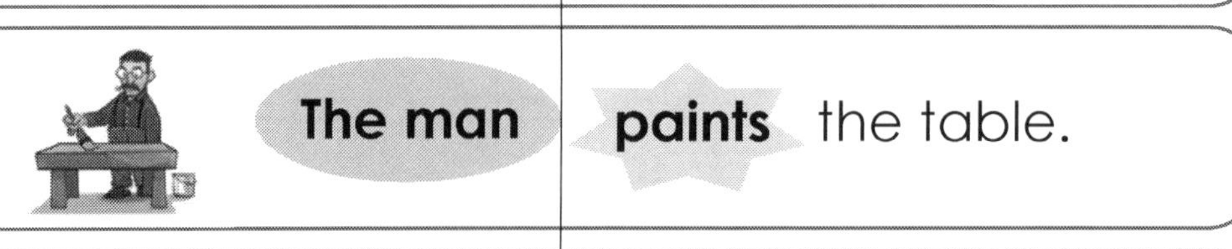

Reteaching Lessons

mechanic

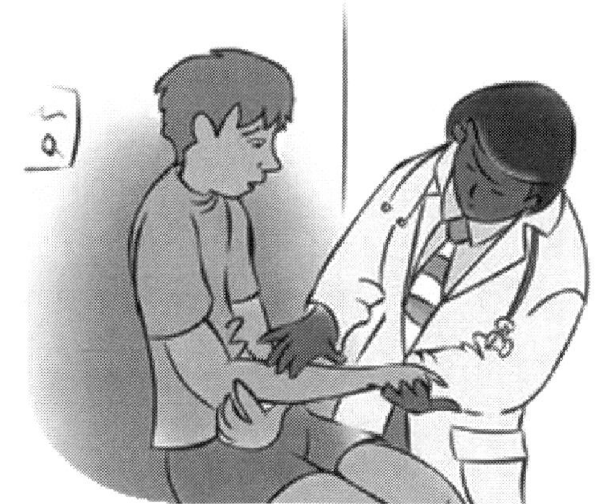

doctor

custodian

builder

electrician

seamstress

Reteaching Lessons

Reteaching Lessons

Example Pip and Rim	play	together.	
Rim 1	digs 1	a big hole. 1	1
The fence 2	breaks 2	in pieces. 2	2
Pip 3	sees 3	the broken fence. 3	3
She 4	fixes 4	it. 4	4
Pip and Rim 5	are 5	happy now. 5	5

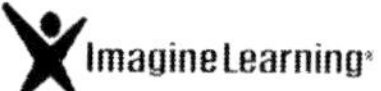

Grade 1

15 min.

CCSS L.1.1.C
TEKS 110.12.b.21.A.i

os

NG OBJECTIVE: Identify and use action verbs correctly.
AGE OBJECTIVE: Use action verbs to describe what people and things do.
QUISITE SKILL: Be able to identify basic nouns.

Overview

eviews rules and examples of action verbs with students. Students practice action verbs in an action en students play a charades game to practice verbs.

Materials	Preparation
nmar Chart on Verbs Chant ure Cards e and Draw Printout (one student)	• Cut out all Picture Cards. • To print materials in color, visit the online Teacher Resources.

ate Prior Knowledge

review the prerequisite skill with students and evaluate their proficiency. If students are not proficient with , complete the corresponding Grammar Lesson before continuing.

: ***Nouns are words that name people, places, and things. I'll say a word. If it is a noun, show me with a up.*** Show thumbs up. ***If it is not a noun, show me with a thumbs down.*** Show thumbs down.

ank: *dog, swim, boy, teacher, jump, cow, pencil, sit, flower, bus, yell, sleep, girl*

h and Model

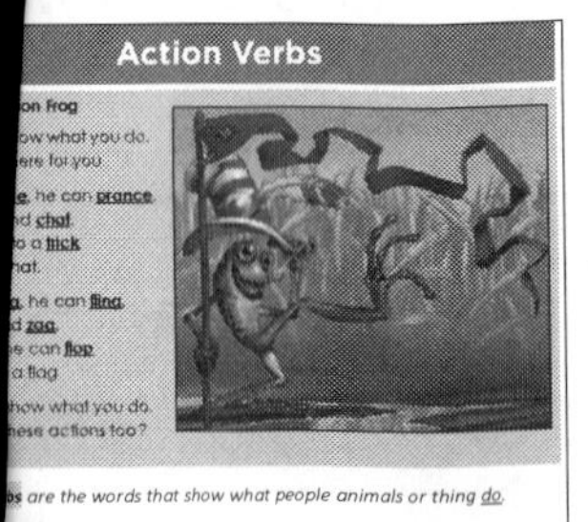

Introduce the grammar principle

The "thumbs down words" you just heard were all verbs: swim, jump, sit, yell, and sleep. Now that you know nouns, let's learn more about verbs.

A verb is a doing word because it shows what people, animals, or things do.

If you can do it, it's a verb. If an animal or thing can do it, it is a verb.

Work through the Grammar Chart

Use the picture and the poem to present the grammar in context.

Read through the rules.

Explore the examples.

Clarify and correct if needed

- ***To find an action verb in a sentence, look at each word and ask yourself, "Can someone or something do this?"***

ided Practice

Now that you know what verbs are, we can practice them with the action verb chant. Let's chant a verse ether. Listen for all the action verbs.

lay the action verbs chant. Have students chorally repeat the verse with you. Call on volunteers to point out action verbs. Then have students stand up. Chant the first verse again, pausing to allow students to act out the s in response to the questions "Can you ....?" Repeat with verses 2 and 3.

A Trip to the Dentis

Question	Answer A	
1	My tooth hurts a lot.	Hurts n
2	Go I to the dentist.	I go to
3	Looks the dentist at it.	The dentis
4	He says it has a cavity.	Says he it h
5	Needs he to fix it.	He needs
6	Fixes the dentist my tooth.	The dentist fixe
7	He tells me to always brush my teeth.	Tells he me to alwa teeth.

Action verbs show what you do.
You can do these actions too.
Can you **blink**? Can you **think**?
Can you **wiggle your nose**?
Can you **spin**? Can you **grin**?
Can you **touch your toes**?

Action verbs show what you do.
You can do these actions too.
Can you **flap**? Can you **clap**?
Can you **reach up high**?
Can you **hop**? Can you **pop**?
Can you **close your eyes**?

Action verbs show what you do.
You can do these actions too.
Can you **skip**? Wiggle your **hips**?
Can you **touch the ground**?
Can you **sneeze**? Can you **freeze**?
Can you **sit back down**?

Independent Practice

Tell students they will play an acting game to practice verbs. Put the Picture Cards in a box or basket. Say: ***Each of you will have a turn to draw a card from this basket. The card will have a picture of a person, an animal, or a thing. Show it to the group and say what it is.***

For example, if there is a monkey on the card, you might say, "This is a monkey," or "It's a monkey."

Then you will think of an action that the person, animal, or thing does or can do. Do not tell us the action. Instead you will act out the verb.

For example, you could act out a monkey climbing, or swinging in a tree, or jumping. Then we will guess the action you are doing.

Ask one student at a time to select a card. Have him or her say the name of the illustration and show the card to the group. Help the student, if needed, to think of a verb that the noun *does* or *can do* and act it out.

When students have guessed the correct action verb, have the actor create a complete sentence using the noun and the verb, such as, "The monkey climbs a tree," or "Monkeys can climb." Write each sentence so students can refer to it again. When every student has had a turn, have students re-read the sentences together and identify the action verbs.

Picture Cards and possible actions:

People:
basketball player (run, jump, shoot, throw, dribble)
artist (paint, draw)
baby (crawl, cry, laugh, sleep, etc.)
clown (frown, smile, laugh, dance, juggle, etc.)
ballerina (twirl, jump, dance)

Animals:
crab (crawl, pinch)
hen (eat, peck, lay eggs, cluck)
horse (eat, gallop, trot, run, neigh)
snake (slither, hiss, bite)
bee (fly, buzz, sting)
bug (crawl, climb)
frog (hop/jump, croak)
dolphin (jump, squeak, swim)

Things:
alarm clock (tick, ring, vibrate)
plane (fly, take off, land)
tail (swish, curl, swing)
stick (poke, tap, break, swish)
door (open, close, slam)

Note: The lines may get a little blurred between people and things doing the action, but as long as the students are focusing on action verbs, allow them to have some freedom on this category.

Reteaching Lessons

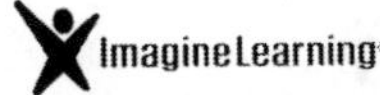

Differentiation

For more support: Have the student with the card hold it up. Have the other students help identify the illustration and suggest possible actions for that noun. Have the student pick one of the suggested verbs and act it out.

For a challenge: Have the group create three sentences for each picture card, using three different action verbs.

Check Progress

Use a sentence-writing activity to check individual progress.

Distribute the Write and Draw sheet. Point out to students that there are four sentences that have been started, but they are all missing an action verb. Read the sentence starters together. Say: ***Your job is to think of an action verb to complete the sentence. Think of something the noun can do and write it in the blank. For example, the girl bakes.*** Invite students to add details to their sentences. For example, "The girl bakes a big cake." ***Then draw a picture that shows what you wrote.***

Assessment Bank:

The girl ________.

The frog ______ .

The cat _______ .

The boy ______ .

Check individual student work. Ask each student to identify the action verbs they've created and explain what an action verb is. If students can do these two things, consider the intervention successful.

Writing Extension

Have students turn the Write and Draw sheet over and create four more squares. Challenge students to write additional sentences with action words on their own. Remind students that a sentence begins with a capital letter and ends with a period. Have them underline the action verb. Allow them to draw the supporting pictures. Consider having them present their favorite sentence with its associated drawing to the class.

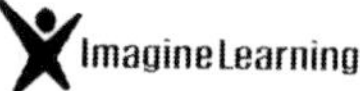

Action Verbs

Action Frog

Action verbs show what you do.
Action Frog is here for you.

Frog can **dance**. He can **prance**.
He can **sing** and **chat**.
He can **kick**, do a **trick**.
He can **tip** his hat.

Frog can **swing**. He can **fling**.
He can **zig** and **zag**.
He can **hop**. He can **flop**.
He can **wave** a flag.

Action verbs show what you do.
Can you do these actions too?

Action verbs *are the words that show what people animals or thing do.*

people	The girl kicks the ball. 
animals	The dog runs. 
things	The boat sails on the water. 

Reteaching Lessons

Action Verbs Chant

Action verbs show what you do.
You can do these actions too.
Can you blink? Can you think?
Can you wiggle your nose?
Can you spin? Can you grin?
Can you touch your toes?

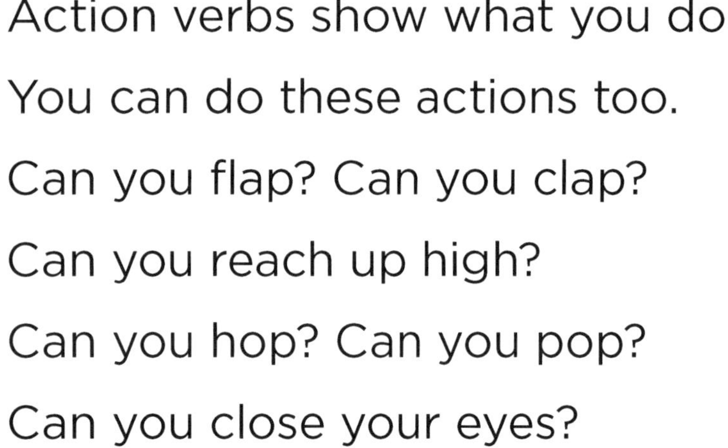

Action verbs show what you do.
You can do these actions too.
Can you flap? Can you clap?
Can you reach up high?
Can you hop? Can you pop?
Can you close your eyes?

Action verbs show what you do.
You can do these actions too.
Can you skip? Wiggle your hips?
Can you touch the ground?
Can you sneeze? Can you freeze?
Can you sit back down?

Write and Draw

The girl ______________________.

The frog ______________________.

The cat ______________________.

The boy ______________________.

Reteaching Lessons

Grammar

To Be Verbs

Grade 1, 3

15 min.

CCSS.L.1.1.E
TEKS 110.12.20.A.i

LEARNING OBJECTIVE: Conjugate the verb *to be* and use it in a sentence.

LANGUAGE OBJECTIVE: Use the verbs *am*, *is*, and *are* to ask and answer questions, talk about bugs, and complete sentences.

PREREQUISITE SKILLS: Understand subjects and pronouns and know basic regular verbs.

Lesson Overview

Teacher reviews rules and examples of *to be* verbs with students. Students guess riddles to practice the forms of the verb *to be*. Then students play a flyswatter game to complete sentences using *am*, *is*, and *are*.

Materials	Preparation
• Grammar Chart • To Be Verbs Picture Prompt • To Be Bug Cards (one per student or one per student pair/group) • Flyswatters (optional) • To Be Bug Sentences printout (optional)	• Cut out To Be Bug Cards. • To print materials in color, visit the online Teacher Resources.

Activate Prior Knowledge

Quickly review the prerequisite skill with students and evaluate their proficiency. If students are not proficient with this skill, complete the corresponding Grammar Lesson before continuing.

SUBJECTS: ***Subjects are nouns that show what or whom a sentence is about. I'll say a sentence. You tell me the subject.***

- ***The teacher stands up.*** (the teacher)
- ***The ants march in a line.*** (the ants)
- ***The students smile.*** (the students)
- ***The flower grows taller.*** (the flower)

PRONOUNS: ***Pronouns can take the place of nouns as the subject of a sentence. Pronouns are words like* I, he, you, they, *and* it. *I'll say a sentence. You tell me if the subject is a noun or a pronoun.***

- ***The teacher stands up.*** (noun: the teacher)
- ***I stand up.*** (pronoun: I)
- ***The ants march.*** (noun: the ants)
- ***They march.*** (pronoun: they)
- ***The flower grows.*** (noun: the flower)
- ***It grows taller.*** (pronoun: it)
- ***You smile.*** (pronoun: you)
- ***The students smile.*** (noun: the students)

SUBJECT VERB AGREEMENT: ***The subject of a sentence needs to match the verb. Add an* -s *to the end of a verb when the subject is* he, she, *or* it. *Don't add the letter* s *to the end of a verb when the subject is* I, you, we, *or* they. *I'll say a sentence with* I, you, we, *or* they. *You will change the subject and add an* -s.**

- ***I stand up. Change the subject to* he.** (He stands up.)
- ***We smile. Change the subject to* she.** (She smiles.)
- ***You march. Change the subject to* the teacher.** (The teacher marches.)
- ***My friend and I stand up. Change the subject to* my friend.** (My friend stands up.)
- ***They grow taller. Change the subject to* it.** (It grows taller.)

Reteaching Lessons

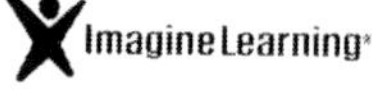

Teach and Model

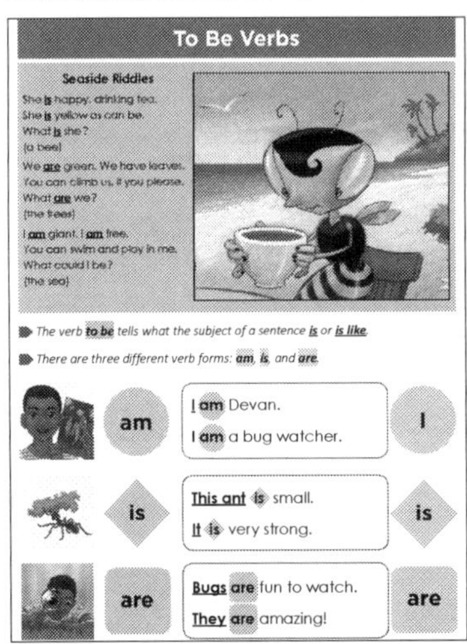

Introduce the grammar principle

Now that you can match verbs and subjects, you are ready to try a more challenging verb: **to be.**

When you match the verb to be with a subject, you do not add **s.** ***Instead, you have three choices:*** **am, is,** ***and*** **are.**

Work through the Grammar Chart

Use the picture and the poem to present the grammar in context.

Read through the rules.

Explore the examples.

Clarify and correct if needed

- ***To be is not an action verb. Using*** **am, is,** ***or*** **are** ***is like using an equal sign.***
- ***The bee is an insect. bee = insect***
- ***The verb to be is often used to start a question. (Am I late? Is he small? Are they in the room?)***

Guided Practice

Tell the students they will use the verbs *am, is,* and *are* to solve riddles about bugs.

Display the To Be Verbs Picture Prompt. Say: ***Look at these bugs. Do you know them all?*** Review the names of each one before beginning: *worm, caterpillars, ladybugs, dragonfly, fly,* butterfly, *crickets, spider, bee, grasshopper, firefly, ants.*

Model the activity using *am* and *are.* Use the sentence frames to help them use ***complete question that includes the verb.*** Say: ***Let's use the verbs*** **am** ***and*** **are** ***to try the first riddle. For example, if I say, "I am green. I am small. I am hungry for apples."*** Point to the sentence frame on the picture prompt. Say: ***You can ask,*** **"Are you a ___?"** Have one or more students ask a question to guess what you are. When a student guesses correctly, say: ***"Yes. I am a worm. What am I?"*** Prompt students to respond, *"You are a worm."*

Read the following riddles aloud as you display the picture prompt.

<u>I am / are you?</u>

- ***I am small but powerful. I am always busy. I am yellow and black.*** (bee)
- ***I am a beetle, but I can fly. I am black. I am bright at night.*** (firefly)
- ***I am beautiful. I am delicate. I am a very good flier.*** (butterfly)

<u>we are / are you?</u>

- ***We are soft. We are fuzzy. We are future butterflies.*** (caterpillars)
- ***We are round. We are good for your garden. We are red and spotted.*** (ladybugs)

Model using is: ***Now I'm going to switch and use*** **is** ***and*** **are** ***to describe the bugs. You use the verbs*** **is** ***and*** **are** ***to solve the riddle. For example, if I say, "It is skinny. It is a speedy flier. It is long and shiny." You can ask, "Is it a ________________?"*** (dragonfly)

Read the following riddles aloud as you display the picture prompt

<u>it, he, she is / is it, he, she?</u>

- ***It can fly. It is noisy. It is good at landing in your food.*** (fly)
- ***She is the best at hiding. She is black. She is dangerous.*** (spider)
- ***He is green. He is a tasty snack in some countries. He is good at jumping.*** (grasshopper)

<u>they are / are they?</u>

- ***They are black or brown. They are awake at night. They are noisy.*** (crickets)
- ***They are workers. They are very strong. They are not welcome at a picnic.*** (ants)

Independent Practice

Tell the students they will play a game to practice using the *to be* verbs.

Display the To Be Bug cards. Explain: ***I will say a sentence with a missing verb. You will know where the missing verb is when you hear the buzzing sound. You must swat the correct "to be bug" to fill in the missing word and complete the sentence.*** Give each student a set of cards or divide the students into pairs or small groups. Have students spread the cards out on a table or desk. Students can use their hands, a rolled up piece of paper, or a flyswatter.

Recite aloud the sentences below. When you get to the blank where a to be verb belongs, say: ***bzzzz***. For example, for the sentence "The students _____ happy," say, ***"The students bzzzz happy."*** Students use their flyswatters to slap the correct to be verb that fits in the sentence. (are) Ask one student to recite the entire sentence, including the correct verb. Students who swatted the correct "to be bug" get a point.

1. I ____ very tall. (am)
2. They _____ Korean. (are)
3. We ____ good students. (are)
4. The book __ small. (is) *
5. My friend _____ nice. (is)
6. I ______ hungry. (am)
7. My eyes _____ blue. (are) **
8. School ______ important. (is)
9. Liz and Steve ____ funny. (are)
10. She _____ an English teacher. (is)
11. We _____ noisy. (are)
12. Mom _____ tired today. (is)
13. They ____ cold and wet. (are)
14. It _____ a fun party. (is)
15. I ______ the best player. (am)
16. Bob ____ the president. (is)
17. The school ____ really old. (is)
18. Bugs ______ interesting. (are)

* Remind students, if needed, that the verb *is* matches the subject *he*, *she* or *it*, and also any singular nouns that can be replaced by these pronouns, such as *book* or *friend*.

** Remind students, if needed, that *are* matches the subjects *we*, *you*, and *they*, but also any plural nouns that can be replaced by these pronouns, such as *eyes* or *Liz and Steve*.

Differentiation

For more support: Use one set of cards for the whole group. Place them on a table for all students to see. Have students take turns catching the "to be bugs." Say a sentence and have a student locate and hold up the card with the correct missing verb. If students still struggle, display the To Be Bug Sentences printout and have students to follow along as you read.

For a challenge: Using the same cards, pair students with a partner. Ask one student to make up a sentence that is missing a to be verb and have the partner swat the card with the correct verb. Have the students swap roles and repeat the activity.

Check Progress

Use the sentences below to check individual progress made on the target skill.

Call on students to answer the questions with short, complete sentences using is, am or are. Questions are grouped below for convenience in assessing responses. Ask questions in a random order.

I am	you are	he/she/it is	we are	they are
Are you a student? Are you happy? Are you good at math? Are you a soccer player?	Am I a bus driver/ Am I tall? Am I the teacher? Am I Japanese?	Is your best friend nice? Is you pet clean? Is today Saturday? Is your house white? Is your shirt blue?	Are we bugs? Are we smart? Are we awake? Are we busy?	Are the chairs soft? Are your friends funny? Are the pencils yellow? Are athletes healthy?

If the student can respond using the correct form of to be, consider the intervention successful.

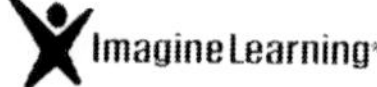

To Be Verbs

Seaside Riddles

She **is** happy, drinking tea.
She **is** yellow as can be.
What **is** she?
(a bee)

We **are** green. We have leaves.
You can climb us, if you please.
What **are** we?
(the trees)

I **am** giant. I **am** free.
You can swim and play in me.
What could I be?
(the sea)

- *The verb **to be** tells what the subject of a sentence **is** or **is like**.*
- *There are three different verb forms: **am**, **is**, and **are**.*

am

I **am** Devan.
I **am** a bug watcher.

I

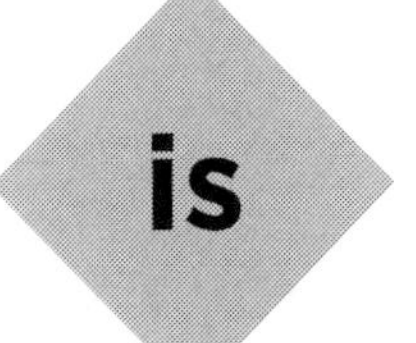

is

This ant **is** small.
It **is** very strong.

he
she
it

are

Bugs **are** fun to watch.
They **are** amazing!

you
we
they

Reteaching Lessons

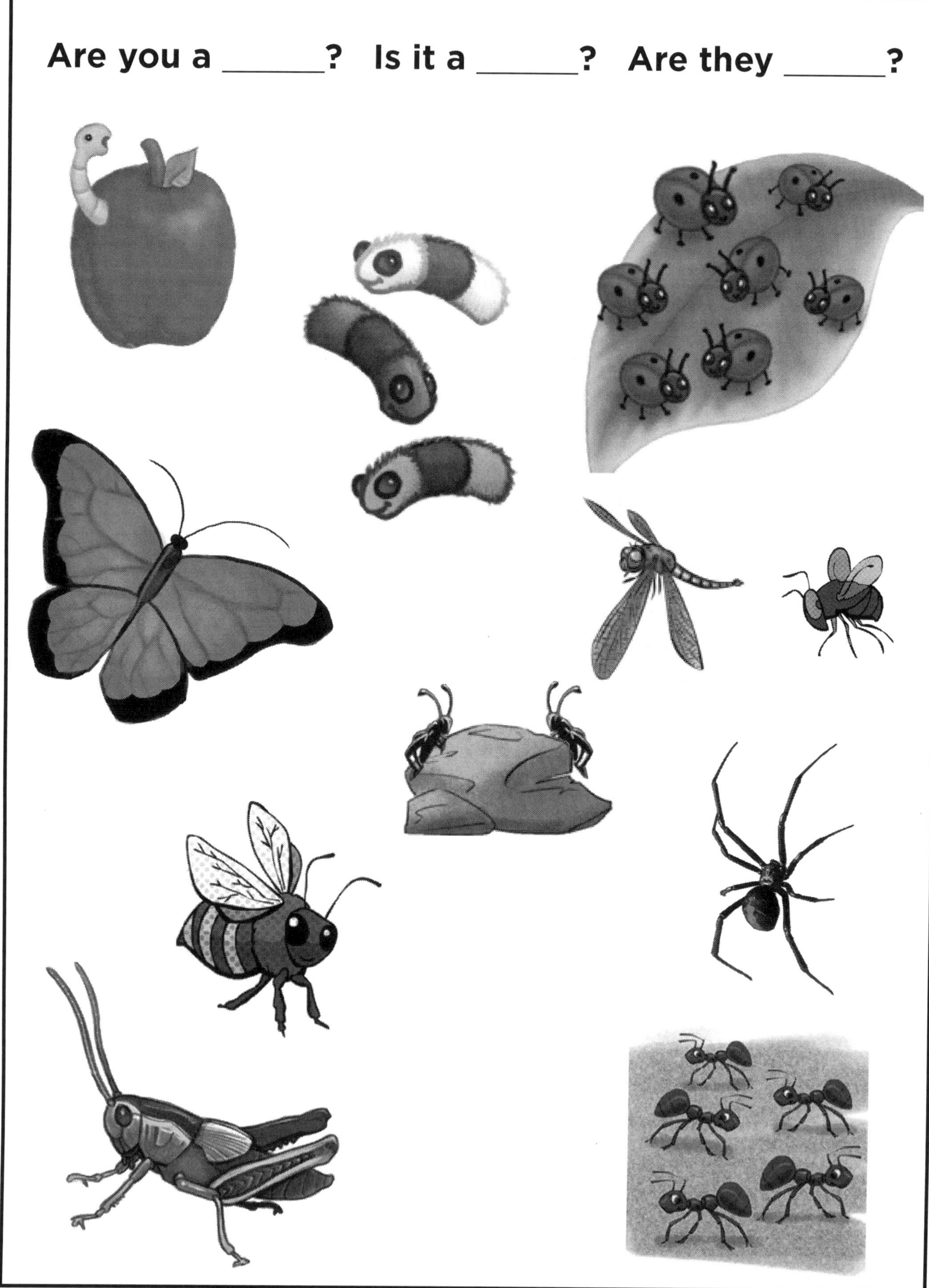

Reteaching Lessons

To Be Verbs Picture Prompt

Imagine Learning

am

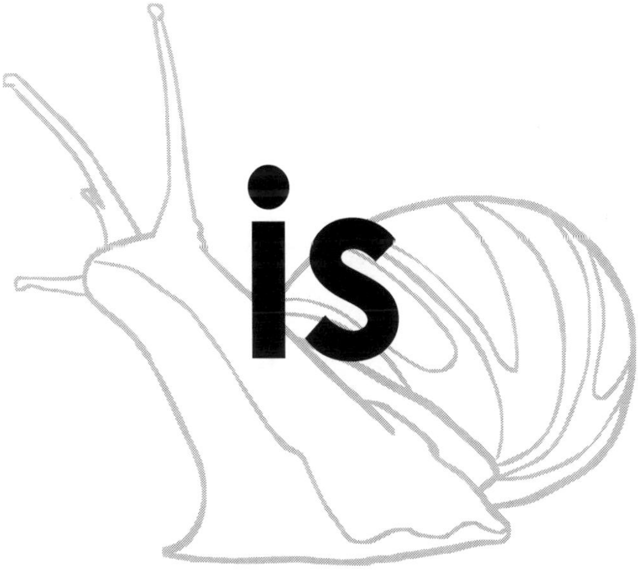

is

are

To Be Bug Sentences

1. I ___ very tall.
2. They _____ Korean.
3. We ____ good students.
4. The book __ small.
5. My friend _____ nice.
6. I ______ hungry.
7. My eyes _____ blue.
8. School ______ important.
9. Liz and Steve ____ funny.
10. She _____ an English teacher.
11. We _____ noisy.
12. Mom _____ tired today.
13. They ____ cold and wet.
14. It _____ a fun party.
15. I ______ the best player.
16. Bob ____ the president.
17. The school ____ really old.
18. Bugs ______ interesting.

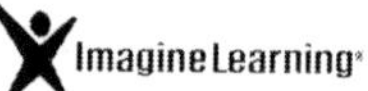

Notes

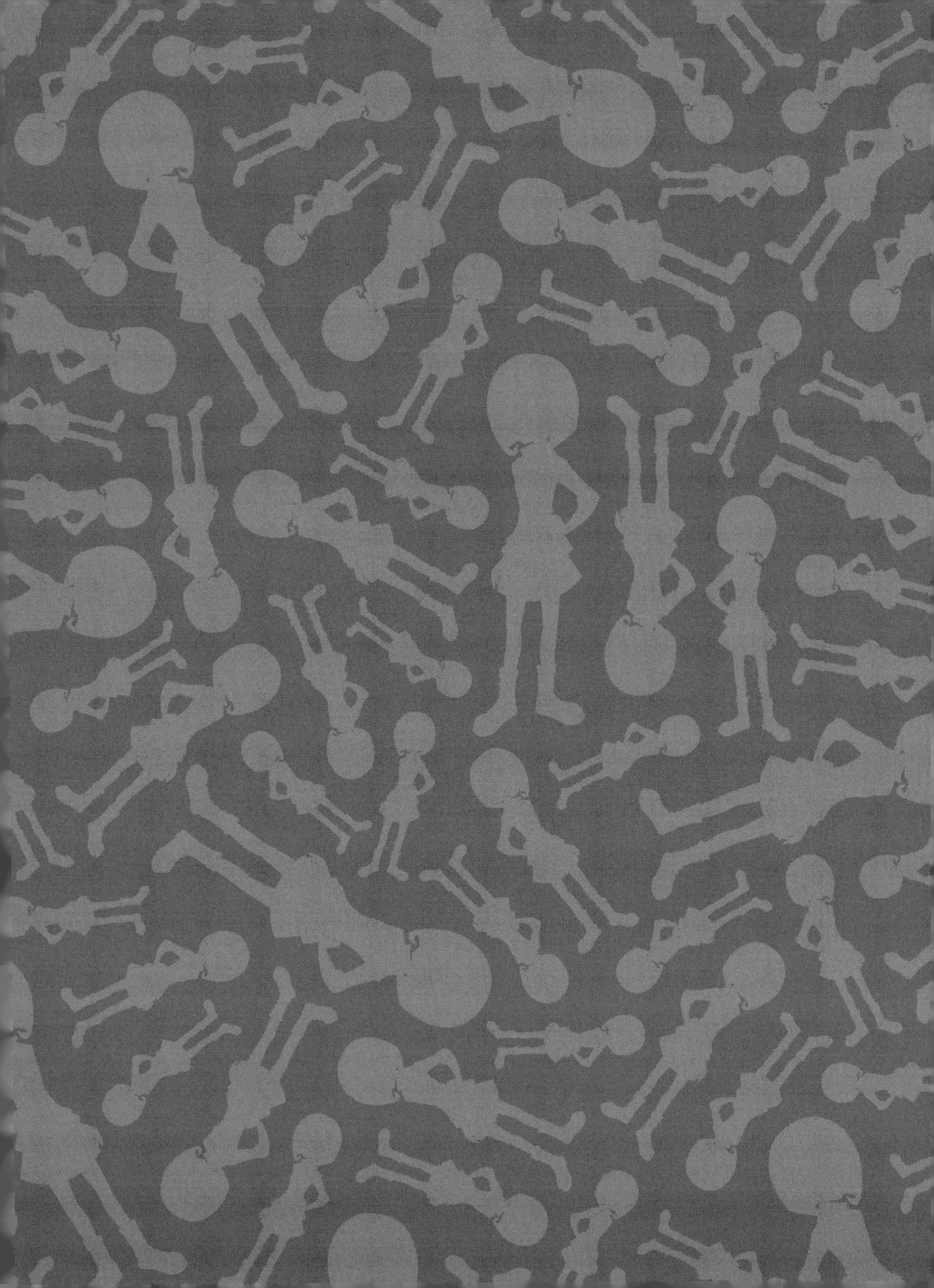

VOCABULARY

CLASSROOM ACTIVITIES

Classroom activities include ideas and resources for whole-class or small-group work to help students develop basic and academic vocabulary. Instruction and practice reinforce what students have learned from the Imagine Learning online curriculum and focus on oral production, providing opportunities for students to actively respond and demonstrate their knowledge.

- Art-rich activities that often include movement to appeal to all learners
- Standards-based materials that require minimal teacher preparation
- Vocabulary words and resources that focus on students' experiences with the world around them

Show Me an Adjective

CCSS.L.1.1F
TEKS 110.11.20.A.iii

LEARNING OBJECTIVE: Use adjectives to describe objects.
LANGUAGE OBJECTIVE: Use adjectives to describe and ask questions about objects.

Activity Overview

Teacher asks questions about objects. Students respond using adjectives to describe objects.

Materials

- music player and music
- ball or soft toy

Explain

Introduce the activity: ***We are going to play a game to practice words to describe things. These words are called adjectives. Let's review them.*** On the board, list all the adjectives shown in the target vocabulary list.

Review words with the class: Use the sentence frame below and insert each adjective and the name of an everyday object. When applicable choose objects that are a good example of each adjective.

____________________ is ____________________. (The clock is round.)

[name of object] **[adjective]**

Play

1. Play music while passing a ball or soft toy around the classroom.
2. Stop the music. Have the student holding the ball or soft toy pick any object visible in the classroom.
3. Using one of the adjectives below, create a describing question. For example, ***"Is the desk square?"***
4. Have the class respond in unison after the count of three.

   For example: Teacher: ***One, two, three.*** Class: "Yes, the desk is square," or "No, the desk is not square." (When dealing with comparisons, use two objects.)
5. Use the same word multiple times, but with different objects in the classroom until you feel the class understands the word.

Word bank: full, empty, round, square, long, short, many, few, blue, brown, black, pink, purple, orange, red, yellow, green, white, same, different, old, new, front, back

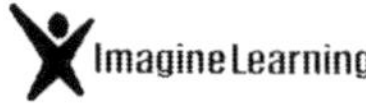

I Can... Can You?

CCSS.L.K.1B
TEKS 110.11.16.A.i

LEARNING OBJECTIVE: Practice verb vocabulary words through dramatization.
LANGUAGE OBJECTIVE: Say and act out action words from a Read-Along Book.

Activity Overview

Students act out verbs from the story, *Can You Do This?*

Materials	Preparation
• *Can You Do This?* Read-Along Book	• Consider projecting *Can You Do This?* using the instructions below.

Explain

Introduce the activity: ***We are going to read a story and then act out the action words we hear. Then we will think of some other words we can act out.*** Project and read the story *Can You Do This?*

Play

1. Have students stand at an arm's distance apart from each other so they have room to move.
2. Project and read the story *Can You Do This?* and have students join in by doing actions as they are read, for example, wink, wink, wink; hop, hop, hop.
3. Have the class think of other action words the class can do.
4. Choose a volunteer to stand in front of the class. Have the student pantomime the action and say the action word as he or she does it. Have the rest of the class say the word aloud and do the action.
5. Choose a new student and repeat the step above.

Action words from story: wink, hop, wiggle, touch, close, stand

To project a book in the classroom, go to the online Activity Menu and then follow this path:

1. Reading Lessons — Click on **Reading Lessons**

2. 

Click on **Read-Along Books**

3. 

Click on the desired book cover

4. 

Choose **Listen and Read**

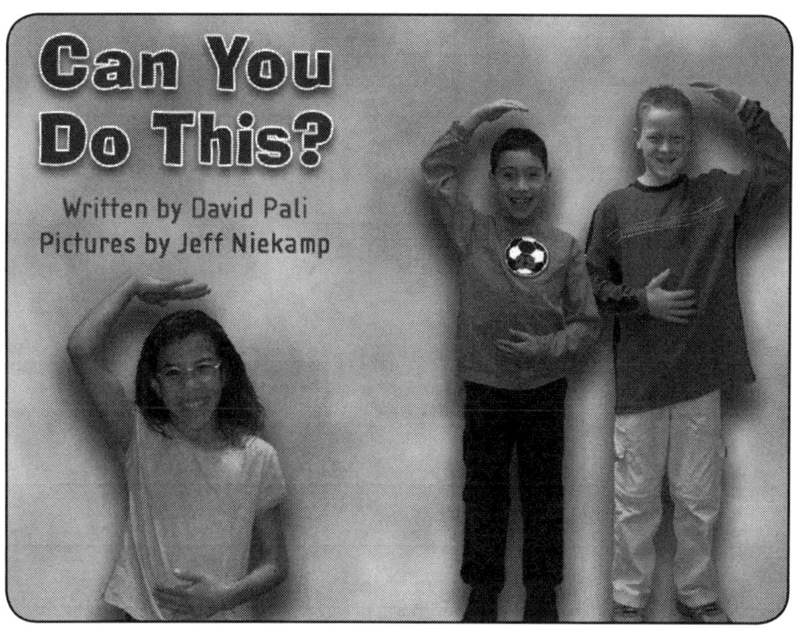

Can You Do This?

Can you close one eye?

Can you wiggle your nose?

Can you stand on one foot?

Can you touch your toes?

Can you do all four things at one time?
Try it.

You look funny!

Can you touch your nose with your thumb?

Can you touch your nose with your tongue?
Try it.

You look really funny!

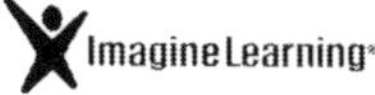

Vocabulary

Sometimes I Feel Happy

CCSS. K.5.C
TEKS 110.11.8.B

LEARNING OBJECTIVE: Use words to describe emotions.
LANGUAGE OBJECTIVE: Use emotion words to talk about feelings.

Activity Overview

Read a story and use words to express emotion.

Materials	Preparation
• *New Baby!* Read-Along Book	• Consider projecting *New Baby* using the instructions below.

Explain

Introduce the activity: ***We are going to read a story and talk about words in the story that help us talk about how we are feeling.***

Read *New Baby!* to the class. Discuss the "feeling" words in the story (*silly, sad, happy, bad, friendly, mad, glad*).

Plays

1. Say the words one at a time (*silly, sad, happy, bad, friendly, mad, glad*), pausing after each word to have the students practice saying the word. Have students help you choose an action they can perform for each word.
2. Have students stand up. Read the story again and pause after every feeling word to allow students to pantomime the action.
3. Repeat the story. As students become more adept at pantomiming, read the story progressively faster.

EXTENSION ACTIVITY: Have students share a time when they have felt one of the emotions from the story.

To project a book in the classroom, go to the online Activity Menu and then follow this path:

1. Reading Lessons — Click on **Reading Lessons**
2. read-along Read-Along Books — Click on **Read-Along Books**
3. Moving — Click on the desired book cover
4. Listen and Read — Choose **Listen and Read**

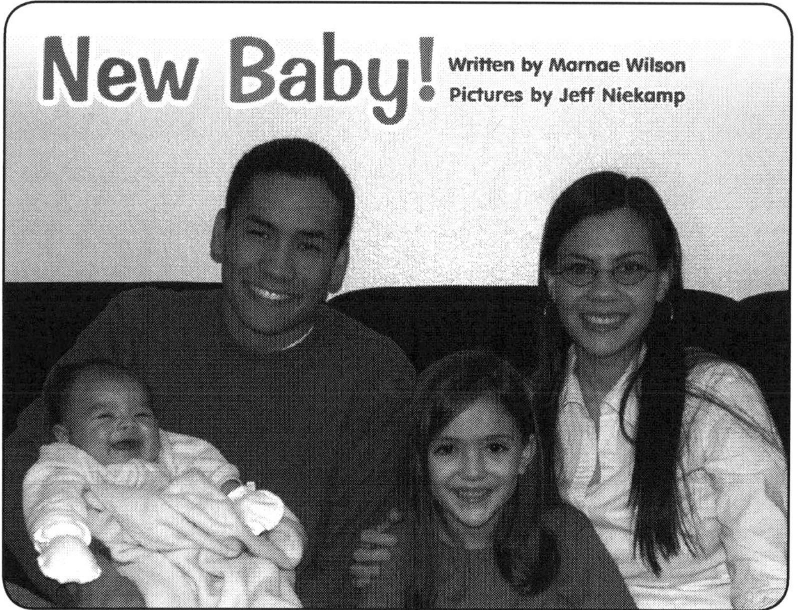

New Baby!

Everything's crazy!

We have a new baby!

Sometimes I feel silly.

Sometimes I feel sad.

Sometimes I feel happy.

Sometimes I feel bad.

Sometimes I feel friendly.

Sometimes I feel mad.

But then I hold my brother,

and I feel glad.

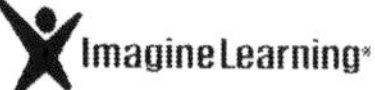

My Own Monster

CCSS.L.K.6
TEKS 110.11.5.C

LEARNING OBJECTIVE: Use vocabulary about the parts of the body and numbers 1–10.
LANGUAGE OBJECTIVE: Use the numbers 1–10 and parts of the body to talk about monsters.

Activity Overview

Review parts of the body and follow directions to draw a monster.

Materials	Preparation
• Parts of the Body Nouns Flash Cards (optional) • My Own Monster printout (1 per student) • crayons	• Cut out Parts of a Body Nouns Flash Cards (at the end of the Classroom Activities section).

Explain

Introduce the activity: ***We are going to learn about parts of the body and then make a monster. I'm going to give you instructions about what to draw. For example, the monster has three eyes. Then we'll see what your monsters look like. Let's review the parts of the body first.***

Review body parts vocabulary with students. Have students say each body part aloud while pointing to their own head, hands, arms, legs, feet, hair, eyes, ears, mouth, and nose. Alternatively, use the Noun Flash Cards of body parts to review the words.

Play

Use the My Own Monster printout, or have students draw two connecting circles on a piece of paper (one for the head of the monster, and one for the body).

1. Have students follow your directions to draw the parts of a body on their monster. Starting with the head, describe a monster with multiple parts of a body. Say: ***The monster has three noses***, or ***The monster has big feet***, and so on. Repeat each detail twice, then allow students time to draw it before going to the next description.
2. If time allows, have students color their monsters.
3. Call on volunteers to show and tell about their monsters, using the target vocabulary.
4. Have a discussion about what is the same or different about the monsters created by the students, for example: ***This monster has three eyes, but one of his eyes is on his arm.*** Display monster pictures in the classroom.

Name

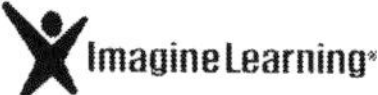

Word Scramble

CCSS.L.K.1B
TEKS 110.11.16.A.ii

LEARNING OBJECTIVE: Build fluency and recognition of vocabulary words.
LANGUAGE OBJECTIVE: Confirm understanding of new words and produce words distinctly.

Activity Overview

Play a game to review basic vocabulary.

Materials	Preparation
• Index cards or Noun Flash Cards (1 per student)	• Write 4–8 vocabulary words on index cards to make flash cards, or cut out Noun Flash Cards (at the end of the Classroom Activities section). Make copies of flash cards so that each word is given to 3–5 students.

Explain

Introduce the activity: ***We are going to play a game with words. First, let's review them.***

Show each flash card. Have all students repeat the word several times. Continue until all words have been reviewed. Add engagement as needed by having students repeat words in a variety of ways. For example, have students whisper the word, say it in a low or high voice, say it to their neighbor, clap the syllables as they say it, etc.

Say: ***You will each be assigned a word. One of you will stand in the middle of the circle. When your word is called, you have to switch chairs.***

Play

1. Place the flash cards so all students can see them for reference.
2. Have students put their chairs in a circle and sit down.
3. Assign a vocabulary flash card to each student.
4. Quickly confirm assignments by saying each word and having the students who were assigned that word stand up.
5. Start the game by having a student stand in the middle of the circle. Take his or her chair out of the circle so you have one less chair than the total number of students.
6. Have the student in the middle of the circle call out one of the words. (The student cannot call out his or her own word.)
7. Students assigned to that word hurry to exchange seats. At the same time, the student in the middle tries to sit in an empty chair.
8. The student left without a chair goes into the center of the circle to begin the next round.
9. If the student in the middle calls out "Scramble!" instead of a vocabulary word, everyone must change chairs.

Vocabulary

Word Search

CCSS.L.K.1B
TEKS 110.11.16.A.ii

LEARNING OBJECTIVE: Practice vocabulary words and directional words.
LANGUAGE OBJECTIVE: Use directional vocabulary to play a searching game.

Activity Overview

Play a game to practice vocabulary words and directional words..

Materials	Preparation
• Index cards or Noun Flash Cards	• Write 10–15 vocabulary words on index cards to make flash cards, or cut out Noun Flash Cards (at the end of the Classroom Activities section).

Explain

Introduce the activity: ***There are words we can use to give someone directions on which way to go or which way to look. If you know them, show me. Which way is up?*** Have students point and then repeat the word *up*. ***Which way is down?*** Have students point and repeat. ***Which way is left? Which way is right?***

Say: ***Now show me these words: Take a step* forward.** Have students point and repeat *forward*. ***Take one step* backward.** Have students point and repeat *backward*.

Say: ***We're going to hide a flash card in the room and have someone find it. As the person is looking, we can say direction words to help. Remember, we can't tell the person where the card is, but we can use any of our direction words to help him or her find it. For example, we can tell the person to look up or down, right or left, or to go forward or backward.***

Play

1. Choose a vocabulary flash card.
2. Review the word with students a few times. Have students repeat the word.
3. Have one student step out of the classroom as you quickly hide the card.
4. Have the student come back in and begin looking for the card.
5. Have the other students in the class give clues using directional words.
6. After the student has found the card, have the class repeat the word and then choose a new one to hide.

VARIATION: Divide the class into two teams and assign each team a side of the room. Send out a student from each team. Hide two cards, one on each side of the room. Have the teams give directions to the player from their team and race to see who can find the card first.

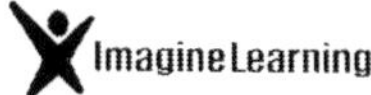

Sort Them Out

CCSS.L.K.5.A
TEKS 110.12.6.D

LEARNING OBJECTIVE: Put nouns into categories.
LANGUAGE OBJECTIVE: Talk about the features of nouns in categories.

Activity Overview

Students sort items into categories to review vocabulary.

Materials	Preparation
• Sorting Cards (1 set per student) • Construction paper (3 sheets per student) • glue	• Cut out the Sorting Cards and column headers. Put each student's set in a sandwich bag or use a paper clip to keep cards together.

Explain

Introduce the activity: ***A good way to learn new words is to sort them into groups.*** Introduce the concept of categories by writing the three category words on the board: animals, people, and food. Name a noun and have students tell you which category it belongs to. Have students brainstorm more words that could go under each category.

Give each student a set of noun cards. Say: ***You each have your own set of noun cards. We have a lot of noun cards here! Let's sort them into groups.***

Play

1. Have students glue each category label to separate pieces of construction paper.
2. Have students sort and glue each word picture under the label it matches.
3. Have students compare their finished pages to a partner's pages.
4. Have students talk about how they created the categories.

Animals 

People 

Food 

police officer

giraffe

sandwich

lion

grapes

diver

rhinoceros

farmer

pie

carrots
fireman
whale
pear
monkey
chef

Vocabulary

Animal Bingo

CCSS.L.K.1B
TEKS 110.11.16.A.ii

LEARNING OBJECTIVE: Practice fluency with animal vocabulary cards.
LANGUAGE OBJECTIVE: Play a game to review animal vocabulary.

Activity Overview

Play animal bingo to review basic vocabulary.

Materials	Preparation
• Bingo Cards (1 per student) • Animal Noun Flash Cards • Bingo card place markers	• Cut out Bingo Cards. • Cut out Animal Noun Flash Cards (at the end of the Classroom Activities section).

Explain

Introduce the activity: ***We are going to play Animal Bingo. First, let's review.*** Use the Animal Noun Flash Cards to review animals with students: bird, cat, dog, duck, fish, chicken, cow, horse, pig, sheep, etc. For variety, have students do an action or sound for each animal.

Play

1. Give each student a bingo card and a set of place markers.
2. Call out an animal. Students with a picture of the animal on their Bingo Card put their fingers on the picture and call out the animal's name. Then they place a marker over the square.
3. Have students call out "Bingo!" when they have all the squares in a row are covered. Rows can be made horizontally, vertically, or diagonally.
4. Have students that shout "Bingo!" name each of the animals in their winning row.

VARIATION: Play again, but this time tell students they must cover all the squares on the card. Have students call out "Black Out!" when all their squares are covered.

FREE
FREE

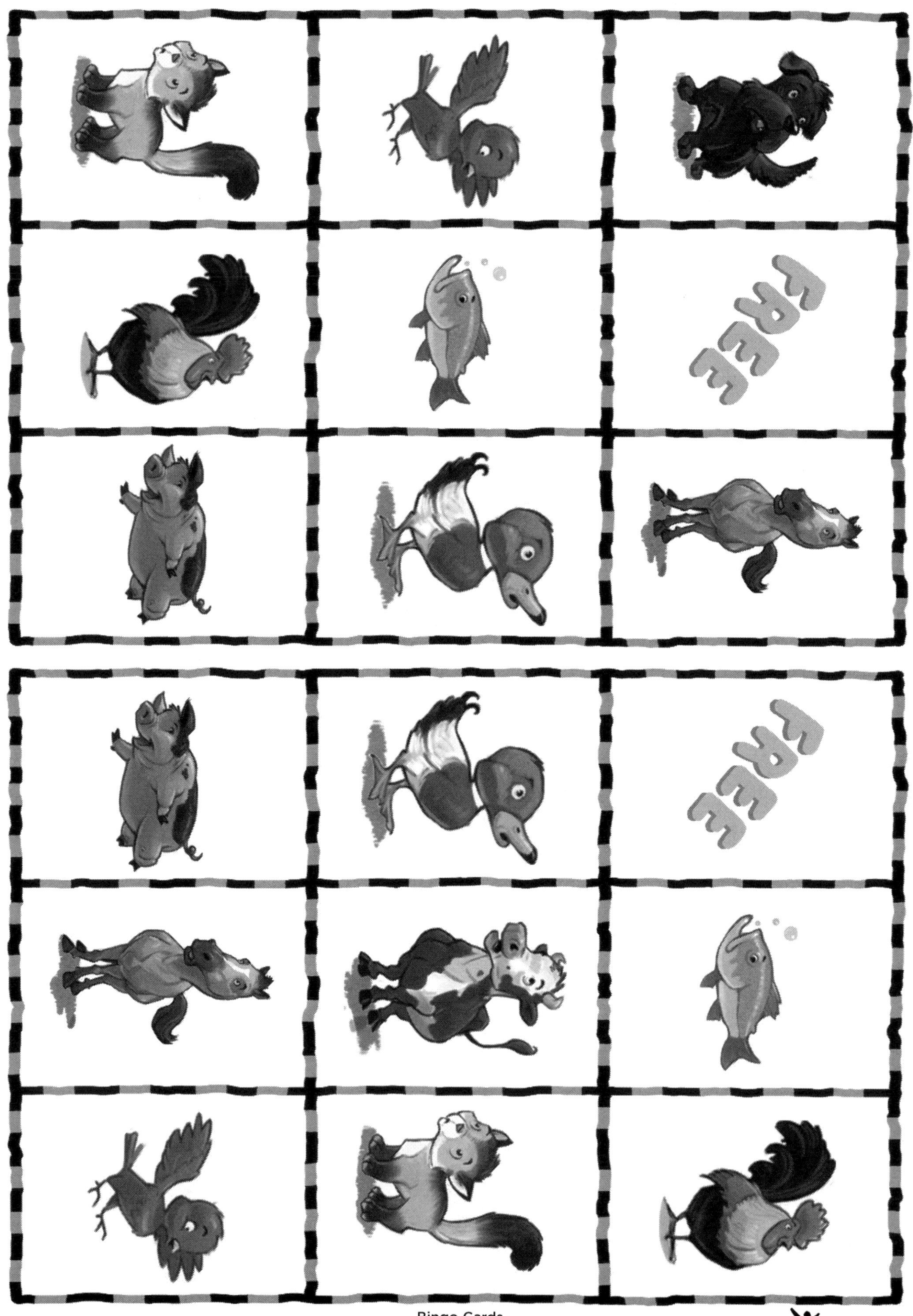

Bingo Cards

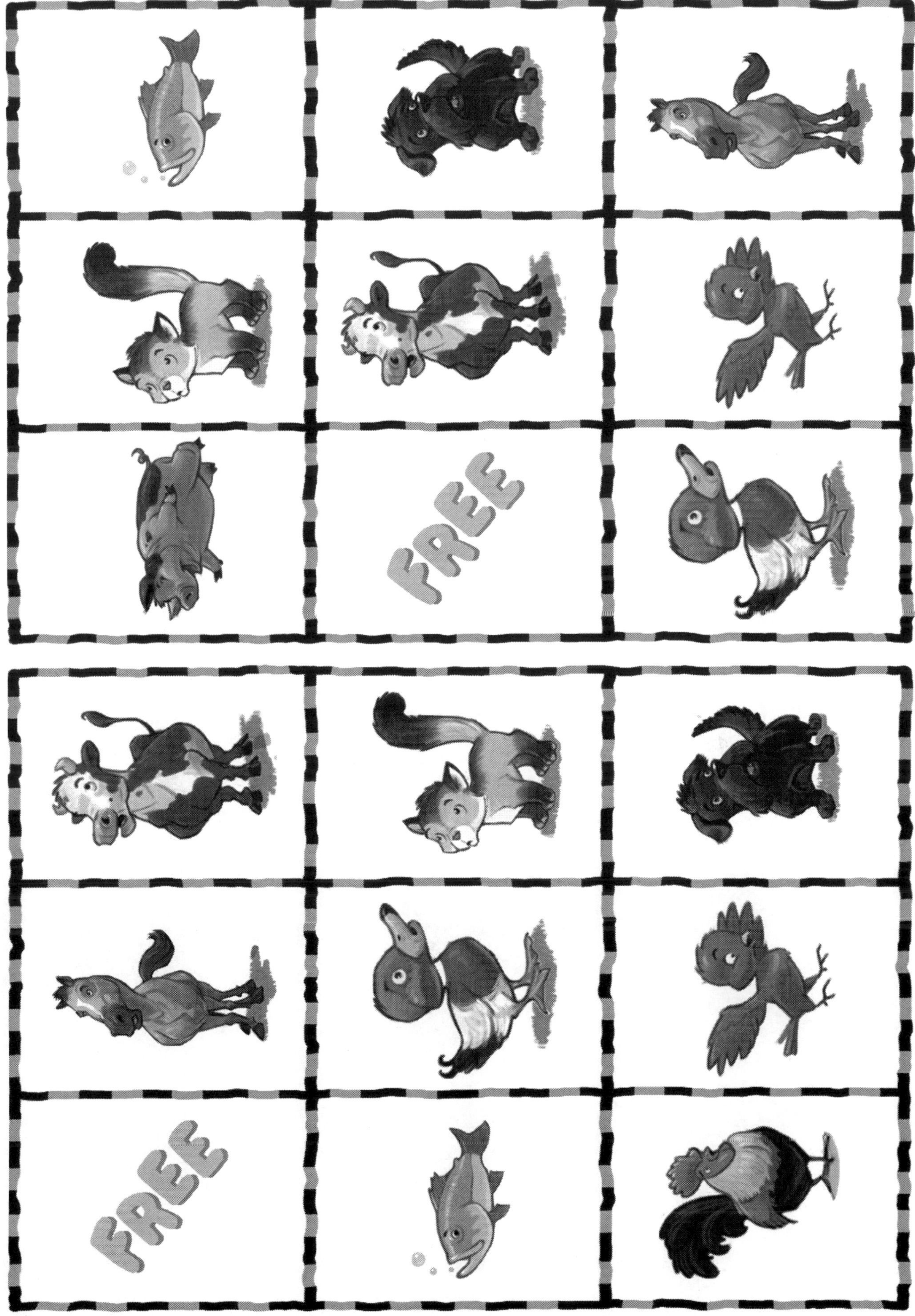
FREE
FREE

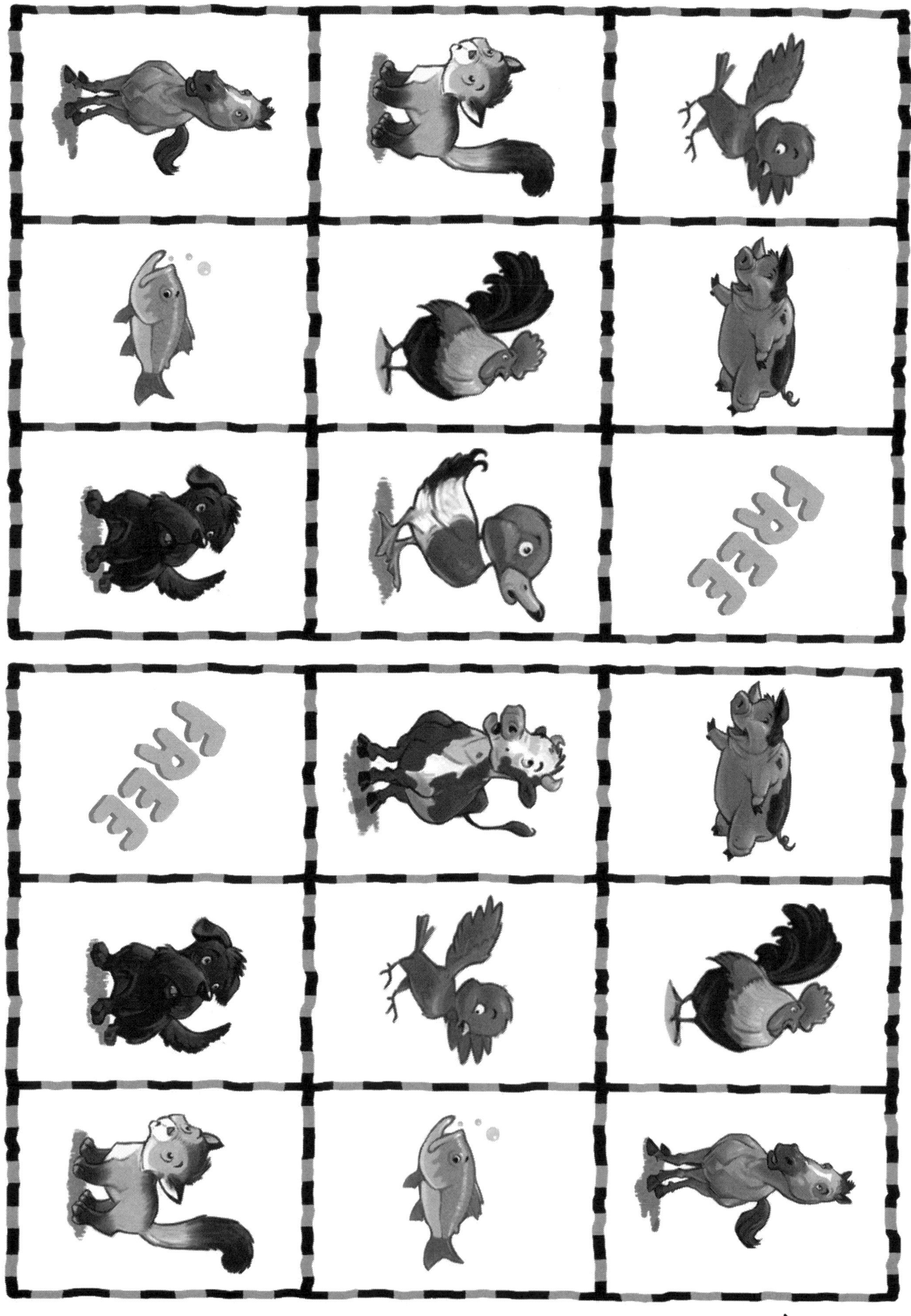
FREE
FREE

FREE
FREE

Bingo Cards

Bingo Cards

FREE
FREE

FREE

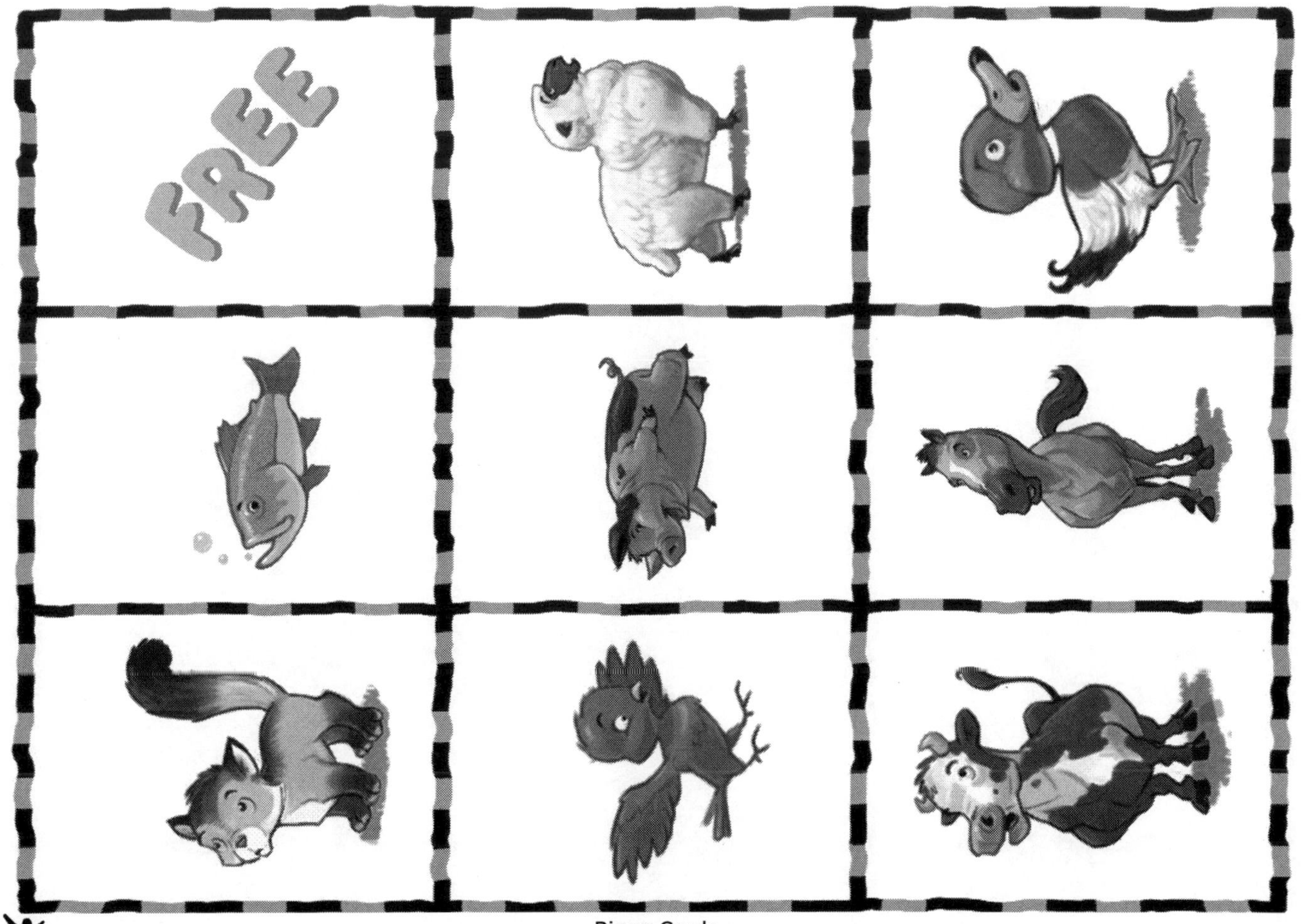

FREE

Bingo Cards

FREE

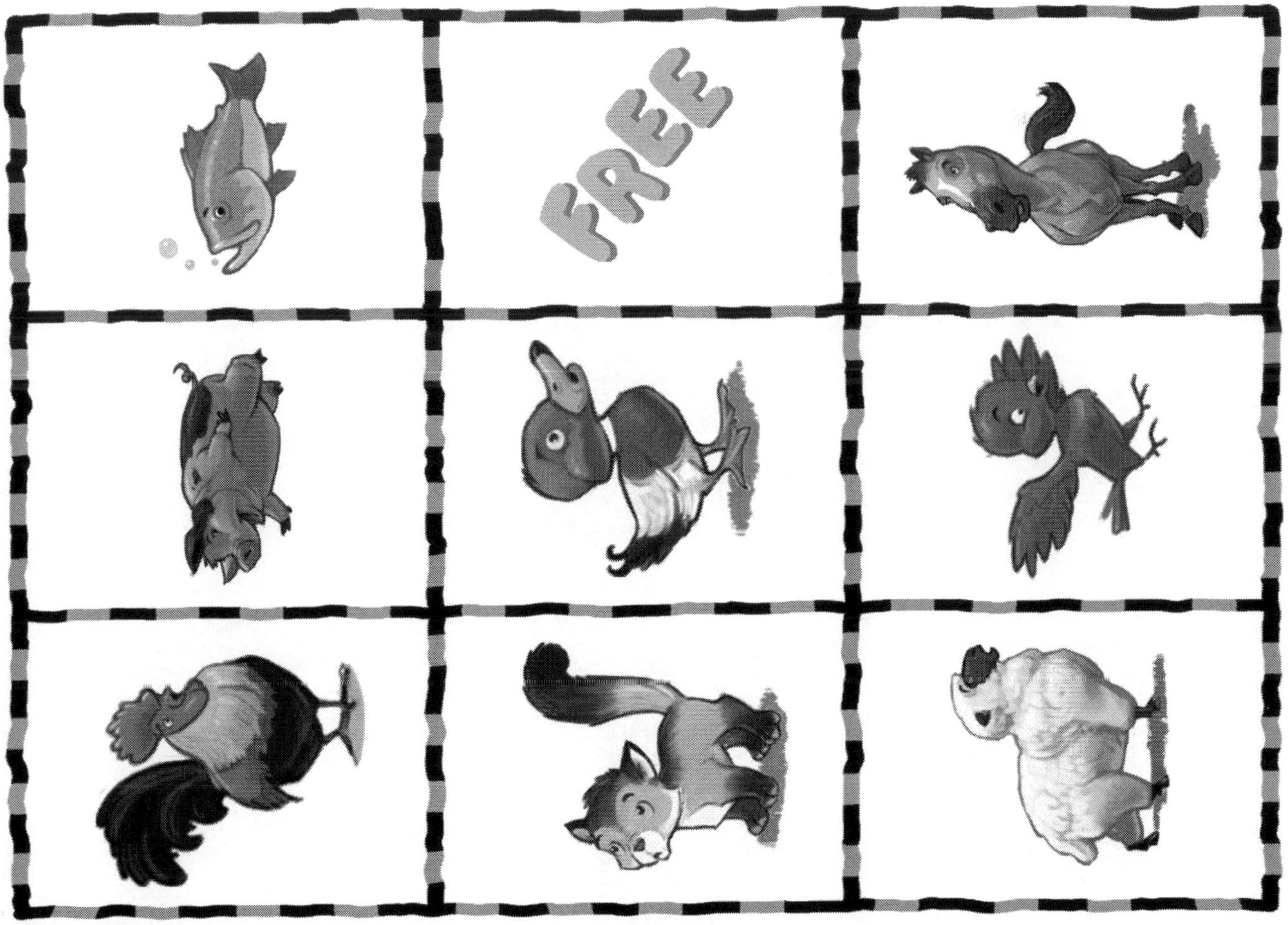

FREE

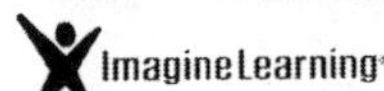

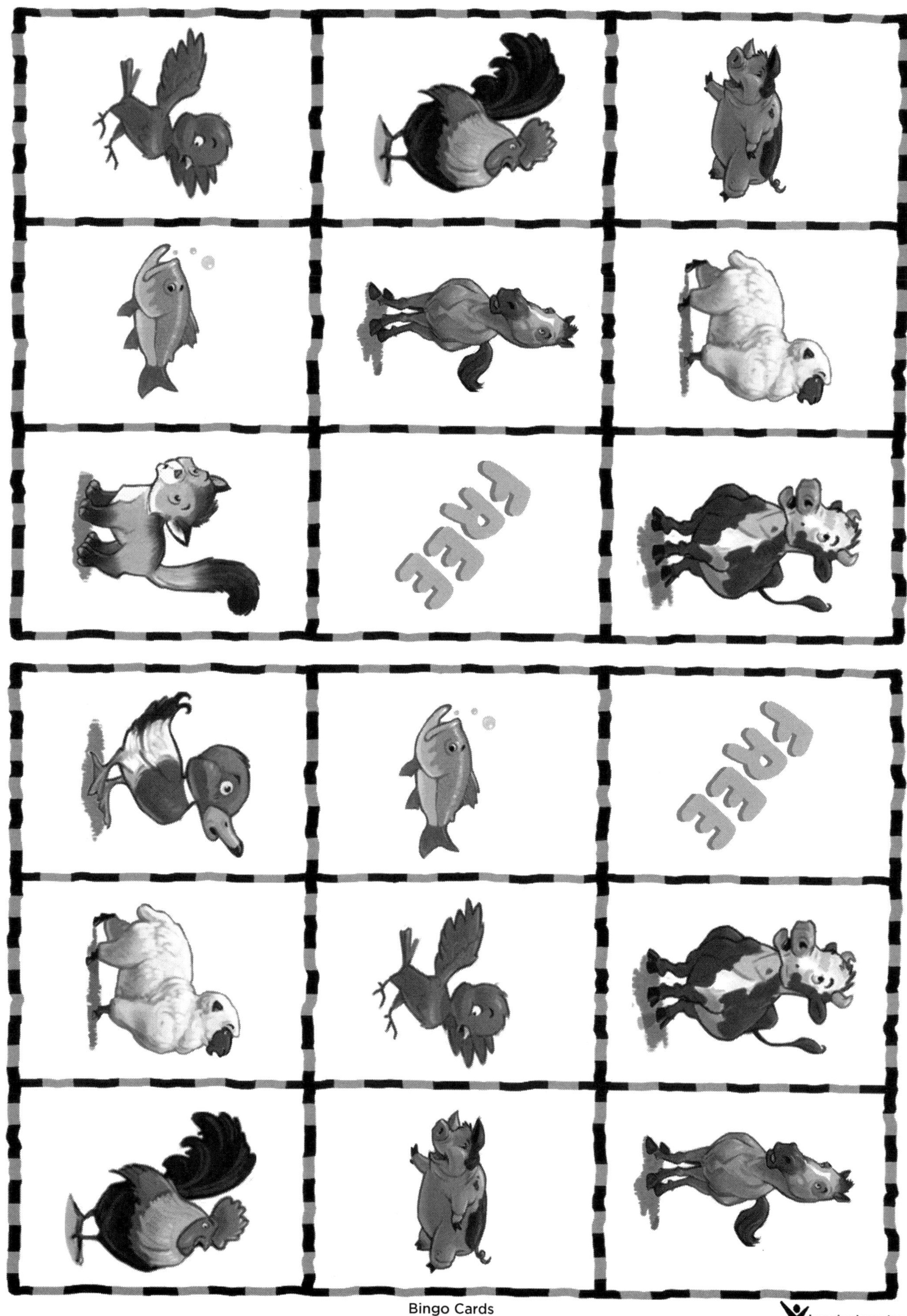
FREE
FREE

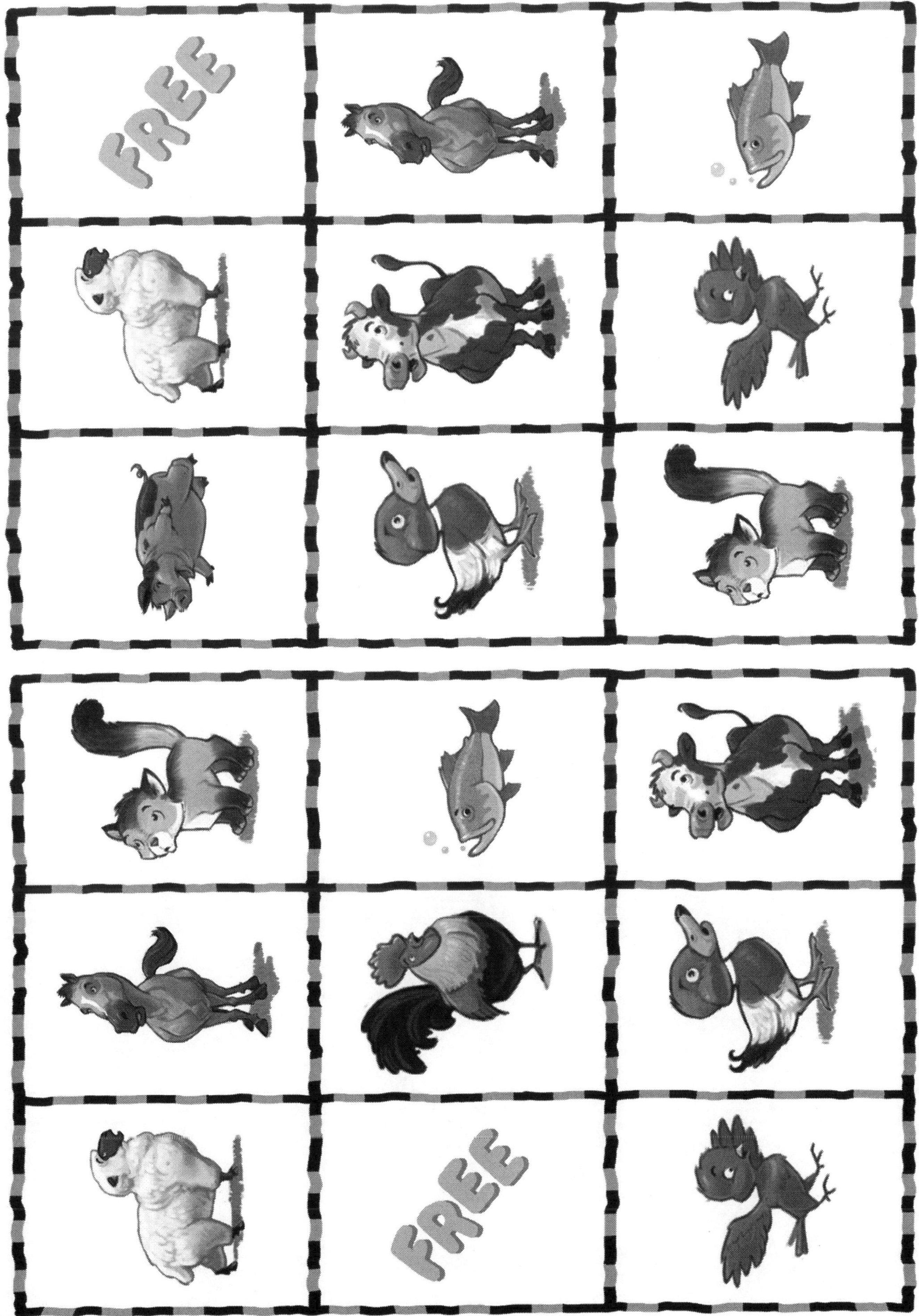
FREE
FREE

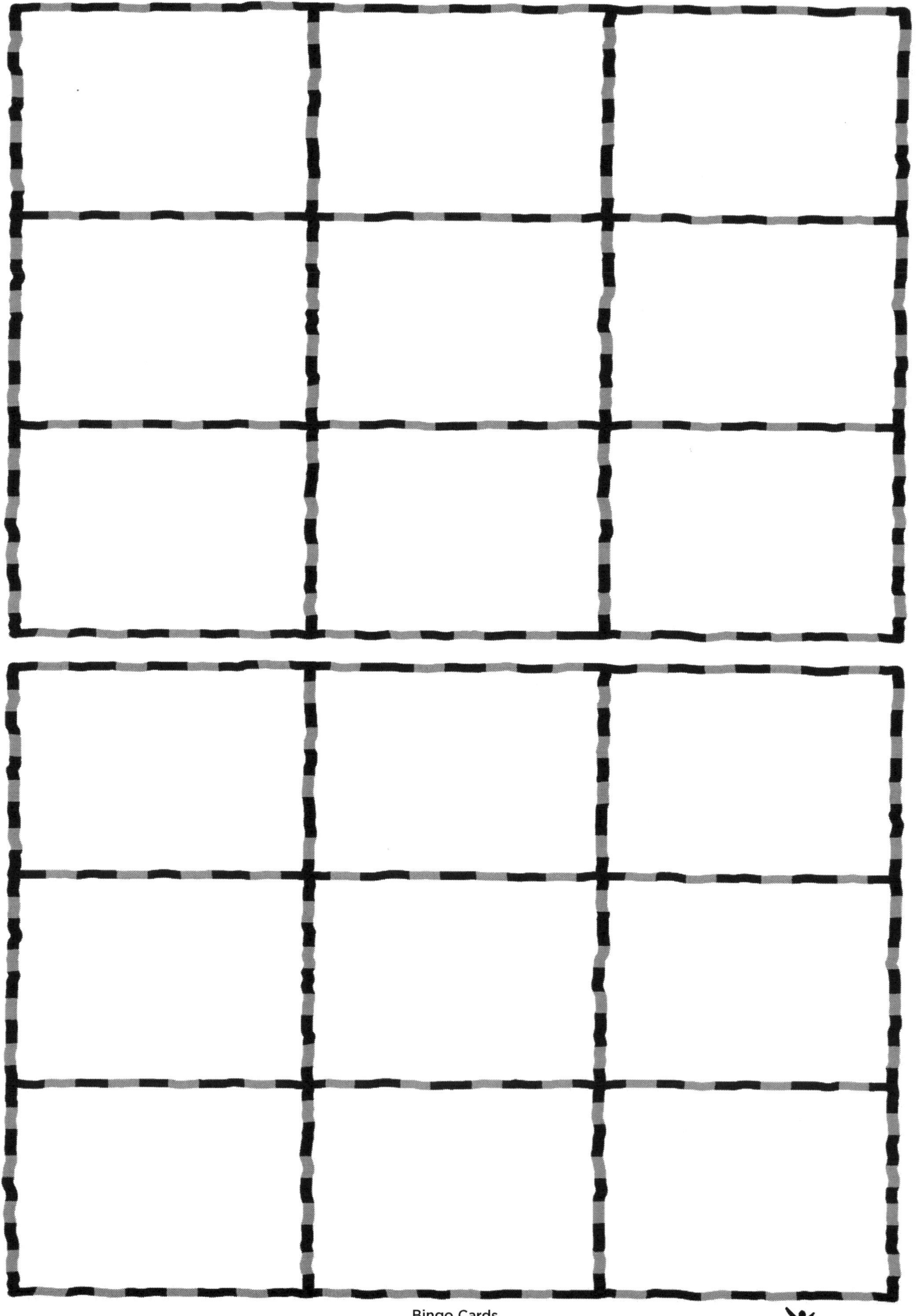

Vocabulary Scenes & Noun Flash Cards Guide

Resource Overview

Each Vocabulary Scene shows five vocabulary words within the context of an illustrated scene. The 25 scenes help students practice Imagine Learning's basic vocabulary words from the following categories:

Animals	Things on a Playground
Body Parts	Things that Go
Clothing	Wild Animals
Food	Landforms
People	Parts of a Book
Things in a Classroom	Places
Things in a House	Weather

Noun Flash Cards for each vocabulary word in the basic vocabulary categories, along with a category heading strip, are also included.

How to Use This Resource in the Classroom

- Have students review newly learned vocabulary by repeating the words and coloring the Vocabulary Scene that illustrates the words.
- Have students work in pairs to review words on Noun Flash Cards and match them with the objects in the Vocabulary Scenes.
- Use basic vocabulary to make simple statements about a Vocabulary Scene ("The man reads a book," or "The trash can is on the bench."). Some of the statements should be true and others should be obviously false. Have the students signal with thumbs up if they think the statement is true and thumbs down if they think the statement is false.
- Have students look at the Vocabulary Scene and say things about it. Decide beforehand whether only complete sentences are accepted or if students can use short phrases. For each correct statement, make a check mark on the board. See how many the class can think of in two minutes.
- Review the words in a Vocabulary Scene with students by pointing to the illustrations and having the students name the objects. Turn the scene over and have students recall objects and describe the scene from memory.
- Have students work in pairs to create a story about a Vocabulary Scene, making sure to include each vocabulary word in the story. Then regroup students so that each is paired with a new partner. Have students retell their stories to their new partner.
- Display a Vocabulary Scene and have students brainstorm adjective-noun combinations from the illustration (black dog, funny cow, etc.). As students suggest phrases, write them in two columns on the board with adjectives in the first column and nouns in the second column. After completing the lists, have students suggest different combinations (black cow, funny dog). Draw a line between the two words. See how many new combinations the class can make.
- Use the category heading strips that accompany the Noun Flash Cards and sort the flash cards into the categories. Use index cards to create new categories and sort vocabulary again. New categories could include: My Favorites, Things with Fur, Things That Fly, Things I Ate This Week, Things I See on My Way to School, etc.
- Choose four sets of Noun Flash Cards. Display the category heading strips and say them aloud to the students. Have students help you sort each noun card into one of the four categories. Then silently choose a word and have students ask yes/no questions to guess the word. Encourage them to begin by

discovering which category the word is in. After the class has guessed the word, remove the used word and have a student whisper to you a new word. Repeat the activity until all vocabulary words have been used.

- Display five Noun Flash Cards. Review the flash cards with students and have them repeat the nouns after you say them. Have students put their heads down or cover their eyes, then take one card away. Have students put their heads up and say which picture is missing. As students become more proficient, take two or three cards away. Choose five different Noun Flash Cards and repeat as time allows.

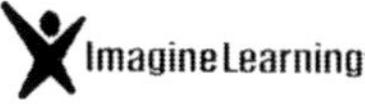

Name

Animals

duck

bird

fish

dog

cat

Name

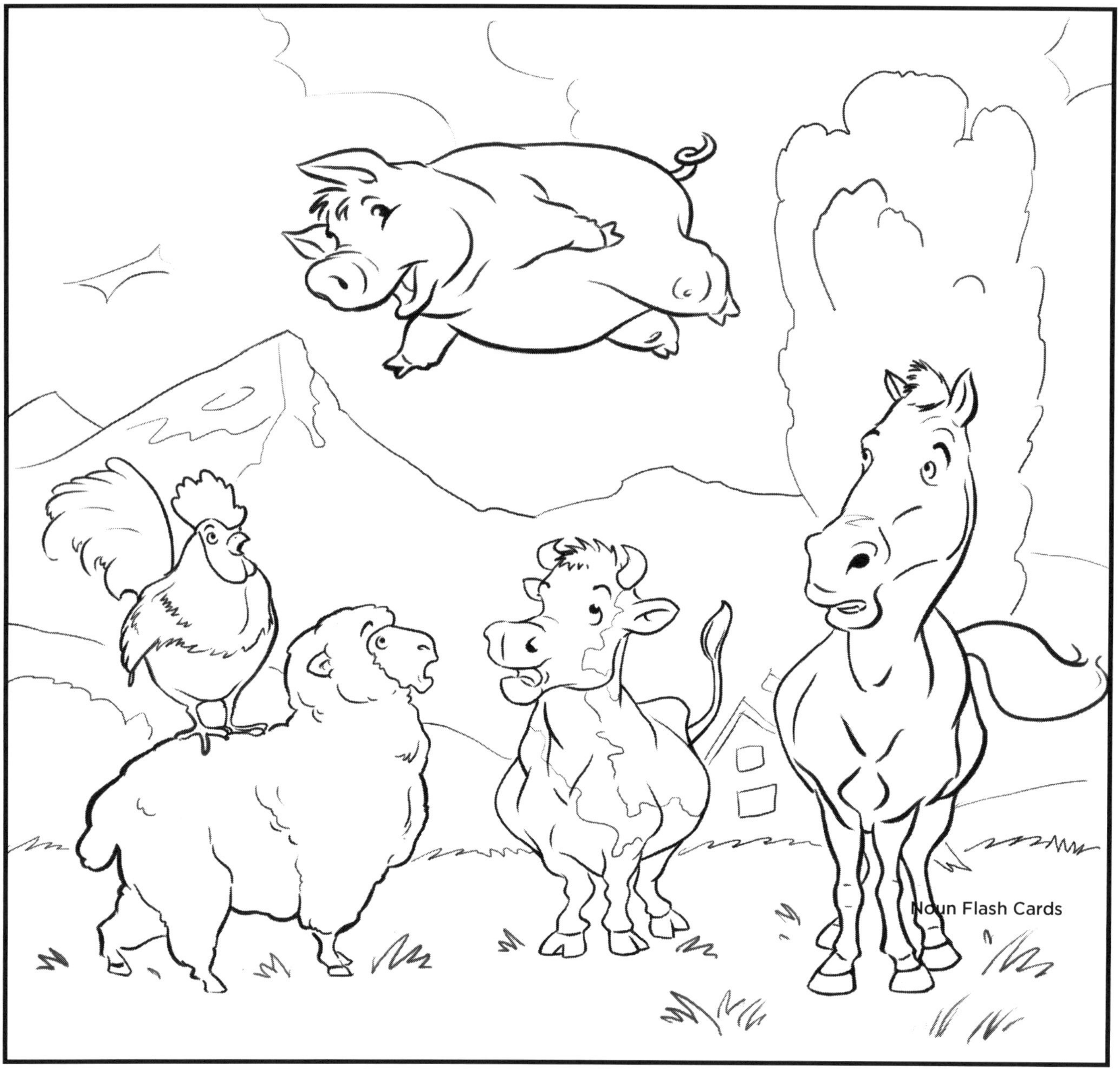
Noun Flash Cards

Animals

chicken

sheep

pig

cow

horse

Imagine Learning

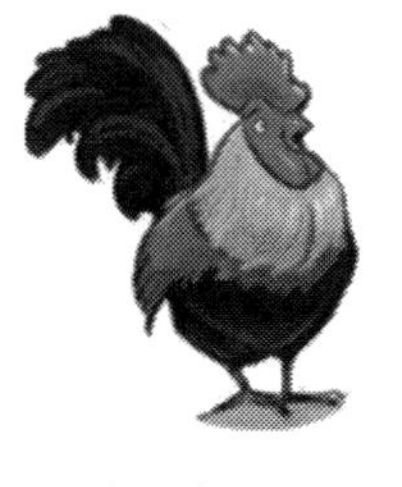

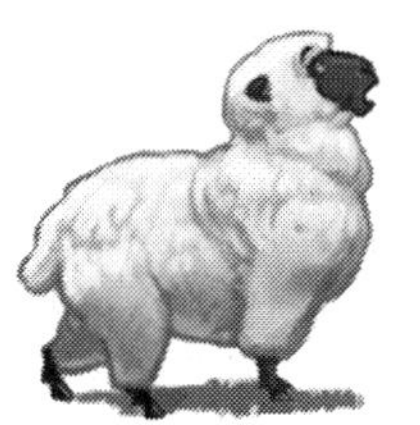

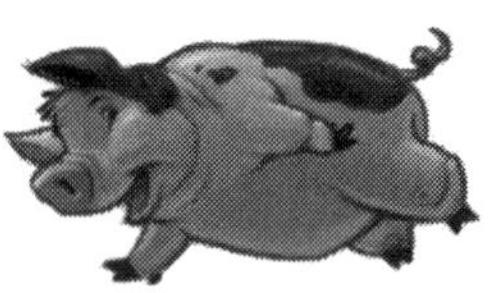

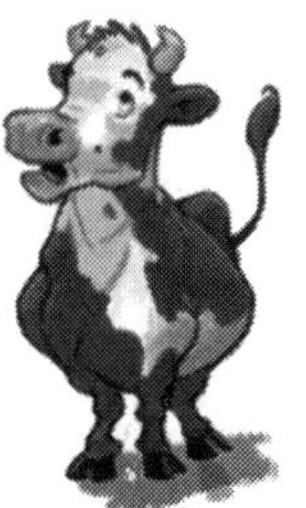

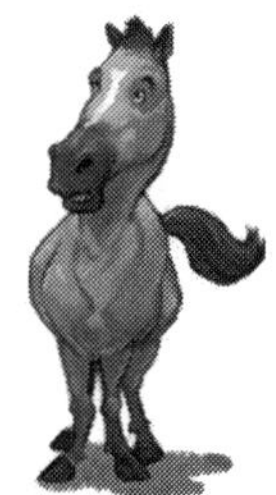

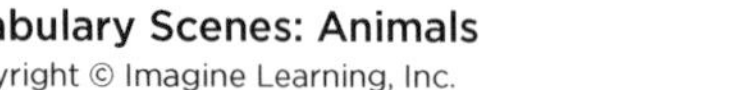

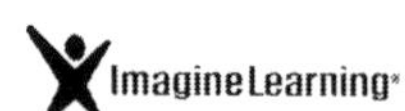

Animals

Category Heading Strip

bird

cat

dog

duck

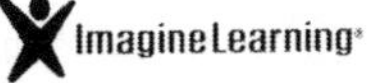

fish

chicken

cow

horse

pig

sheep

Name

Parts of a Body

head arms hands feet legs

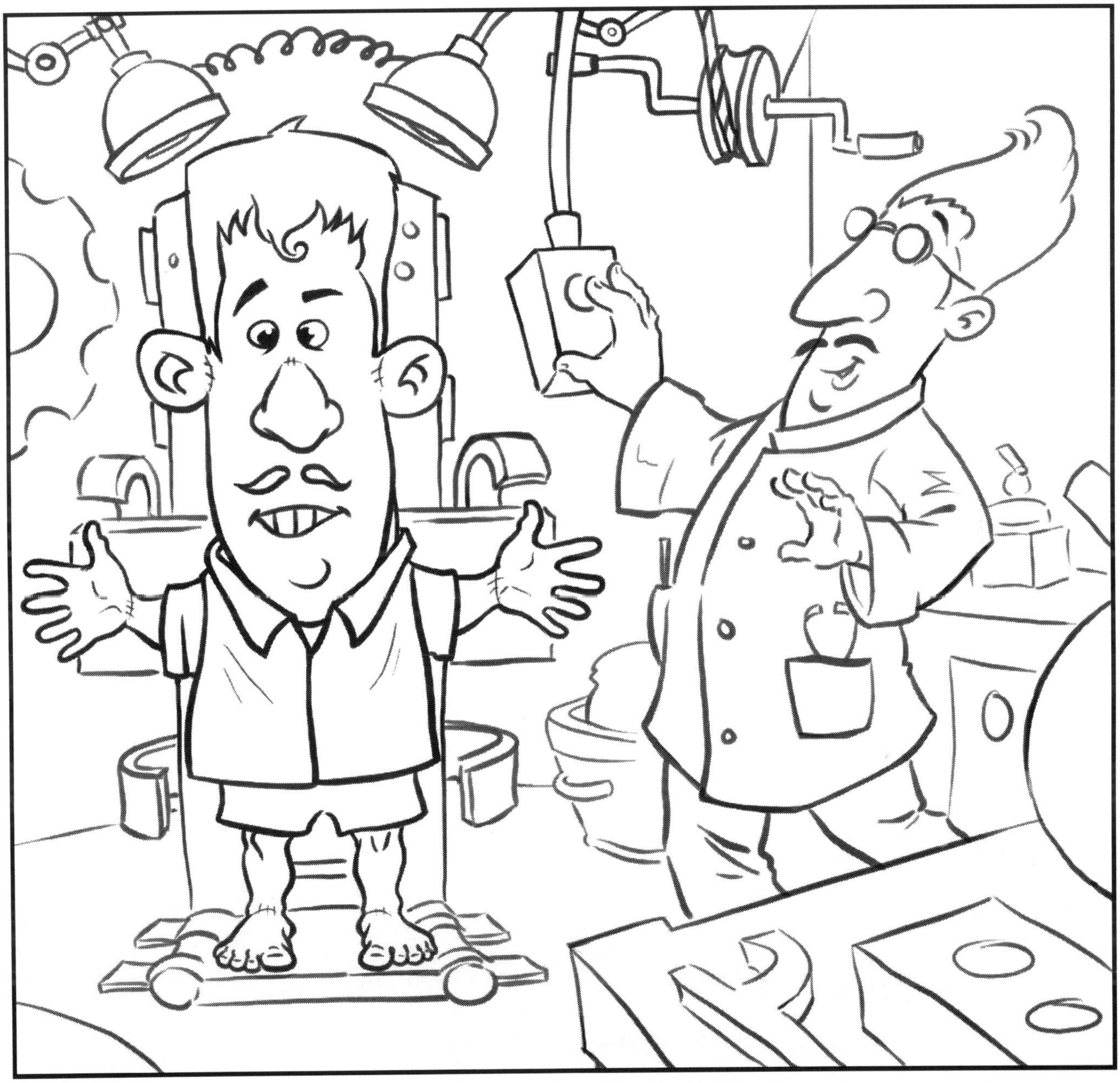

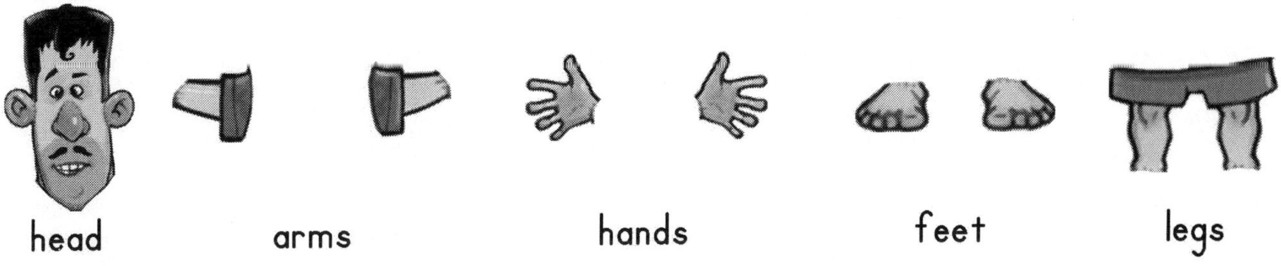

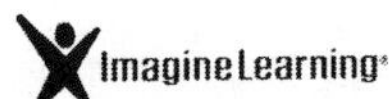

Name

Parts of a Body

shoulders

elbows

chin

eyebrow

fingers

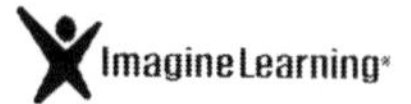

Name

Parts of a Body

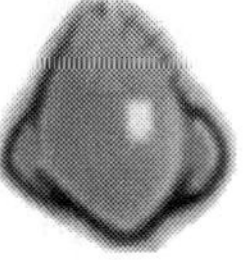

ears eyes hair mouth nose

Parts of a **Body**

Category Heading Strip

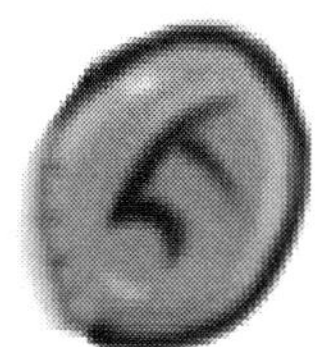

ears

eyes

hair

mouth

nose

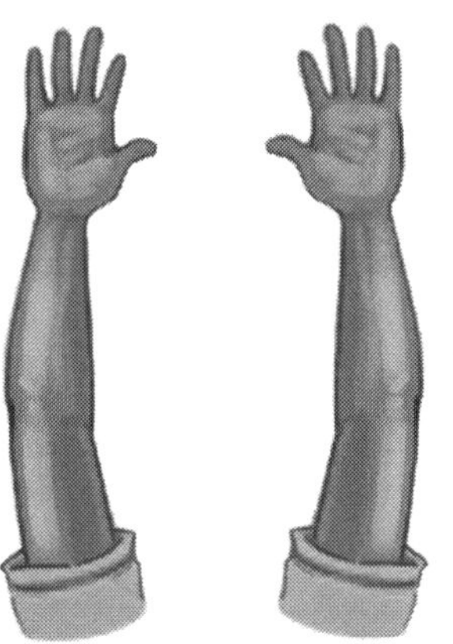

arms

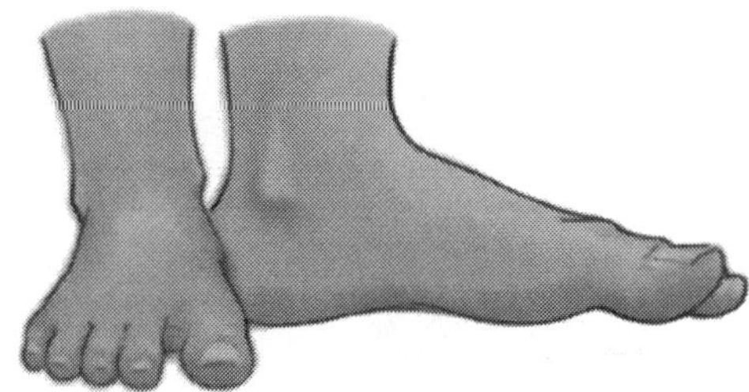

feet

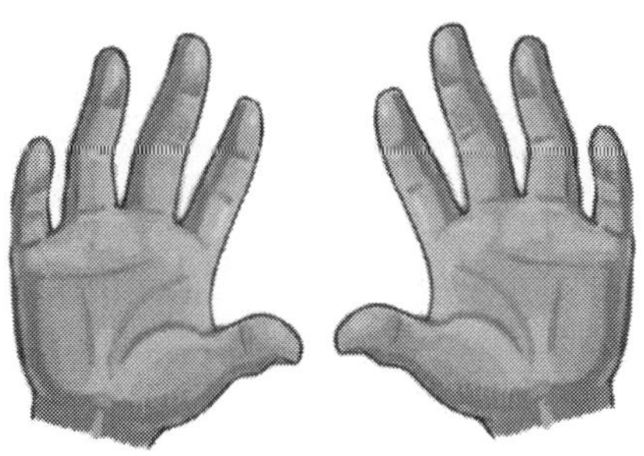

hands

head

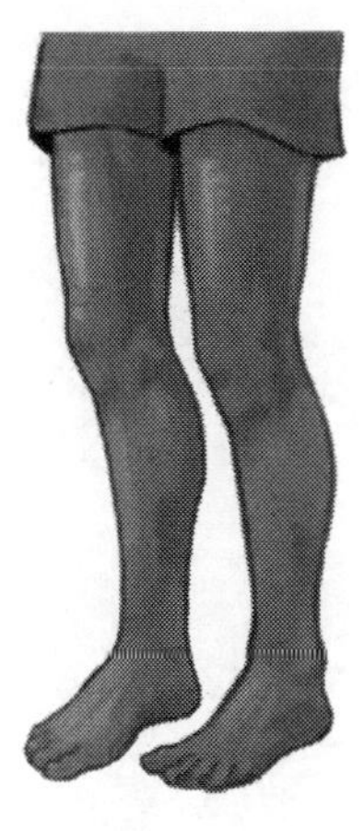

legs

chin

elbows

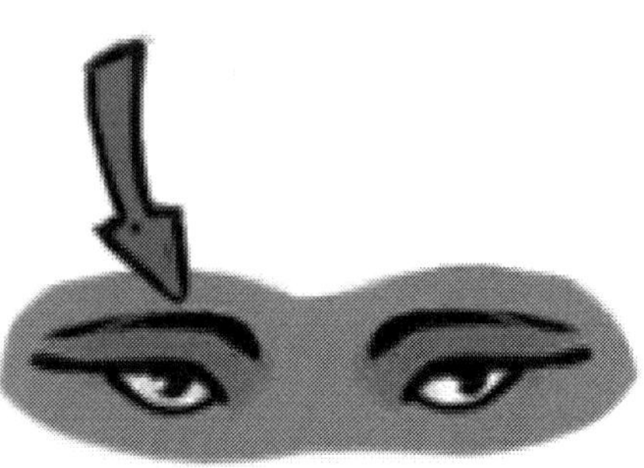

eyebrow

fingers

shoulders

Noun Flash Cards: Parts of a Body

Name

Clothing

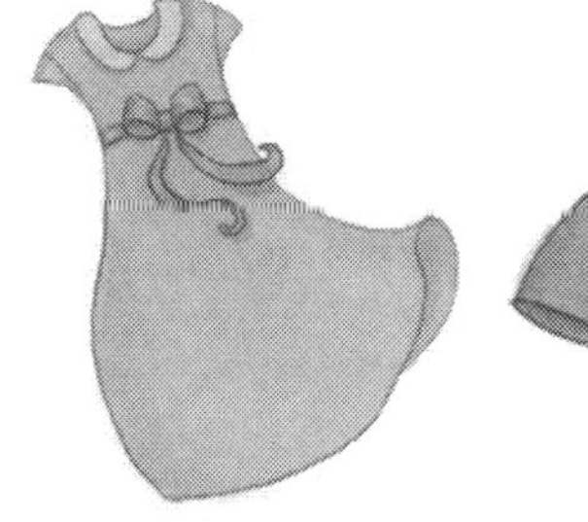

dress

shirt

pants

socks

shoes

Name

Clothing

pajamas sweater coat shorts hat

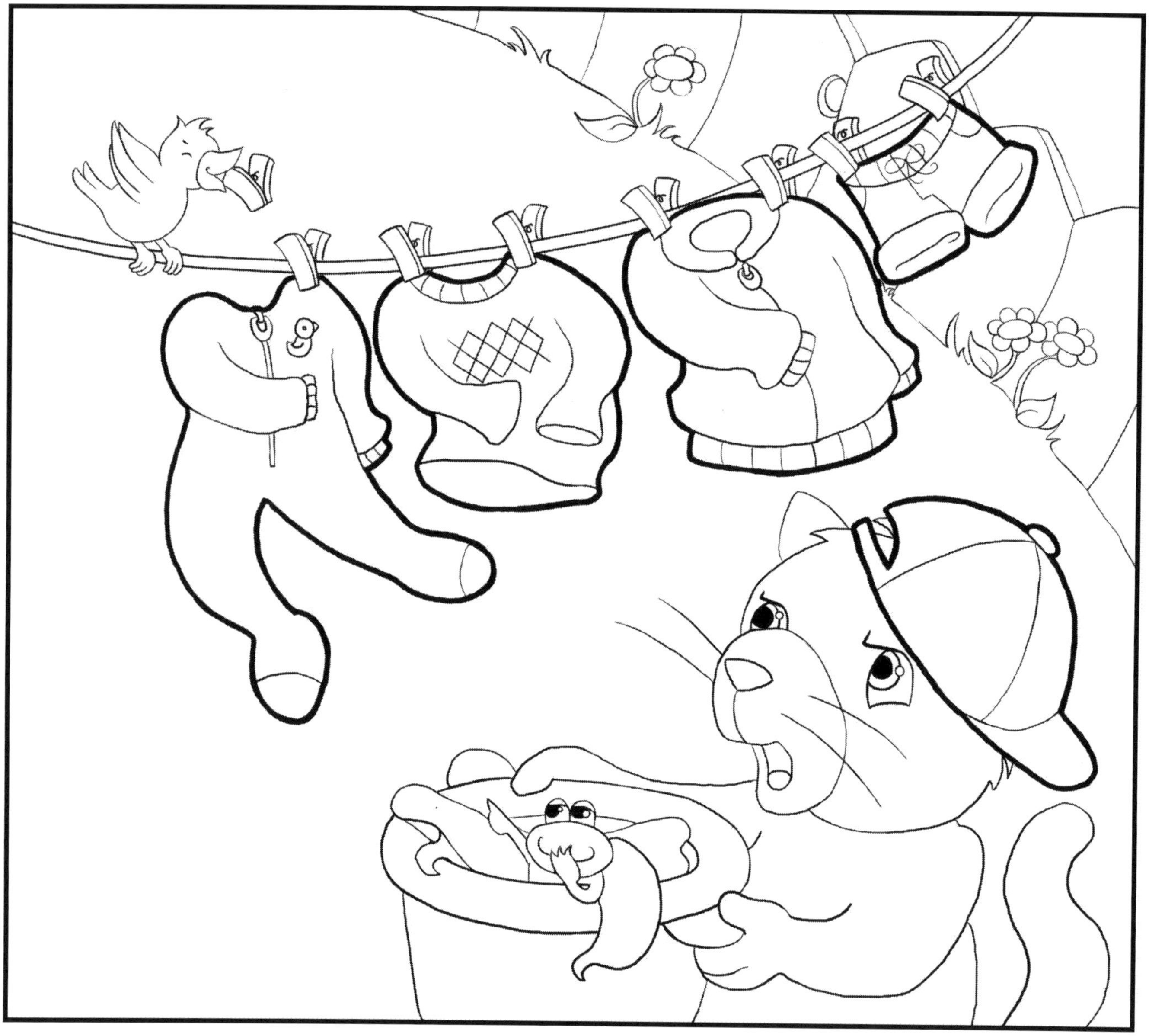

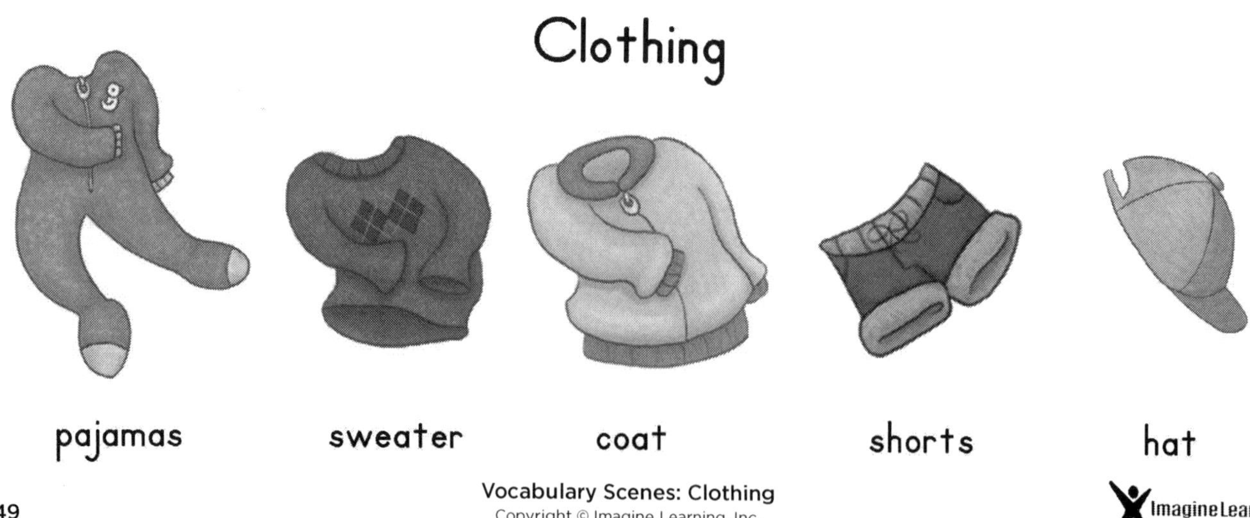

Clothing

Category Heading Strip

shirt

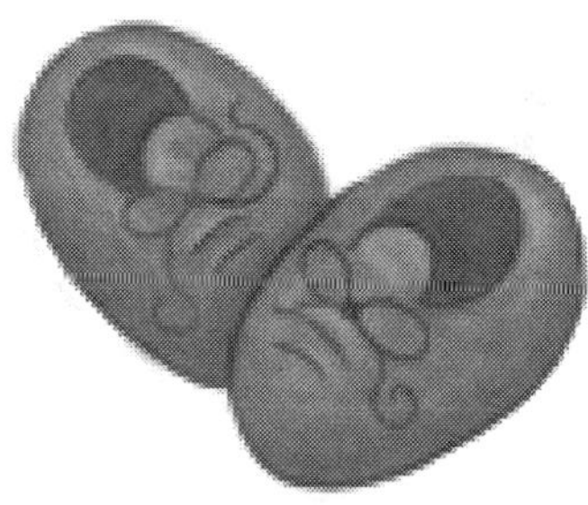

shoes

socks

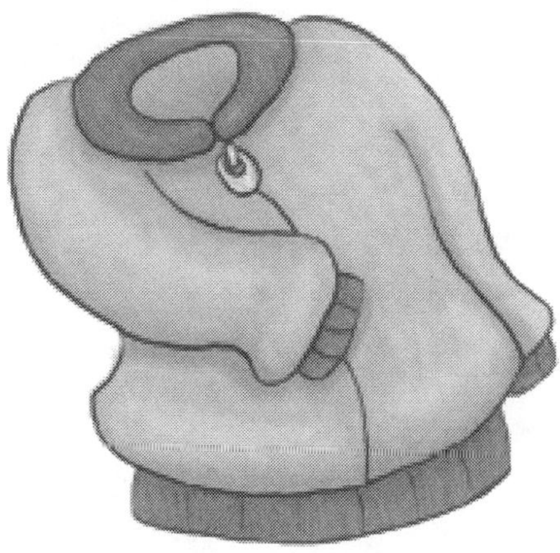

coat

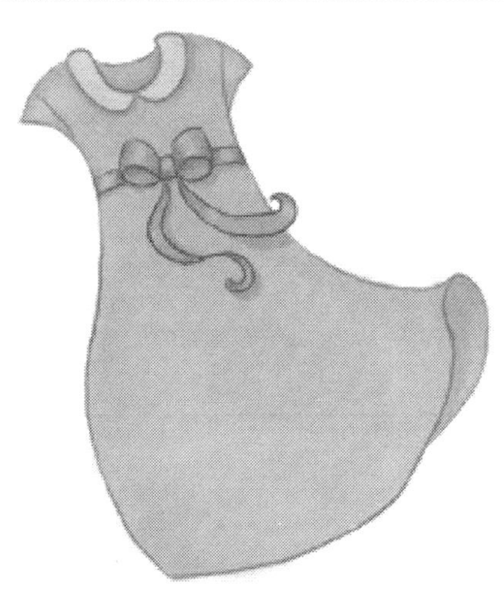

dress

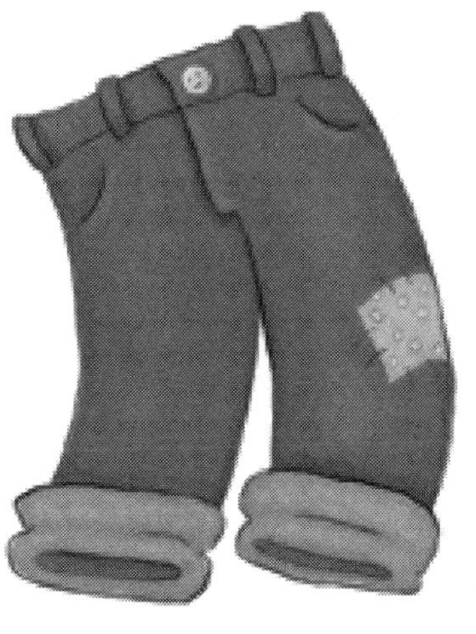

pants

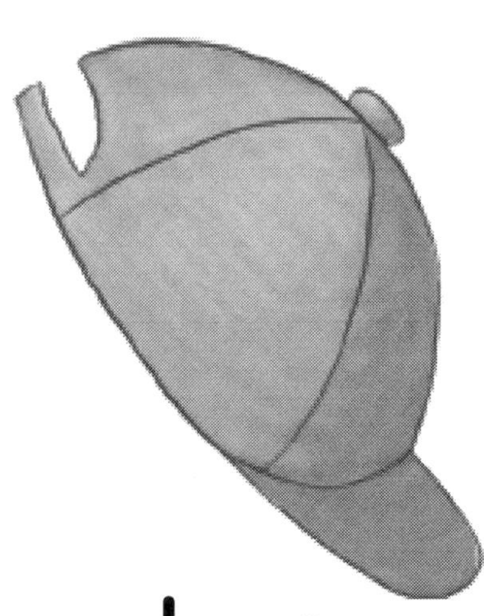

hat

pajamas

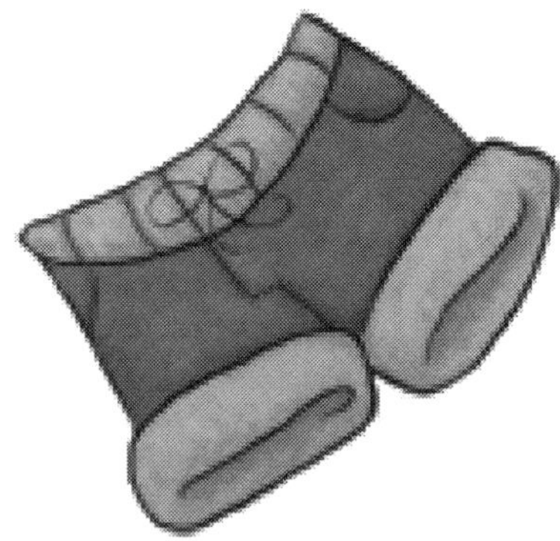

shorts

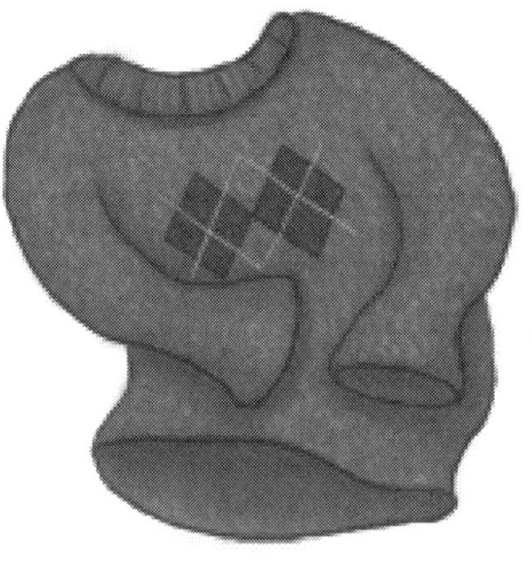

sweater

Name

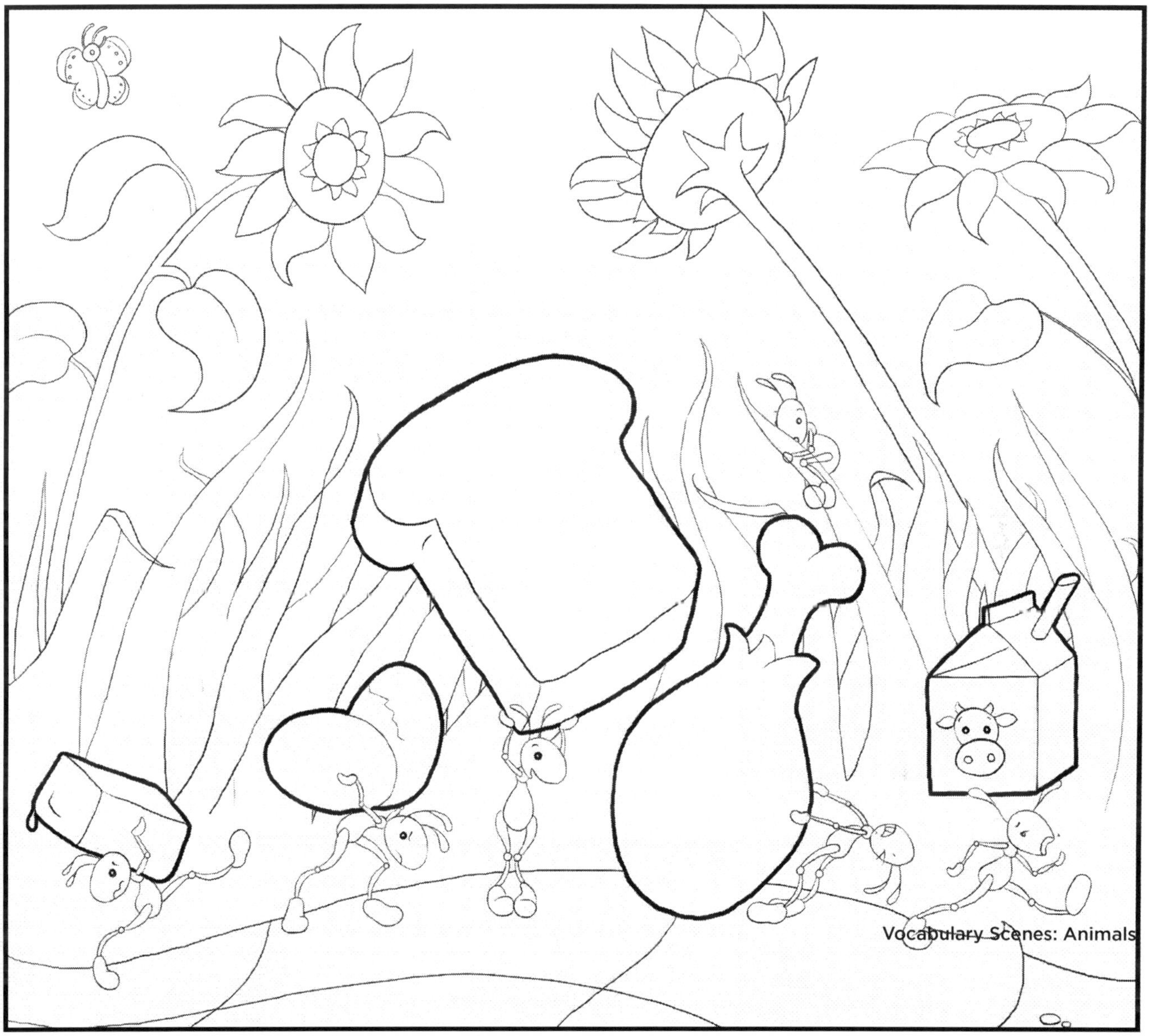
Vocabulary Scenes: Animals

Food

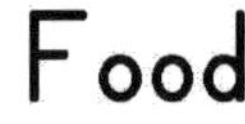

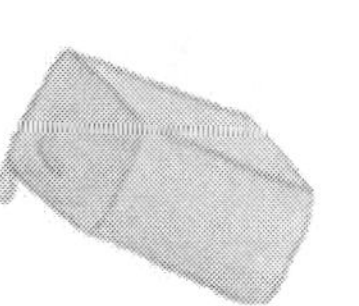

butter

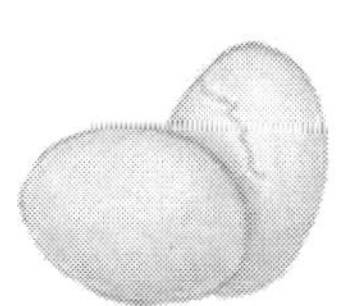

eggs

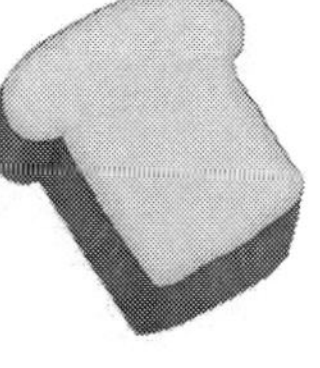

bread

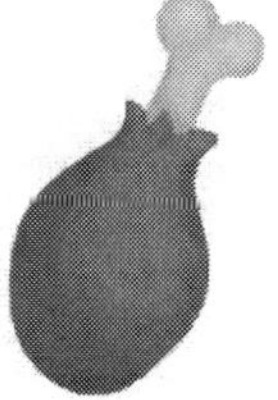

meat

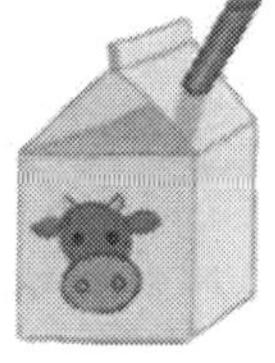

milk

Name

Food

orange

lemon

grapes

peach

apple

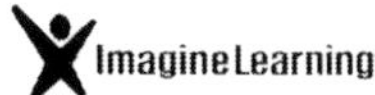

Food

Category Heading Strip

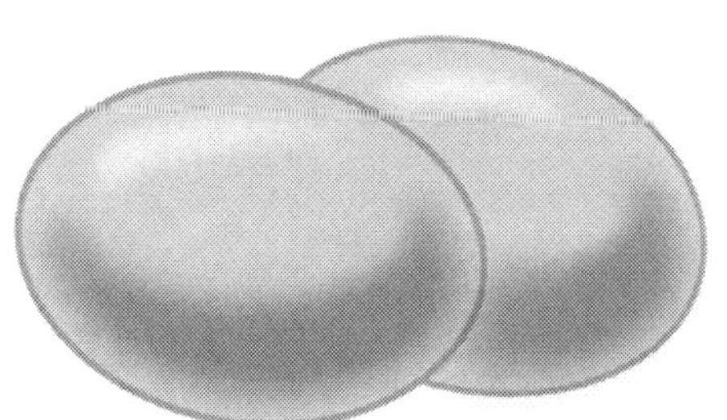

eggs

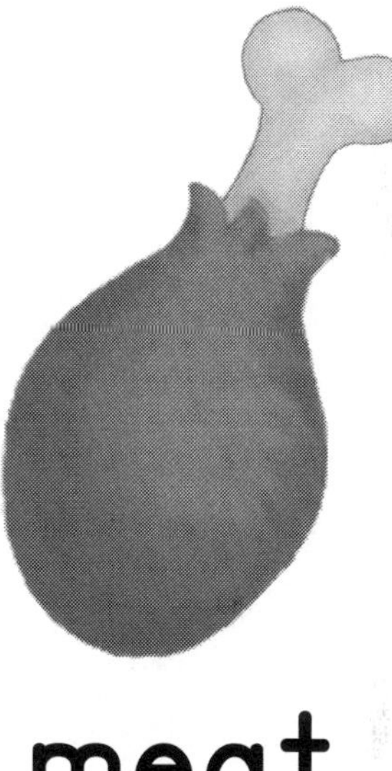

meat

milk

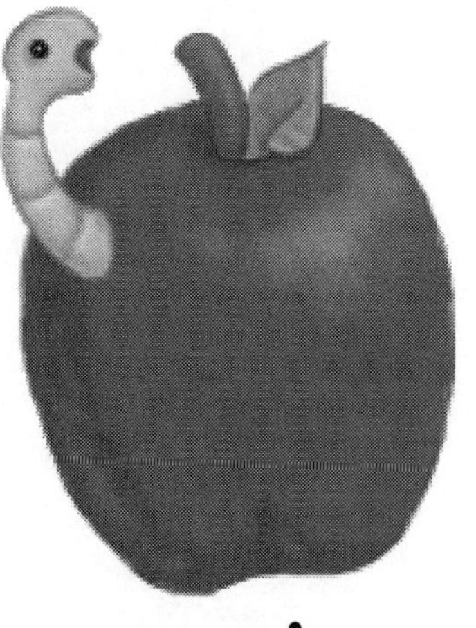

apple

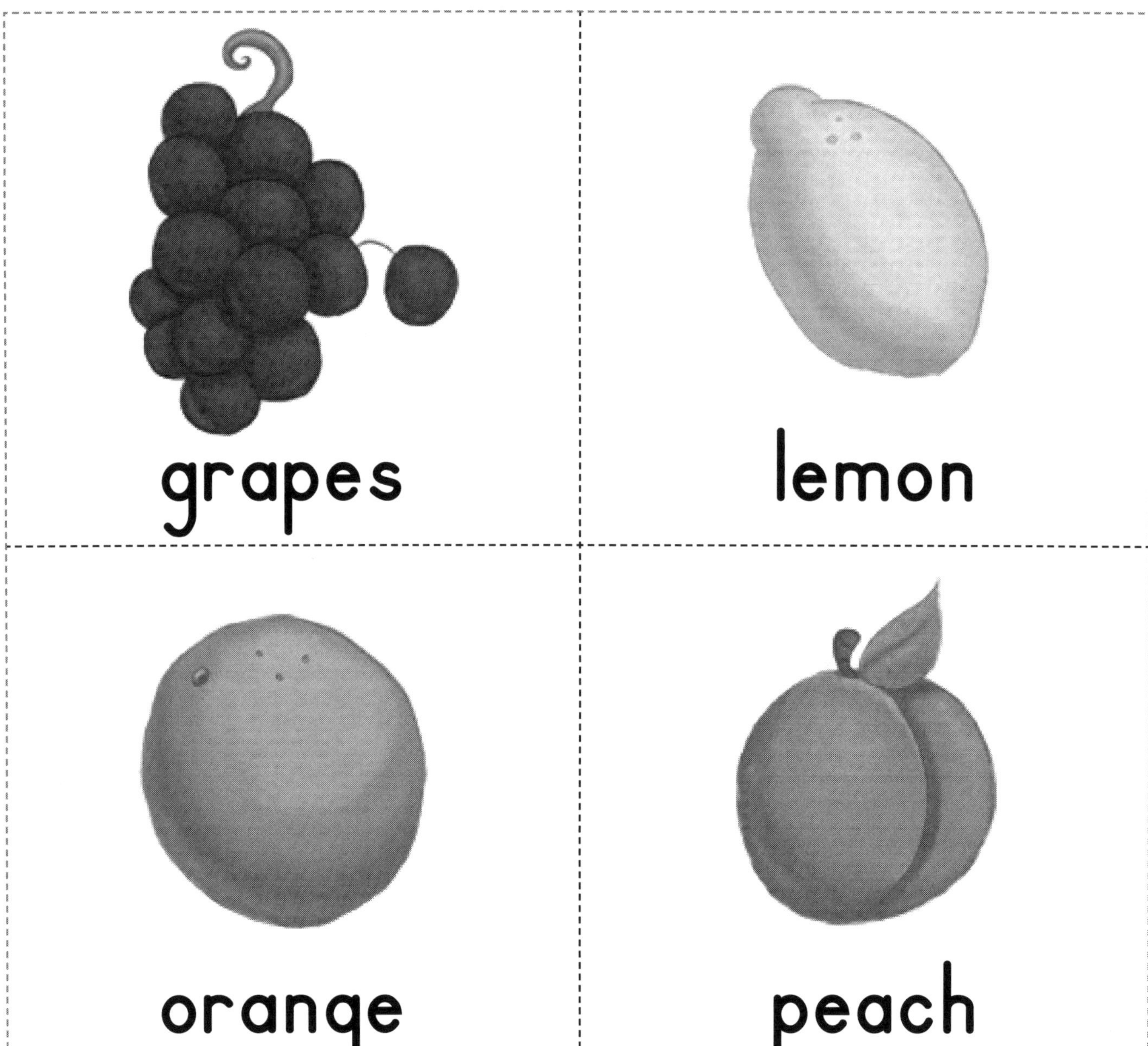
grapes
lemon
orange
peach

Name

People

dad

sister

brother

mom

baby

Name

People

police officer

doctor

girl

boy

bus driver

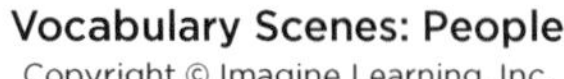

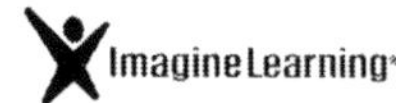

People

Category Heading Strip

baby

brother

sister

dad

mom

boy

girl

bus driver

doctor

police officer

Name

Aa Bb Cc Dd Ee Ff Gg Hh Ii Jj Kk Ll Mm Nn Oo

Aa

Things in a Classroom

computer

desk

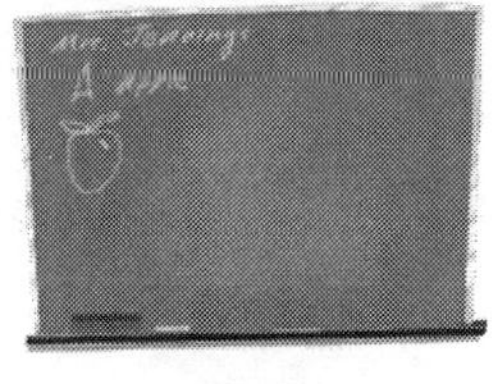
board

teacher

shelves

Name

Things in a Classroom

book

pencil

crayon

pen

paper

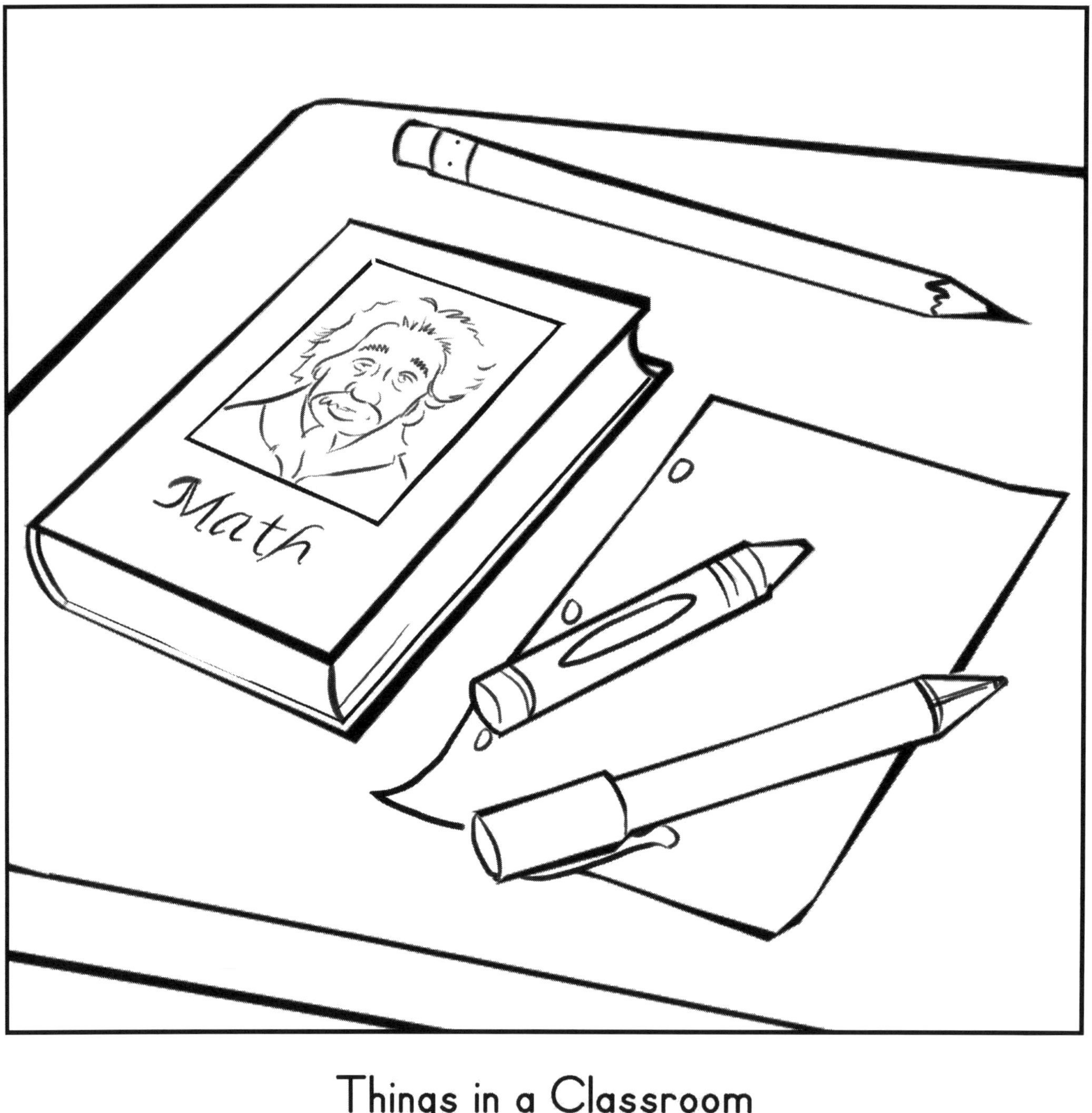

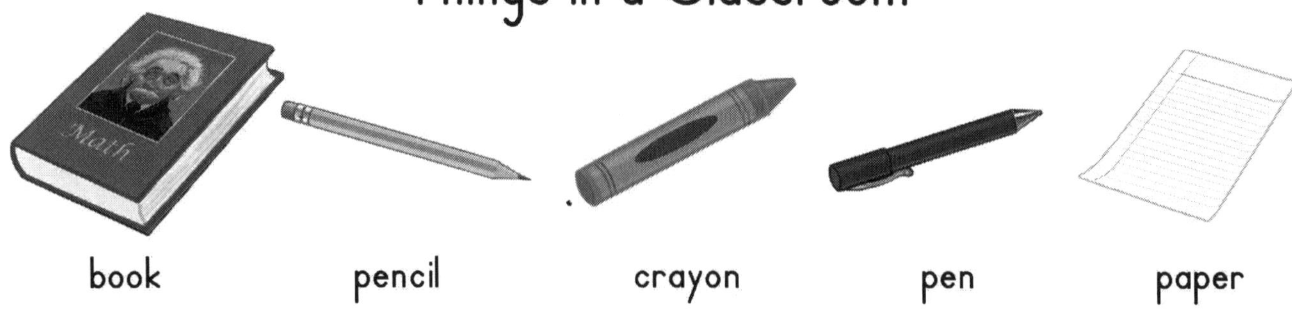

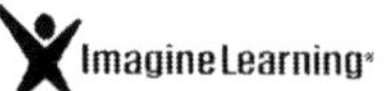

Things in a
Classroom

Category Heading Strip

teacher

board

computer

desk

shelves

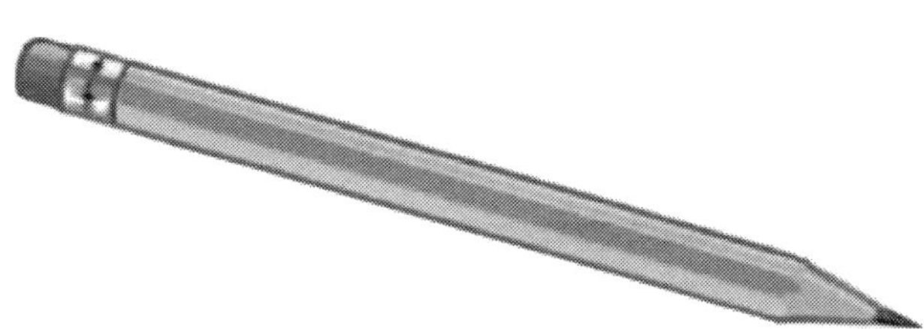

pencil

book

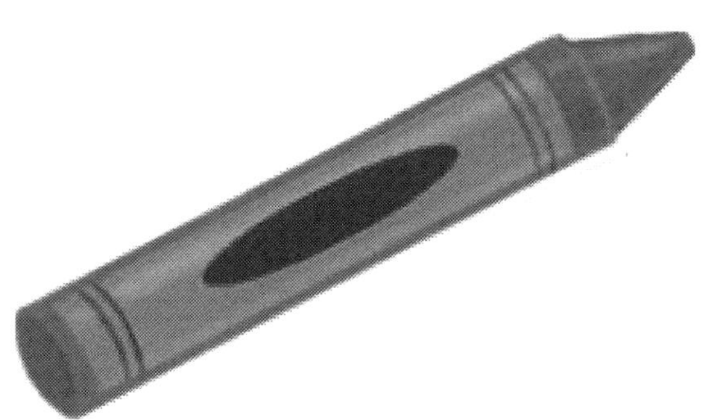

crayon

paper

pen

Noun Flash Cards: Things in a Classroom

Name

Things in a House

door

window

bed

lamp

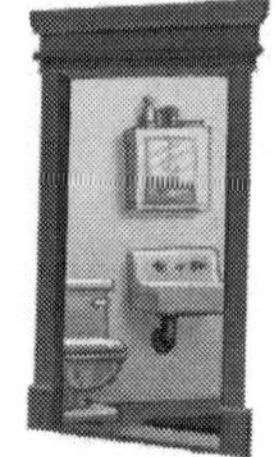

bathroom

Classroom Activities

Name

Things in a House

oven

chair

table

fridge

sink

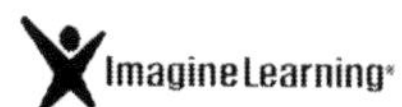

Things in a House

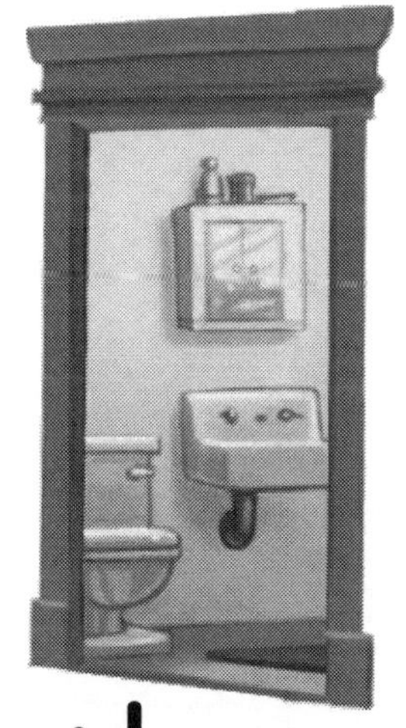

bathroom

bed

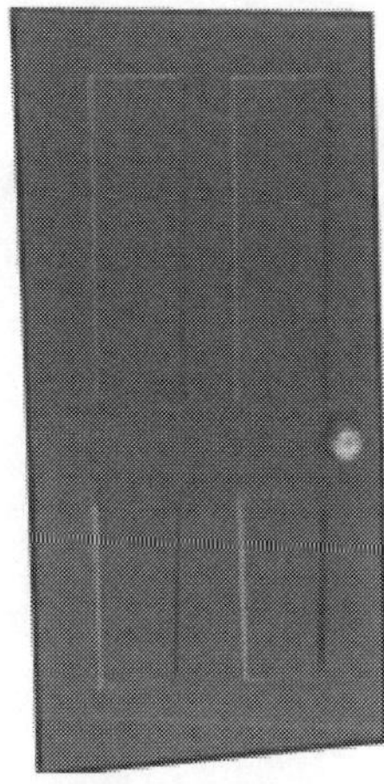

door

lamp

window

chair

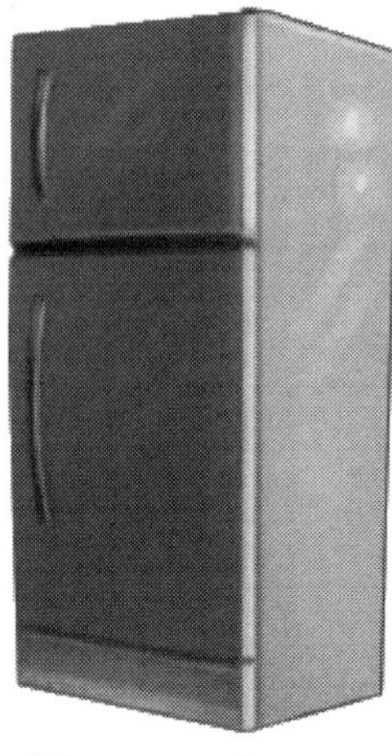

fridge

oven

sink

table

Name

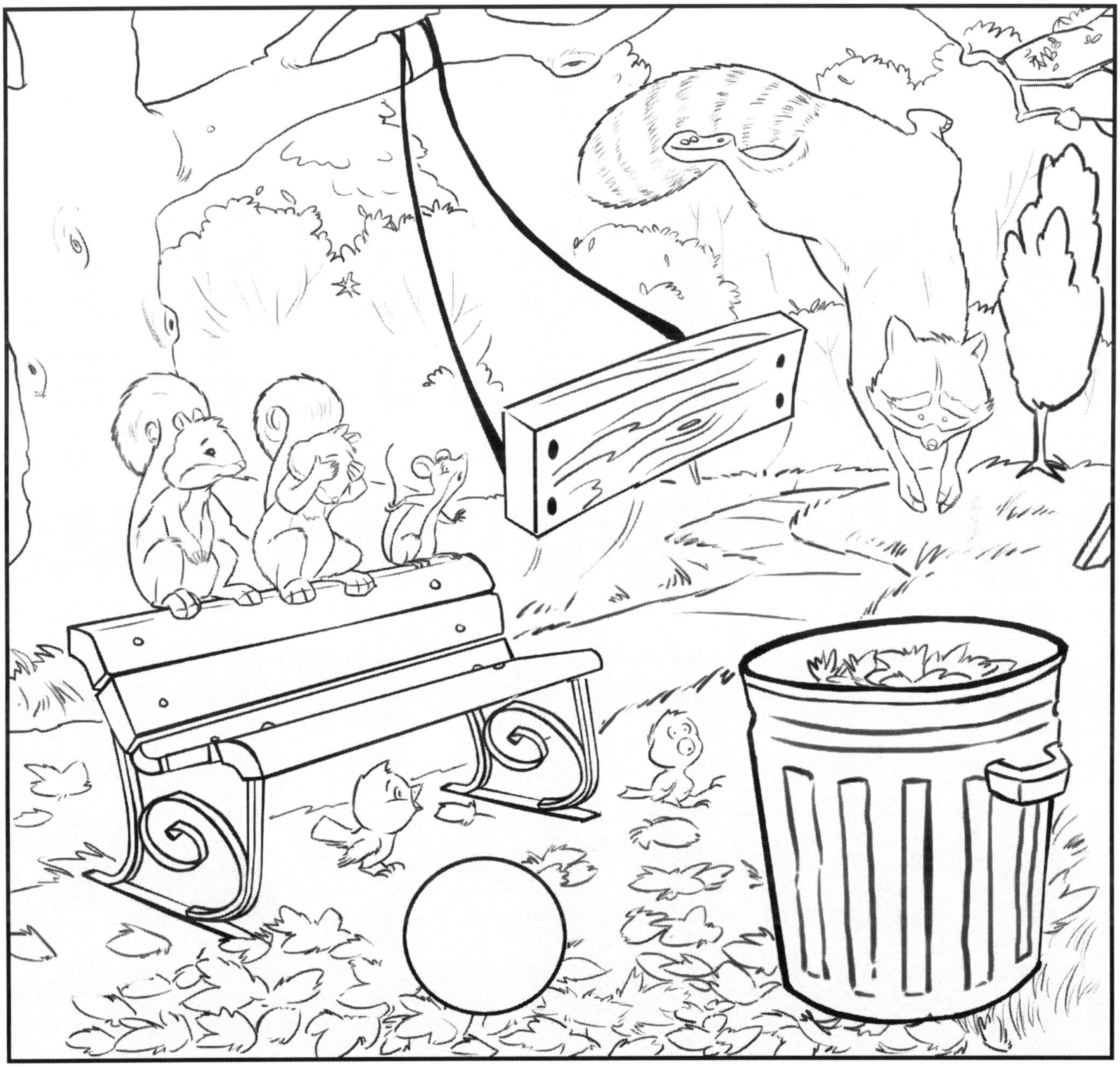

Things on a Playground

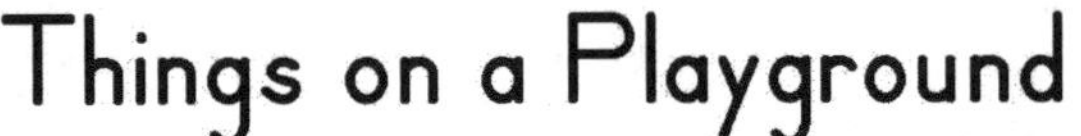

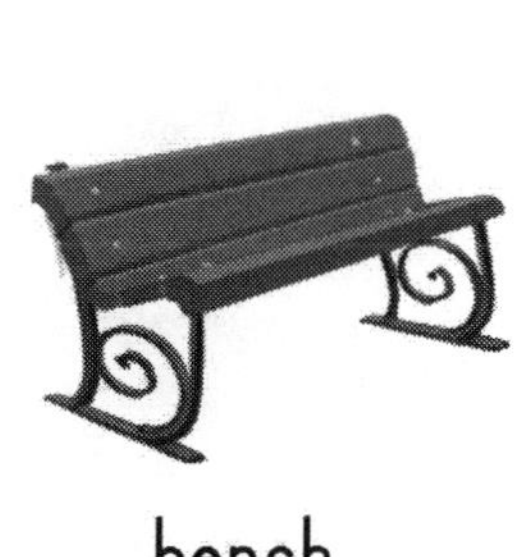

bench

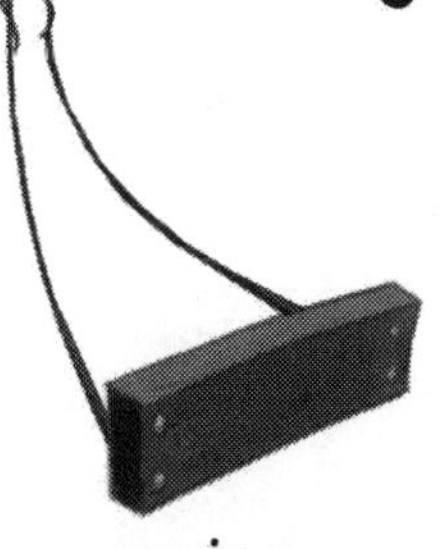

swing

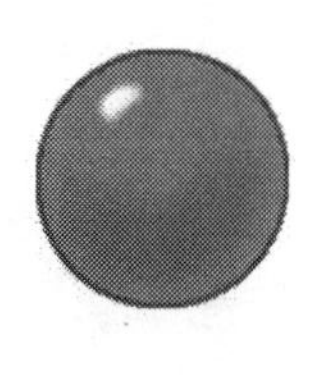

ball

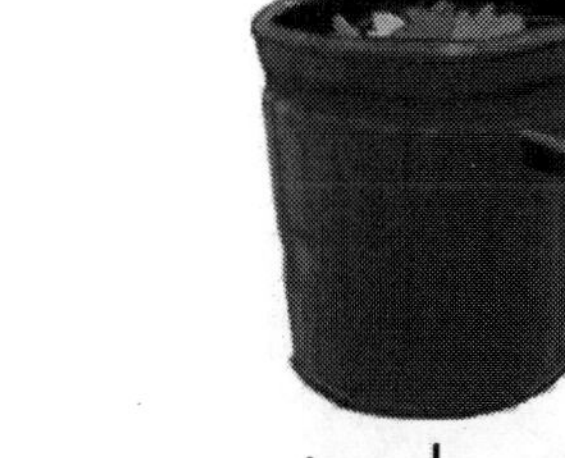

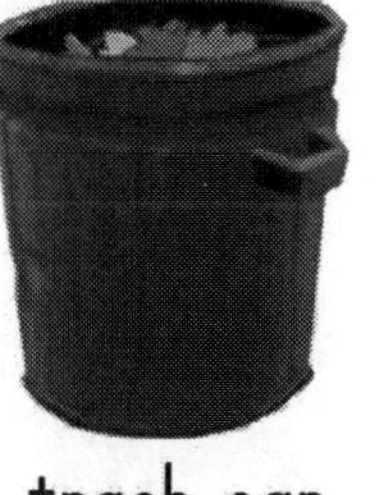

trash can

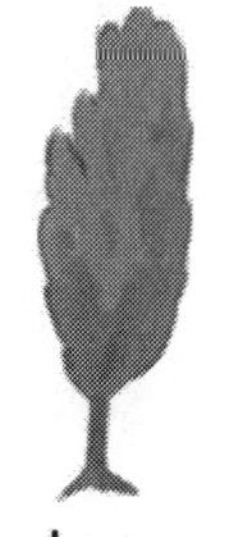

tree

Name

Things on a Playground

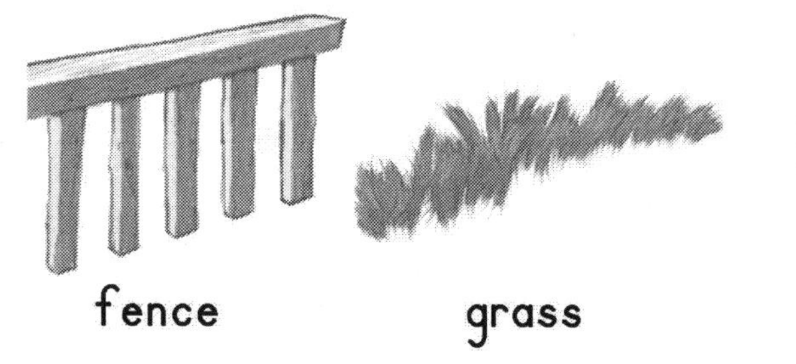

fence grass

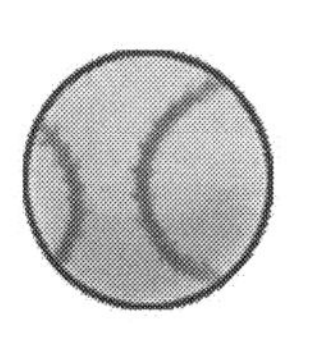

baseball

slide

soccer ball

Things on a Playground

Category Heading Strip

bench

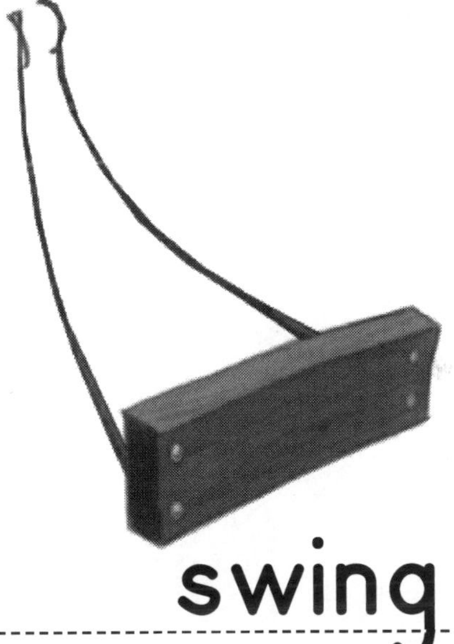

swing

trash can

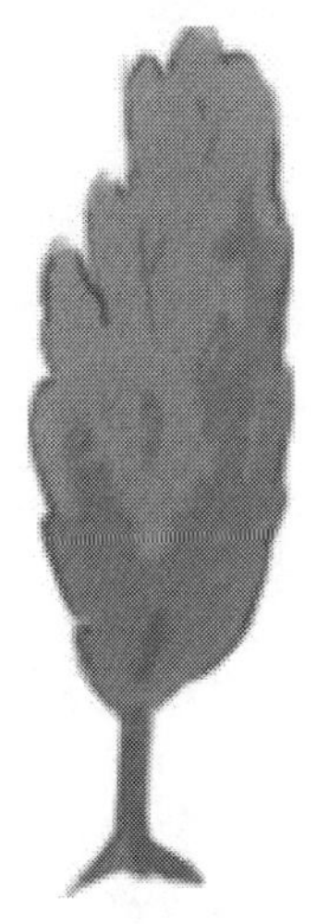

tree

ball

soccer ball

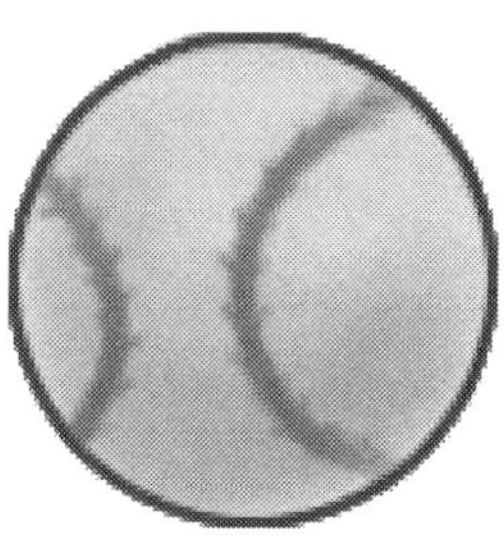

baseball

fence

grass

slide

Name

Things That Go

truck

train

airplane

bus

car

Name

Things That Go

boat

bike

helicopter

van

motorcycle

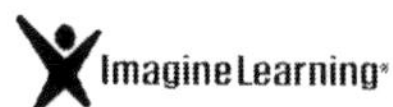

Things that
Go

Category Heading Strip

bus

car

train

truck

airplane

bike

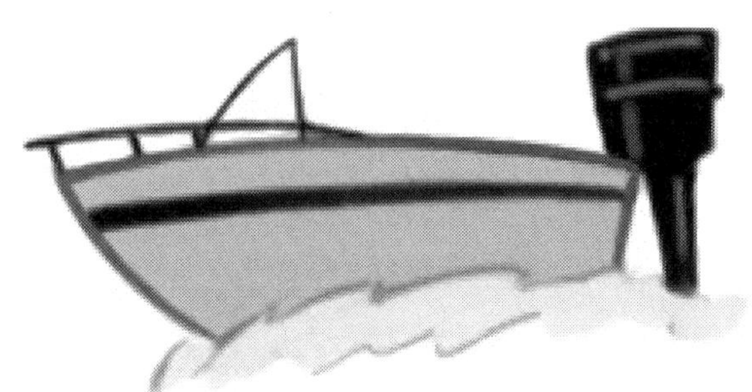

boat

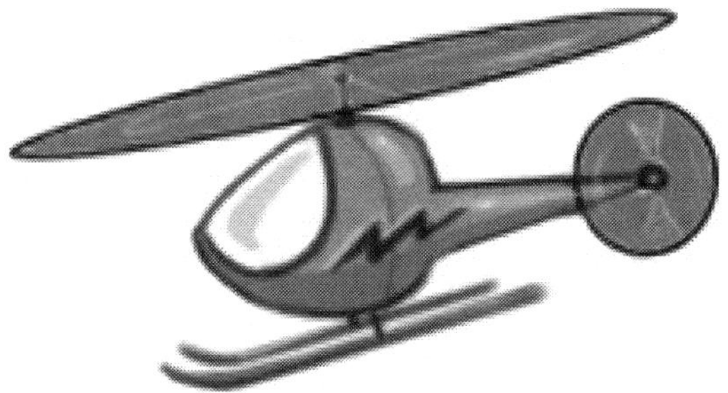

helicopter

van

motorcycle

Noun Flash Cards: Things That Go

Name

Classroom Activities

Wild Animals

elephant

zebra

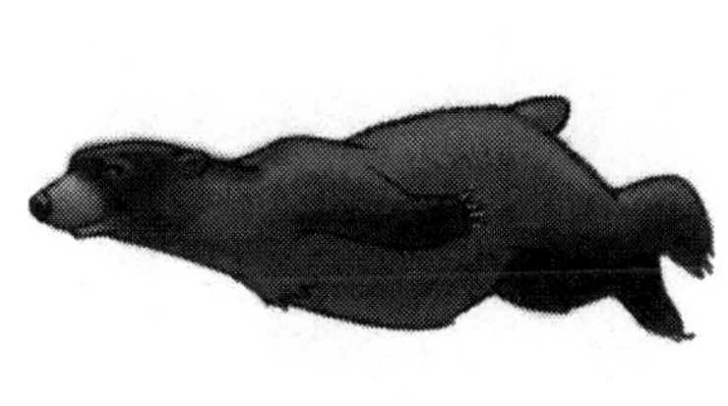
bear

lion

monkey

Name

Wild Animals

lizard

spider

snake

bug

butterfly

Wild Animals

Category Heading Strip

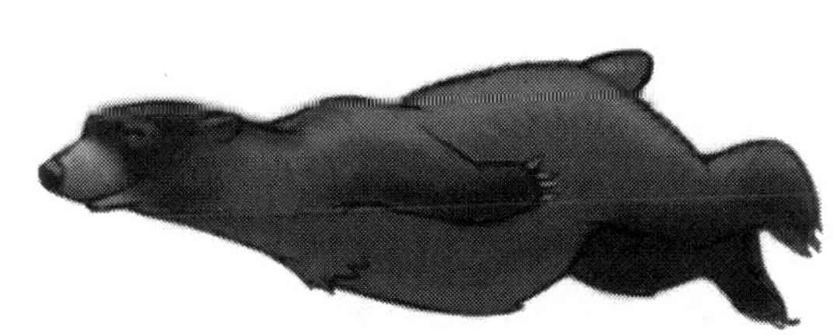

bear

elephant

lion

monkey

zebra

bug

lizard

snake

spider

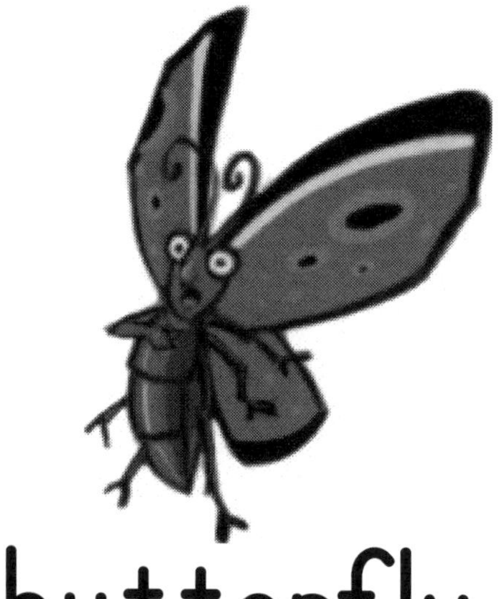

butterfly

Landforms

Parts of a

Book

Places

Weather

Classroom Activities

Name

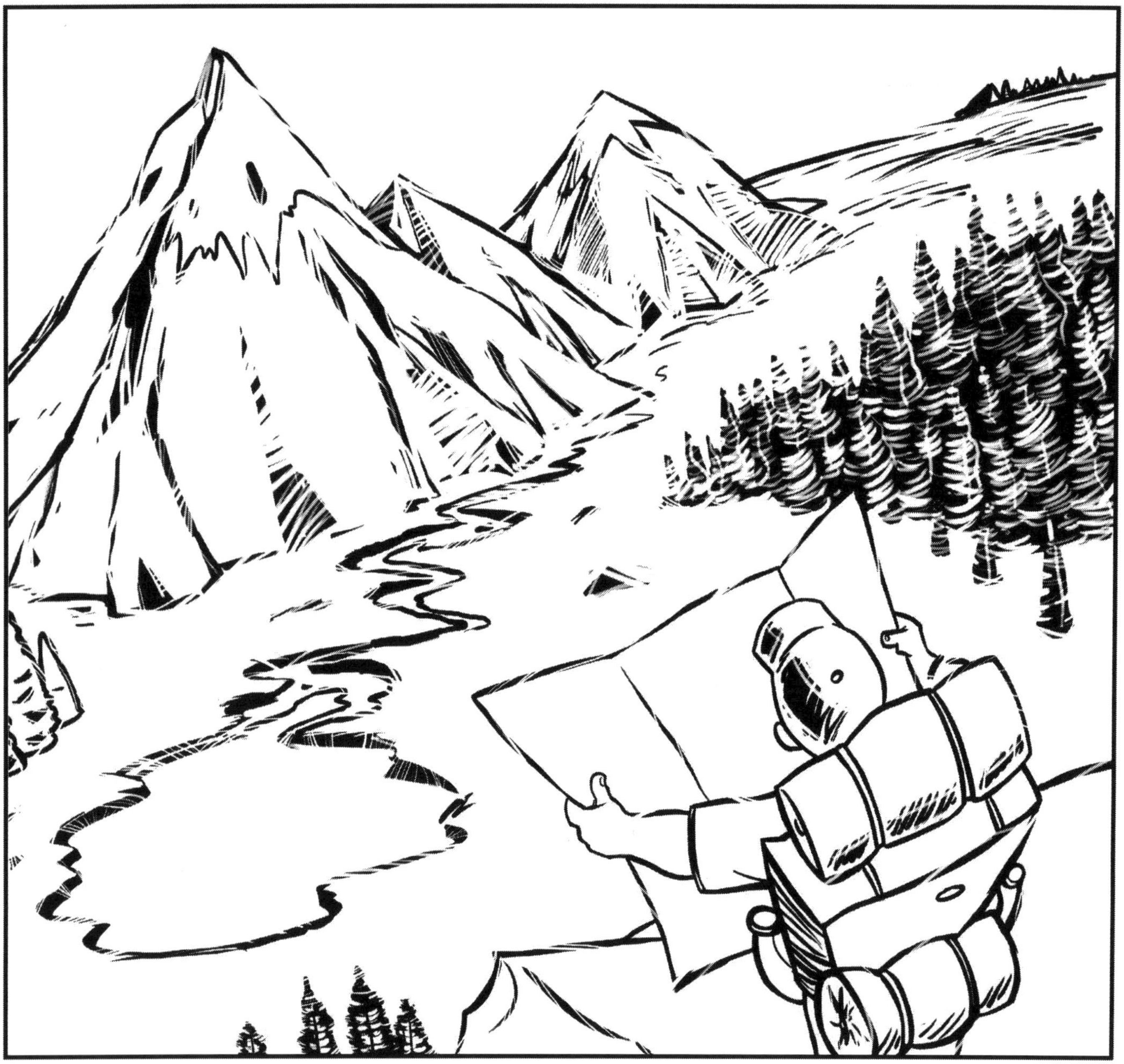

Landforms

lake

river

mountain

map

forest

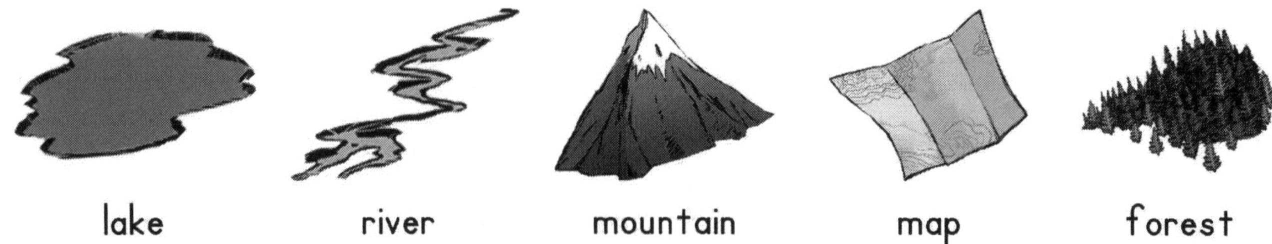

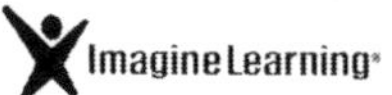

mountain

river

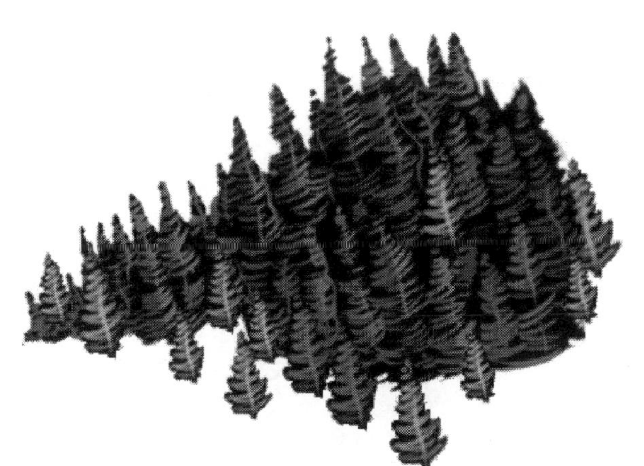

forest

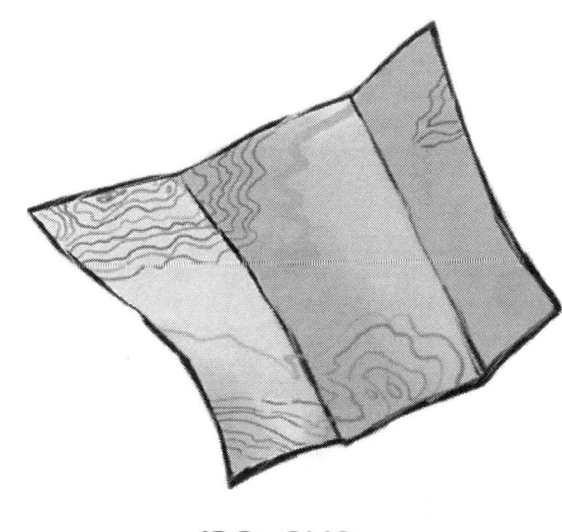

map

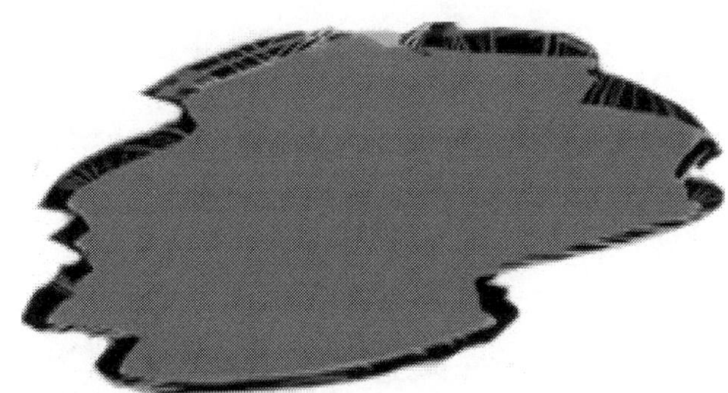

lake

Name

Parts of a Book

illustrator

picture

author

pages

title

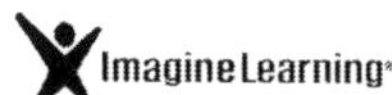

author

illustrator

pages

picture

title

Name

Places

hospital

library

restaurant

post office

fire station

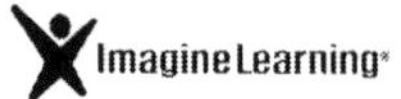

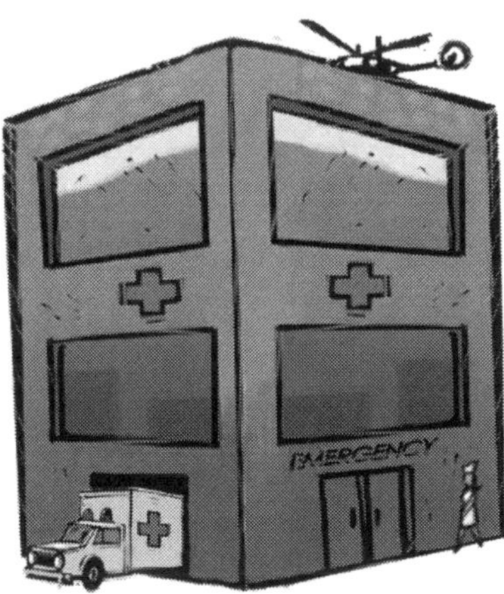

hospital

fire station

post office

library

restaurant

Name

Weather

cloud

rain

sun

wind

snow

cloud

rain

snow

sun

wind

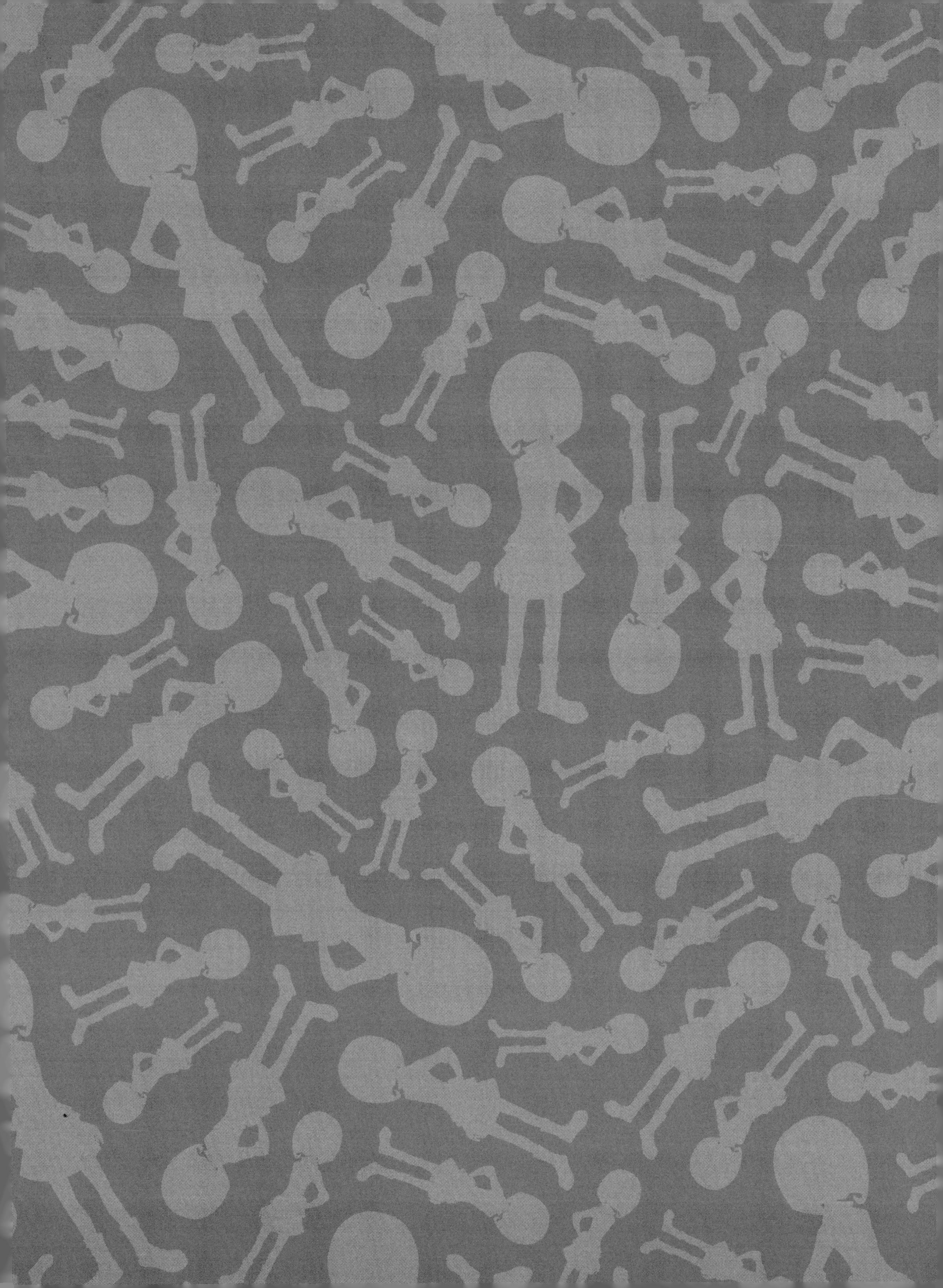

VOCABULARY

RETEACHING LESSONS

Developed with research-based methods, these instructional routines provide engaging activities and print-ready supporting materials to help students develop productive academic vocabulary. Each vocabulary routine emphasizes oral language production and can be used for small group intervention or adapted for whole-class use. Also included in this section is a master list of vocabulary words taught in the Imagine Learning online curriculum.

Analyze data in the Imagine Learning Action Areas Tool to identify groups of students who struggle with vocabulary and use the Reteaching Lessons to provide additional support.

- Complete lesson plans that include modeling, practice, and assessment
- Master vocabulary list with student-friendly definitions and example sentences for hundreds of beginning, intermediate, and advanced academic vocabulary words
- Lesson format that allows teachers to substitute easier or more challenging words, based on the individual needs of students
- Flexible grouping and suggestions for implementing differentiated instruction

Progress Tracking Sheet

Date	Student Name	Lesson/Skill	Intervention Successful (Y/N)	Notes

---

Progress Tracking Sheet

Date	Student Name	Lesson/Skill	Intervention Successful (Y/N)	Notes

Notes

Reteaching Lessons

Beginning Academic Vocabulary (K–2)

Word	Definition	Example Sentence
above	(prep) Illustrate this word by putting your hand above your head. Have the students put their hands above their heads or above different objects near them.	The light is above my head
accident	(noun) something that happens but wasn't planned or expected	I dropped my lunch tray by accident.
across	(adv) When something moves from one side to the other	I ran across the playground.
add	(verb) to find the total of two or more numbers.	When you add 2 and 3, you get 5.
address	(noun) the number and street that tells where a place is.	My address is 229 Main St.
against	(prep) Illustrate this word by leaning against a wall or leaning a book against something.	I leaned my bike against the house.
age	(noun) Illustrate this word by telling the students their age.	When the nurse asked my age, I told her I was 6.
ahead of	(prep) Illustrate this word by having students line up. Point out who is ahead of each other.	My friend is ahead of me, so he will get his lunch first.
alike	(adj) the same in one or more ways.	My brother and I are alike. We both have brown hair and brown eyes.
area	(noun) Illustrate this word by identifying the different areas in the classroom.	We can play in this area.
army	(noun) a group of people who fight for a country.	Our army protects us.
around	(prep) Illustrate this word by walking around your desk, and draw attention to a scarf, necklace, or belt around your neck or waist.	He put chairs around the table.
arrive	(verb) to get to the place you are going.	You arrive at school at 7:30 in the morning.
away from	(adv) Illustrate this by having a student move away from the group.	I moved away from the dog when it growled at me.
begin	(verb) to start something.	When I say "Start," you can begin the test.
beginning	(noun) the first part of something.	At the beginning of the poem Humpty Dumpty sat on the wall.
behind	(prep) Illustrate this word by having the students line up and then identify who they are behind.	I was behind my friend in the lunch line so she got her lunch first.
below	(prep) Illustrate this word by having the students put an object below their hands or chair.	I can put my hands below my chair
beneath	(prep) Illustrate this word by telling students that beneath and below are synonyms and have them put something beneath their chairs.	The floor is beneath your feet.
beside	(prep) Illustrate this word by having the students identify the person beside them.	Sit beside your partner so you can read the book together.
best	(adj) better than all the others.	I won the race, so I'm the best!

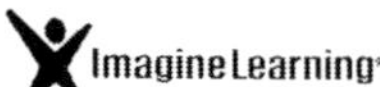

Beginning Academic Vocabulary (K–2)

Word	Definition	Example Sentence
between	(prep) Illustrate this word by having three students stand in a line and identify the student that is between the other two, or by giving them two numbers and identifying what number is between them.	Four is the number between three and five.
both	(various) Illustrate this word by identifying something two students have in common.	Although they are very different animals, both cats and dogs make good pets.
bridge	(noun) a bridge is built over a river, a road, or some other space to help people get from one side to another.	We crossed the high bridge over the rushing river.
by	(prep) Illustrate this word by having two students stand by each other.	We line up by the door before going to lunch. .
calendar	(noun) Illustrate this word by having the students identify the calendar in the classroom. Ask students what they learn from a calendar.	I found the 4th of July on the calendar.
capital	(noun) the city where a state or country's main government is.	The capital of the United States is Washington D.C.
center	(noun) Illustrate this word by having the students stand in a circle and then have them take turns standing in the center.	There are seeds in the center of an apple.
change	(verb) to make something different.	You can change red to purple by adding blue. The leaves change colors in the fall.
city	(noun) an area where lots of people live and work.	In the city where I live there are lots of people, cars, and places to shop.
climate	(noun) the weather that is normal for an area.	The climate here is hot most of the year.
coast	(noun) Illustrate this word by pointing to the coast on a map or globe in the classroom.	From the boat I could see the coast.
complete	(verb) to finish.	The teacher told us we must complete and turn in our reports today.
continent	(noun) Illustrate this word by showing the continents on a map or globe in the classroom.	We live on the North American continent.
copy	(verb) to make something that looks like another thing.	I will copy the math problem on the board in my notebook.
corner	(noun) Illustrate this word by pointing to the corner of a piece of paper, the classroom, or a book.	A triangle has three corners and a square has four.
correct	(adj) without any mistakes.	That answer is correct.
country	(noun) an area of land that has one government.	Our country is the United States of America.
cover	(noun) something that goes over another thing to protect it.	The book's cover kept the pages safe from the rain.
crop	(noun) plants that are grown on a farm.	This year we had a big crop of corn.
cross out	(verb) to draw a line through something.	Let's cross out the wrong answer.
date	(noun) Illustrate this word on your classroom calendar.	Today's date is ___________.
difficult	(adj) hard to do.	The puzzle was difficult, so I asked my dad for help.

Reteaching Lessons

Beginning Academic Vocabulary (K–2)

Word	Definition	Example Sentence
direction	(noun) the way something or someone is looking or going.	This map will help you find the direction you need to go to get to my school.
discover	(verb) to find or learn for the first time.	The scientist hopes to discover a new planet.
E/earth	(noun) the planet we live on.	I wonder what Earth looks like from space.
edge	(noun) Illustrate this word by pointing to the edge of a book, paper, or table.	Don't put your glass on the edge of the table, because it might get knocked off.
end	(noun) the last part of something.	At the end of the story, Golidlocks sees the three bears standing over her and she gets scared and runs away.
equal	(adj) the same amount or weight.	Our pieces of cake are the same size, so they are equal.
equator	(noun) an imaginary line around the middle of the Earth.	The weather is very hot on the equator.
example	(noun) Illustrate this word by explaining that there are many kinds of fruit. Then ask students to give you examples. Ask if corn is an example. Ask students why not.	This example on the test helped me know how to answer the rest of the questions.
explore	(verb) to travel to different places to learn new things about them.	In a few years we might explore Mars.
far from	(adv) a long distance away from something.	My friend sits at the back of the class so she is far from me.
farm	(noun) a place where plants and animals are raised.	Cows live on the farm.
favorite	(adj) something you like more than other things.	I have read my favorite book four times.
fill in	(verb) to give information that is missing.	On the test, we had to fill in the words that were missing.
find	(verb) to discover something, especially after looking for it. (noun) a discovery.	I hope I can find the money I lost.
finish	(verb) to end or complete something.	I must finish my homework before I can watch TV.
fix	(verb) to make something work as it should.	My bicycle tire is flat, but I can fix it.
follow	(verb) to go after or behind someone or something.	We follow the leader.
fraction	(noun) a small part of a larger thing.	This piece of cake is a fraction of the whole cake.
give	(verb) Illustrate this word through a demonstration of giving something to a student.	I give my dog a treat when he is being good.
globe	(noun) Illustrate this word by pointing to a picture of a globe in the classroom.	Turn the globe until you see the United States.
government	(noun) people who make laws and important decisions for a city, state, or a country.	I have to wear a safety belt in the car, because the government made it a law.
grade	(noun) a score or letter given on schoolwork that shows how well you did.	I work hard in school and get good grades.

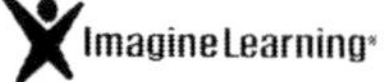

Beginning Academic Vocabulary (K-2)

Word	Definition	Example Sentence
greater than	Illustrate this word by putting the students into unequal groups or drawing unequal groups of circles and identify the group that is greater than the other.	Four is greater than two.
group	(noun) some people or things that belong together.	My reading group meets everyday.
guess	(verb) to think something without knowing for sure	I don't know the answer, so I'll have to guess what it is.
half	(noun) Illustrate this word by folding a piece of paper in half.	We made two groups, so we'd have half the class on each team.
hear	(verb) to be aware of sounds.	I like to hear birds singing.
holiday	(noun) a day of celebration when many people do not go to school or work.	We don't go to school today because it's a holiday.
human	(noun) a person.	People are human, but animals and plants are not.
husband	(noun) a married man.	When my grandpa married my grandma, he became her husband.
imagine	(verb) to think of a thing that isn't real.	I like to imagine that I am an astronaut floating in space.
in	(prep) Illustrate this word by putting an object in a container.	My book is in my backpack.
in front of	(prep) Illustrate this word by having the students line up and identify one student who is in front of another.	I am in front of you in line, so I will get lunch first.
incorrect	(adj) not right, wrong.	My teacher made me fix my incorrect answer to the question.
inside	(prep) Illustrate this word by putting an object inside a container.	There was no light inside the cave.
into	(prep) Illustrate this word by having the kids walk into the room, or by putting an object into a container.	He walked into the room.
island	(noun) land that has water all around it.	We sailed in our boat all the way around the island.
last	(adj) coming in after others.	I was the last to eat lunch, because I was at the end of the line.
leader	(noun) someone that other people follow.	We followed the line leader back to class.
less than	Illustrate this word by putting the students into unequal groups or drawing unequal groups of circles and identify the group that is less than the other.	Two is less than four.
line	(noun) Illustrate this word by drawing a line or pointing to a line in the classroom.	I write my name on the line at the top of my paper.
machine	(noun) something we make to do work.	A dishwasher is machine that washes and dries the dishes.
measure	(verb) to find out the size, length, or weight of something.	I measure my foot with a ruler to see how long it is.
message	(noun) information given or sent to someone.	My mom sent a message that she would get me after school.

Beginning Academic Vocabulary (K–2)

Word	Definition	Example Sentence
middle	(noun) Illustrate this word by having three or more students line up. Identify the student(s) in the middle.	Lunch is in the middle of the day.
mistake	(noun) something a person did wrong.	I made a mistake working out the math problem and got the wrong answer.
money	(noun) paper or metal coins used to pay for things.	I have two dollars. How much money do you have?
month	(noun) one of the twelve parts of a year.	January is the first month of the year.
move	(verb) Illustrate this word by moving something from one place to another.	I move the books from the shelf to my desk.
near	(prep) Illustrate this word by moving yourself near someone or something in the classroom.	I like to sit near my friend, so we can read together.
neighbor	(noun) a person who lives near you.	My girl in the house next door is my neighbor.
next to	(prep) Illustrate this word by moving yourself next someone or something in the classroom.	I sit next to the door, so I am always the first one in line.
nothing	(noun) Illustrate this word by showing the students a container with nothing in it, than with something in it.	I need a drink, but my cup is empty.
number	(noun) tells how many or which one.	I counted the number of plates we need for dinner.
ocean	(noun) Illustrate this word by finding the ocean on a map or globe in the classroom.	Big ships sail on the ocean.
off	(prep) Illustrate this word by having someone turn off a light switch.	The heater was off, so we all had to wear our coats in the classroom.
on	(prep) Illustrate this word by putting your hand on your head, on the table, etc.	The book is on the table.
on top of	(prep) Illustrate this word by drawing a square and then putting a triangle on top. Add more shapes or ask students to find things in the classroom that are on top of other things.	The candles are on top of the cake.
once	(adverb) one time.	We go on vacation once a year.
out of	(prep) Illustrate this word by putting something in a closed container (box) and ask a student to take the item out of the container.	Carefully take the eggs out of the carton.
outside	(prep) Illustrate this word by taking a crayon outside of a box, or have students take something outside of their backpacks.	The doors were locked so we waited outside the school.
over	(prep) Illustrate this word by putting your hand over and under things.	The cloud is over us.
parents	(noun) someone who is a mother or father.	My parents help me with my homework.
piece	(noun) a part that is taken away from something larger.	I ate a small piece of the pie.
planet	(noun) large, round object that orbits a star.	Earth is a large planet.
print	(verb) Illustrate this word by printing your name and writing your name in cursive.	I can print my name.
pull	(verb) to hold onto something and move it toward yourself.	I can pull the chair.

Beginning Academic Vocabulary (K–2)

Word	Definition	Example Sentence
push	(verb) to use force and move something away from you.	I had to push my bike up the steep hill.
quarter	(noun) Illustrate this word by folding a paper in half and then half again, pointing out that each section is a quarter of the whole paper.	Four of us each had a quarter of the pizza.
real	(adj) something that is imaginary.	Elephants are real.
rectangle	(noun) a four-sided shape.	The top of the table is a rectangle.
report	(noun) Information about a topic or event that is shared with others	I am giving a report to the class about Mars.
ruler	(noun) Illustrate this word by showing a ruler and use it to measure something and use it to draw a straight line.	This ruler is twelve inches long.
score	(noun) a number that shows how many points a person or team makes in a game.	The soccer score was 5–3.
season	(noun) parts of year called spring, summer, winter, or autumn.	Winter is my favorite season.
sentence	(noun) a sentence has a subject and a verb and gives a complete thought.	This is a sentence: The puppy licked my hand.
settle	(verb) to make a home in a place.	My family settled here because it is such a friendly place.
shape	(noun) Illustrate this word by pointing out different shapes in the classroom.	This shape is a rectangle.
show	(verb) Illustrate this word by revealing something special such as a book the class will be reading or a picture of something engaging.	I want to show you a new magic trick I've learned.
side	(noun) Illustrate this word by pointing to the side of the room, the side of an object, and the side of a line shape, such as an octagon.	We have bookcases on one side of our classroom and computers on the other side.
smell	(verb) to use your nose to sense smells.	I smell cookies baking.
space	(noun) the area between things or the area for something special.	On book covers there is space for the name of author and illustrator.
spell	(verb) to write or say letters in a word in the right order.	How do you spell your name?
stand	(verb) to be on your feet.	All the seats were taken so I had to stand for the whole game.
street	(noun) a road in a city or town.	The school bus stops on the street in front of my apartment.
take away	(verb) to subtract.	If I have five apples and you take away two, I'll only have three left.
taste	(verb) to sense if food is sweet, sour, salty, or bitter using your mouth.	Please taste the soup and see if it needs more salt.
team	(noun) a group of people who work together.	We have ten good players on our team.
tell	(verb) to talk about something to someone.	I like to tell jokes to my friends.
temperature	(noun) a measurement that tells you how hot or cold something is.	The weatherman says the temperature is dropping, so I'm going to wear a coat today.
think	(verb) to use your mind get ideas or solve problems.	I like puzzles because it's fun to think about different ways to solve them.

Beginning Academic Vocabulary (K–2)

Word	Definition	Example Sentence
touch	(verb) to put your hand or other part of the body on something.	When I touch an ice cube it feels really cold.
triangle	(noun) a shape that has three sides Illustrate this word by pointing out triangles in the classroom.	My slice of pizza is shaped like a triangle.
turn	(verb) to change direction.	If you go to end of the hall and turn right, you'll see the lunchroom.
twice	(verb) two times	I will say this twice. I will say this twice.
under	(prep) Illustrate this word by placing a book under a desk or by placing your hand under a book.	I couldn't find my pencil because it was under my chair.
underline	(verb) to draw a line under something.	I will underline the words that I spelled wrong.
unequal	(verb) Illustrate this word by cutting a piece of paper in equal parts (halfs). Then cut another paper into unequal parts. Have students explain the concept of unequal. You can also assign easy tasks to a small group and a large group.	I complained when my brother cut the cake into unequal pieces.
vote	(verb) to make your choice known when deciding something with other people.	Let's vote for reading more books. I voted for reading time after lunch.
wait	(verb) to stay in one place.	We had to wait in the lunch line for a long time.
week	(noun) seven days.	If I read four pages every day for seven days, I will finish this book in a week.
whole	(noun) complete or full.	No one wanted a piece of pizza, so I at the whole pizza by myself.
wife	(noun) a married woman.	When my grandpa married my grandma, she became his wife.
work	(verb) to get something done.	Taking care of a pet is hard work.
wrong	(adj) when something is not true.	1 + 1 = 3 is wrong.
year	(noun) Illustrate this word by showing 12 months on a calendar to show the whole year.	It takes a whole year for the earth to orbit the sun.
zero	(noun) the number 0; nothing at all.	Our team had zero points until I scored.

Intermediate Vocabulary (3–4)

Word	Definition	Example Sentence
agree	(verb) to feel the same way as someone else.	Ella and I agree that chocolate ice cream is the best kind of ice cream.
apologize	(verb) to say you're sorry.	I apologize for being mean to you.
apostrophe	(noun) an apostrophe is used to make two words into one word.	These words all have an apostrophe: can't, won't, we're.
assignment	(noun) something that someone has given you to do.	The teacher gives us a homework assignment every day.
audience	(noun) a group of people who watch or listen to something.	The audience clapped loudly when the play ended.
backward	(adv) toward the back; facing the opposite direction of the front.	If you can see your tag and you can't see your buttons, your shirt is on backward.
balance	(verb) to make two or more things even or steady.	Can you balance the two buckets of water?
blank	(adj) without any writing, drawing, or other marks.	There is a blank space at the top of the test where you need to write your name.
bold	(adj) having thicker, darker letters, usually to make a word different from the rest of a text.	The bold vocabulary words are easy to spot because they are darker than the rest of the text.
category	(noun) a group of things that are alike.	I like lots of different movies, but I won't watch any from the "horror" category.
century	(noun) one hundred years.	The buildings started to look old and dirty a century after they were built.
chapter	(noun) one of the main parts of a book that usually has a number or title.	My favorite part of the book is in chapter seven, when the robots take over the cafeteria.
chart	(noun) a table, graph, or image that explains something.	This chart compares how all the third-grade classes did with the canned food drive.
check	(verb) to make sure something is correct.	When I take a test, I check my answers twice before I turn it in.
choose	(noun) to pick something.	Mom lets me choose what we eat for dinner on my birthday.
classify	(verb) to group things together because they have something in common.	Scientists classify different snails by the size and shape of their shells.
collect	(verb) to gather something together, to gather and keep a particular kind of thing, usually as a hobby.	My aunt knows I like to collect rocks, so every week she brings me a new one.
column	(noun) a long, vertical space where things can be written.	When you add more than two numbers together, be careful to make the column of numbers line up perfectly.
combine	(verb) to put things together.	I combine red and white paint to make the color pink.
compare	(verb) to look at how things are similar or different from one another.	If you compare my brother and me, you'll find that he is taller, and I am better-looking.
connect	(verb) to join one or more things together.	He connected the power cords and the television finally turned on.
consonant	(noun) a letter of the alphabet that is not a vowel (vowels are *a*, *e*, *i*, *o*, and *u*).	The letter *l* is a consonant.

Intermediate Vocabulary (3-4)

Word	Definition	Example Sentence
contraction	(noun) a shortened form of a word or words that uses an apostrophe to show that letters have been taken out.	You can make the contraction "haven't" from the words "have" and "not."
create	(verb) to make.	In art class, I created a huge painting that my teacher hung on the wall.
culture	(noun) the things that a group of people who live in the same area do and think.	People in my culture like bright colors and fast music.
decade	(noun) ten years.	It took a decade to build the new office building.
decide	(verb) to make a choice.	I decided to wear a jacket since it was snowing outside.
decimal	(noun) a period placed in a number between the unit and tenths place.	In a price, like $2.45, the dollars go to the left of the decimal and the cents go to the right.
decrease	(verb) to go from larger to smaller in size or number.	If I decrease the amount of hours I sleep, I will be tired all day.
defend	(verb) to protect.	I have to defend my sandwich from my older brother, otherwise he'll eat it.
definition	(noun) what a word means.	I didn't know the definition of a word, so I looked it up in the dictionary.
describe	(verb) to tell about something.	The party was so great, I couldn't wait to go home and describe it to my mom.
diagram	(noun) a drawing or a written plan that explains the different parts of something.	This diagram shows some of the different parts of a flower: the stem, the petals, the leaves, and the roots.
dictionary	(noun) a book or online resource that tells what words mean.	If you want to know what a word means, look it up in a dictionary.
direction	(noun) the way something faces, the way something is going.	The bus driver drove the wrong direction and had to turn around.
disagree	(verb) to think something different from someone else.	I think goldfish make the best pets, but my sister disagrees because birds are her favorite.
discuss	(verb) to talk about.	There's no time to talk about it now–we'll discuss this later.
dissolve	(verb) to disappear by scattering; to melt something completely, usually with liquid.	The piece of cotton candy dissolved in my mouth as soon as I took a bite.
document	(noun) a piece of writing that gives information.	You can't drive a car unless you have a document called a driver's license.
double	(adj) twice as many/much.	I love pepperoni so I always ask for double pepperoni on my pizza.
dozen	(dozen) twelve of something.	Eggs are sometimes sold by the dozen.
draft	(noun) a piece of writing that needs to be worked on more.	The first draft of the paper is due today, and the final paper is due next week.
edit	(verb) to make changes to something, usually a picture or piece of writing.	My first draft is too long, so I will need to edit it to make it shorter.
encyclopedia	(noun) a book or online resource that gives information on many subjects.	I looked in the encyclopedia for information on lions.
equation	(noun) a math problem.	2 + 2 = 4 is an equation.
estimate	(verb) to guess how many or how much.	I estimate this building is forty feet high.

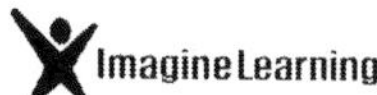

Intermediate Vocabulary (3-4)

Word	Definition	Example Sentence
even	(adj) numbers that end with 0, 2, 4, 6, or 8 are even numbers.	Two is an even number.
exclamation mark	(noun) a punctuation mark that is used to show that something should be read with a lot of emotion.	If you use a lot of exclamation marks, it can look like your writing is shouting.
experiment	(noun) a test you do to learn something new.	We do experiments in science class to figure out how things work.
final	(adj) last.	You are the last person in line, so you are the final one.
forward	(adv) ahead.	They couldn't drive the car forward because there was a large rock in front of it.
glossary	(noun) a list of words from a piece of writing and their definitions.	I was confused about the meaning of a word I read, so I looked in the book's glossary for the definition.
graph	(noun) a picture or chart that shows how two or more things are alike or different.	This graph shows how many perfect scores the class has earned each month.
heading	(noun) a word or phrase used at the beginning of some text.	The heading tells me what this part of the article is about.
headline	(noun) a title written in large letters about a story in a newspaper.	The headline of the article was written in huge letters.
height	(noun) a measurement of how tall something is.	My dad measures my height each year to see how much taller I've grown.
illustrate	(verb) to draw pictures that describe something else.	Artists illustrate books to show you what is happening.
inch	(noun) a way to describe how long something is.	This ruler is 12 inches long.
increase	(verb) to become greater in size or number.	I want to increase my score on the next math test, so I will study extra hard this week to prepare.
instrument	(noun) a tool used to do something.	The dentist uses special instruments to check teeth.
introduce	(verb) to have someone meet someone else.	I'd like to introduce you to my friend, Paul.
italicize	(verb) to make words slant to the right or left.	You italicize the title of a book or movie when you write about it.
label	(verb) to put a word or name on something to identify it.	Please label the boxes by putting the names on them.
length	(noun) the distance from the start of something to the end of it; how long it is.	We measured the length of the room to see if the new couch would fit.
liquid	(noun) a thing that is able to flow freely like water.	Apple juice is a kind of liquid.
list	(verb) to write things down in order.	The art teacher went to the blackboard and listed all the supplies we would need for our next project.
magazine	(noun) a thin book that has stories and articles about a specific thing that is published every week or month.	Every story in this magazine is about animals in Africa.
margin	(noun) the space between the writing and the edge of the paper.	If you have a question or a note, write it in the margin of your paper.

Intermediate Vocabulary (3–4)

Word	Definition	Example Sentence
microscope	(noun) a tool used for making very small things visible.	You can't see human cells without using a microscope.
muscle	(noun) parts of your body that allow you to move by contracting and expanding.	Runners have very strong leg muscles.
odd	(adj) numbers that end with 1, 3, 5, 7, or 9 are odd numbers.	3 is an odd number.
paragraph	(noun) a group of sentences that describe one thing.	The first paragraph of this story introduces the main character.
passage	(noun) a small piece of writing.	First we read a short story, and then we talked about the author.
period	(noun) a length of time that starts and ends.	Recess only lasts for a short period.
plus	(prep) used when describing two things being added together.	Two plus two equals four.
practice	(verb) to do something over and over to become better at it.	I want to be a better reader, so I practice reading each day.
prewrite	(verb) to plan out your writing before starting the first draft.	I prewrite to get out every idea I have before writing my final essay.
price	(noun) how much you have to pay to get something.	The price of this water bottle is fifty cents.
problem	(noun) something that is difficult to deal with.	The problem with the bike is that the tire is flat.
pronounce	(verb) to say a word, usually clearly and correctly.	The name of that street is difficult to pronounce.
publish	(verb) to produce something for sale, like a book or magazine.	You can publish a book, movie, or game.
punctuation	(noun) marks used with words to make them easier to understand.	A period, exclamation point, and comma are all examples of punctuation.
question mark	(noun) a mark used at the end of a sentence to show a question.	I could not tell that what he wrote was a question because he didn't use a question mark.
quotation marks	(noun) marks used to show the beginning and end of a quote.	Every time a character speaks in your story, you need to put quotation marks around what he or she says.
repeat	(verb) to say or do something again.	I didn't hear what you said, can you repeat it please?
research	(verb) to study something carefully to learn something new.	I am researching sharks for my report next week.
revise	(verb) to make changes to correct or improve something.	There are too many mistakes in this paper–it needs to be revised.
section	(noun) one of the parts that make something.	May I have one section of your orange?
select	(verb) to choose something from a group.	They looked at many different types of cars and finally selected the blue truck.
shaded	(adj) an area of darkness that is made when something blocks light.	A tree provides a cool and shaded area on a hot sunny day.
similar	(adj) when two things are almost the same.	Those two brothers look so similar that it is hard to tell them apart.
single	(adj) when something is alone.	You can't buy a single egg at the store; you have to buy a carton of twelve.

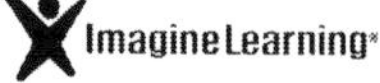

Intermediate Vocabulary (3–4)

Word	Definition	Example Sentence
skeleton	(noun) all of a person's bones put together.	We all have skeletons inside us.
sort	(verb) to put things in groups in a particular order.	We sorted the laundry into two piles: dark clothes and light clothes.
stage	(noun) a platform where shows or events are shown.	They decorated the stage to look like a forest for the fall play.
symbol	(noun) an object, event, or action that reminds you of an idea or thing.	In class, we use symbols to draw how we are feeling–a smiley face when we are happy, and a frowny face when we are sad.
table	(noun) a set of rows and columns with information in them.	On this table put the number of boys on one row and the number of girls on the next row.
total	(noun) complete; after everything is counted.	She worked for three hours and earned a total of thirty dollars.
unusual	(adj) not normal.	It is unusual for the weather to be warm in the winter.
usually	(adverb) most of the time.	Usually we go to the park on Wednesdays, but this week it rained so we couldn't.
vowel	(noun) a letter sound made with your mouth open (*a*, *e*, *i*, *o*, *u*, and sometimes *y*).	*A* and *o* are vowels.
weight	(noun) a measurement of how heavy something is.	Stand on the scale and we'll see what your weight is.
width	(noun) the distance from one side of a thing to the other side.	We need to measure the width of the box to be sure it can fit through the door.

Advanced Vocabulary (4–6)

Word	Definition	Example Sentence
analyze	(verb) to study something very carefully so you can understand it.	We can analyze this plant to learn more about it.
annual	(adj) happening every year.	The school has bake sales every other month, but the book fair is an annual event.
apply	(verb) to fill out papers for a job or a chance to do something special.	I have to apply if I want to be a volunteer at the animal shelter.
approximately	(adv) almost; nearly the right number or amount.	The kids moved so fast they were hard to count, but there were approximately 30 of them on the field.
article	(noun) a kind of writing usually found in newspapers, magazines, or on the Internet that explains or describes something.	This article in my new magazine is about buffalo.
assume	(verb) to believe something is true without any proof.	I assume he likes pizza, but we should ask him to make sure.
average	(adj) about the same as everyone else. (noun) a number found by adding a list of amounts, then dividing the total by the number of items on the list.	(adj) The average person likes pizza. (noun) The average of 2, 4, 6, and 8 is 5.
based on	(adj) using ideas from something else.	This movie was based on a book.
characteristic	(noun) things about a person, place or thing that make it unique.	A characteristic that easily separates Asian elephants from African elephants is their much smaller ears.
comment	(noun) a short thought or feeling you share with others. (verb) to share a short thought or feeling with others.	Casey's comment that my shoes looked cool made me feel better.
communicate	(verb) to share information or ideas, usually by talking or by writing.	My friend lives far away, so now we communicate by writing letters to one another.
complex	(adj) made of many different parts that are hard to understand.	The inside of the computer was very complex, with lots of circuits, chips, wires and fans.
comprehend	(verb) to understand.	When Mrs. Ochoa explains word problems I find them much easier to comprehend.
conclusion	(noun) a carefully thought-out decision that something is true or not true.	Mary listened to both stories then came to the conclusion that Jose was right.
conflict	(noun) a problem or disagreement between people or countries.	Conflict between England and France went on for many centuries and resulted in several wars.
consist of	(verb) to be made of two or more things.	Lemonade consists of water, lemon juice, and sugar.
contrast	(verb) to show how things are different.	If you contrast the two plans you will see how mine is better.
convince	(verb) to get someone to believe you or do what you want.	Can I convince you to jump up and down?
data	(noun) pieces of information, such as facts or numbers.	We can collect data about our class.
define	(verb) to tell what a word means.	I don't know that word, can you define it for me?

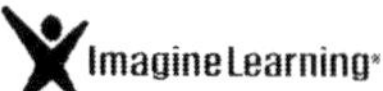

Advanced Vocabulary (4-6)

Word	Definition	Example Sentence
demonstrate	(verb) to show or explain clearly.	My little brother didn't know how to tie his shoe, so I demonstrated it for him several times.
economy	(noun) the way a country makes, buys, and sells things.	When you spend money, you are part of the economy.
emphasize	(verb) to make something seem more important than other things.	My parents emphasize working hard, because they know if I do, I will succeed.
entry	(noun) a note that is added to a document, usually in a list, dictionary, or journal.	Every day she writes a new entry in her journal, even if it's just to say, "Today was okay."
error	(noun) something that is wrong; a mistake.	The error you made when you added up the first numbers caused you to get the whole problem wrong.
event	(noun) something that happens, especially something important or exciting.	Parades are an event I enjoy.
eventually	(adv) after a long time.	Eventually, we will get to Mars.
evidence	(noun) facts that prove something is true or real.	His fingerprints on the doorknob are evidence that he was at the house.
except	(adv) used to say that something is left out of the group.	All months have 30 or 31 days, except for February.
experience	(noun) an event in your life where you learned something.	Getting lost in the woods was a terrible experience, but I learned a lot from it.
explain	(verb) to tell something so clearly that it is easy to understand.	Can anyone explain how the internet works?
express	(verb) to tell or show how you think or feel.	Let me express how proud I am of you.
feature	(noun) a part or quality of something.	A feature of this book is the cover.
file	(noun) a collection of information you store in a paper folder or on a computer.	She kept all the old letters and pictures in a file.
future	(noun) a time that has not come yet.	I wonder how small phones and computers will be in the future.
general	(adj) having to do with a whole group of things; not detailed or specific.	The general opinion is that the movie was bad, but I saw it and I liked it.
goal	(noun) something you want and are trying to get.	My goal is to finish this assignment.
horizontal	(adj) straight across, level, and flat.	This table is horizontal.
identify	(verb) To tell what something is or who someone is.	She can identify different kinds of trees by looking at their leaves and their bark.
in order to	(prep phrase/adv) a phrase you use when one thing must happen before another.	In order to teach you this word, I have to use an example.
include	(verb) to put something into a group or let someone be part of a group.	We should include the story about the bat in our report.
individual	(noun) one person.	Twins like it when you treat each one as an individual.
influence	(verb) to help change the way someone feels, thinks, or acts without making them change.	How can you influence others to be nice?
instead of	(prep) a phrase that means you did one thing but not something else.	Instead of doing math, we are learning about words.

Advanced Vocabulary (4–6)

Word	Definition	Example Sentence
interpret	(verb) to translate one language into another. (verb) to explain the meaning of something.	Maya did a better job on the project after I helped her interpret the directions.
investigate	(verb) to look carefully for information to find out why something happened. (verb) To learn hidden facts about something.	Detectives learn what happened when they investigate a crime scene and find clues.
legal	(adj) allowed by the law.	Stealing is not legal.
locate	(verb) to find where a place or object is.	When I locate Alaska on a map, I realize that it's very, very far away.
main	(adj) biggest or most important.	The main purpose of school is learning.
mention	(verb) to talk or write about someone or something in a quick way without giving away any details.	I can mention this book without telling you what it's about.
method	(noun) the way something is done.	My friend learned a very different method of long division while she lived in Germany.
natural resources	(noun) things found on the earth that are useful such as land, lakes, and minerals.	Water and wood are examples of natural resources.
obvious	(adj) describes something that is easy to see or understand.	I can't believe I missed that one; the answer is so obvious.
occur	(verb) to happen.	Most tornadoes occur in flat country.
organize	(verb) to put plans, ideas, or things into some kind of order.	I like to organize my books in alphabetical order by author.
paraphrase	(verb) to use your own words to describe what someone else has said or written	I don't remember his whole speech, but I can paraphrase the main ideas for you.
permit	(verb) to let someone do something; to allow.	I can permit you to use the bathroom.
phrase	(noun) a group of words that is not a complete sentence.	"Pie in the sky," is a phrase.
plot	(noun) the events that happen in a story.	Every episode of that cartoon has the exact same plot.
previous	(adj) earlier in order or time.	I worked very hard on this book report because my previous one got a bad grade.
procedure	(noun) a group of actions done in a certain order or way.	To solve a difficult math problem correctly, you need to follow a procedure.
process	(noun) a method of doing things that leads to a certain result.	Learning to read is a process.
produce	(verb) to make something.	That cherry tree produces very sour cherries.
receive	(verb) to get or be given something.	I like to receive gifts.
refer	(verb) to look somewhere for information, like a book or your notes.	I can refer to a dictionary if I don't know the word.
region	(noun) a large area of land.	You're from New England? I've never been to that region.
represent	(verb) to speak or act for another person or group.	I represent the fifth grade at our school's student council meetings.
require	(verb) to need something.	The teacher requires a signed permission form before I can go on the field trip.
resources	(noun) things that are used to make something else.	We need a new school but we don't have the resources to build one.
response	(noun) an answer to a question.	I asked her if she likes vegetables and her response was "yes."

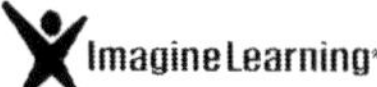

Advanced Vocabulary (4–6)

Word	Definition	Example Sentence
responsibility	(noun) a job you are required or expected to do.	Feeding the dog is my responsibility.
result	(noun) something that is caused by something else.	The result of eating too much cake is a stomachache.
reveal	(verb) to make something known or to show something.	You can ruin a good story when you reveal the ending too soon.
sample	(noun) a piece of something that gives you more information about the thing you took the piece from.	If you don't know which flavor of ice cream you want, ask for a sample to try.
scarce	(adj) very small in amount or number.	Seats are scarce on the crowded bus.
selection	(noun) the thing chosen from a group.	The paragraph I want to read is a selection from my favorite book.
series	(noun) a number of similar things that come one right after another.	During Spirit Week, the school will have a series of events to get students excited.
setting	(noun) the place and time of the story; place where something occurs.	The setting of Little Red Riding Hood is a forest.
situation	(noun) all of the facts, events, and conditions that affect something at a certain time and place.	We read several news stories to understand the situation better.
solution	(noun) something that solves a problem.	When we didn't have enough crayons, Ms. Brown's solution was to break all the crayons in half to make more.
source	(noun) the place where something comes from.	The stream was a source of water for many animals in the forest.
specific	(adj) a way of describing a certain thing.	He didn't want just any shoes, he wanted a very specific style of shoes.
statement	(noun) something that is said or written.	After this important event, we expect the President to make a statement.
strategy	(noun) a plan for reaching a goal.	I won the game because I had a better strategy.
subject	(noun) a person or thing being described or discussed.	The subject of this lesson is new words.
substance	(noun) a special kind of solid, liquid, or gas.	Helium is a substance that makes balloons float.
succeed	(verb) to complete a task correctly.	We're working hard on this topic because we want to succeed on the test.
suggest	(verb) to give an idea about what to do.	I suggest you work hard on your report.
support	(verb) to help a person or an idea be successful.	I support the idea that everyone should treat each other nicely.
the following	(phrase) a phrase that shows something that is coming next.	The following is a color: blue.
theory	(noun) an idea about why or how things happen that hasn't been proven.	To prove a theory, you need to do a lot of research and experiments.
topic	(noun) the subject you are writing about or giving a speech about.	The topic of this lesson is new words.
tradition	(noun) an idea, belief, or way of doing something that has been done by a group of people for a long time.	My family has a tradition of eating waffles on New Years Day.
vertical	(adj) positioned up and down.	When you stand, you are vertical. When you lie down, you are horizontal.

Vocabulary Routine: Rate the Word

CCRA.L.4, CCRA.L.6
TEKS 110.18.2

LEARNING OBJECTIVE: Acquire and use general, academic, and domain-specific vocabulary.

LANGUAGE OBJECTIVE: Correctly pronounce and use target vocabulary orally and in writing to deepen understanding of the words and acquire word-learning strategies.

Research

Vocabulary acquisition is essential to reading comprehension and general academic success. Intentional vocabulary instruction helps students acquire new vocabulary and word-learning strategies (Honig et al., 2013). The different levels of word knowledge identified by Edgar Dale in 1965 can be a useful tool for students to rate their knowledge of vocabulary. Follow-up instruction should be robust and allow students to engage actively with the words in a variety of ways (Beck et al., 2002).

Lesson Overview

Students rate their knowledge of the target vocabulary and actively engage with the words to deepen their understanding of meanings.

Materials	Preparation
• Vocabulary List • Vocabulary Rating Cards (one set per student) • Word journals or notebooks (one per student)	• Cut out all Vocabulary Rating Cards, or have students cut out their cards. • Prepare prompts and questions for the target vocabulary. Use the Active Engagement with Vocabulary chart as a guide.

Introduce the Activity

Tell students you will introduce some new vocabulary words and ask them to show how much they know about the words.

Display a set of the Vocabulary Rating Cards. Explain: ***When I introduce a new vocabulary word, you will hold up one of these cards to show how much you already know about the word. Then you will learn more about the word and use the cards again to show how much you learned.***

Distribute a set of the Vocabulary Rating Cards to each student. Then read them aloud together and explain each rating:

1. "I don't know it" means you have never seen or heard this word before.

2. "I have seen it or heard it" means you have read or heard this word before but can't explain what it means.

3. "I'm an expert" means you know the word well and can use it and explain its meaning.

Introduce the Target Word

Use the following routine to introduce each new word from the Vocabulary List.

1. **Say the Word** Display the vocabulary word and model the pronunciation. Have students say the word aloud.
2. **Rate the Word** Prompt students to hold up a Vocabulary Rating Card to show how well they know the word.
3. **Explain Word Meaning** Invite students who rated the word with a 3 to share what they know about the word. Follow up student responses, as needed, by explaining the word in student-friendly, everyday language.
4. **Provide Context** Use the word in sentences to demonstrate how it might be used in general and academic contexts. Invite volunteers to use the word in a sentence of their own.
5. **Actively Engage with the Word** Share a prompt or question for the vocabulary word. Then have students turn to a partner and discuss. After partner discussion, invite volunteers to share their responses.
6. **Rate the Word** Prompt students to rate the word again using the Vocabulary Rating Cards.

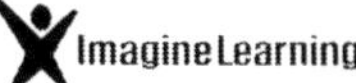

Active Engagement with Vocabulary

Engagement activities provide short, upbeat opportunities for students to interact with the word and deepen their understanding of its meaning.

Activity	**Examples** **Target Word: public**
Questions	***What is your favorite place to go in public?*** ***What is something you would never do in public?***
Example or Non-Example	***Which of these two sentences tells about ways to serve the public?*** • ***You can help clean up a nearby park.*** • ***You can clean your bedroom.***
Finish the Idea	***I didn't want to go out in public today because ____.***
Have You Ever . . . ?	• ***Have you ever made an announcement in public? What was it?*** • ***Have you ever been embarrassed in public? What happened?***
Choices	***If what I say is something that is normal to do in public, say* okay. *If it is something that looks silly if you do it in public, say* no.** • ***meet a friend*** (okay) • ***brush your teeth*** (no) • ***eat at a restaurant*** (okay) • ***ride a bike*** (okay) • ***climb on furniture*** (no)

Check Progress

To check individual progress, observe students during group and pair work and as they rate the word a second time. If students can accurately use the target vocabulary in context or explain the meaning, consider the intervention successful.

Have students work independently to record the words in a word journal. Encourage students to:

- ***Write the word's meaning.***
- ***Write the word in a context sentence.***
- ***Draw a picture to illustrate the word's meaning.***

Meet with each student individually to review their word journals. Use one of these prompts to have students demonstrate understanding of the words:

- (nouns) ***What is a ____?***
- (verbs) ***What does it mean to ____?***
- (adjectives) ***What might you describe using ____?***
- (adverbs) ***What does it mean if you do something ____?***
- (prepositions) ***Use ____ to tell where something is.***

Beck, I. L., McKeown, M.G., & Kucan, L., (2002). *Bringing Words to Life.* New York: Guilford.

Honig, B., Diamond, L., & Gutlohn, L., (2013). *Teaching Reading Sourcebook (updated 2nd ed.).* Novato, CA: Arena Press.

Reteaching Lessons

Vocabulary Rating Cards

1

I don't know it.

1

I don't know it.

2

I have seen it or heard it.

2

I have seen it or heard it.

3

I'm an expert.

3

I'm an expert.

Vocabulary Routine: Four Corners

CCRA.L.4, CCRA.L.6
TEKS 110.18.2

LEARNING OBJECTIVE: Tap into prior knowledge to connect vocabulary to other words and concepts using a graphic organizer.

LANGUAGE OBJECTIVE: Use target vocabulary in context and explain meaning orally and in writing.

Research

Students need opportunities to process word meanings in multiple ways to extend their word knowledge beyond isolated pieces of information. This ensures that the words become part of their working vocabulary (Honig et al., 2013). Four Corners vocabulary cards encourage students to interact with a word in multiple ways, creating visual representations that include word meanings and context (Echevarria, Vogt & Short, 2012).

Lesson Overview

Students create a Four Corners Vocabulary Card to define a word, tell what it's like, and give examples.

Materials	Preparation
• Vocabulary List • Four Corners Vocabulary Cards (one per student for each word) • Word journals or notebooks (one per student; optional)	• Select a target vocabulary word to use with the Four Corners graphic organizer. If time allows, select additional words and repeat steps 3 and 4 of the routine. • Prepare a student-friendly definition and a context sentence for the target vocabulary to be used in step 1.

Introduce the Activity: Creating a Four Corners Card

Tell students they will make a vocabulary chart that shows their understanding of a vocabulary word. Explain: ***In this activity you are making a personal connection with the word. You get to be creative and draw your own picture, write your own sentence, and explain the meaning in your own words.***

1. **Assign a Vocabulary Word** Display the target vocabulary word and guide group discussion about its meaning. Say a student-friendly definition of the word. Then prompt volunteers to restate the meaning in their own words. Say the word in a sentence and invite students to say the word in a sentence of their own.
2. **Model a Four Corners Card** Display the Four Corners Vocabulary Card Samples. Use one of the samples shown and explain how to complete each corner of the graphic organizer.
3. **Complete the Graphic Organizer** Distribute a copy of the Four Corners Vocabulary Card to each student, or have them draw and complete a four corners graphic organizer in their word journals. See **Differentiation** suggestions.
4. **Share Word Knowledge** Invite students to share one corner of their completed graphic organizers with the group.

Differentiation
Below Level Pair beginner students with a more proficient partner. Have the beginner student in each pair complete just the top two corners of their own graphic organizer, writing the word with partner help and drawing a picture.
On Level Have students work with a partner to complete a shared graphic organizer.
Above Level Have students complete the graphic organizer individually. Encourage them to say or write two to three additional sentences using the target word.

Check Progress

Check each student's Four Corners Vocabulary Card and use the following activity to check progress.

Meet with students individually to review their graphic organizers. Then use these prompts to have students describe their assigned vocabulary word:

- ***What does the word mean?***
- ***Say a sentence using the word.***
- ***How does your picture show the meaning of the word?***

If students can accurately describe the target vocabulary, consider the intervention successful.

Honig, B., Diamond, L., & Gutlohn, L., (2013). *Teaching Reading Sourcebook (updated 2nd ed.).* Novato, CA: Arena Press.

Echevarria, J., B., Vogt, M., & Short, D., (2012). *Making Content Comprehensible for English Learners: The SIOP ® Model, 4th edition*. Boston, MA: Pearson.]

Four Corners Vocabulary Card Samples

Word	Picture or Symbol
dollar	$
Word in Sentence	**Meaning**
It costs one dollar to buy a balloon.	a kind of money

Word	Picture or Symbol
inspect	
Word in Sentence	**Meaning**
My dad inspects my room to make sure it is clean.	to look at something closely

Four Corners Vocabulary Cards

Word	Picture or Symbol
Word in Sentence	Meaning

Word	Picture or Symbol
Word in Sentence	Meaning

Four Corners Vocabulary Cards

Picture or Symbol

Meaning

Word

Word in Sentence

Picture or Symbol

Meaning

Word

Word in Sentence

Picture or Symbol

Meaning

Word

Word in Sentence

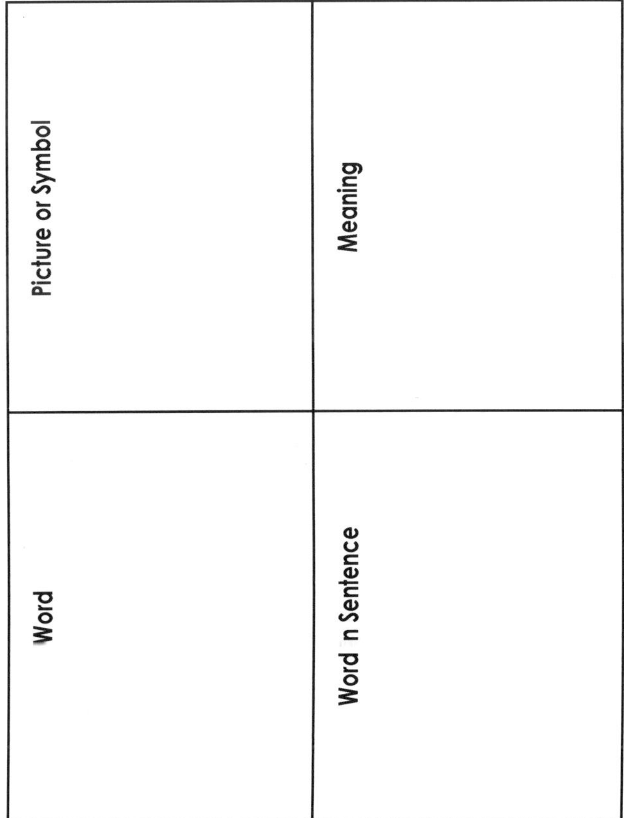

Reteaching Lessons

Vocabulary Routine: Graphic Organizers

CCRA.L.4, CCRA.L.6
TEKS 110.18.2

LEARNING OBJECTIVE: Use graphic organizers to deepen understanding of vocabulary.

LANGUAGE OBJECTIVE: Describe connections between the target vocabulary word and information recorded in a graphic organizer.

Research

Word webs and other graphic organizers provide a visual representation of words and their meanings. Graphic organizers allow students to explore a variety of meanings and contexts associated with vocabulary, deepening their understanding of the word (Beck et al., 2002; Honig et al., 2013).

Lesson Overview

Students complete a graphic organizer with information related to a target vocabulary word.

Materials	Preparation
• Vocabulary List • Printouts of the Graphic Organizer (one per student) • Word journals or notebooks (one per student; optional)	• Select a target vocabulary word and a graphic organizer to use with the word (see the Sample Graphic Organizers). • Prepare a student-friendly definition and context sentence for the target vocabulary. Note synonyms/antonyms and examples for the word as required by the chosen graphic organizer.

Introduce the Activity: Using a Vocabulary Graphic Organizer

Tell students they will complete a graphic organizer that shows their understanding of a vocabulary word. Explain: ***In this activity, you should think about the word's meaning, how it's used in the classroom and everyday conversations, and how it relates to other words.***

1. **Assign a Vocabulary Word** Display the target vocabulary word and guide group discussion about its meaning.
   - Say a student-friendly definition of the word. Then prompt volunteers to restate the meaning in their own words.
   - Say the word in a sentence and invite students to say the word in a sentence of their own.
   - If appropriate for the chosen graphic organizer, say an example, a non-example, a synonym (words with the same meaning), and an antonym (words with opposite meanings). Prompt students to think of other related words.
2. **Model Creating the Graphic Organizer** Display the Sample Graphic Organizers on page 3 and explain how to complete each section of the chosen graphic organizer.
3. **Complete the Graphic Organizer** Distribute a copy of the blank graphic organizer to each student, or have them draw and complete the graphic organizer in their word journals. See **Differentiation** suggestions.
4. **Share and Discuss** Invite students to share one part of their completed graphic organizer with the group.

If time allows, select additional words and repeat steps 3 and 4 of the routine.

Differentiation
Below Level Guide the group to create a shared graphic organizer for the target word. Add information with input from students.
On Level Have students work with a partner to complete a shared graphic organizer.
Above Level Have students complete the graphic organizer individually. Encourage them to say or write a few sentences using the target vocabulary and other words and phrases from the completed graphic organizer.

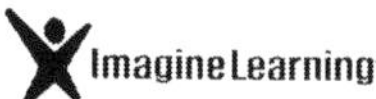

Check Progress

To check individual progress, observe students during group sharing and discussion of the graphic organizers.

Meet with each student individually to review their graphic organizer. Then use these prompts to have students describe their assigned vocabulary word:

- ***What does the word mean?***
- ***Can you use the word in a sentence?***
- ***How does your graphic organizer help you remember the meaning of the word?***

If students have accurately represented the target vocabulary in their graphic organizer and can show understanding of the word, consider the intervention successful.

Beck, I. L., McKeown, M.G., & Kucan, L., (2002). *Bringing Words to Life.* New York: Guilford.

Honig, B., Diamond, L., & Gutlohn, L., (2013). *Teaching Reading Sourcebook (updated 2nd ed.).* Novato, CA: Arena Press.

Reteaching Lessons

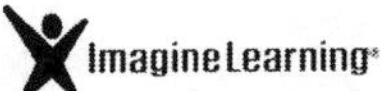

Sample Graphic Organizers

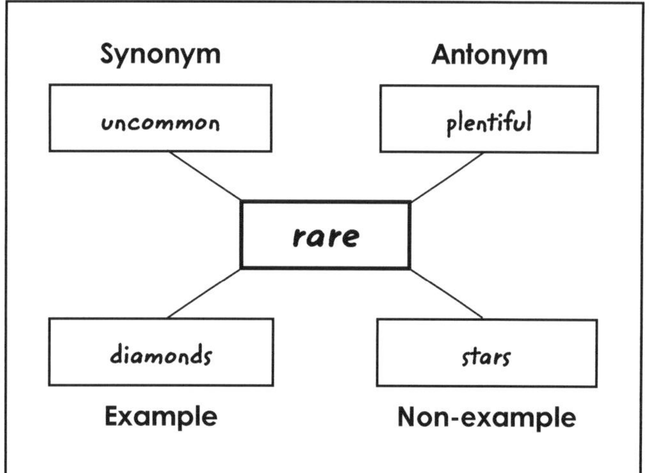

Synonym/Antonym Map

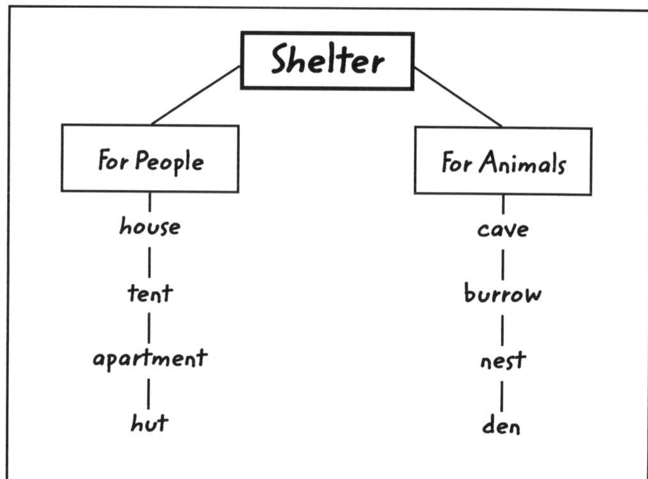

Semantic Map

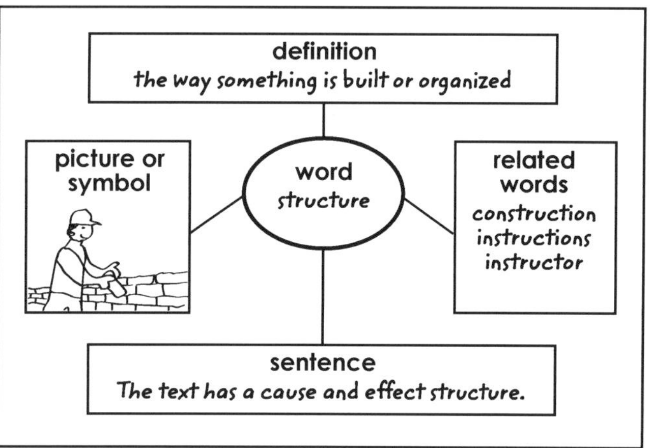

Connections Map

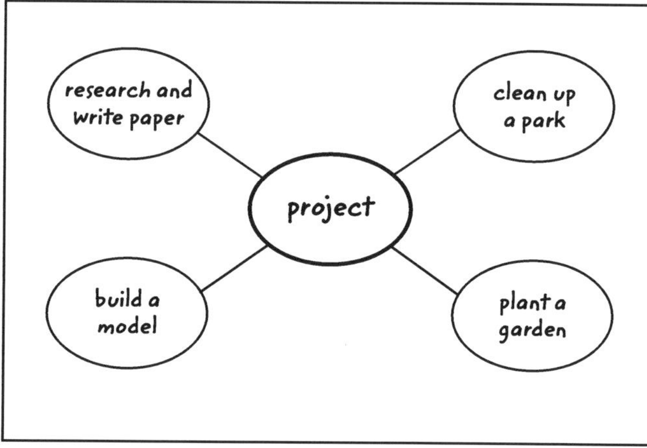

Example Web

Reteaching Lessons

Imagine Learning

Name: ____

Synonym/Antonym Map

Antonym

Non-example

Synonym

Example

Reteaching Lessons

Name: ____

Semantic Map

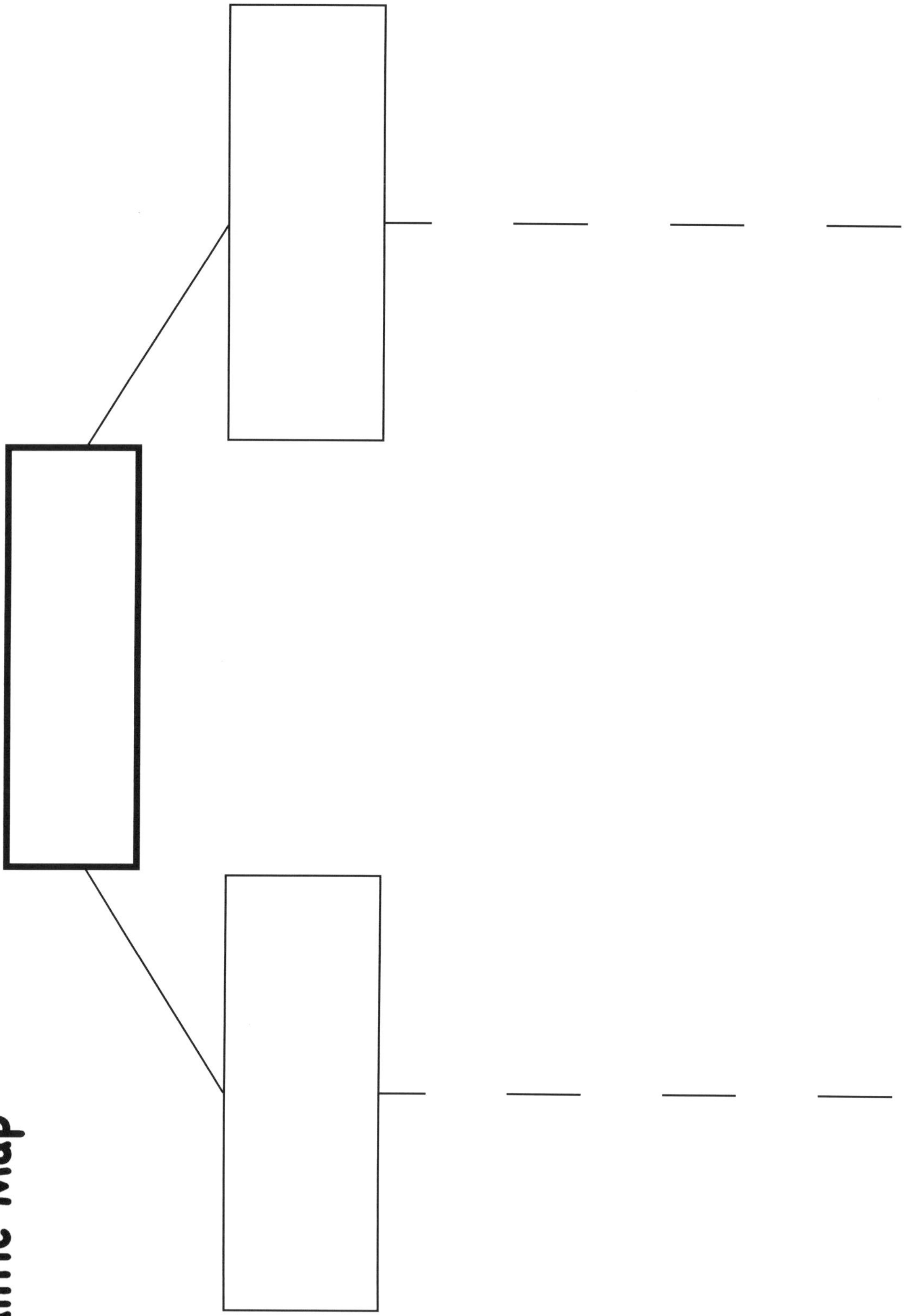

✓ Reteaching Lessons

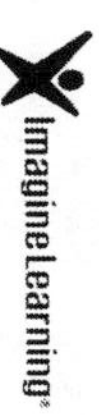

Connections Map

definition

picture or symbol

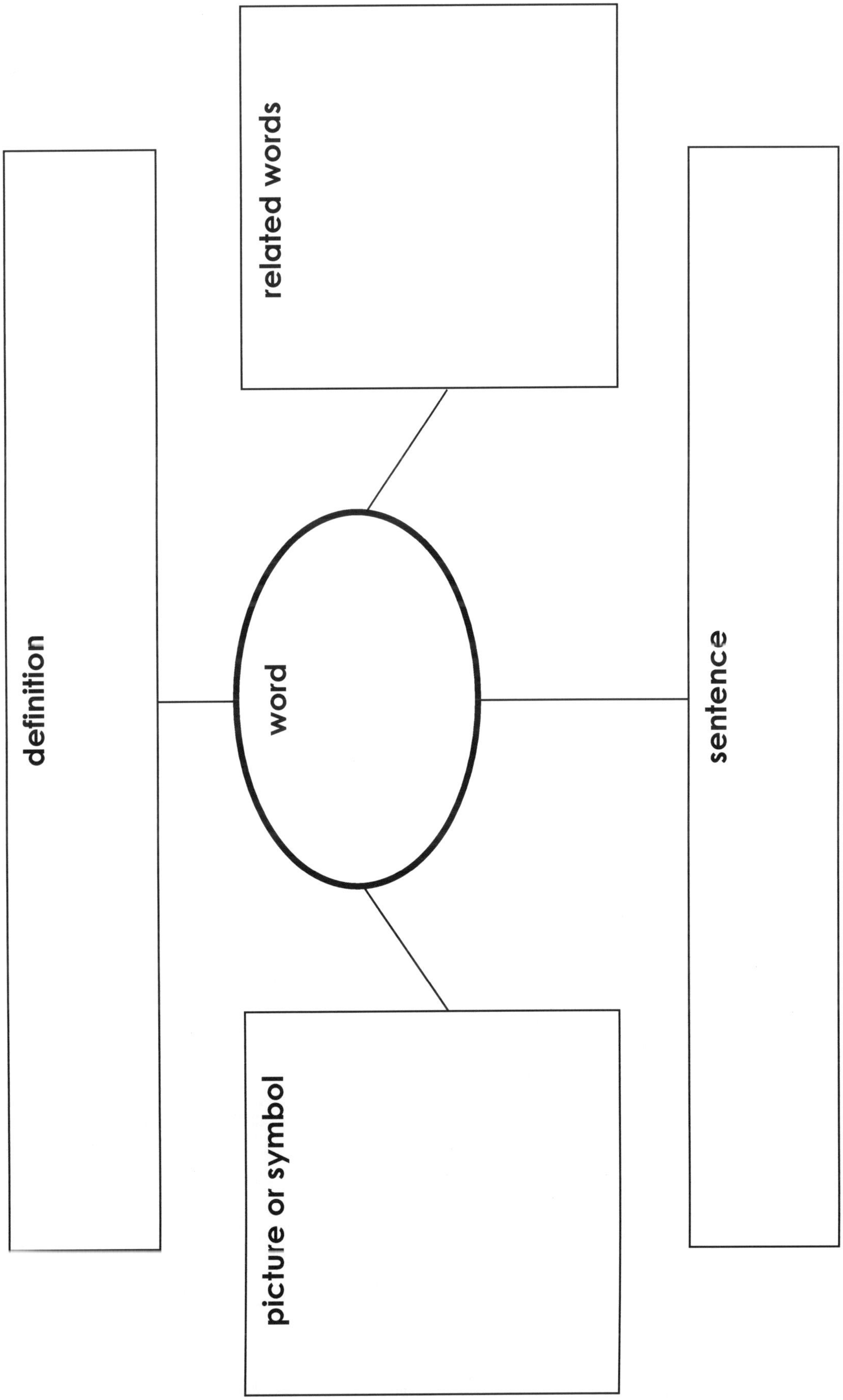

word

related words

sentence

Reteaching Lessons ✓

Name: ______________________________

Name: ______________________________

Example Web

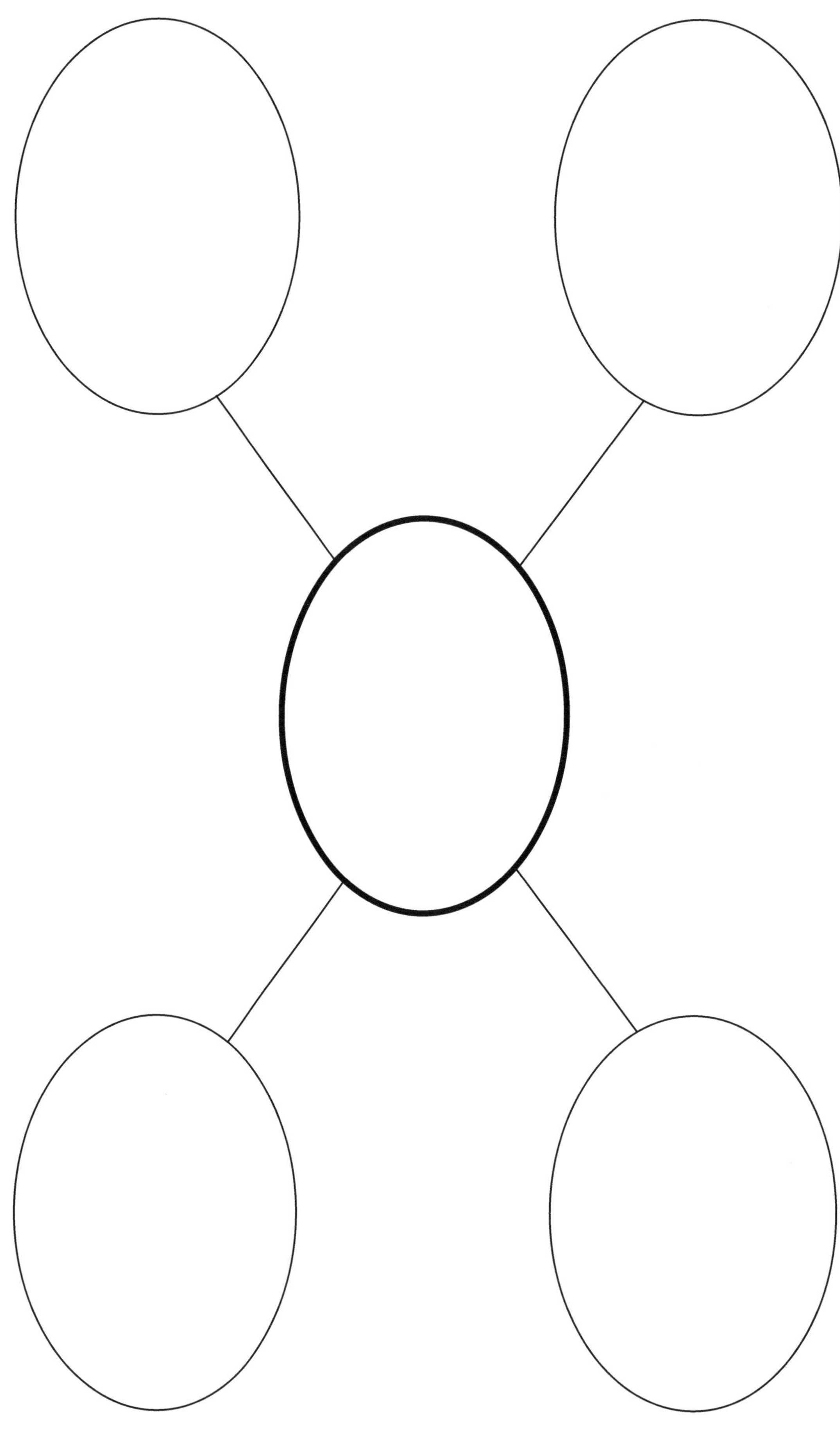

Vocabulary Routine: 3-D Graphic Organizers

CCRA.L.4, CCRA.L.6
TEKS 110.18.2

LEARNING OBJECTIVE: Use three-dimensional graphic organizers to deepen understanding of vocabulary.

LANGUAGE OBJECTIVE: Describe connections between the target vocabulary word and information recorded in a three-dimensional graphic organizer.

Research

Three-dimensional graphic organizers help students analyze and communicate word meanings and connect concepts for deeper understanding (Beck et al., 2002; Honig et al., 2013). They also give kinesthetic learners the opportunity to organize information in a hands-on way. Kinesthetic activities foster analytical skills and information retention (Lengel & Kuczala, 2010).

Lesson Overview

Students complete a three-dimensional graphic organizer with information related to the target vocabulary.

Materials	Preparation
• Vocabulary List	• Select a target vocabulary word and a 3-D graphic organizer to use with the word (see the sample 3-D Graphic Organizers). • Prepare a student-friendly definition and context sentence for the target vocabulary. Prepare examples and related words as required by the chosen 3-D graphic organizer. • Some students may have difficulty accurately folding a sheet of paper into thirds for the trifold. Consider preparing a sheet of paper for each student in advance, marking where they should fold the paper.

Introduce the Activity: Creating a 3-D Graphic Organizer

Tell students they will create a 3-D graphic organizer that shows their understanding of a vocabulary word. Explain: ***We will make a 3-D graphic organizer by folding paper to create different sections. In each section, you will fill in different kinds of information that relate to the word. I will guide you step-by-step to create your 3-D graphic organizer.***

1. **Assign a Vocabulary Word** Display the target vocabulary word and guide group discussion about its meaning.
    - Say a student-friendly definition of the word. Then prompt volunteers to restate the meaning in their own words.
    - Say the word in a sentence and invite students to say the word in a sentence of their own.
    - If appropriate for the chosen 3-D graphic organizer, give an example or a related word. Prompt students to think of other examples or related words.
2. **Model Creating the 3-D Graphic Organizer** Display the page with a sample of the chosen 3-D graphic organizer. Explain how the information in each section relates to the vocabulary word.
3. **Create the 3-D Graphic Organizer** Use the directions to guide students in making a 3-D graphic organizer with information about the target vocabulary word. See Differentiation suggestions for grouping.
4. **Share and Discuss** Invite students to share one part of their completed 3-D graphic organizer with the group.

If time allows, select additional words and repeat steps 3 and 4 of the routine.

Differentiation
Below Level Guide the group to create a shared 3-D graphic organizer for the target word. Add information with input from students.
On Level Have students work with a partner to create a shared 3-D graphic organizer for the target word.
Above Level Have students work individually to create a 3-D graphic organizer. Encourage them to say or write a few sentences using the target vocabulary and other words and phrases from the completed graphic organizer.

Check Progress

To check individual progress, observe students during group sharing and discussion of the 3-D graphic organizers.

Meet with students individually to review their 3-D graphic organizers. Then use these prompts or similar questions to quiz students on the vocabulary word:

- ***What does the word mean?***
- ***Can you use the word in a sentence?***
- ***How does your 3-D graphic organizer help you remember the meaning of the word?***

If students have accurately represented the target vocabulary in their graphic organizer and can show understanding of the word, consider the intervention successful.

Beck, I. L., McKeown, M.G., & Kucan, L., (2002). *Bringing Words to Life.* New York: Guilford.

Honig, B., Diamond, L., & Gutlohn, L., (2013). *Teaching Reading Sourcebook (updated 2nd ed.).* Novato, CA: Arena Press.

Lengel, T. & Kuczala M., (2010). *The Kinesthetic Classroom: Teaching and Learning through Movement.* Thousand Oaks, CA: Corwin Press.

Half Book

a tool for looking at things far away

definition

I saw the Moon through a telescope.

context sentence

INSTRUCTIONS

1

Fold a sheet of paper in half like a hamburger, lining up the top corners of the paper with the bottom corners.

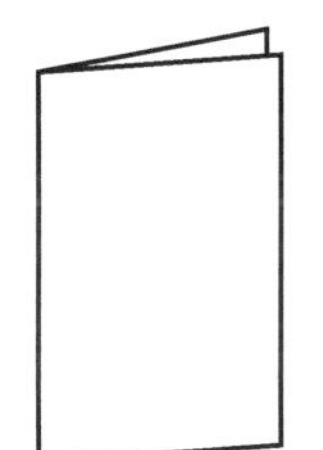

2

Make a crease at the center point.

Trifold

invention

word

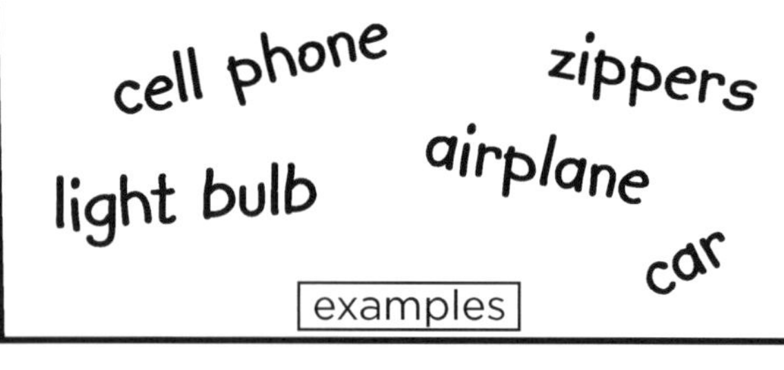

a new tool
or machine

definition

The Wright brothers
tested their invention in 1903.

context sentence

INSTRUCTIONS

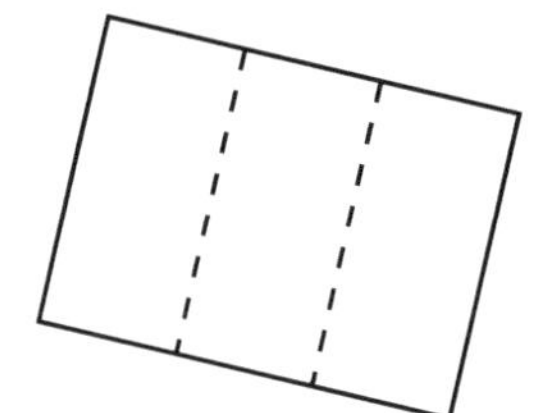

1

Fold a sheet of paper into thirds.

2

Bring in the top corners to meet the fold of the bottom half of the paper. Make a crease at each of the two folds

Shutter Fold

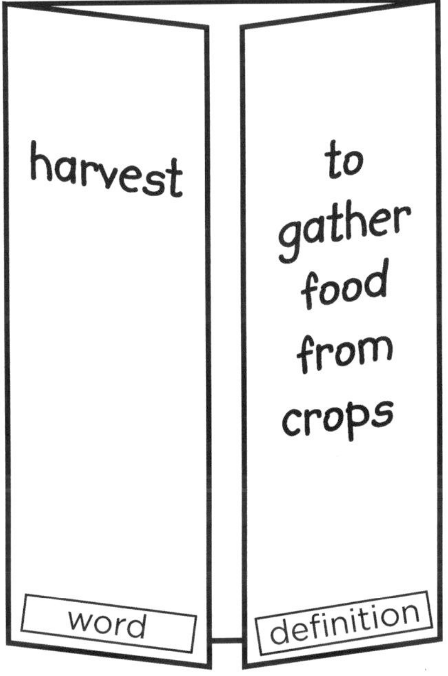

INSTRUCTIONS

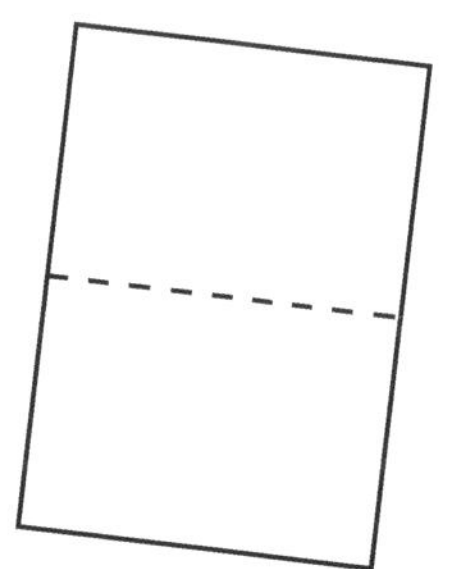

1

Line up the top corners of the paper with the bottom corners, folding it like a hamburger, but without making a crease. Pinch each side of the paper to mark the center point.

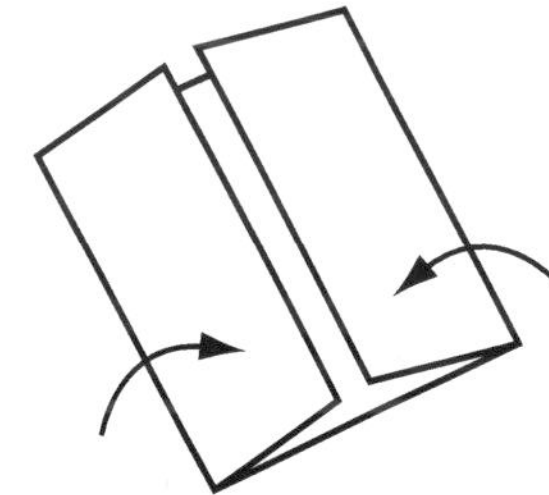

2

Lay the paper flat again, then fold each outer edge of the paper to meet at the center point.

Matchbook

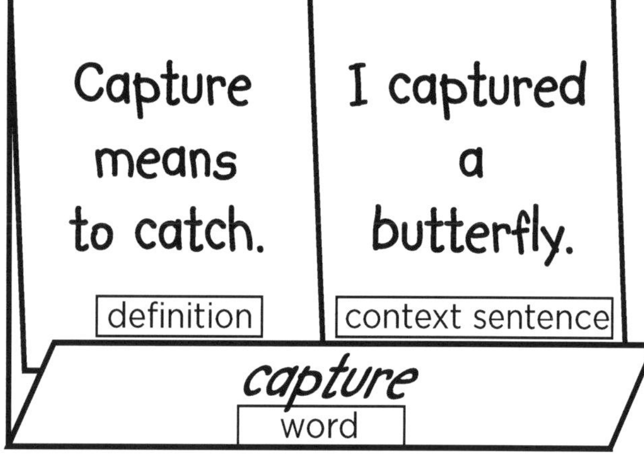

INSTRUCTIONS

1
Fold the bottom edge of a sheet of paper up and make a crease about one inch away from the edge.

2
Fold the top corners of the paper down to meet the fold on the bottom. Tuck the top fold into the bottom fold.

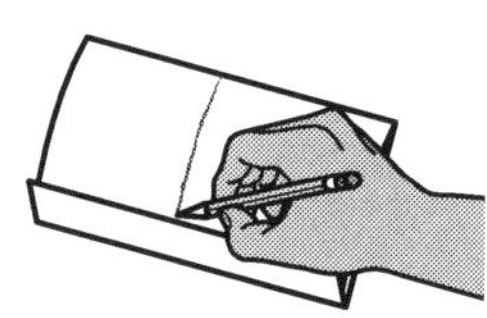

3
Draw a center line from the top fold to the edge of the bottom fold.

✓ Reteaching Lessons

Vocabulary Routines: Vocabulary Games

CCRA.L.4, CCRA.L.6
TEKS 110.18.2

LEARNING OBJECTIVE: Tap into prior knowledge to connect vocabulary to other words and concepts.

LANGUAGE OBJECTIVE: Correctly pronounce target vocabulary and orally define the word, give examples, or use the word in a sentence.

Research

Research indicates that playing interactive games helps students acquire new knowledge related to vocabulary words (Bear et al., 2016; Beck et al., 2002; Honig et al., 2013).

Lesson Overview

Students practice identifying and describing vocabulary words by playing vocabulary games.

Around the World

Materials

- Vocabulary List

How to Play

1. **Designate a Traveler** The designated traveler faces off with the student nearest to him or her. The winner of the face-off advances to challenge the next student in the group, and so on, until one challenger has successfully traveled all the way "around the world."
2. **Give the Clue** Give the traveler and the challenger a clue by stating a definition or giving examples. For example, for the word *team* you might say: ***It's a group of people or animals who work together.*** Or you might give these examples of a team: ***soccer players, horses pulling a wagon, sled dogs, firefighters.*** The traveler and the challenger try to be the first to say the correct vocabulary word. If the traveler wins, he continues to the next challenger. If the traveler loses, the challenger takes his place and becomes the traveler.
3. **Keep Traveling** The first traveler to travel all the way back around to his or her seat wins.

Check Progress

Give a clue for each vocabulary word. Have a student identify the correct words for the clues. If students can correctly identify the vocabulary words, consider the intervention successful.

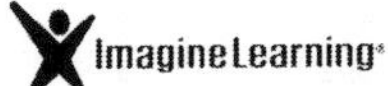

Concentration

Materials	Preparation
• Vocabulary List of 5–10 words • Index Cards (2 for each word per student pair)	• For each student pair, write each vocabulary word on an index card, or have students create their word cards. • For each student pair, write the definition of each vocabulary word on an index card, or have students create their definition cards.

How to Play

1. **Pair Students** Assign students to a partner to play the game. Give each pair a set of vocabulary cards and definition cards.
2. **Students Shuffle the Cards** Have partners shuffle their cards and lay them facedown in a grid.
3. **Play the Game** Students take turns turning over two cards and reading them aloud. If the player turns over two matching cards (a word and the matching definition), he or she says the word in a sentence and keeps the two cards. If the two cards don't match, the player turns the cards facedown again and the turns ends. The player with the most cards in the end wins the game.

Check Progress

Name each vocabulary word. Prompt a student to give the definition. If students can give accurate definitions of the words, consider the intervention successful.

Picture It

Materials

- Vocabulary List of 5–10 words.

How to Play

1. **Display the Vocabulary Words** Display a list of vocabulary words for students.
2. **Draw the Word** Choose one student to go first. The student should choose a vocabulary word without telling anyone which word he or she has chosen. Without talking, the student draws pictures as clues to help the other students guess the word.
3. **Score Points** The first student to guess the word gets one point. He or she scores one more point for correctly using the word in a sentence.
4. **Continue the Game** Continue the game until each student has had a turn drawing clues.

Check Progress

Name each vocabulary word. Prompt a student to use the word in a sentence. If students can correctly use the words in a sentence, consider the intervention successful.

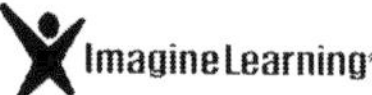

Clue Me In

Materials	Preparation
• Vocabulary List of 8–10 words • Index Cards	• Write each vocabulary word on an index card.

How to Play

1. **Draw a Card** Assign students to a partner to play the game. Each pair of students is a team.
2. **Draw a Card** Place the vocabulary cards facedown in a stack. Choose a team to go first. Have one member of the first team draw a card.
3. **Student Gives Clues** The player who draws the card gives clues about the word. The student can define the word or give examples but can't say the word or any part of it. This player has 15 seconds to get his or her partner to say the vocabulary word. The team scores a point if the correct word is guessed in the time.
4. **Continue the Game** Continue with the next pair of students. Have students play until all the cards are used.

Check Progress

Name each vocabulary word. Prompt a student to give a clue for the word by defining or giving examples. If students can give accurate clues for the words, consider the intervention successful.

Vocabulary Bingo

Materials

- Vocabulary List of 9 words
- Printout of Vocabulary Bingo (one per student)
- Small items to use as Bingo markers

How to Play

1. **Display the Vocabulary** Display the Vocabulary List.
2. **Prepare Vocabulary Bingo Sheets** Distribute a Vocabulary Bingo sheet to each student. Have students fill in each square of the Vocabulary Bingo sheet with a vocabulary word in random order.
3. **Give Clues** Say a clue about a vocabulary word by giving a definition or examples. For example, for the word *crop* you might say: ***It means food grown by farmers.*** Or you might give these examples of crops: ***corn, wheat, hay, apples, beans.***
4. **Students Place Markers** Students identify the word and place a marker on the corresponding square of their Vocabulary Bingo sheets.
5. **Bingo!** The first student to place three markers in a row calls, "Bingo!" Check that the student has correctly identified each vocabulary word. Ask the student to choose one word from the winning row and use it in a sentence.

Check Progress

Give a clue for each vocabulary word. Have a student identify the correct word for the clue. If students can correctly identify the vocabulary words, consider the intervention successful.

Bear, D., Invernizzi, M., Templeton, S., Johnston, F. (2016). *Words Their Way (6th edition).* Pearson Education.

Beck, I. L., McKeown, M.G., & Kucan, L., (2002). *Bringing Words to Life.* New York: Guilford.

Honig, B., Diamond, L., & Gutlohn, L., (2013). *Teaching Reading Sourcebook (updated 2nd ed.).* Novato, CA: Arena Press.

Name ___________________________________

Vocabulary Bingo

Write a different vocabulary word in each square. Words should be written in random order. Listen for clues and place a marker on the correct vocabulary word. Say "Bingo!" when you have placed 3 markers in a row.

Notes

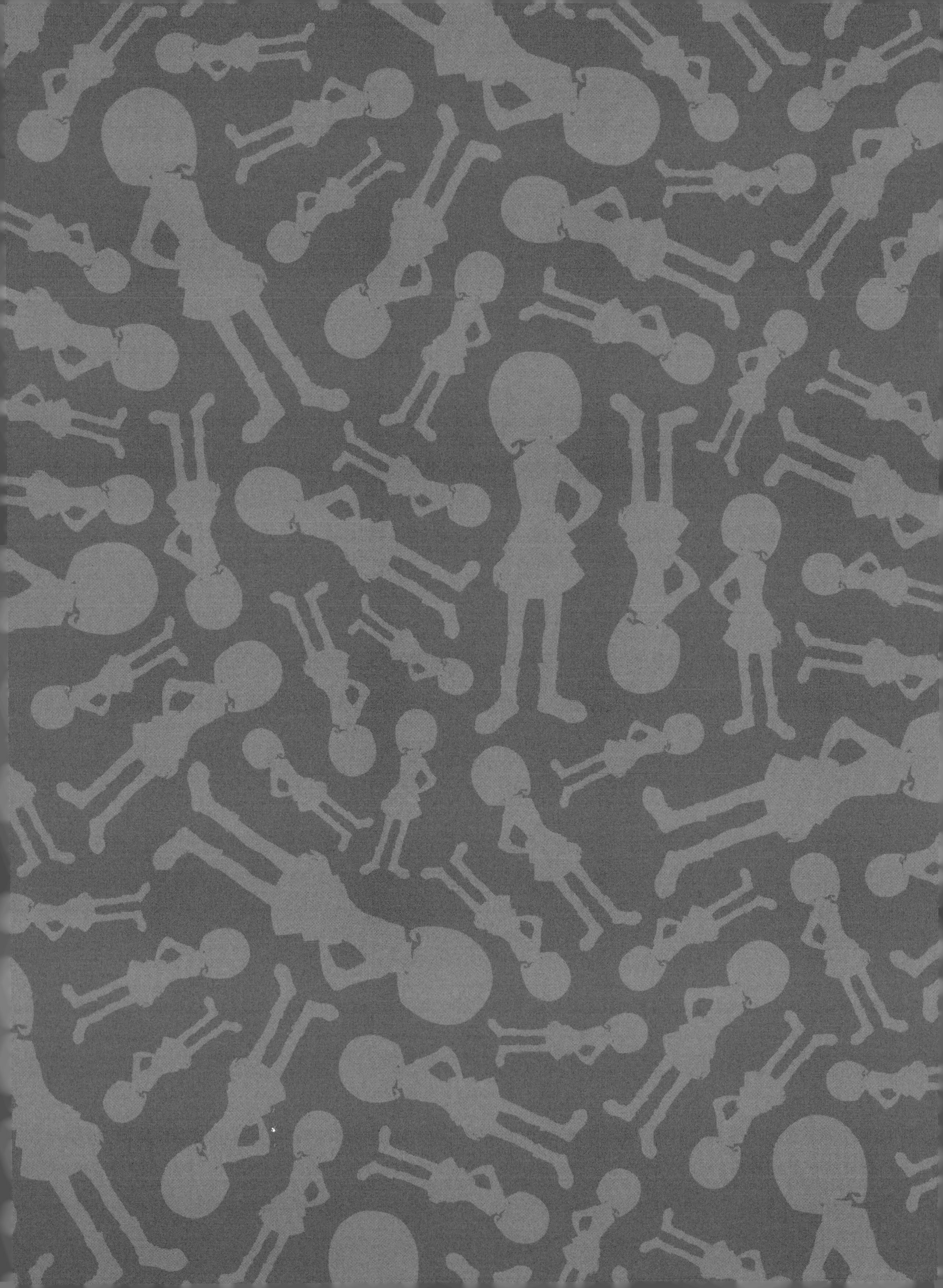

SPEAKING AND LISTENING

CLASSROOM ACTIVITIES

Classroom activities include ideas and resources for whole-class or small group work to help students develop skills in speaking and listening. The engaging activities support language production, listening comprehension, and conversation, and extend the skills students learn from the Imagine Learning online curriculum.

- Language-focused activities based in real-world, everyday language
- Standards-based materials that require minimal teacher preparation
- Interactive activities to help English Language Learners build confidence in their speaking and listening abilities
- Printouts of Imagine Learning chants to help with language acquisition

My Own Calendar

CCSS.L.K.5.C
TEKS 110.11.5.A

LEARNING OBJECTIVE: Learn to read a calendar.
LANGUAGE OBJECTIVE: Use calendar vocabulary to talk about dates and days.

Activity Overview

Students fill out a calendar and use it to review numbers and calendar vocabulary.

Materials

- Calendar printout (1 per student, plus 1 for modeling)
- sample calendar
- crayons or markers

Explain

Introduce the activity: ***You are going to make your own calendar today, and we'll review the words we see.*** Show the class a calendar and turn to the current month. Explain that a calendar shows the weeks and days for each month. Give each student a blank Calendar printout. Use a printout to model each step or create a large, blank calendar on poster paper.

Ask: ***What goes at the top of a calendar page?*** (The month) ***How many months are there in a year?*** (twelve) ***What month is this?*** Write the name of the current month at the top of your calendar poster. Have the students repeat the name of the current month and write it on their calendars.

Ask: ***What goes across the first line of the calendar?*** (days of the week) ***How many days of the week are there?*** (seven) Have the students repeat the days of the week as you write them on your calendar. Have the students write the days of the week on their calendars.

Ask: ***What goes in each box?*** (dates, calendar days) ***How many days does each month have?*** Explain that each month has twenty-eight, thirty, or thirty-one days in it. (See Variation.) Write the numbers for the current month on your poster. Have students write the date numbers on their calendars. When all students have finished writing the numbers, repeat them together.

Fill in any special holidays or activities happening during the month.

Play

Introduce the game: ***Let's play a find and point game. I'll ask you a question. You point to the answer on your calendar.***

Ask these questions and have students respond by pointing to their calendar. When all students are showing a response, call on a volunteer to say the answer aloud. Then have all students repeat the answer together.

- ***What are the first three letters in the name of this month?*** Point out that the names of the months are often shortened to the first three letters.
- ***What is the third day of the week?*** (the first, the last, the fifth, etc.)
- ***What day of the week comes before Thursday?*** (after Monday, between Tuesday and Thursday, etc.)
- ***What day of the week is the 10th of this month?*** (5th, 23rd, etc.)
- ***What is the date of the 2nd Tuesday of this month?*** (the third Friday, the last Saturday, the first Sunday, etc.)
- ***How many Fridays are there in this month?*** (how many Wednesdays, how many holidays, etc.)
- ***What days do you go to school?*** (what days do you stay home)
- ***What day is your favorite? Why?***

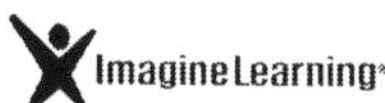

VARIATION: Have the students repeat the words to this poem:

Thirty days are in September,
April, June, and November;
All the rest have thirty-one,
But February stands alone,
It has twenty-eight days time,
In leap years, it has twenty-nine.

EXTENSION ACTIVITY

Have students add colors or illustrations to their calendar. At the beginning of each day, ask students to find the current day on their calendars and cross it out.

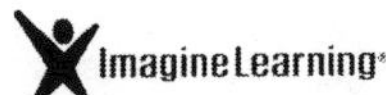

Calendar

1-2-3 Find the Color

CCSS.L.K.5C
TEKS 110.11.5.C

LEARNING OBJECTIVE: Comprehend and use color words.

LANGUAGE OBJECTIVE: Use color words to talk about objects in the classroom.

Activity Overview

Find items of certain colors in the classroom to review color words.

Materials

- 9 sheets of colored paper, one for each color in the game

Play

1. Put the sheets of colored paper where all students can see them.
2. Review the names of the colors while pointing to each paper. Have students repeat the color words as you review them.
3. Demonstrate how to play the game. Say: ***"1-2-3. Find the color yellow."*** At first you may want to point to the colored paper. Students look around the room for something yellow, and then go touch it.
4. Tell students that when they hear colors repeated, they need to choose something they have not touched before. They must find something else that color. No more than five students should touch the same item.

VARIATION: Have one student call out a color and the other students find items of that color.

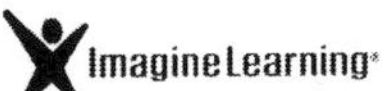

Names and Numbers

CCSS.L.K.5.C
TEKS 110.11.5.A

LEARNING OBJECTIVE: Express personal Information.
LANGUAGE OBJECTIVE: Use vocabulary about addresses and phone numbers in a role play.

Activity Overview

Students role-play conversations about addresses and phone numbers.

Materials	Preparation
• list of students' addresses and phone numbers from school directory	• Assign students to memorize their full names, addresses, and phone numbers.

NOTE: If you do not want to share your own personal information with your students, you could choose to use a puppet to model the phrases.

Explain

Introduce the activity: ***It's important to know your name, your address, and your phone number. We are going to learn about them and practice using them.***

Say: ***My name is [teacher's name]. What's your name?***

Have students turn to a partner and exchange names using the sentence frame, "My name is _____." Have students turn to a different partner and exchange names.

Say: ***My full name is [teacher's full name]. What's your full name?*** Discuss with students where the family name is placed in English. Discuss how different countries might place it differently. If applicable, have students share examples from different countries.

- In Spanish-speaking countries, it is common to have two family names, like Luis Martinez Lago. In this example, *Martinez* is the father's surname and *Lago* is the mother's. The child uses both names.
- In China, names start with the family name, followed by the person's first name.

Say: ***What's your full name?*** Have students turn to a partner and exchange full names using the sentence frame, "My full name is _____." Have students turn to a different partner and exchange names.

Say: ***My address is [teacher's address]. What's your address?*** Discuss with students that most addresses have a house or building number, street, city, state, and zip code. Someone who lives far from a city might have an address that is just name of the road they live on.

Say: ***What's your address?*** Have students turn to a partner and exchange addresses using the sentence frame, "My address is _____." Have students turn to a different partner and tell say their addresses.

Say: ***My phone number is [teacher's phone number].*** Discuss with students that In the United States, your phone number is 10 digits. In New Zealand, your phone numbers might be 8 digits. In other places, your phone number might be 11 digits.

Say: ***What's your phone number?*** Have students turn to a partner and exchange phone numbers using the sentence frame "My phone number is _____." Have students turn to a different partner and tell them their phone number.

Play

Let's do a role play using names, addresses, and phone numbers.

1. Discuss different situations where students would need to give personal information. Possible situations might include:
    - Student and a friend want to get together after school.
    - Student is at a new school and gives their information to a school secretary.
    - Student is lost and approaches a store clerk or a police officer.
    - Student is planning a party and wants to send invitations.
2. Divide students into pairs. Assign each pair a situation. Have students role play the situation either in groups or in front of the class.
3. Students reverse roles so that each student has a chance to recite personal information.

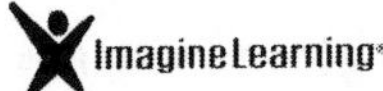

What Happened?

CCSS.L.K.5.C
TEKS 110.11.5.A

LEARNING OBJECTIVE: Review ordinal numbers.
LANGUAGE OBJECTIVE: Use ordinal numbers to tell a story.

Activity Overview

Use a story sequence to review ordinal numbers.

Materials	Preparation
• *Zoo Day*, or another short picture book with a clear sequence of events • Ordinals Flash Cards	• Cut out Ordinals Flash Cards. • If using *Zoo Day*, project the book to the class using the instructions below.

Explain

Introduce the activity: Write the numbers 1–10 across the board. ***When we count, we say numbers like this: one, two, three. . .*** Continue through ten.

Under each number place the ordinal flashcard that matches it: first under 1, second under 2, and so on to tenth.

Say: ***Numbers can also tell us the position or place of a person or object. For instance, in a race, someone comes in first, someone comes in second, and someone comes in third.*** Point to ordinal number words as you say them.

Ask for other examples of when we count using the words, *first*, *second*, *third*, etc. (what grade someone is in at school, how many times you do something, birthdays, things in a list, etc.)

Have students repeat the ordinal numbers after you as you point to them several times. Explain that stories often have an order. Something happens first, then the second thing happens, etc. Tell students that you are going to read them a story to see if they can figure out what happens first, second, and so on.

Play

Let's do a role play using names, addresses and phone numbers.

1. Read *Zoo Day* or another short picture book that has a clear sequence of events.
2. As you read, emphasize ordinal words in the story.
3. After reading, have students repeat the ordinals as you show pictures from the book.
4. Tell students that now it is their turn to tell a story called *My Day*.
5. Have a volunteer tell a short story about a typical sequence of things in their day using ordinal numbers (getting ready for school, what they did last night, etc.).
6. Have students turn to a partner and tell a short story about a typical sequence of things in their day using ordinal numbers.

To project a book in the classroom, go to the online Activity Menu and then follow this path:

1. Reading Lessons — Click on **Reading Lessons**
2. read-along Read-Along Books — Click on **Read-Along Books**
3. Moving — Click on the desired book cover
4. Listen and Read — Choose **Listen and Read**

Number Race

CCSS.L.K.5.C
TEKS 110.11.5.A

LEARNING OBJECTIVE: Review ordinal numbers.
LANGUAGE OBJECTIVE: Recite and put ordinal numbers in order.

Activity Overview

Team members race to get in ordinal number order.

Materials	Preparation
• Ordinals Flash Cards (1 set per team)	• Cut out and shuffle Ordinals Flash Cards.

Explain

Introduce the activity: ***We are going to play a game to review ordinal numbers.***

Play

1. Organize students into teams of ten (or adapt game to a different number of students per team).
2. Review ordinals by writing the numbers from one to ten across the board. Under each number write the ordinal that matches it.
3. Have students repeat the ordinal numbers after you.
4. Give each team a set of Ordinals Flash Cards.
5. Each student on a team takes a card from the pile, and then all students on the team line up in the order of their cards.
6. Have students recite the ordinals to check the accuracy of their order.
7. Repeat the team line up, but make it a race. Mix up each team's set of flash cards, then place the flash cards in piles at the front of the classroom.
8. Have one team member from each team race to the front of the room, collect their card set, and return to the team. Then, each team member takes a card. The team must arrange themselves to stand in order from first to tenth.
9. Have students recite the ordinals when they think they have lined up in the correct order. The game ends when a team becomes the first to line up in correct order.

first

second

third

fourth

fifth

sixth

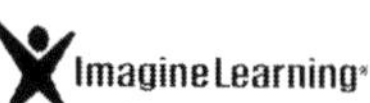

seventh

eighth

ninth

tenth

Good Morning

CCSS.L.K.6
TEKS 110.11.22

LEARNING OBJECTIVE: Practice common conversational phrases.
LANGUAGE OBJECTIVE: Use common conversational phrases.

Activity Overview

Play a game to review common phrases.

Materials

- 3 different colored soft balls or bean bags

Explain

Introduce the activity: ***We are going to play a game to practice greetings. Each ball (or bag) stands for a different greeting. When you get the ball (or bag), say the greeting that goes with it.***

Play

1. Have students form a circle.
2. Have each item represent a phrase. For example, the blue ball represents *Good morning*, the red ball represents *How are you?*, and the green ball represents *I'm fine. And you?*
3. Have students gently toss the ball to another student who then says the phrase connected with that ball.
4. Have students practice with one ball first, then gradually add another ball until all three balls are in play.
5. Add new phrases each time students play.

Bank of phrases:

Phrase 1	**Phrase 2**	**Phrase 3**
Good morning.	How are you?	I'm fine. And you?
These are my friends.	It's nice to meet you.	It's nice to meet you too.
Who are they?	This is my father (mother).	This is my sister (brother).
What's up?	Not much.	How about you?
Hello.	Do you speak English?	I speak English.
What are you doing?	We are shopping.	I'm reading a book.
What are they doing?	They are playing basketball.	They're exercising.
What are you going to do?	I'm going to work.	I'll help you.
May I help you?	Thank you.	You're welcome.
How old are you?	I am ten years old.	I am too.
It's 12:00.	It's time for lunch.	Let's eat.
Do you like it?	Yes. Good job.	I'm finished.

Speaking & Listening

What Is Your Name?

CCSS.L.K.6
TEKS 110.11.22

LEARNING OBJECTIVE: Practice the phrase, "What is your name?"
LANGUAGE OBJECTIVE: Use conversational questions with peers.

Activity Overview

Play a guessing game to review the conversational phrase "What is Your Name?"

Materials

- one chair

Play

1. Have a student sit in a chair in the front of the room with his or her back to the class.
2. Ask a student in the class, "What is your name?"
3. The teacher points to a student. Have that student answer, "My name is _________." The student can either say his or her own name or the name of someone else in the class. (The student in the chair cannot see who is speaking.)
4. Say, ***Is it [name student said]?*** Have the student in the chair answer, "Yes, it is," or "No, it isn't."
5. If the student in the chair guesses correctly, he or she stays in the chair. If he or she guesses incorrectly, the student who fooled the student in the chair gets a turn in the chair.

Note: Students can take turns being the teacher and pointing to the other students. For even more fun, suggest that students disguise their voices.

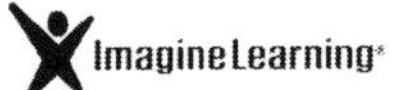

Tell Me a Story

CCSS.RL.K.2
TEKS 110.11.8.A

LEARNING OBJECTIVE: Retell a story.
LANGUAGE OBJECTIVE: Use puppets to retell a story.

Activity Overview

Use puppets to reenact a story.

Materials	Preparation
• *What If...* Read-Along Book (1 per student) • Puppets (1 per student) • Crayons • Glue • large craft sticks (1 per student)	• Cut out puppets. • Consider projecting *What If...* for the class to read using the instructions below.

Explain

Introduce the activity: ***We are going to make puppets that will help us re-tell a story. Then you can take the puppets home and tell the story to your family.***

Play

1. Read the story to students.
2. Have students color the puppets and glue a craft stick to the back of each puppet.
3. Read the story again. Have students use their puppets in the appropriate spots in the story.
4. Have students volunteer to retell the story using their puppets.
5. Send the puppets and a copy of the story home with students so they can retell the story to their families.

To project a book in the classroom, go to the online Activity Menu and then follow this path:

1. Reading Lessons — Click on **Reading Lessons**
2. read-along Read-Along Books — Click on **Read-Along Books**
3. Moving — Click on the desired book cover
4. Listen and Read — Choose **Listen and Read**

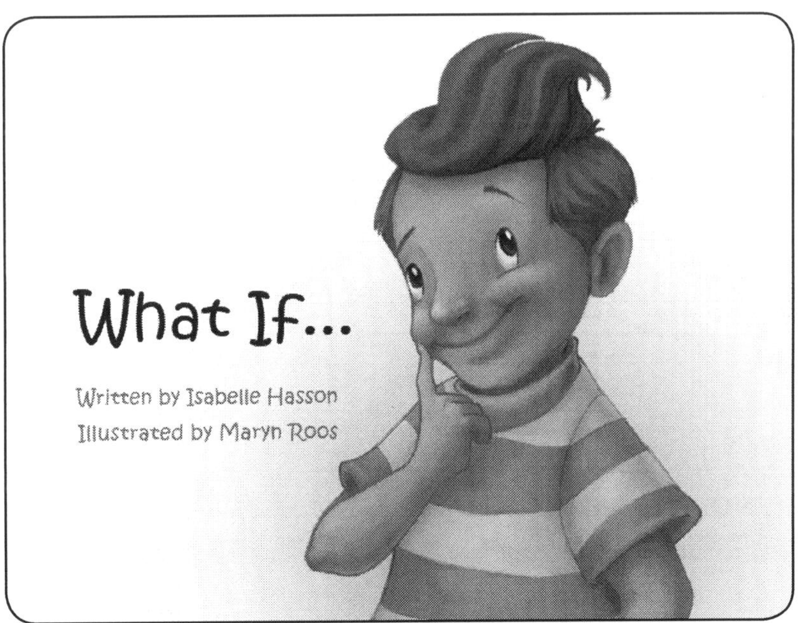

What If...

What if a horse....
had an elephant's nose?

What if a cow...
had a lizard's toes?

What if a dog...
had a fish's tail?

What if a pig...
had a bear's fingernails?

What if a bird...
had a crocodile's teeth?

What if a duck...
had a tiger's feet?

What if these animals grew and grew?
I'd want to see them. Wouldn't you?

Puppet

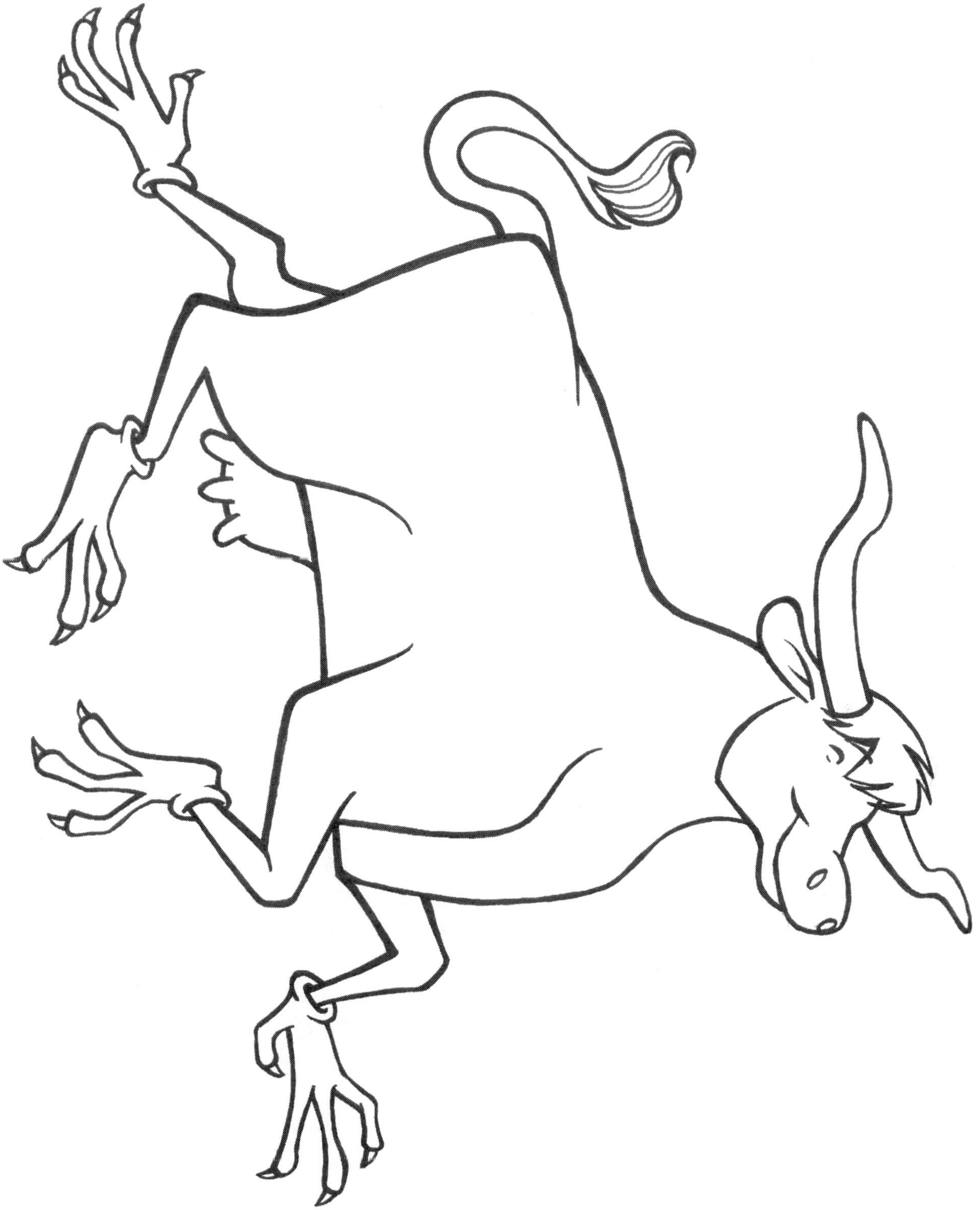

Puppet

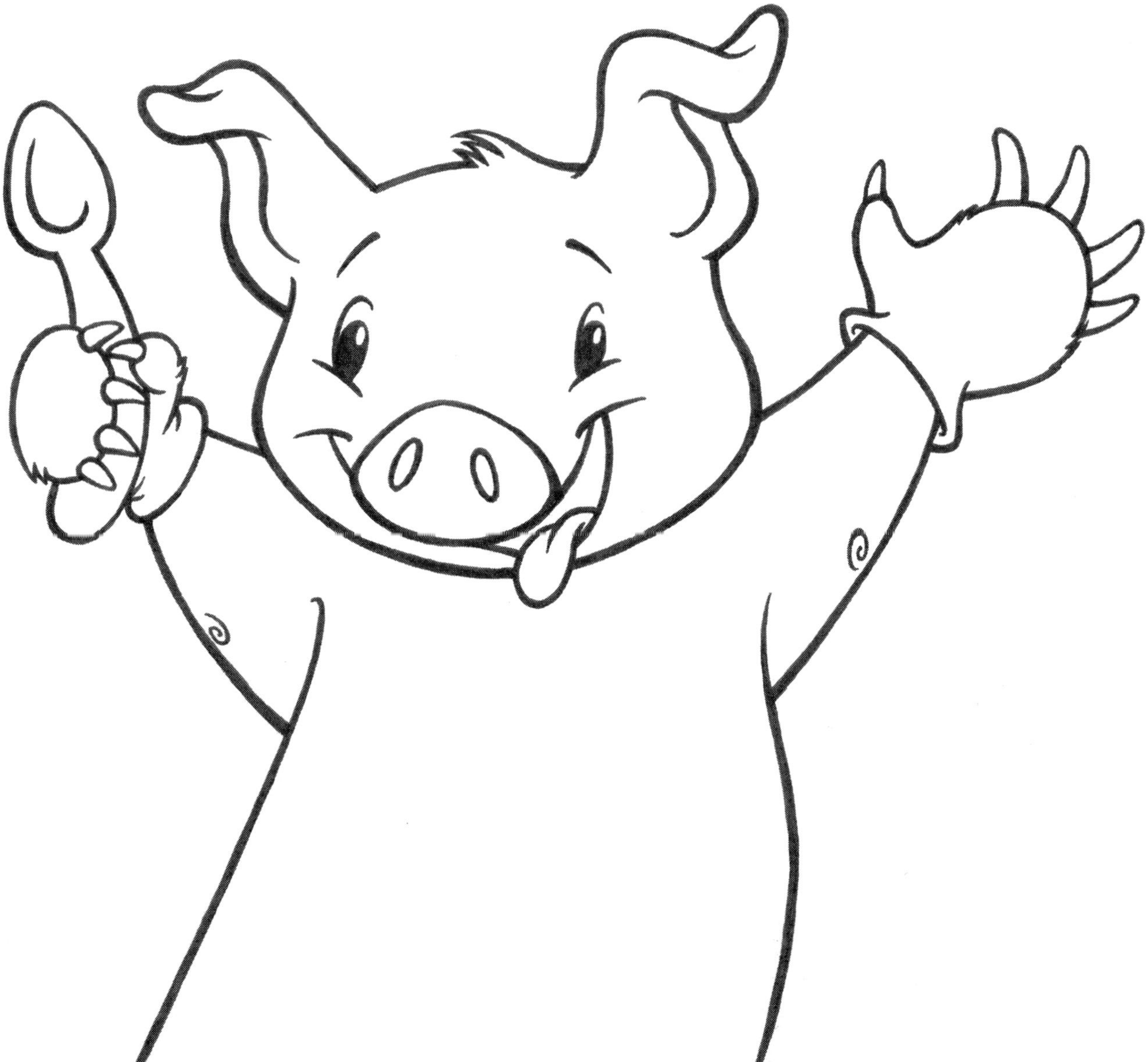

Tell it Again

CCSS.RL.K.10
TEKS 110.11.4.A

LEARNING OBJECTIVE: Students will listen to and reenact a story.
LANGUAGE OBJECTIVE: Listen to and reenact a story.

Activity Overview

Students listen to and then reenact a story.

Materials	Preparation
• Picture Cutouts (1 per student) • one-inch-wide paper strips for headbands (1 per student) • crayons • glue or stapler • craft sticks (optional) • *The Pesky Mosquito* Read-Along Book	• Measure a paper strip to fit around each student's head, then paste or staple the ends of the strip together so it makes a headband. • Consider projecting *The Pesky Mosquito* using the instructions below.

Play

1. Give at least one Picture Cutout to each student (there are eight items total: chair, me, frog, log, mosquito, tree, sock, and rock).
2. Have students color their picture.
3. Have students paste their colored item onto their headband (or craft stick).
4. Choose nine students for the first reenactment. The remaining students become the audience.
5. Read the story, *The Pesky Mosquito*, while students act it out.
6. Read the story again using a different group of students. (For variety, you can ask students to act out the story without words, or you can ask a student to retell the story.)
7. Encourage students to take their headbands home and retell the story to their families.

To project a book in the classroom, go to the online Activity Menu and then follow this path:

1. 

Click on **Reading Lessons**

2. 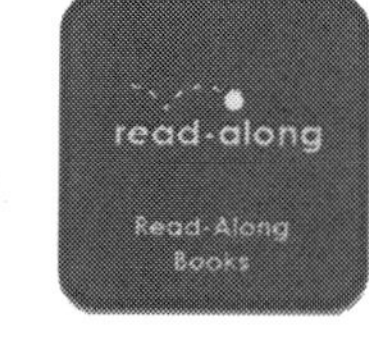

Click on **Read-Along Books**

3. 

Click on the desired book cover

4. 

Choose **Listen and Read**

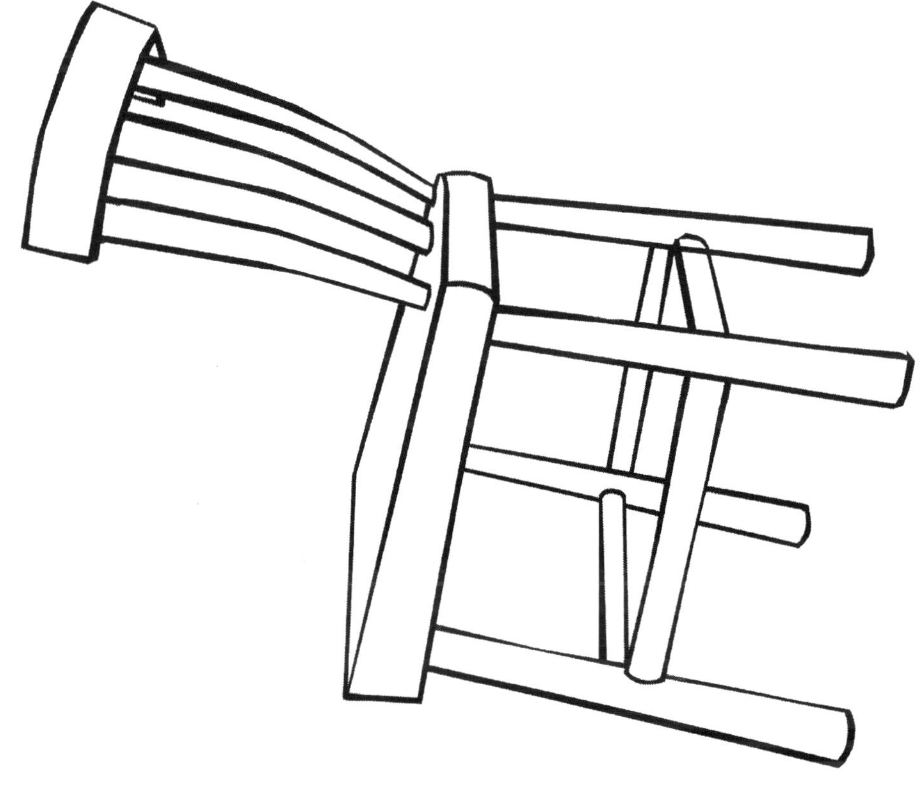

chair

me

frog

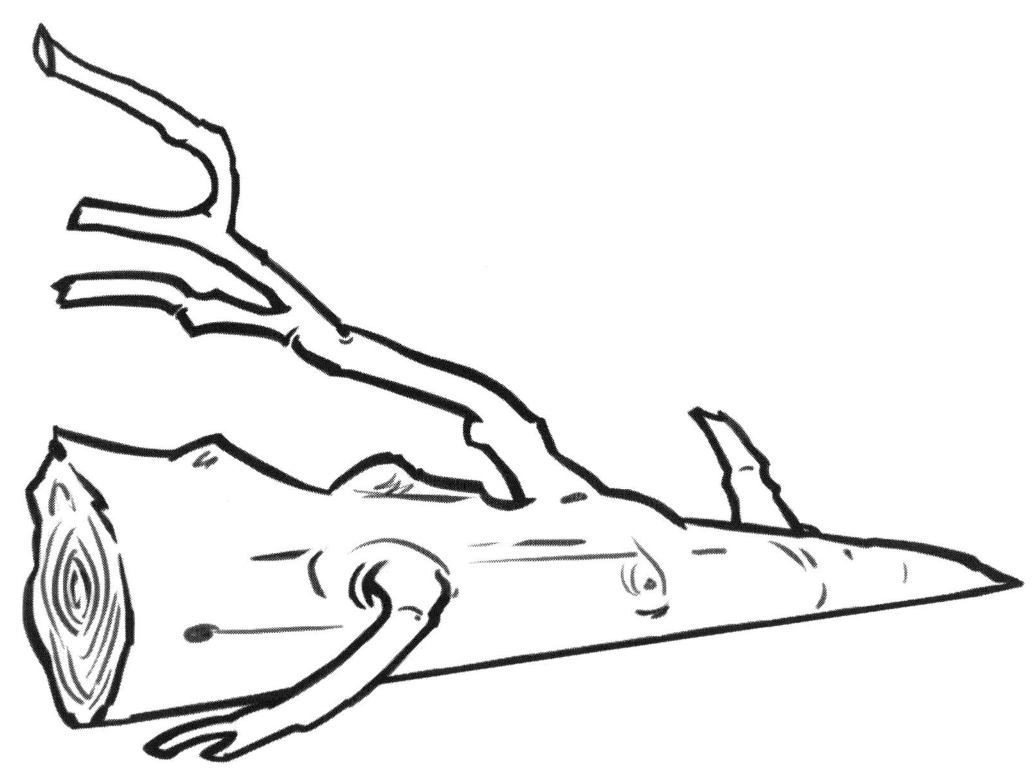

log

mosquito

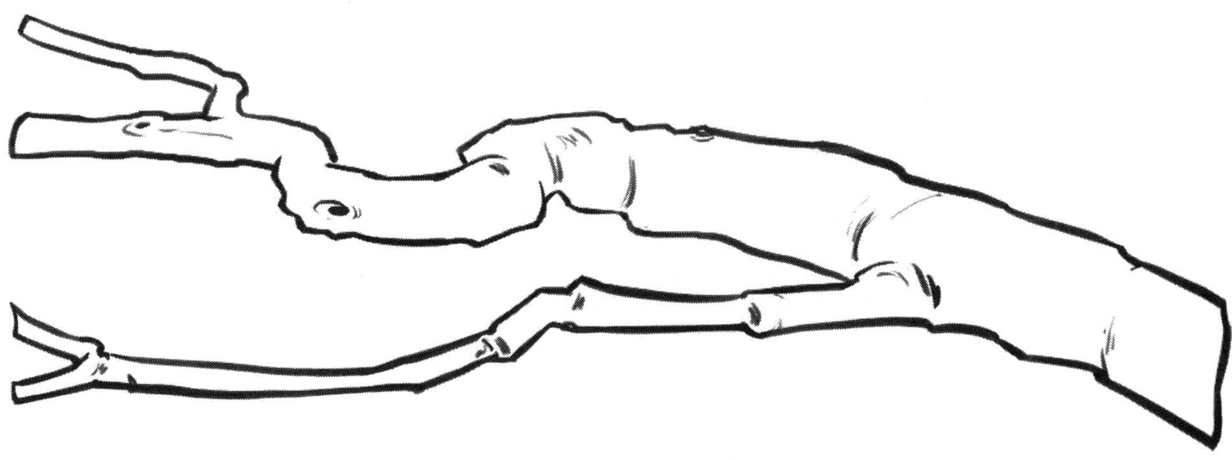

tree

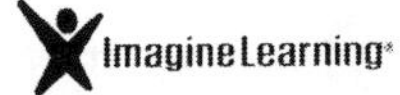

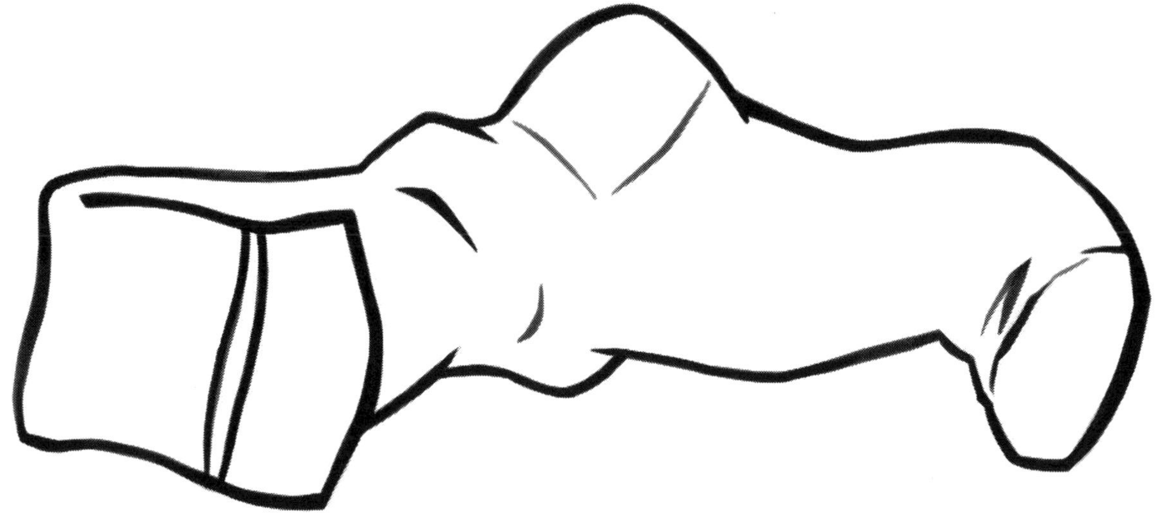

sock

rock

Sequence Stories Guide

Resource Overview

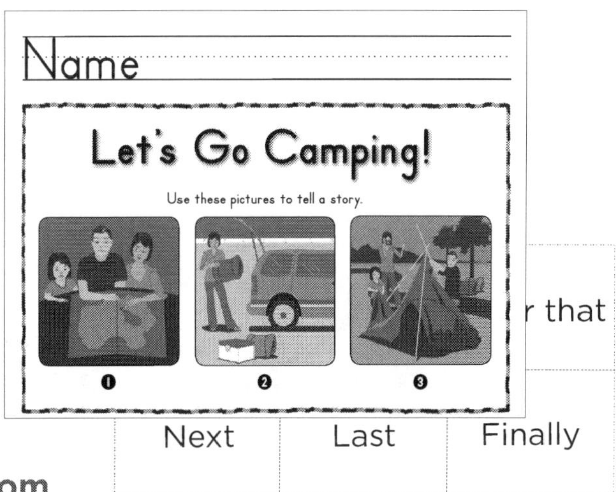

Sequence Stories are blackline masters of short stories that are told in three pictures. Understanding sequence helps students organize information and ideas efficiently. The pictures feature topics and details that allow the students to tell the story in the format that is best suited to their linguistic ability. Sequence stories can be used as they are, with the pictures in order and numbered 1, 2, and 3, or the pictures can be cut apart and used as Sequence Picture Cards.

Sequence Word Cards show words that students can use while talking about sequence. The word cards provide language support to help students more confidently speak about an order of events.

How to Use This Resource in the Classroom

Sequence Story printout

- Give each student a Sequence Stories Printout. Have students work with a partner and use sequencing words to tell the story using the pictures.
- Talk through the story as a class. Then cover one of the images. Have one student retell the story in sequence and describe the missing scene as he or she tells the story. Cover a different image and have another student tell the story again.
- Use Sequence Word Cards to teach sequence words and phrases before using the sequence stories. Ask students to think of a common event that happens in their home in a certain order (getting ready for bed, leaving the house to go to school, washing or feeding a pet, setting the table for a meal). Ask a volunteer to describe one of these events using the prompts you provide. Use the Sequence Word Cards to prompt the telling of the event. For example, hold up the card that says *First* and read it aloud. Then, have the student complete the sentence: "First I brush my teeth."

Sequence Picture Cards

- Display the Sequence Picture Cards for one story in order. Talk through the story as a class. Scramble the cards so they are out of order, and ask for volunteers to place the cards back in order.
- Organize the students into groups of three. Give each group a different story, and assign each student a separate Sequence Picture Card. Have students look at the picture and come up with their part of the story. Then, have them stand next to each other in order. Ask each student to tell his or her part of the story in order.
- Organize the students into groups of three. Give each group a different story, and assign each student a separate Sequence Picture Card. Ask the groups to determine the sequence for their cards. Then have each person prepare to act out the action pictured on the card. Have each group come to the front of the room and perform the actions in order. Have the rest of the class guess what each actor is trying to demonstrate, and then have volunteers tell the sequence of events based on the actions performed.
- Scramble the Sequence Picture Cards. Place the cards on a table or in a pocket chart. Pass out Sequence Word Cards to each student. Have students place their word cards under the pictures. Ask a volunteer to rearrange the pictures and corresponding sequencing labels so they are in chronological order from left to right. Have a volunteer tell the story using the sequencing phrases to confirm that the pictures are in the right order.
- Mix together Sequence Picture Cards from several stories and distribute the cards among the students. Have students move around the room, searching for pictures that would come before or after theirs in a series. When all students have found their story set and are grouped with two other students, have them work together to tell the sequence story in their groups or in front of the class.

Name

Let's Go Camping!

Use these pictures to tell a story.

1

2

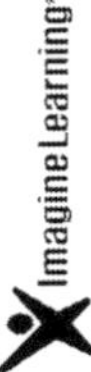

Name

It's Raining!

Use these pictures to tell a story.

1

2

Name

Ouch!

Use these pictures to tell a story.

1

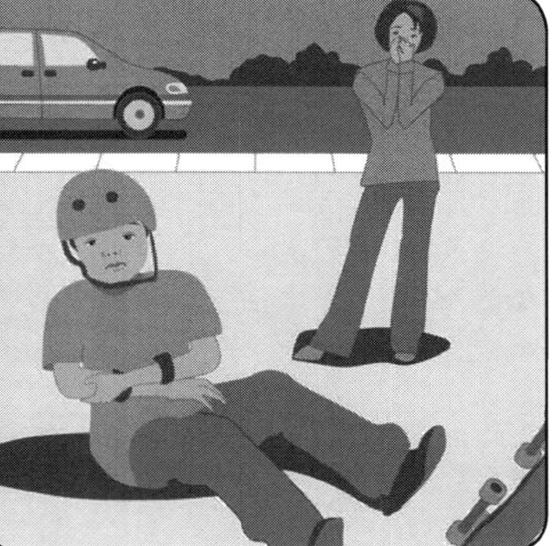

2

3

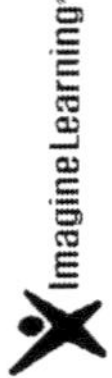

Name ________________________________

A Game in the Park

Use these pictures to tell a story.

1

2

3

Name

I Want That Book!

Use these pictures to tell a story.

1 2 3

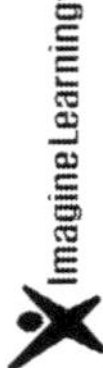

At first	Then	After that
Next	Last	Finally
First	Second	Third

1	2	3
a	b	c
Beginning	Middle	End

Songs and Chants Guide

Resource Overview

These printouts are the songs and chants used in the Imagine Learning online program. Students learn songs and chants to help them acquire language and literacy skills and promote oral language. The Song and Chants printouts can be used in a variety of ways to enhance language learning and production in the classroom. Song lyrics are filled with sound devices that can help young students explore the sounds of language and, as they view the printouts, develop print and phonemic awareness. Songs and Chants also expose students to words in a meaningful context, and the repetition of lyrics can be more engaging than traditional vocabulary worksheets or flash cards. Songs and Chants can also provide struggling readers with opportunities to read connected text at their independent or instructional level.

This Is the Way

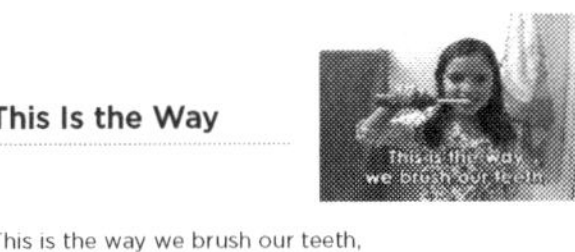

This is the way we brush our teeth,
Brush our teeth, brush our teeth.

This is the way we brush our teeth,
So early in the morning.

This is the way we comb our hair,
Comb our hair, comb our hair.

This is the way we comb our hair,
So early in the morning.

This is the way we go to school,
Go to school, go to school.

This is the way we go to school,
So early in the morning.

Online Resource Overview

To project a song or chant in the classroom, go to the online Activity Menu and then follow this path:

1. Speaking & Listening

   Click on **Speaking & Listening**

2. Songs & Chants

   Click on **Songs & Chants**

3. Be Verbs

   Click on the desired song or chant

How to Use This Resource in the Classroom

The following ideas can help you tap into students' natural love for language and rhythm.

Develop print and phonemic awareness

- Practice letter-sound recognition by reading the words to a song or chant and having students signal each time they hear the sound in the song.
- Practice letter recognition by choosing a letter that is repeated often in a song or chant. Give students printouts and have them look at the words on the printout and circle the letter on the printout any time it appears.

Improve fluency and pronunciation and practice vocabulary

- Each time you sing through a song, have the student listen for key words, rhyming words, or repeated words.
- Ask a student to pick one word from the song or chant to leave out. Sing the song or chant again, but this time, have the students clap instead of saying the word that has been chosen.
- Display a word list and have students find and circle the words on the printout. Play the song or chant and have students stand up or signal as they hear the words in the song.
- Blank out selected vocabulary words on the printout before you make copies to create a cloze activity. Play the song or chant and have students listen and fill in the blanks.

Engage student and help them to remember new concepts

- Sing songs and chants frequently.
- Incorporate songs into daily routines and transition times.
- Repeat songs in a variety of ways. On popsicle sticks or index cards, write different ways you can sing a song (in a whisper, loudly, girls only, boys only, etc.). Have a student draw a card/stick to decide which way you will sing the song or chant.

Teach reading and writing

- Print or display lyrics and encourage repeated readings.
- Make word strips of each phrase of the song. Display them in the wrong order or place them around the room and have students put them in order as they sing the song several times.
- Have students listen to a song and then write a one-line summary, fill in a story map, or complete a graphic organizer using the lyrics.
- Use lines from the songs as writing prompts.

Create shared language experiences and encourage group participation

- Divide students into groups. Have one group sing the song while the other group thinks of a question that is answered in the song. Write questions on the board that can be answered as the students sing the song.
- Blank out three unknown or new words from the song or chant. Display the song and have the students work in groups to guess the missing words. Fill in the words and sing the song or chant. Have groups discuss the meanings of the words.

A, E, I, O, U

Vowels are letters that change sounds.

A, E, I, O, U

Vowels in every word are found.

A, E, I, O, U

Short or long, they're all around.

A, E, I, O, U

These are called the vowels.

A, E, I, O, U

Sometimes Y is too.

A, E, I, O, U

Alphabet Soup

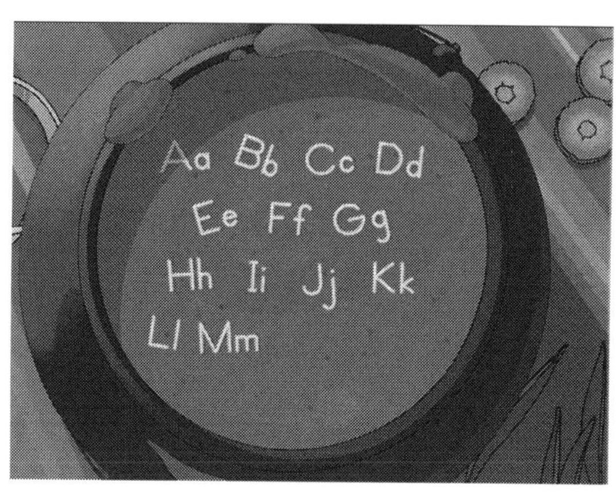

A - B - C - D - E - F
G - H - I - J - K - L - M
N - O - P - Q - R - S - T - U
V - W - X - Y - Z

The alphabet is fun to sing.

I sing it every day.

From a to z or z to a,

I sing it either way.

Z - Y - X - W - V - U
T - S - R - Q - P - O
N - M - L - K - J - I - H - G
F - E - D - C - B - A

Be Verbs

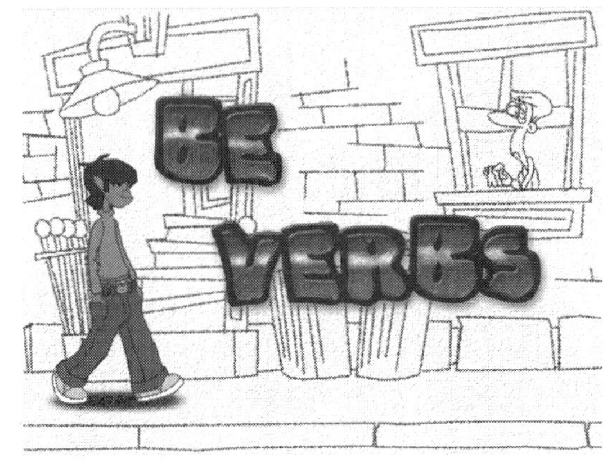

I am happy. He is sad.
We are scary. We are bad.
She was worried. They were mad.
These are called the Be Verbs.

am, is, are, was, were
These are called the Be Verbs.

Action, action—not with these verbs.
am, is, are, was, were
Be Verbs!

Classroom Activities

Buckle My Shoes

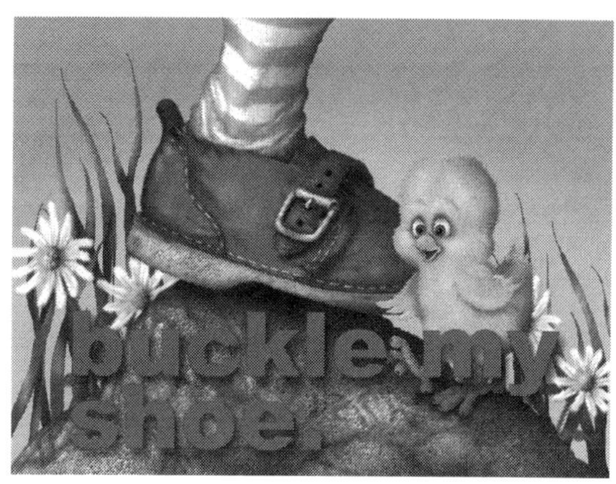

One, two, buckle my shoe.

Three, four, shut the door.

Five, six, pick up sticks.

Seven, eight, open the gate.

Nine, ten, big fat hen.

Colors

The sun is yellow.
The sky is blue.
The grass is green,
And the trees are, too.

The flowers are orange.
The water is blue.
The apples are red,
And the birds are, too.

Counting Is Fun

One, one, counting is fun.
Two, two, baking with you.
Three, three, three eggs for me.

One, two, three.
Let's count from one to ten.

Four, four, need one more.
Five, five, five cups piled high.
Six, six, six spoons to mix.

One, two, three, four, five, six.
Let's count from one to ten.

Seven, seven, into the oven.
Eight, eight, eight, fill each plate.

Nine, nine, it's tasting time.
Ten, ten let's do it again.

One, two, three, four, five, six,
seven, eight, nine, ten.

Let's count from one to ten!

Days of the Week

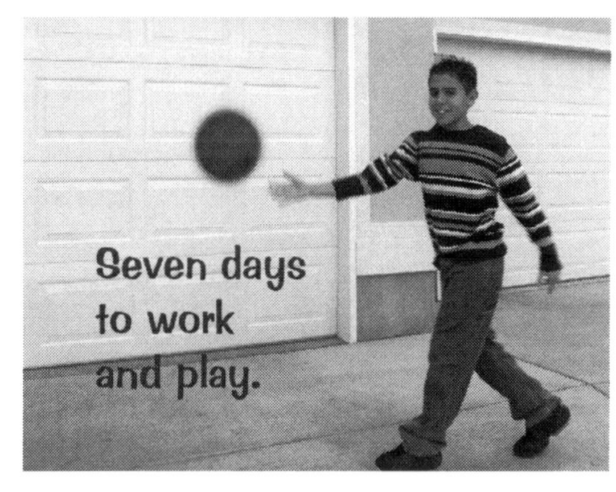

Classroom Activities

Sunday, Monday,

Tuesday, Wednesday,

Thursday, Friday, Saturday.

Seven days are in a week.

Yes, seven days to work
and play.

Fuzzy Wuzzy

Fuzzy Wuzzy was a bear.
Fuzzy Wuzzy had no hair.
Fuzzy Wuzzy wasn't fuzzy,
Was he?

Good Morning, Good Evening

The sun comes up,
Good morning!

The sun comes up,
Good morning!

The sun comes up,
Good morning!

Wake up!
Get out of bed!

The sun goes down,
Good evening!

The sun goes down,
Good evening!

The sun goes down,
Good evening!

Time to go to sleep.

Hickory, Dickory, Dock

Hickory, dickory, dock.
The mouse ran up the clock.
The clock struck one.
The mouse ran down!
Hickory, dickory, dock.

If You're Happy and You Know it

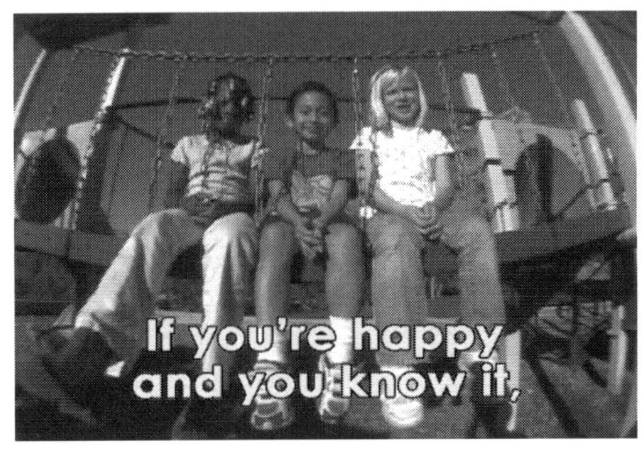

If you're happy and you know it,
Clap your hands.

If you're happy and you know it,
Clap your hands.

If you're happy and you know it,
Then your face will surely show it.

If you're happy and you know it,
Clap your hands.

It's Mine

We use pronouns to play games.
Pronouns take the place of names.

He has it. It's his.
She has it. It's hers.
he—his
she—hers

We use pronouns to play games.
Pronouns take the place of names.

They have it. It's theirs.
We have it. It's ours.
they—theirs
we—ours

I have it. It's mine.
Better luck next time.

We use pronouns to play games.
Pronouns take the place of names.

Keep Counting

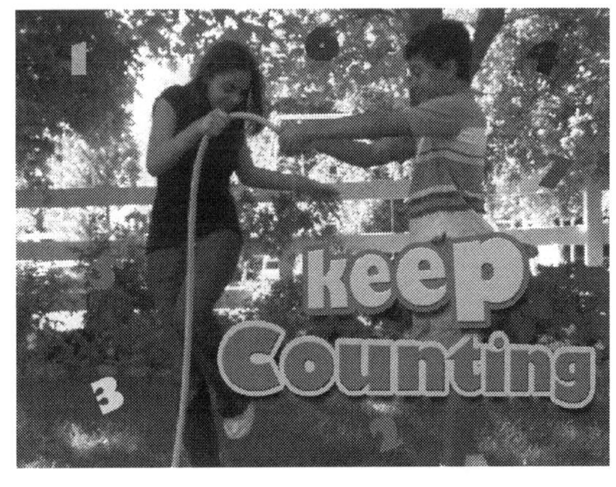

Classroom Activities

I can count from one to ten.
If there's more, what happens then?

Eleven, twelve next are seen.
Then you simply add a teen:
Thirteen, fourteen, fifteen, sixteen,
Seventeen, eighteen, nineteen, twenty.

I can count to twenty now.
If I have more, tell me how.

You say twenty, twenty-one,
Twenty-two, and on and on.

Then there's thirty, forty, fifty,
Sixty, seventy, eighty, ninety.
Ninety-one and ninety-two.
Reach one hundred and you're through.

Let's Talk

Let's talk, let's talk,
Let's talk, talk, talk.
Let's talk real fast.
Let's talk real slow.
Let's talk real high.
Let's talk real low.
Let's talk about all the words you know.
Let's talk!

Letter Sound Sing-Along

/a/ ant.../a/, /a/, ant
/b/ bear.../b/, /b/, bear
/k/ cat... /k/, /k/, cat
/d/ donkey.../d/, /d/, donkey
/e/ elephant.../e/, /e/, elephant
/f/ frog.../f/, /f/, frog

Chorus:
Here's a little song.
You can sing along.
Letter sounds are fun.
Come on everyone!

/g/ goat.../g/, /g/, goat
/h/ horse.../h/, /h/, horse
/i/ inchworm.../i/, /i/, inchworm
/j/ jaguar.../j/, /j/, jaguar
/k/ kangaroo.../k/, /k/, kangaroo
/l/ lion.../l/, /l/, lion

Chorus

/m/ monkey.../m/, /m/, monkey
/n/ newt.../n/, /n/, newt
/o/ otter.../o/, /o/, otter
/p/ penguin.../p/, /p/, penguin
/kw/ quail.../kw/, /kw/, quail
/r/ raccoon.../r/, /r/, raccoon

Chorus

/s/ skunk.../s/, /s/, skunk
/t/ tiger.../t/, /t/, tiger
/u/ bug.../u/, /u/, bug
/v/ vole.../v/, /v/, vole
/w/ walrus.../w/, /w/, walrus
/ks/ fox.../ks/, /ks/, fox

Chorus

/y/ yak.../y/, /y/. yak
/z/ zebra.../z/, /z/. zebra

Lots of letter sounds.
Hear them all around!
It's been so much fun.
Now our song is done!

Places

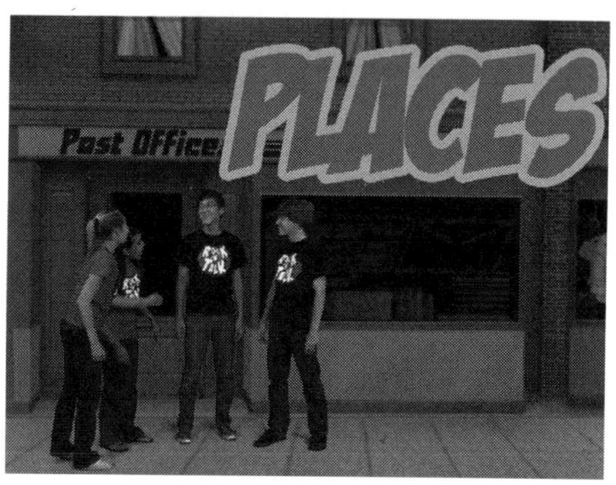

Let's catch the bus and go to town.
Follow me, we've got places to see!

The post office—
You can mail a letter.

The hospital—
If you are sick, you'll get better.

Now turn left,
Then go straight.

A restaurant—
The food is great.

There's still a lot more for us to explore.
Follow me, we've got places to see!

The park—
A place to play.

The bakery—
The treats are sweet.

Turn at the corner
And cross the street.

At the school,
The kids are cool.

Don't forget all the places we've seen.
Now we're done. Hope you had fun!

Plurals

Plural means it's more than one.
Here's a way to get it done:

Make it plural—add an s.
Make it plural—add an s.

cat—cats
brick—bricks

Plural means it's more than one.
Here's another way it's done:

Make it plural—add es.
Make it plural—add es.

fox—foxes
match—matches

Plural means it's more than one.
Now you know just how it's done.

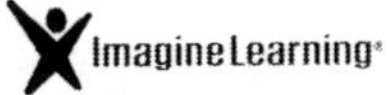

Question Words

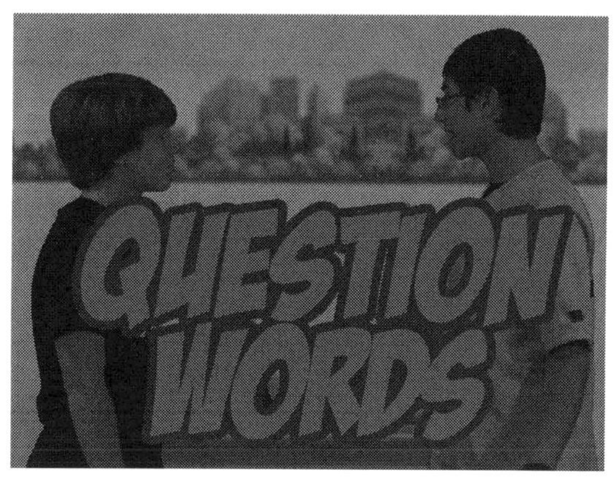

Want to ask a question?
Here's our suggestion:

All you need
Is who, what, where, when,
why!

Who, who?
Who are you?
I am number 32.

What, what?
What is your name?
My name? My name is
Shane.

Where, where?
Where's the game?
The game is here—in the
park.

When, when?
When does it start?
It starts at three, at three
o'clock.

Oh no! We are late.

Why, why?
Why are we late?
At three fifteen, they close
the gate.

Want to ask a question?
Well, here's our suggestion:
All you need
Is who, what, where, when,
why!

Row, Row, Row Your Boat

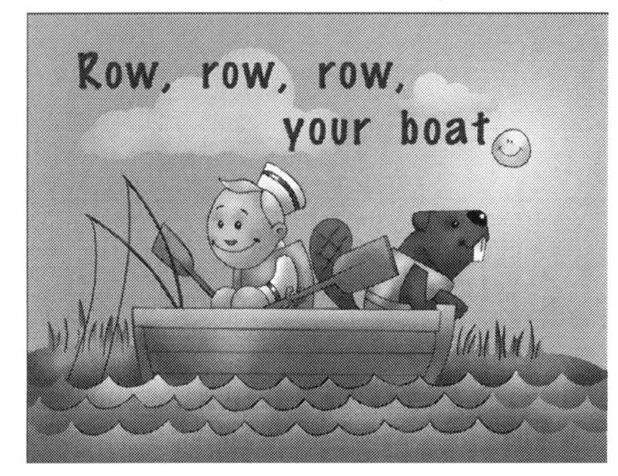

Row, row, row your boat

Gently down the stream.

Merrily, merrily, merrily, merrily,

Life is but a dream.

The Opposite Song

Come on everyone,
Let's sing the opposite song.

Happy, sad;
Awake, asleep;
High, low;
In and out;
Up and Down.

That's what opposites are all about.
Yeah, that's what opposites are all about.
Fast, slow;
Long, short;
Front, back;
In and out;
Up and Down.

That's what opposites are all about.
Yeah, that's what opposites are all about.
(Repeat)

There Was a Turtle

There was a little turtle
Who lived in a box.

He swam in the puddles,
And climbed on the rocks.

He snapped at the mosquito.
He snapped at the flea.

He snapped at the minnow,
And he snapped at me.

He caught the mosquito.
He caught the flea.

He caught the minnow,
But he didn't catch me!

Classroom Activities

This and That

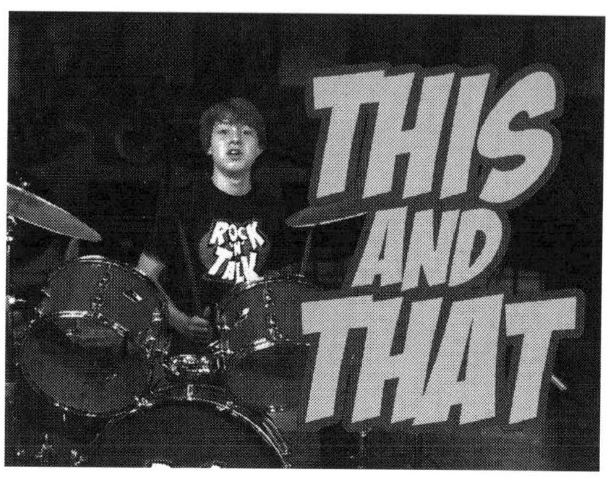

This or that, these or those.
How do you know which word to use?

This is near, that is far.
This is near, that is far.

I'm gonna be a rock star!

These are near, those are far.
These are near, those are far.

I'm gonna be a rock star!

This or that, these or those.
Now you know the word that goes.

This Is the Way

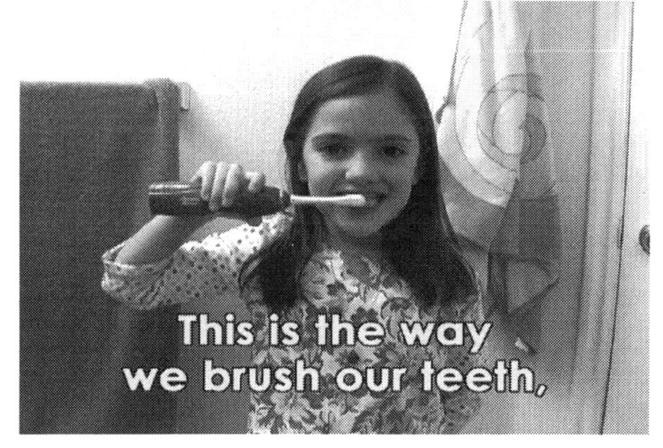

This is the way we brush our teeth,
Brush our teeth, brush our teeth.

This is the way we brush our teeth,
So early in the morning.

This is the way we comb our hair,
Comb our hair, comb our hair.

This is the way we comb our hair,
So early in the morning.

This is the way we go to school,
Go to school, go to school.

This is the way we go to school,
So early in the morning.

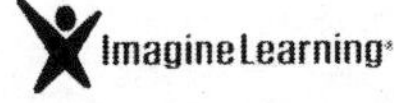

Underwater ABC

A - B - C - D

E - F - G

H - I - J - K

L - M - N - O - P

Q - R - S

T - U - V

W - X - Y and Z.

Now I know my ABCs.

Next time won't you sing with me?

*Note: The Circus ABC, Western ABC, and Space ABC songs also use these lyrics.

What Do You Mean?

Would you rock a rock?
Could you sock a sock?
Does a tap tap?
Can a bat bat?

rock—rock
sock—sock
tap—tap
bat—bat

Watch the words that you are reading.
Some of them might have two meanings.

Would you pound a pound?
Could the ground be ground?
Can a shot be shot?
Is a top on top?

pound—pound
ground—ground
shot—shot
top—top

Watch the words that you are reading.
Some of them might have two meanings.

You're Dancing

Flip-flops slap and slide.
Hands raise to the sky.
Knees bend and elbows fly.
Now you're dancing!
Yes, you are.

Jump up. Touch the ground.
Twist, twist. Turn around.
Boogie, boogie to the sound.
Now you're dancing!
Yes, you are.

Notes

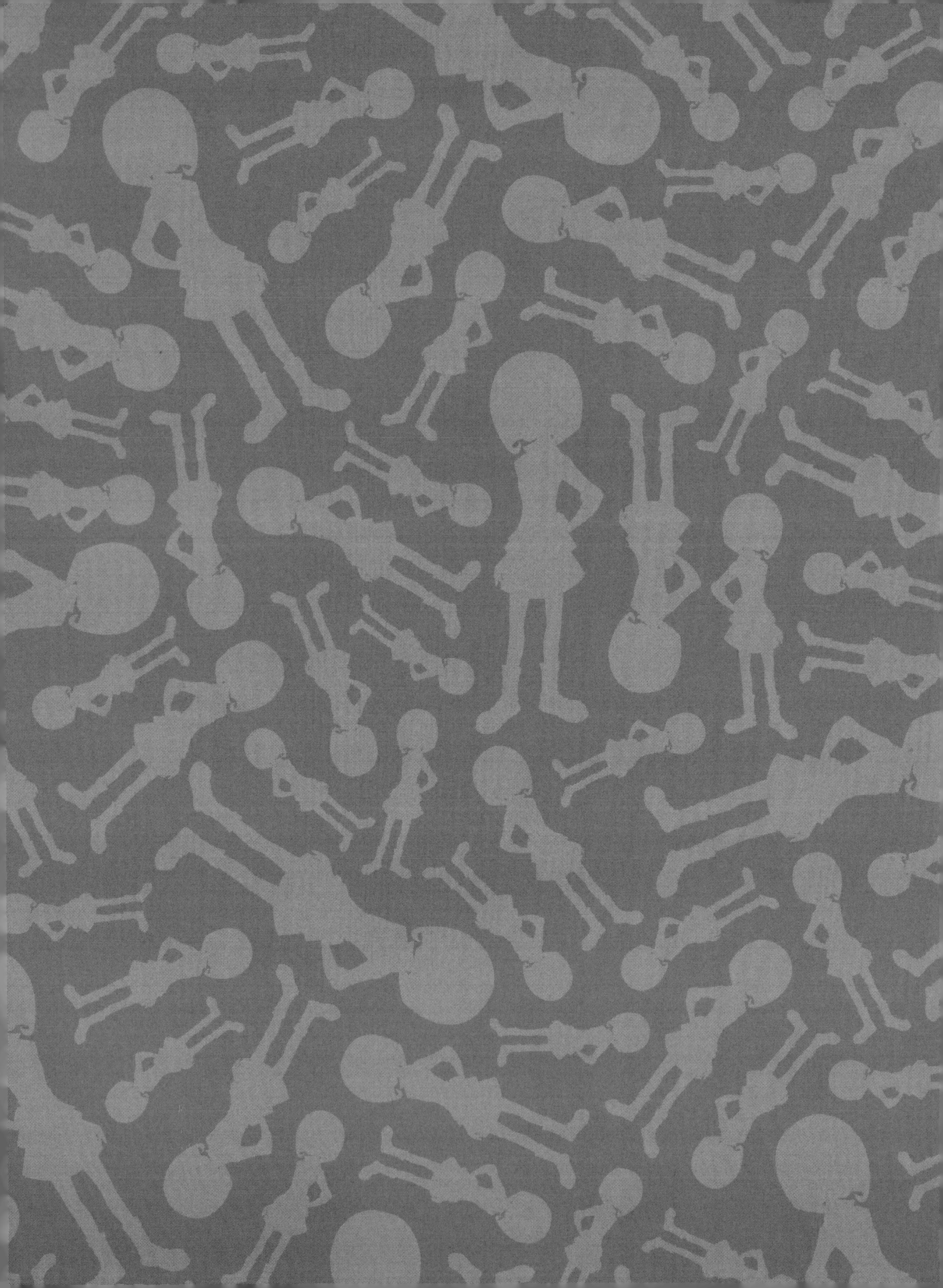

SPEAKING AND LISTENING

RETEACHING LESSONS

Developed with research-based methods, these lessons provide engaging activities and print-ready supporting materials to help students develop skills in speaking and listening. Each lesson can be used for small group intervention or adapted for whole-class use. Lessons are designed to maximize oral language production.

Analyze data in the Imagine Learning Action Areas Tool to identify groups of students who struggle with speaking and listening and use the Reteaching Lessons to provide additional support.

- Complete lesson plans that include modeling, practice, and assessment
- Activities that provide speaking opportunities to build students' confidence
- Lessons support language comprehension with gestures and realia
- Standards-based materials that require minimal teacher preparation

Progress Tracking Sheet

Date	Student Name	Lesson/Skill	Intervention Successful (Y/N)	Notes

Progress Tracking Sheet

Date	Student Name	Lesson/Skill	Intervention Successful (Y/N)	Notes

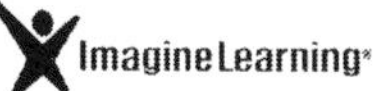

Notes

Nouns in Sentences

LEARNING OBJECTIVE: Identify nouns in a spoken sentence.
LANGUAGE OBJECTIVE: Listen closely to identify nouns in spoken sentences and say them aloud.

Lesson Overview

Students practice identifying nouns in spoken sentences by selecting the corresponding picture cards and saying the nouns aloud.

Materials	Preparation
• Picture Strips (one set) • Picture Cards (one set per student pair)	• Cut out all Picture Strips. • Cut out all Picture Cards. (Note that the extension activity for Find It, Show It requires one set of Picture Cards per student.)

NOTE: The nouns represented in the Picture Strips and Picture Cards have all been taught as part of Basic Vocabulary lessons in the online Imagine Learning Curriculum.

Teach and Model: Listen for Nouns

Use gestures and realia as you explain the concept of nouns: ***A noun names a person*** (point to yourself)***, a place*** (gesture to point out the classroom)***, or a thing*** (touch an object such as a pencil or chair)***.***

Place a white sheet of paper in front of students. Say: ***Listen for the noun as I say a sentence. The paper is white.*** Hold up the paper and say: ***The noun is* paper. *I am talking about the paper. The paper is white. What is the noun?*** (paper)

Invite students to demonstrate understanding. Place the paper and a pencil separately in front of students. Say: ***Listen for the noun as I say a sentence. When you hear the noun, say it and point to it on the table. The pencil is for writing. What is the noun in the sentence?*** (Students point to and say *pencil.*) ***The paper is on the table.*** (Students point to and say *paper.*) ***I have a new pencil.*** (Students point to and say *pencil.*) ***My pencil is long and yellow.*** (Students point to and say *pencil.*)

Explain: ***Listening for nouns can help you understand what people are saying.***

Expand on the concept of nouns in sentences. Hold up two fingers and say: ***Sometimes a sentence has two nouns. Listen for two nouns as I say a sentence. The teacher sits in a chair. What is the first noun?*** (Students point and say *teacher.*) ***What is the second noun?*** (Students point and say *chair.*) Restate the sentence emphasizing the nouns.

Practice and Apply: Find that Noun

Display the Picture Strips. Review the nouns with the students: Point to the noun in each picture. Ask: ***What is this?*** After students respond, point again and have the students chorally repeat the word. (*bear, dog, door, window, fish, duck, shelves, glass, bug, shoes*)

Set aside the *bear* and *dog* Picture Strip. Distribute the other strips to each student or pair of students. Have the students place their strips faceup in front of them. Introduce the activity: ***I will say a sentence. Listen carefully for the noun. Then look at your pictures. If you have the strip with that noun, touch the picture and say the word aloud.***

Model the activity using the *bear* and *dog* Picture Strip. Say: ***The bear is sleeping.*** Then touch the picture of the bear and say **bear**. Say: ***The dog is sleeping.*** Then touch the picture of the dog and say **dog**.

Prompt students with these sentences:

- ***The window is open.***
- ***The fish is swimming.***
- ***The glass is empty.***
- ***The bug is small.***

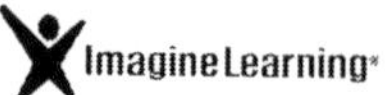

Then have students or pairs exchange strips. Repeat with these sentence prompts:

- ***The door is open.***
- ***The duck is swimming.***
- ***The shelves are empty.***
- ***The shoes are small.***

EXTENSION ACTIVITY: Have students take turns choosing a picture and repeating the sentence or making up their own sentence.

Practice and Apply: Find It, Show It

Give each pair of students one set of the Picture Cards. Have student pairs mix up their cards and divide the set equally between them. Each student should have four cards.

Explain: ***I will say a sentence. Listen carefully for the two nouns. Then look at your pictures. If you have the picture that goes with the sentence, place the card on the table and say the two nouns.***

Use these sentence prompts:

- ***My mom is painting the bench.***
- ***My dad is painting the bench.***
- ***The boy is riding in a boat.***
- ***The boy is riding a bike.***
- ***The horse is jumping the fence.***
- ***The sheep is jumping the fence.***
- ***The bread is on the table.***
- ***The grapes are on the table.***
- ***The girl is raising her eyebrows.***
- ***The girl is raising her hands.***

EXTENSION ACTIVITY: Give each student a set of picture cards. Have students take turns choosing a Picture Card and repeating the sentence or making up their own sentence for the group. Have the other students try to be the first to find the correct Picture Card in their own set.

Check Progress

Observe each student during practice and use the following activity to check progress made on the target skill. If the student can correctly identify the noun(s) in two sentences, consider the intervention successful.

Say a sentence for each student. Have the student identify the noun(s) in each sentence and say the noun(s) aloud. Repeat until each student has had two opportunities. Use the following sentences:

- ***Close the window.***
- ***Put the books on the shelves.***
- ***The boy is running.***
- ***The ducks and sheep are asleep.***
- ***My hands are cold.***
- ***The girl is drinking from the glass.***
- ***The horse is running.***
- ***My mom is talking to my dad.***
- ***The boat is fast.***
- ***His bike is by the bench.***

The bear is sleeping.

The dog is sleeping.

The door is open.

The window is open.

The fish is swimming.

The duck is swimming.

The shelves are empty.

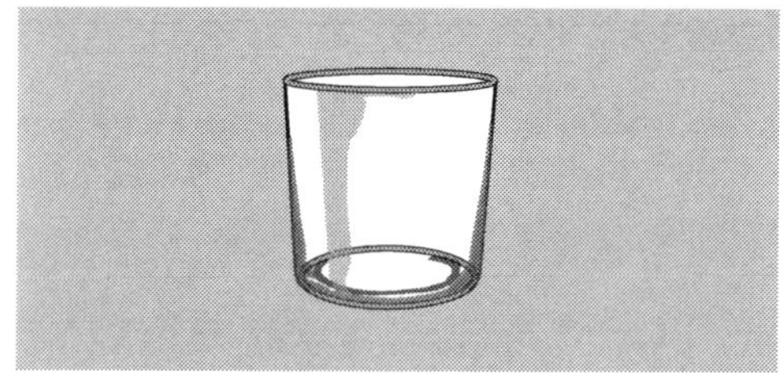

The glass is empty.

The bug is small.

The shoes are small.

My mom is painting the bench.

My dad is painting the bench.

The boy is riding in a boat.

The boy is riding a bike.

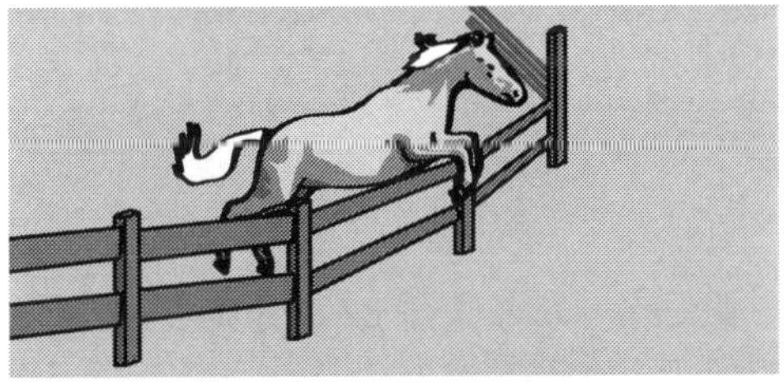

The horse is jumping the fence.

The sheep is jumping the fence.

The bread is on the table.

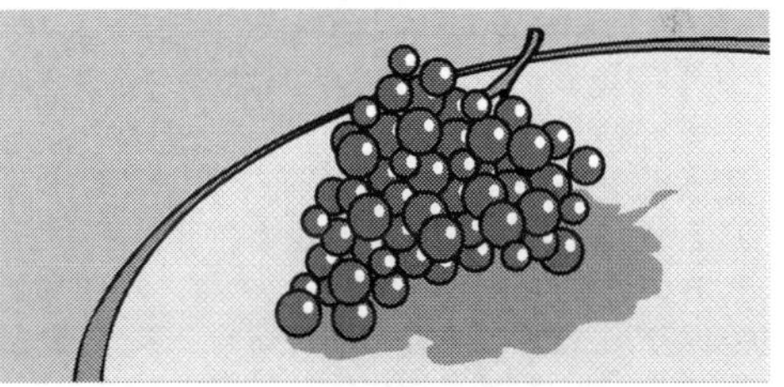

The grapes are on the table.

The girl is raising her eyebrows.

The girl is raising her hands.

Speaking & Listening

Verbs in Sentences

15 Min. | CCSS.SL.2.2

LEARNING OBJECTIVE: Identify verbs in a spoken sentence.
LANGUAGE OBJECTIVE: Listen closely to identify verbs in spoken sentences and say them aloud.

Lesson Overview

Students practice identifying verbs in spoken sentences by selecting the corresponding picture cards and saying the verbs aloud.

Materials	Preparation
• Picture Strips (one set) • Picture Cards (one set per student pair)	• Cut out all Picture Strips. • Cut out all Picture Cards. (Note that the extension activity for Find It, Show It requires one set of Picture Cards per student.)

NOTE: The verbs represented in the Picture Strips and Picture Cards have all been taught as part of Basic Vocabulary lessons in the online Imagine Learning Curriculum.

Teach and Model: Listen for Verbs

Use gestures as you explain the concept of verbs: ***A verb is an action word. A verb tells you what someone or something does. I am talking.*** (Gesture *talking* with hand.) ***The verb is* talking.** (Cup hand to one ear.) ***You are listening. What is the verb?*** (*listening*)

Invite students to demonstrate understanding. Say: ***I will say a sentence. Listen for the verb. When you hear the verb, you say the word and do the action. My students are smiling.*** (Students say *smiling* and smile.) ***The verb is* smiling. *Now listen for the verb in this sentence. Say the verb and do the action. Your hands are shaking.*** (Students say *shaking* and shake their hands.) ***Listen again. Everyone is bending their arms.*** (Students say *bending* and bend their arms.)

Explain: ***When you listen, pay attention to important words. Listening for verbs can help you understand what people are saying.***

Practice and Apply: Listen for the Verb

Display the Picture Strips. Review the verbs with the students: Say: ***Say the verb that shows the action in the picture.*** Point to each picture and have students chorally say the correct verb. (*crawling, swinging, climbing, sliding, swimming, walking, drawing, reading, playing, eating*)

Set aside the *crawling* and *swinging* Picture Strip. Distribute the other Picture Strips to each student or pair of students. Have students place their strips faceup in front of them. Introduce the activity: ***I will say a sentence. Listen carefully for the verb. Then look at your pictures. If you have the Picture Strip with that verb, touch the picture and say the word aloud.***

Model the activity using the *crawling* and *swinging* Picture Strip. Say: ***The baby is swinging.*** Then touch the picture of the baby swinging and say **swinging**. Say: ***The baby is crawling.*** Then touch the picture of the baby crawling and say **crawling**.

Prompt students with these sentences:

- ***My sister is climbing.***
- ***My mom is walking.***
- ***My brother is drawing.***
- ***The cat is eating.***

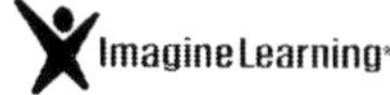

Then have students or pairs exchange cards. Repeat with these sentence prompts:

- ***My sister is sliding.***
- ***My mom is swimming.***
- ***My brother is reading.***
- ***The cat is playing.***

Extension Activity

EXTENSION ACTIVITY: Have each student take turns choosing a picture and repeating the sentence or making up their own sentence.

Practice and Apply: Find It, Show It

Assign students to work with a partner. Give each pair of students a copy of the Picture Cards. Have partners mix up their cards and divide the cards equally between them. Have students place their cards on the table in front of them.

Explain: ***I will say a sentence. Listen carefully for the verb. Then look at your pictures. If you have the picture that goes with the sentence, hold it up and say the verb.***

Use these sentence prompts:

- ***The little boy is walking to his dad.***
- ***The little boy is smiling with his dad.***
- ***The girl is pointing to a tree.***
- ***The girl is climbing a tree.***
- ***The cat is sleeping by the fence.***
- ***The cat is jumping from the fence.***
- ***My sister is kicking the soccer ball.***
- ***My sister is drawing a soccer ball.***
- ***The horse is drinking from the river.***
- ***The horse is running by the river.***

Extension Activity

EXTENSION ACTIVITY: Give each student a set of picture cards. Have students take turns choosing a Picture Card and repeating the sentence or making up their own sentence for the group. Have the other students try to be the first to find the correct Picture Card in their own set.

Check Progress

Observe each student during practice and use the following activity to check progress made on the target skill. If the student can correctly identify the verb in each sentence, consider the intervention successful.

Say two sentences for each student. Have the student identify the verb in each sentence and say the it aloud. Use the following sentences:

- ***Sara is drinking a glass of milk.***
- ***She is swimming in the pool.***
- ***My mom is reading my favorite book.***
- ***He is drawing a picture for the teacher.***
- ***Dad is walking to the park with me.***
- ***Uncle John is playing a game with us.***
- ***We are eating eggs for breakfast.***
- ***Martin is running to the playground.***
- ***My brother is climbing a big tree.***
- ***The teacher is pointing to me.***

Reteaching Lessons

Reteaching Lessons

The baby is crawling.

The baby is swinging.

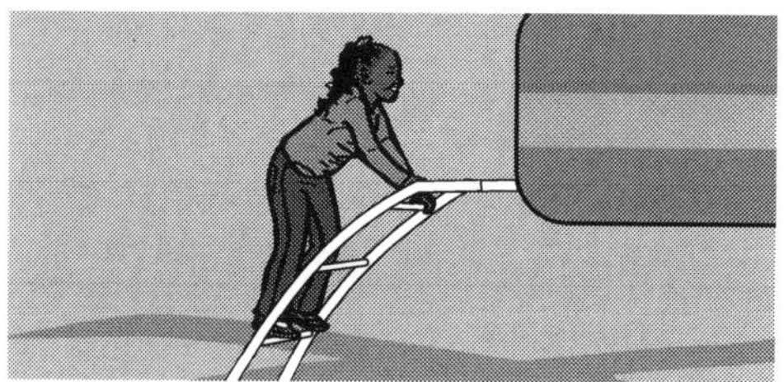

My sister is climbing.

My sister is sliding.

My mom is swimming.

My mom is walking.

My brother is drawing.

My brother is reading.

The cat is playing.

The cat is eating.

The little boy is walking to his dad.

The little boy is smiling with his dad.

The girl is pointing to a tree.

The girl is climbing a tree.

The cat is sleeping by the fence.

The cat is jumping from the fence.

My sister is kicking the soccer ball.

My sister is drawing a soccer ball.

The horse is drinking from the river.

The horse is running by the river.

Adjectives in Sentences

15 Min. | CCSS.SL.2.2

LEARNING OBJECTIVE: Identify adjectives in a spoken sentence.
LANGUAGE OBJECTIVE: Listen closely to identify adjectives in spoken sentences and say them aloud.

Lesson Overview

Students practice identifying adjectives in spoken sentences by selecting the corresponding picture cards and saying the adjectives aloud.

Materials	Preparation
• Picture Strips (one set) • Picture Cards (one set per student pair)	• Cut out all Picture Strips. • Cut out all Picture Cards. (Note that the extension activity for Find It, Show It requires one set of Picture Cards per student.)

 NOTE: The adjectives represented in the Picture Strips and Picture Cards have all been taught as part of Basic Vocabulary lessons in the online Imagine Learning Curriculum.

Teach and Model: Listen for Adjectives

Use gestures as you explain the concept of adjectives: ***An adjective is a word that describes a person, place, or thing.*** (Gesture *big* with hands.) ***The ball is big. The adjective is* big.** (Gesture *tiny* with two fingers.) ***The ball is tiny. The adjective is* tiny**. (Gesture *round* with two hands.) ***The ball is round. What is the adjective?*** (round)

Invite students to demonstrate understanding. Say: ***I will say the sentences again. Listen for the adjectives. Then say the sentence and show me with your hands. The ball is tiny.*** (Students say the sentence and gesture *tiny*.) ***The ball is round.*** (Students say the sentence and gesture *round*.) ***The ball is big.*** (Students say the sentence and gesture *big*.)

Explain: ***When you listen, pay attention to important words. Listening for adjectives can help you understand what people are saying.***

Practice and Apply: Listen for the Adjective

Display the Picture Strips. Review the adjectives with the students: Say the name of the adjective that describes a picture. Call on one volunteer to touch the correct picture. Then have students chorally repeat the word. Say: ***I will say an adjective. You touch the picture that shows the adjective. Then we will all say the adjective together.*** (*asleep, cold, dirty, clean, new, short, straight, black, old, tall*). Model with the first picture.

Set aside the Picture Strip for *asleep* and *cold*. Distribute the Picture Strips to each student or pair of students. Have students place their Picture Strips faceup in front of them. Introduce the activity: ***I will say a sentence. Listen carefully for the adjective. If you have a picture of that adjective, touch the picture and say the word aloud.***

Model the activity using the *asleep* and *cold* Picture Strip. Say: ***The man is asleep.*** Then touch the picture of the sleeping man and say **asleep**. Say: ***The man is cold.*** Then touch the picture of the shivering man and say **cold**.

Prompt students with these sentences:

- ***His shirt is <u>clean</u>.***
- ***The pencil is <u>new</u>.***
- ***Her hair is <u>black</u>.***
- ***The fence is <u>tall</u>.***

Then have students exchange strips. Repeat with these sentence prompts:

- ***He has a <u>dirty</u> shirt.***
- ***The pencil is <u>short</u>.***
- ***She has <u>straight</u> hair.***
- ***The fence is <u>old</u>.***

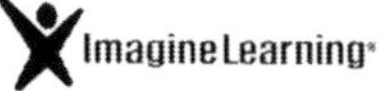

EXTENSION ACTIVITY: Have students take turns choosing a picture and repeating the sentence or making up their own sentence. Remind students to use an adjective to describe the noun in the picture.

Practice and Apply: Find It, Show It

Give each pair of students one set of the Picture Cards. Have student pairs mix up their cards and divide the cards equally between them. Each student should have four cards.

Explain: ***I will say a sentence. Listen carefully for the adjective. Then look at your pictures. If you have the picture that goes with the sentence, place the card on the table and say the adjective.***

Use these sentence prompts:

- ***My brother has a small dog.***
- ***He is walking with a big dog.***
- ***She is playing with the black car.***
- ***My sister is playing with a white car.***
- ***Her dress is wet.***
- ***My sister is wearing a long dress.***
- ***The little boy is playing with a helicopter.***
- ***The tall boy is playing with a helicopter.***

EXTENSION ACTIVITY: Give each student a set of picture cards. Have students take turns choosing a Picture Card and repeating the sentence or making up their own sentence for the group. Have the other students try to be the first to find the correct Picture Card in their own set.

Check Progress

Observe each student during practice and use the following activity to check progress made on the target skill. If the student can correctly identify the adjective in each sentence, consider the intervention successful.

Say two sentences for each student. Have the student identify the adjective in each sentence and say it aloud. Use the following sentences:

- ***Mom and Dad have a new car.***
- ***My dog was wet after jumping in the lake.***
- ***The cats are asleep.***
- ***My dad is tall.***
- ***I like to play with small cars.***
- ***My brother is a little baby.***
- ***There is a long path through the forest.***
- ***I have short hair.***
- ***She must wash her dirty dress.***
- ***Dad will sell his old car.***

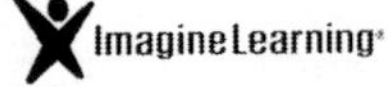

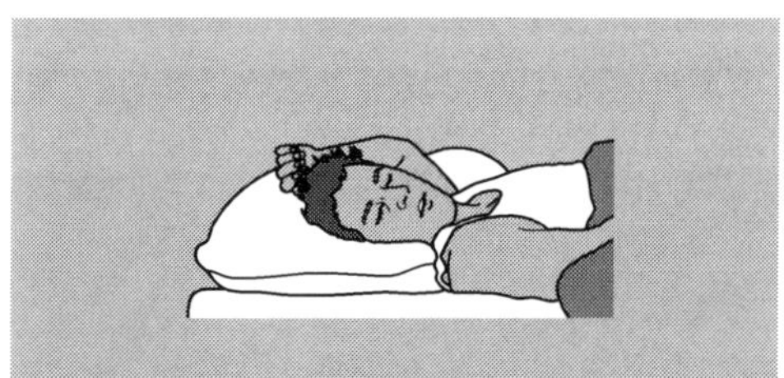

The man is asleep.

The man is cold.

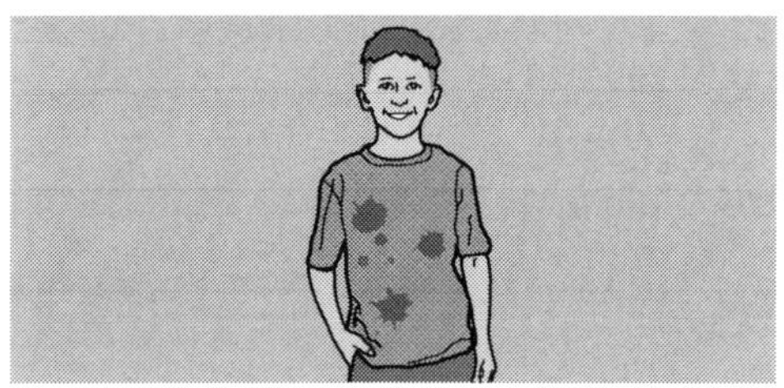

He has a dirty shirt.

His shirt is clean.

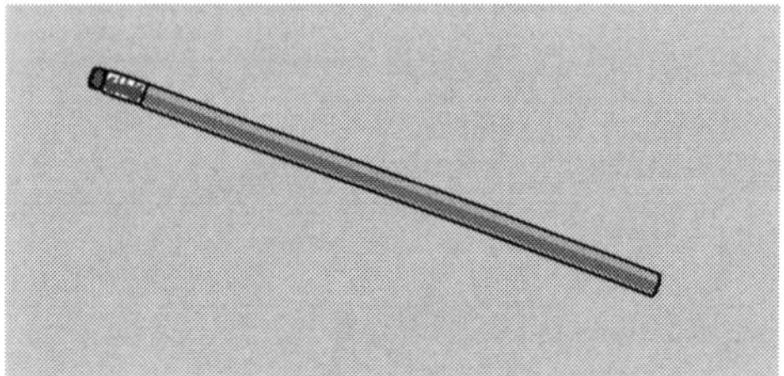

The pencil is new.

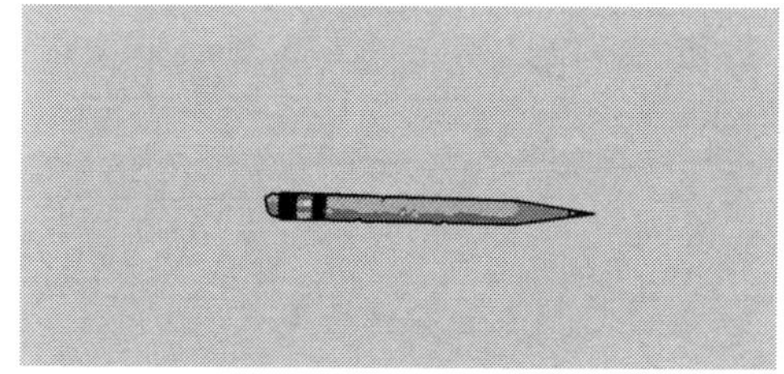

The pencil is short.

She has straight hair.

Her hair is black.

The fence is old.

The fence is tall.

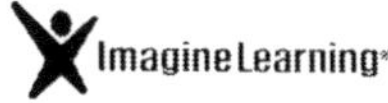

My brother has a small dog.

He is walking with a big dog.

She is playing with the black car.

My sister is playing with a white car.

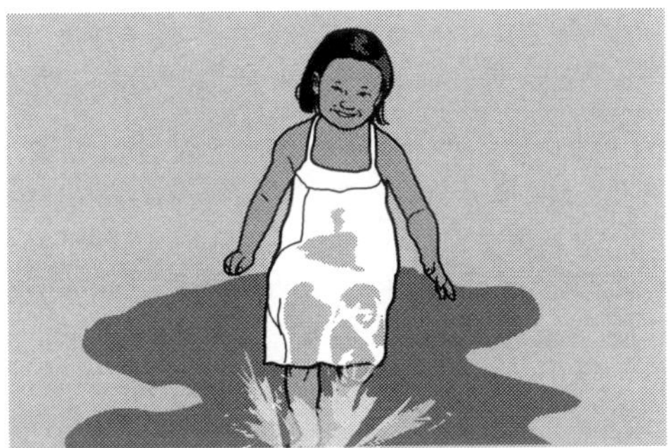

Her dress is wet.

My sister is wearing a long dress.

The little boy is playing with a helicopter.

The tall boy is playing with a helicopter.

Reteaching Lessons

Listening for Meaning

LEARNING OBJECTIVE: Recall key ideas and details from a passage read aloud.

LANGUAGE OBJECTIVE: Use listening skills to comprehend a text read aloud and orally answer comprehension questions with picture support.

Lesson Overview

Students listen to passages read aloud and select picture cards to answer comprehension questions about each passage.

Materials

- Printout of Story Pictures
- Printouts of Picture Bingo (one per student, plus one for modeling)

Teach and Model: Listening for Meaning

Review the concept of listening for key words in spoken sentences: ***You learned to listen for nouns, verbs, and adjectives when you hear a sentence. Listening for these important words can help you understand the overall idea.***

Expand the concept: ***Sometimes people use many sentences when they speak or tell a story. You can use your listening skills to understand what they say.***

Say: ***I will read a short passage. Listen for the nouns, verbs, and adjectives to help you understand.***

Read the following passage aloud:

> Tom takes good care of his dog. He gives his dog food and water. Tom also washes his dog when it gets dirty. When they go out to play, Tom throws a ball to the dog and the dog runs after it.

Say: ***Now I will ask some questions about what you heard***.

Display the Story Pictures. Point to the pictures in the first row. Ask: ***What kind of pet does Tom have?*** Model how to choose the correct answer: ***One of the important words in the passage is a noun:* dog. *Did you hear the nouns* monkey *or* cat *in the passage?*** (no) ***So which picture shows the correct answer?*** (dog)

Point to the pictures in the second row. Call on one student to answer this question: ***What does Tom do when the dog gets dirty?*** (Student points to the boy washing the dog.) Prompt students to identify the verb: ***What is Tom doing in that picture?*** (washing the dog)

Point to the pictures in the third row. Call on one student to answer this question: **What does the dog do when Tom throws the ball?** (Student points to the dog running after the ball.) ***What is the dog doing in that picture?*** (running after the ball)

Practice and Apply: Picture Bingo

Distribute a copy of Picture Bingo to each student. Introduce the activity: ***Listen for the important words as I read a passage. Circle the four pictures that show the ideas from the passage. You will use the pictures to answer questions about what you heard.***

Model with the first sentence from the passage. Say: ***Listen as I read the first part of the passage: "Ling went to the store with her Aunt Mei this morning." I heard the word* store. *There is a picture of a store on the Picture Bingo sheet. Find the picture of the store and circle it.***

Read the passage aloud:

> Ling went to the store with her Aunt Mei this morning. They went shopping for clothes first. Aunt Mei bought Ling a new dress to wear.
>
> Ling asked, "Can we buy some grapes, too?"
>
> Aunt Mei said, "Yes, we can."
>
> On their way home, they walked by the river. "Shhh!" said Aunt Mei. Then she pointed to two white ducks sleeping in the grass.

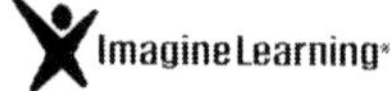

Circle the correct answers on a clean Picture Bingo sheet. (grapes, store, white ducks sleeping, dress). Display the correct answers for other students and explain: ***If you circled the correct pictures, you should have four circled pictures that line up.*** Draw a diagonal line through the circled pictures. Say: ***If you have four pictures that line up like this, call "Bingo!"***

Call on students to use their Picture Bingo sheet to answer one of the questions below.

- ***Where did Ling and Aunt Mei go first?*** (to the store)
- ***What did Aunt Mei buy for Ling to wear?*** (a new dress)
- ***What did Ling ask Aunt Mei to buy?*** (grapes)
- ***Where did Aunt Mei buy the dress and the grapes?*** (at the store)
- ***What did Aunt Mei see by the river?*** (two white ducks)
- ***What were the ducks doing?*** (sleeping)
- ***Where were they sleeping?*** (in the grass)

Check Progress

Observe each student during practice and use the following activity to check progress made on the target skill.

Play another round of Picture Bingo using the same sheets. In this round, have students draw a box around the important words as you read the following passage aloud to the group.

> Martin and his mom planned to go to the lake. Mom decided to carry apples with them for a snack. She wore her big hat. Martin wore his favorite black pants. They talked together as they walked to the lake. Then they ate apples as they watched white ducks swimming by.

Meet with students individually to check their Picture Bingo sheets. Prompt each student to answer two questions:

- ***Where did Martin and his mom go?*** (to the lake)
- ***What did Mom carry with them for a snack?*** (apples)
- ***What did Martin wear?*** (pants)
- ***What color were his pants?*** (black)
- ***Where did they eat their snack?*** (at the lake)
- ***What animals did they see?*** (ducks)
- ***What color were the ducks?*** (white)
- ***What were the ducks doing?*** (swimming)

If the student circles the correct pictures and can correctly answer the questions, consider the intervention successful.

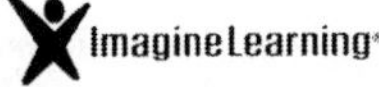

Story Pictures

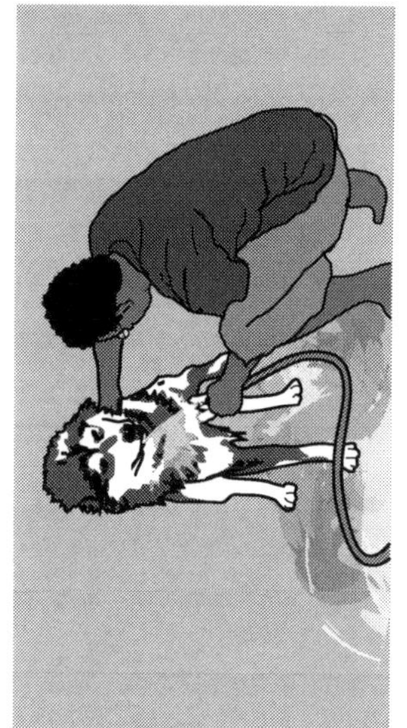

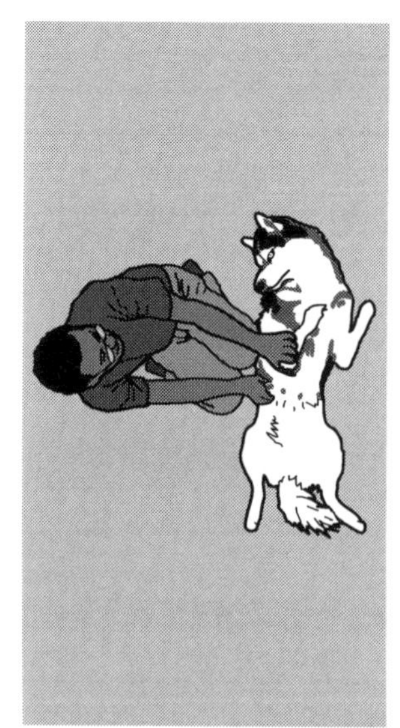

Name ____________________

Picture Bingo

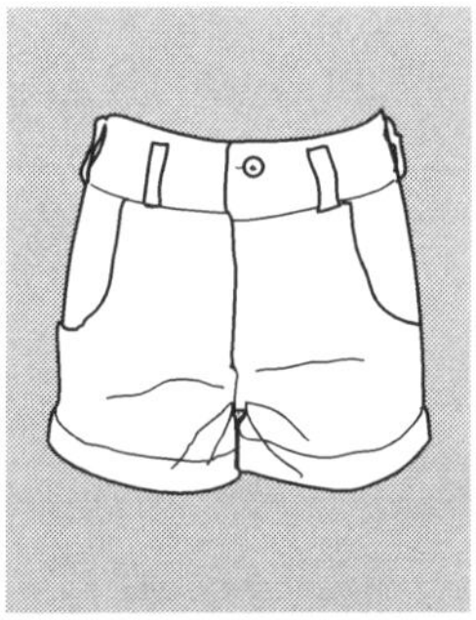

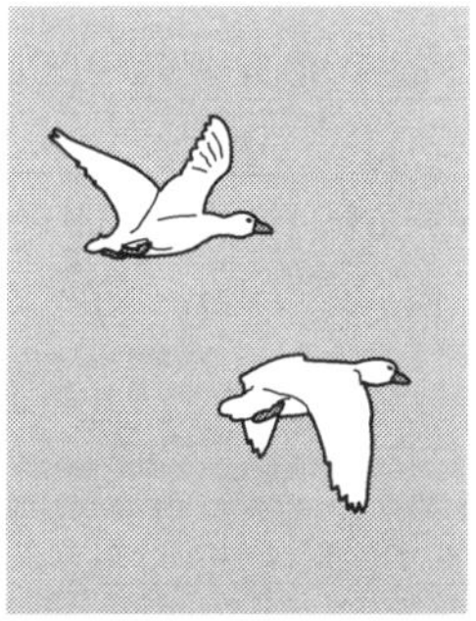

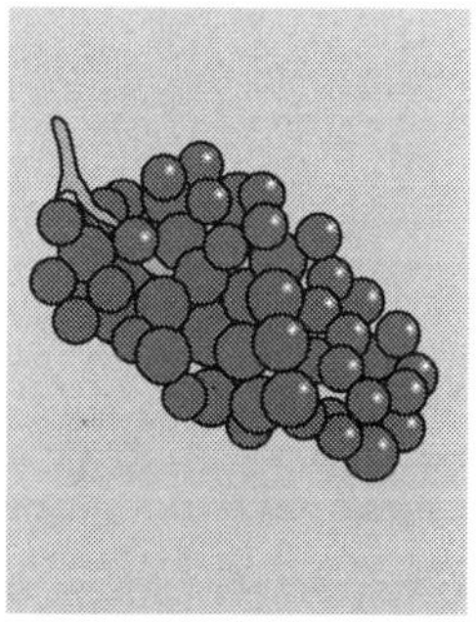

GENERAL STORE

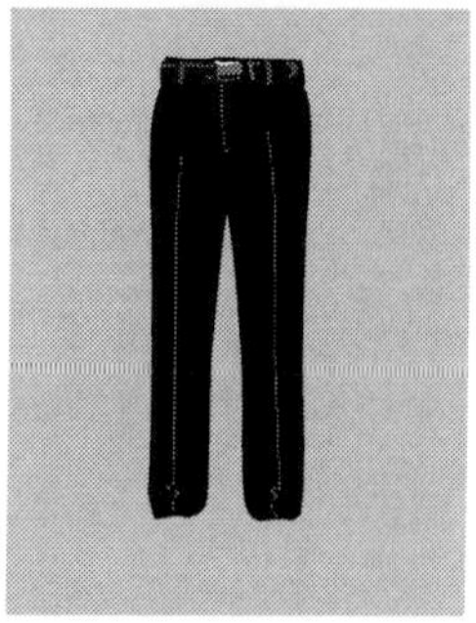

Reteaching Lessons ✓

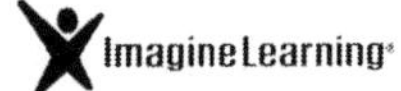

Made in the USA
Columbia, SC
13 September 2018